WHO MAKES PUBLIC POLICY?
The Struggle for Control between Congress and the Executive

Edited by

ROBERT S. GILMOUR and ALEXIS A. HALLEY

with Original Case Studies by

Diana Evans
Robert S. Gilmour
Alexis A. Halley
G. Calvin Mackenzie
Thomas L. McNaugher
Eric Minkoff
Roger L. Sperry
James A. Thurber

Sponsored by the
National Academy of Public Administration
Washington, D.C.

Chatham House Publishers, Inc.
Chatham, New Jersey

WHO MAKES PUBLIC POLICY?
The Struggle for Control between Congress and the Executive

CHATHAM HOUSE PUBLISHERS, INC.
Post Office Box One
Chatham, New Jersey 07928

Copyright © 1994 by Chatham House Publishers, Inc.

PUBLISHER: Edward Artinian
PRODUCTION SUPERVISOR: Katharine Miller
COVER DESIGN: Lawrence Ratzkin
COMPOSITION: Bang, Motley, Olufsen
PRINTING AND BINDING: R.R. Donnelley & Sons Company

Library of Congress Cataloging-in-Publication Data
Who makes public policy? : the struggle between Congress and the
  Executive / Robert S. Gilmour and Alexis A. Halley, editors ;
  contributors, Diana Evans ... [et al.].
      p.   cm.
  "Case studies from the National Academy of Public Administration,
  Washington, D.C."
  Includes bibliographical references and index.
  ISBN 1-56643-004-6
    1. Executive power—United States—Case studies. 2. Separation of
  powers—United States—Case studies. 3. United States. Congress.
  4. United States—Politics and government—1945—Case studies.
  5. Policy sciences—Case studies. I. Gilmour, Robert S. (Robert
  Scott), 1940– . II. Halley, Alexis A. III. Evans, Diana, 1947– .
JK585.W48 1994
320.473′04—dc20   93-34362
                                                            CIP

Manufactured in the United States of America
        10 9 8 7 6 5 4 3 2 1

Contents

Foreword

When James Madison wrote of the need for "auxiliary precautions"—checks and balances—more than two centuries ago, the threat was the tyranny of one branch over the other. Today, after the decades-long accretion of power to the presidency, followed by an accumulation of "precautions" taken by Congress to check the executive, the greater threat may be managerial paralysis: the inability of the government to do its work. This has led to great concern about the government's institutional capacity to function.

As in other nations, the capacity to govern in the United States is affected by a global economy, transformations wrought by advances in information technology, a decaying social infrastructure, scarce fiscal resources, an increasing number of players in the process of governing, a much richer network of interactions among public and private organizations, and often inadequate structures and processes to develop coherent policies and programs. A major factor in whether a consensus can be reached on any agenda for improvement and whether the means can be found for carrying it out is the relationship between Congress and the president, as well as the executive branch departments and agencies he oversees. Distrust of government and skepticism toward elected officials dominate the relationship U.S. citizens have with their national government, especially the legislative and executive branches. Work is now required to repair the distrust and reverse the skepticism. Public confidence in government needs to be restored if the United States is to overcome the immense challenges that lie ahead. A first step is to renew and reform the relationship between Congress and the executive branch.

In responding to this concern, the Academy undertook a two-year study of congressional-executive relations. *Beyond Distrust: Building Bridges Between Congress and the Executive,* published in January 1992, was prepared by a bipartisan panel chaired by James R. Jones. The panel's charge was to recommend ways to strengthen congressional-executive working relationships in order to improve the management and implementation of programs of vital concern to the American people. According to Jones:

New attitudes and new devices are urgently needed in this critical relationship. We know that improved relations between Congress and the Executive Branch offer only one source for solutions to America's problems. New approaches must be tried soon if our political system is to retain the confidence of the American people and respond effectively to pressing national and international needs.

The ten cases presented in this book were used as evidence by the panel, in addition to its collective expertise, in reaching its conclusions and recommendations. These cases provide provocative and revealing examples that could be used as benchmarks in rebuilding bridges of trust and capacity between these branches.

In addition to *Beyond Distrust,* the National Academy of Public Administration, over its twenty-five years serving the nation, has conducted more than three hundred studies and undertaken hundreds of other initiatives aimed at fostering excellence in public management. In 1989 the Academy issued its first report focused directly on Congress; the report addressed the oversight of regulatory programs. Shortly thereafter the Academy convened a group of current and former members of Congress, congressional staff, and senior executive branch officials at the U.S. Capitol to begin to think through and debate ways in which relationships between the branches could be improved. Drawing from this discussion, Academy staff began to develop the blueprint for *Beyond Distrust.* In addition, another Academy panel prepared a report for the 1989 presidential transition that contained a chapter on congressional-executive relations.

This case book provides additional insights into the relationship between the branches through in-depth treatment of specific issues and problems confronting them. Robert Gilmour and Alexis Halley have pulled together the case studies in a manner that provides a direct look at the motivation, means, and effects of detailed congressional intervention in the administration of policies and programs—traditionally regarded as a prerogative of the executive branch. As Congress became further involved, the dynamics and outcomes of these federal policies and programs were greatly affected. This book illustrates how and why.

This fascinating book is must reading for practitioners and scholars alike. The insights illustrated in the case studies and the conclusions reached by Gilmour and Halley add much to the research and literature on congressional-executive relations.

The National Academy will continue to explore ways of improving the relationship between the branches as integral to renewing the nation's system of governance.

— R. Scott Fosler, President
National Academy of Public Administration
Washington, D.C.

Acknowledgments

In a book with eight authors, a complete list of acknowledgments would be unduly long. As the editors, we thank our coauthors for their major contributions in developing the framework of this study as well as the individual cases. Their drive to probe the nature and results of congressional intervention in program implementation, their willingness to use the case-analysis approach, and their investment of energy and commitment over a period of three years made this effort possible.

The case-study research owes much to the initiative and leadership of the National Academy of Public Administration's Panel on Congress and the Executive and its Project Advisory Board. James R. Jones, chairman and chief executive officer of the American Stock Exchange, and former member of Congress, provided intellectual and organizational leadership in framing the overall Academy study and guiding it to conclusion. Ray Kline, president of the Academy during the study, supported its initiation and provided counsel, encouragement, and critical questions at key junctures throughout the research process. R. Scott Fosler, current president of the Academy, urged separate, scholarly publication of the case studies that now appear in this volume.

Panel members and their advisers participated in the selection of the cases and provided counsel on the reporting of the findings and interpretation of results. The panel members and their advisers included Thomas H. Boggs, Jr., Richard Bolling (deceased), Alan S. Boyd, Hale Champion, Roger Davidson, Martha Derthick, John N. Erlenborn, Joseph L. Fisher (deceased), Alton Frye, Harry S. Havens, Matthew Holden, Frank Horton, Melvin R. Laird, Howard Messner, Terry Sanford, Allen Schick, James Sundquist, Alair Townsend, Richard Wegman, and Joseph R. Wright, Jr.

During preparation of the ten cases presented here, the authors interviewed well over three hundred officials, former officials, and close observers who were actively involved in or who had important perspectives on policy and administrative aspects of relevant issues as they unfolded. These respondents—from executive branch departments and agencies; from Congress, including elected members, former members, and professionals from the personal and committee staffs of both houses and the congressional support agencies; from specialized associations and groups from both the public and private sectors; from academia and research foundations; and from independent consulting agencies—were invaluable to the research. Their efforts frequently involved critical reviews of materials in preparation, and for two of the cases, participation in roundtable evaluations of the draft policy and program development reports. Without their involvement, the case research and analysis presented here would not have been possible. In most situations anonymity was promised to protect our respondents and to encourage candor. The masks have been preserved, yet our debt for the time, effort, and insights of these firsthand observers and commentators is enormous and undiminished by their anonymity. Several authors have acknowledged individuals who gave special assistance in the preparation of their cases. We add our thanks here as well.

Staff of the Congressional Research Service, the U.S. General Accounting Office, the Brookings Institution, the Council on Foreign Relations, and the American Enterprise Institute were especially helpful in briefing the research team on a wide range of policy issues during the early stages of the study and, subsequently, providing a greater in-depth understanding of the issues selected.

The case-study research was supported by grants to the National Academy of Public Administration from the Ford Foundation, the Hewlett Foundation, the Prudential Foundation, and State Farm Mutual Insurance Companies. Other funding was furnished by the Academy's endowment.

We would also like to thank the people at Chatham House, publisher Ed Artinian, production supervisor Katharine Miller, and Betty Seaver, consultant for overall copy editing of the book, for their invaluable assistance and encouragement in bringing this volume to print. But, of course, final responsibility for what appears in the text, and in particular, for any errors or omissions, rests with the editors and authors.

Robert S. Gilmour   Alexis A. Halley
Storrs, Connecticut   Washington, D.C.

Contributors

Diana Evans is associate professor of political science at Trinity College in Hartford, Connecticut. Her research and publications deal with Congress and interest groups as well as congressional policy making in transportation.

Robert S. Gilmour is professor of political science at the University of Connecticut and a member of the District of Columbia bar. He is a former senior professional staff member of the Senate Committee on Governmental Affairs, and was director of the Congress and Executive project sponsored by the National Academy of Public Administration. He is the author or co-author of numerous articles and books on congressional-executive relations, including *Politics, Position, and Power: From the Positive to the Regulatory State* (4th edition, 1986) with Harold Seidman.

Alexis A. Halley is a senior management consultant addressing questions of leadership, governance, and change in the public sector. She is director of the John C. Stennis Congressional Fellows Program for senior congressional staff, sponsored by the Stennis Center for Public Service and the Council for Excellence in Government. She served as associate director of studies and project co-director of the Congress and Executive project at the National Academy of Public Administration. She has written or edited numerous publications, including *Delivering Human Services: A Learning Approach to Practice* (3d edition, 1992).

G. Calvin Mackenzie is the Distinguished Presidential Professor of American Government at Colby College. He has worked in both the legislative and executive branches, and his books include *The House at Work, The Politics of Presidential Appointments,* and *American Government: Politics and Public Policy.*

Thomas L. McNaugher is senior fellow in the foreign policy studies program at the Brookings Institution. He is a former policy analyst at the Rand Corporation. His books include *The M16 Controversies: Military Organizations and Weapons Acquisition; Arms and Oil: U.S. Military Strategy* *and the Persian Gulf;* and *New Weapons, Old Politics: America's Military Procurement Muddle.*

Eric Minkoff is a management analyst with the Justice Management Division in the U.S. Department of Justice. He formerly served as project coordinator and research associate on numerous reports, projects, and studies for the National Academy of Public Administration, including *Beyond Distrust: Building Bridges Between Congress and the Executive; The Executive Presidency: Federal Management for the 1990s;* and *Organizing the Administration of Surface Transportation Policies and Programs to Meet National Needs.*

Roger L. Sperry is director of management studies at the National Academy of Public Administration. He is a former professional staff member with the Senate Committee on Governmental Affairs and a GAO consultant to the Congressional Joint Committee on Atomic Energy. He is the author of *GAO 1966–1981—An Administrative History* and numerous journal articles on public management topics.

James A. Thurber is professor of government and director of the Center for Congressional and Presidential Studies at the American University. He is editor of *Divided Democracy: Cooperation and Conflict Between the President and Congress* and coauthor of *Setting Course: A Congressional Management Guide.* He is a former professional staff member of the Senate Committee on Committees and the Commission on the Administrative Review of the U.S. House of Representatives.

Introduction

I

The Struggle for Control of Policy and Program Development

ROBERT S. GILMOUR AND ALEXIS A. HALLEY

Public policy making in the United States is at best an art form, usually involving a Byzantine and somewhat arcane set of processes and procedures and often a bewildering array of participants. Broadly considered, public policy making encompasses the implementation of discrete governmental programs as well as the development of grand strategic designs. The president and Congress, as well as their staffs, agencies, committees, and councils; the federal judiciary at all levels; sprawling and almost uncountable departments, agencies, and other subunits of the executive branch; "fourth-branch" independent regulatory commissions; thousands of politically active interest groups and lobbies; the mass and specialized communications media, both print and electronic; state and local officials and their organizations; hosts of quasi-governmental agencies, special authorities, and government contractors; and even a few academics—all are players in ongoing scenes of the policy-making process. This case book focuses primarily on the two branches of government—Congress and the executive—that are most often at the center of national policy and program development.

The working relationship between Congress and the executive branch is critical to the success or failure of U.S. policies and programs. Neither branch acts alone at any stage of policy and program development. Both play essential roles in the processes of planning, setting, paying for, executing, monitoring, and evaluating national policy. From the purchase and sale of multibillion-dollar weapons systems and the commitment of troops in foreign fields, to the rental of government office space or the processing of a social security claim, Congress and the executive branch are engaged in a daily struggle for control of the overall leadership and management of public policy.

Although both branches periodically proclaim the importance of "greater interbranch cooperation" in addressing the nation's domestic and international challenges, strong but differing institutional orientations toward their respective constituencies, a need for the protection of political

3

turf, partisan loyalties, and outside interests have discouraged that cooperation. These structural tendencies toward disagreement are generally exacerbated by the phenomenon of divided government—one party in control of the presidency and the other dominant in either one or both houses of Congress—and by an unusually high level of ideological tension between the two branches.

Policy Making between the Branches

Despite the overall complexity of the substance and process of U.S. policy, the development of specific policies and programs is remarkably limited and specialized in focus. The structure of congressional committee and executive and independent agency jurisdictions and the understanding in these institutions of the appropriate scope of particular programs hold their limits to a narrow gauge.

In large measure, U.S. domestic policies—and most foreign policies as well—have been developed by joint-branch (Congress and executive branch) implementation of specialized programs. The implementation has been piecemeal, with many different and to some extent competing legislative, executive, judicial, and quasi-public or private institutions and individuals involved. Continuing concerns for the *input* to these programs—definitions, personnel resources, and dollars budgeted, appropriated, and disbursed —have largely dominated the action. Far less attention has been given to alternative (or duplicative) program choices or to a comprehensive policy perspective in light of a broader understanding of relative priorities among public needs. As a result, public policy is more likely to be the residue of accumulated programs and arrangements than the calculated results of intentional design. Carefully intellectualized and articulated policies such as "containment," "massive retaliation," and "flexible response" in strategic foreign policy are exceptions. For the most part, distinctions between "policy" and "programs" have been either formalistic and artificial or purposely left vague in the real-world interplay of politics and administration.

Characteristically, policy making has been accorded greatest attention at the macro level: bold strategies or campaigns in foreign and military affairs; grand legislative departures defining new domestic agendas; and the introduction of major new economic theories. Consequently, the primary focus of national policy debates has run from major issues of the Cold War ("containment" and "mutually assured destruction," for example) to the nature and desirability of the Vietnam and Persian Gulf wars; to New Deal and Great Society approaches to domestic problems; and to the merits and results of Keynesianism, monetarism, or supply-side economics as guiding frameworks. In most governmental circles the implementation of policy—in the details of program development and management—was regarded as important but not, in the order of things, at the highest level of attention and concern. Generally, assessment of implementation was left to after-the-fact administrative oversight and to program evaluation, if attended to at all.

Over more than a decade, however, resources for major (usually expensive) new departures in public policy have largely been unavailable. Caught in the squeeze between automatically escalating entitlement programs (social security, Medicare and Medicaid, and a variety of pension programs), compounding interest on the federal debt, and relatively stagnant levels of federal revenues, anticipated annual increases in existing domestic "controllable" programs were scaled back dramatically. During the early 1980s, some were actually cut in terms of base-year dollars appropriated. A few were ended altogether. With the thaw and finally the end to four decades of Cold War, once-sacrosanct defense programs also became "controllable" and subject to the constraining pressures of spiraling national budget deficits. By 1985 expensive, large-scale policy departures of any kind had become matters of rhetoric, not of action.

By the mid to late 1980s as well, various signs warned unmistakably that many existing policies and programs were wholly misguided (the savings and loan regulatory system and the federal farm credit system), egregiously mismanaged (a variety of programs at the Department of Housing and Urban Development), antiquated and dangerous (nuclear production and waste disposal), hugely expensive and wasteful (Medicare and Medicaid), even falsely represented and dysfunctional (numerous military acquisitions programs, including the Army's Sergeant York gun, the Navy's A-12 stealth aircraft, and the Air Force's B-1 strategic bomber).

In congressional quarters, gradual realization dawned, beginning even in the 1970s, that broad delegations of relatively uncharted and unchecked policy-making power to the executive branch may have been misplaced. Members of Congress and their staffs increasingly understood that traditional passive and ad hoc methods of administrative oversight were not only unappealing politically but likely to be inadequate to the tasks of redirecting policies believed to be wrong-headed, reordering priorities for governmental attention, or realistically evaluating the effectiveness of programs thought to be foundering. As such realizations became more widespread, intensified particularly by the ideological divide of the Reagan years, members of Congress and their staffs evidently came to believe that they must respond—at least in part—with ever-more-detailed program directives, specifications, deadlines, and managerial controls.

Opinions vary widely about the scope, methods, legitimacy, and results of the role Congress plays—along with the executive—in the detailed day-to-day development, direction, and management of federal policies and programs. Yet, there has been little in the way of evenhanded, case-specific exploration of that role. The cases of this volume were chosen and researched specifically to that end.

Separate Powers and Modern Governance

When James Madison wrote over two centuries ago of the need for "auxiliary precautions"—checks and balances between the branches of government—the threat to be countered was the tyranny of one branch over the other and, ultimately, the threat of one-branch tyranny over the people. By constitutional design, legislative and executive powers were divided in broad but imprecise mandates with respect to both policy making and administration. Power was set against power in what E.S. Corwin years ago termed "an invitation to struggle."[1]

Although governmental functions appear to be separated—"All legislative powers ... vested in a Congress"; "The executive power ... vested in a President"—in fact they are both separate and shared. The long list of enumerated legislative powers in the Constitution is tempered by the presidential veto power and vice-presidential authority to preside over the Senate and to vote in the event of a tie. The powers of the president in foreign affairs and as commander in chief of the military are offset by a senatorial role in treaty-making and congressional powers not only to declare war but also to govern, regulate, organize, arm, discipline, and call forth the militia. The power of the president to appoint "officers of the United States" is tempered not only by senatorial "advice and consent" but also by congressional power to establish such offices and to vest appointment power otherwise. Even the president's constitutional direction to "take care that the laws be faithfully executed" must be weighed against the congressional power "to make all laws ... necessary and proper for carrying into execution the foregoing [enumerated congressional] powers."

Before the advent of the Constitution, the Continental Congress had responsibility for executive, legislative, and judicial functions. It should come as no surprise, then, that Congress was involved with executive issues—the implementation of public policy—from its first session. In 1789, when Congress created the five original federal departments, it legislated in very great detail, identifying each job and setting each job's salary by statute.[2] Two of those departments, War and Foreign Affairs, were described in only the most general terms, whereas Treasury was given a detailed statutory scheme. Because of its constitutional powers over the purse, from the first, Congress had a great deal of interest in managing the Treasury.[3] At the same time, however, the Treasury Department, in the person and presence of Alexander Hamilton, was felt directly in congressional chambers during the crafting of Treasury's enabling act[4] as well as in the development of early taxation statutes.[5]

Details can be important building blocks of public policy.[6] Yet, in 1885 a young Woodrow Wilson chided Congress for "entering more and more into the details of administration until it has virtually taken into its own hands all the substantial powers of government."[7] However, Wilson was also "inclined to think that the enlarged powers of Congress are more the fruits of an immensely increased efficiency of organization than of any definite and persistent scheme of conscious usurpation."[8] Wilson's complaint has persisted through more than one hundred years of U.S. government.

The question of the proper nature and extent of congressional involvement in the details of policy development and implementation is central to debates about the meaning of the separation of powers as a criterion for carrying out the Constitution. The reality is that there are two principles: a system of separation of powers and a system of checks and balances. Separation of powers creates three institutional branches; checks and balances are mechanisms enabling separate institutions to ensure that no one of them accrues the whole power to run the government. Congress and the executive branch are separate but interdependent institutions collectively responsible to develop and implement federal programs as well as to raise the revenue to pay for them. In short, the system is one of separate institutions sharing certain powers—a design intended to prevent tyranny, protect liberty, and promote good government. The history of the nation's governance since adoption of the Constitution has been marked by a continuing debate on how to preserve the constitutional system while enabling it to adapt to a modern world and accommodate a plurality of ideologies and multiplicity of interests.

Executive issues have also become important to the success of Congress—indeed, to the success of the government. All the major policy questions today have important executive dimensions. The budget deficit, trade imbalance, drugs, AIDS, national security, health care, abortion, weapons procurement, education, energy, and environment all require that implementation matters be considered when policy is formulated. In fact, implementation often determines what policies actually result. Joint participation of Congress and the executive branch in the implementation of national policy and the management of government programs is inevitable, largely because (1) neither the executive branch nor Congress, as separate institutions, constitutes "the government" or "the manager of government"; (2) Congress and the executive branch have a shared constitutional mandate in the direction, organization, finance, and staffing of federal programs; (3) policy implementation is a continuous process requiring both branches to be constructively engaged; and (4) contemporary issues require less by way of problem solution and more by way of ongoing problem management.

Pendulum Swings of Government Power

The history of the nation's governance since adoption of the Constitution has been marked by pendulum swings of government power, especially between the legislative and executive branches.[9] Throughout much of the nineteenth century Congress often played a dominant role in the execution as well as the development of public policy. In the twentieth century until the 1970s, however, government power was concentrated in the executive branch as the recipient of generally broad congressional delegations. Following the Vietnam war and the Watergate scandal, Congress reacted to a public perception of growing presidential insensitivity, remoteness, and excessive power. A number of politicians from both parties ran campaigns in the early 1970s declaring that they would make Congress a true voice for the people in their districts. Congress passed, for example, the War Powers Resolution of 1973 and the Congressional Budget and Impoundment Control Act of 1974[10] and imposed a large number of legislative veto provisions on discretionary executive actions.[11] To be more responsive—and to counter executive branch expertise—Congress added the Congressional Budget Office and the Office of Technology Assessment to its support agencies, expanded the Congressional Research Service, and over several decades markedly increased the numbers of congressional staffs and subcommittees.[12] Reacting to concerns about an overcentralization of power in Congress itself, legislators dethroned three House committee chairmen and dispersed their authority to subcommittees. Also during the 1970s Congress began to curtail or withdraw its sweeping, open-ended grants of unchecked executive authority—over national health care, environmental protection, consumer and transportation safety, occupational health, foreign aid, and military weapons acquisitions, to name a few. Many congressional requirements of executive agencies were made more detailed and precise.[13]

The trend continued in the 1980s and 1990s. Policy and program difficulties and disputes were not, of course, the only incentives for congressional retrieval of prior, broad delegations. Earlier, in an era of more abundant national resources, sweeping legislation was enacted to conquer poverty, environmental pollution, poor health, and other social problems. Later, as glaring budget deficits, technologically intractable problems, and discordant national priorities between the branches signaled a new reality, many in Congress changed their approach.

Ambivalence about Congressional Oversight

The congressional oversight role is often misunderstood.[14] Article I (secs. 1 and 8) of the Constitution makes clear that the central function of Congress is to legislate. Inherent in this legislative power to authorize programs, create agencies, and appropriate funds is a corollary responsibility to exercise control over the agencies of the executive branch. Authority to determine the objectives of executive action implies some responsibility to ensure that adequate steps are taken to achieve those objectives. Accordingly, the role of congressional oversight has evolved as an essential part of the separated and shared powers system: Congress is to be concerned with the *how* as well as the *what* of executive action. Congress must consider how policies are being executed, whether they are accomplishing the desired results, and, if not, what action it should take.[15]

Reforms enacted by Congress to enhance oversight capacity—most pointedly in 1970, 1974, and 1978—repeatedly ran counter to members' desires for an increasingly decentralized committee and subcommittee structure. Hortatory language extolling the virtues of oversight was adopted, but strong proposals to centralize the oversight agenda and legislative follow-through were not. Members instead chose to protect their emerging individual prerogatives and powers, which were developing most notably in the proliferating subcommittee environments. Centralized oversight functions ran against that grain. For example, in 1974 the House Select Committee on Committees (the Bolling committee) proposed to strengthen the House Government Operations Committee by empowering it to develop an oversight agenda for the entire House and to offer privileged amendments, based on oversight findings, to bills reported by other committees. At about the same time, House and Senate reforms to strengthen the subcommittee structure and staff, the so-called subcommittee bill of rights, made centralizing reforms for enhanced oversight (or for any other purpose) seem even less attractive to newly ensconced subcommittee chairmen and ranking members. The Bolling committee's oversight proposals, as well as many others, were watered down, rejected, or ignored.

Congressional ambivalence toward the oversight function is likely to reflect the tension among the range of roles Congress can play in carrying it out. For example, at one extreme, Congress can be a passive reviewer-overseer focusing on implementation after the fact. At the other, Congress can be an active participant, boldly and proactively involved in direct and detailed implementation and execution of policy and programs.

The Swing toward Congressional Micromanagement

More than a decade has passed since Congress last conducted a comprehensive examination of how it conducts oversight. Despite Congress's own 1946 mandate to its standing committees to "exercise continuous watchfulness of the execution of the administrative agencies" and repeated congressional reaffirmations "that comprehensive and systematic oversight *ought* to be conducted,"[16] by almost all accounts such sentiments have not prevailed in practice.[17] Major changes have occurred nonetheless. With the return of divided party control of the two branches and other forces of political, social, economic, and international change in the 1980s and early 1990s, the pendulum has swung to a new extreme as Congress, according to its critics, accelerated its interest in oversight, "micromanaged," or intervened excessively in the details of administration. Criticism came from numerous sources: President Reagan's Private Sector Survey on Cost Control (also known as the Grace commission after its chairman, J. Peter Grace), the Heritage Foundation, and the American Enterprise Institute. David Kirkpatrick in *Fortune* magazine put the case bluntly: "Congress has strayed from its historic role of helping to set the overall direction for the nation. Instead, in the name of oversight, it too often busies itself with 'micromanagement' —mucking with the petty details of policy execution. The agencies won't ever function well unless Congress gets off their backs."[18]

Observers both inside and outside government lament a "myopic legislature," a "micromanaging legislature" that places an abundance of strictures on direct government operations.[19] According to these views, multiple control systems, personnel ceilings and freezes, budget austerity, legislative requests by phone for data from executive agencies, legislatively mandated reports from executive agencies, time spent by top management of agencies repeating the same testimony before multiple committees and subcommittees, and a host of other rigid administrative requirements have robbed executive managers of the flexibility and discretion necessary for effective performance.[20] Such constraints, it is argued, coupled with judicial restrictions and requirements on executive performance, lead to "managerial paralysis"—the inability of the government, especially the executive branch, to do its work.

Congressional micromanagement is a relatively new term used by some to express a very old complaint: intervention by Congress in administrative details.[21] According to James Q. Wilson:

> Congress is commonly criticized for micromanaging government agencies; it does and it always has. Because of its right to authorize programs, appropriate funds, confirm presidential appointees, and conduct investigations, Congress can convert any bureaucratic decision into a policy choice. What is new—and what is obscured by scholarly writings—is that the form of this micromanagement seems to have changed. Congress is somewhat less likely today than formerly to make administrative decisions and more likely to enforce congressional constraints on how those decisions are made. Congressional micromanagement takes the form of devising detailed, elaborate rules instead of demanding particular favors for particular people.[22]

Congressional micromanagement has come to represent a hodgepodge of observations and charges about the proper role of Congress in executive issues. The term is neither wholly concerned with lawmaking nor wholly concerned with oversight, nor even with Congress's legitimate role of representation. The term *micromanagement* has taken on a life of its own, illustrating rather pointedly how Congress's roles of lawmaking, oversight, and representation have become so blurred that it is often impossible to distinguish them in practice.

One person's micromanagement of federal programs is another person's effective directions that ensure administrative compliance with legislative intent in setting the course of public policy.[23] What for one person is administrative discretion to manage is for another a bureaucracy out of control. Fingers are repeatedly pointed at Congress as contributor to or creator of the problems. Yet, from the outset of the research on the cases of this volume, the evidence suggested that the reasons for weaknesses and outright failures in national policy development, implementation, and program management were too complex to be captured by one-sided slogans about congressional micromanagement or deficiencies in congressional oversight. A major objective of this study is to begin to sort out (1) the different means that Congress uses to intervene directly in the details as well as the broad outlines of policy development, implementation, and program management, and (2) the results of direct and detailed congressional intervention—as understood by those most closely involved—for policy and the policy-making process, for program management, and for the institutional roles and performance of Congress itself.

Development and Organization of the Book

Penetrating congressional involvement in the details of public policy and program development is hardly confined to a particular area. Congressional responsibility, curiosity, and committee jurisdictions run the gamut of domestic, defense, and foreign policy concerns. So do Congress's direct actions. Hence, the selection of specific cases, among the thousands of possible examples, is necessarily limited and somewhat arbitrary, including even the determination of the major policy areas to be sampled.

Before introducing the case studies of this volume, two caveats should be stated at the outset. First, the scope of the cases explored here encompasses yet goes beyond specific instances of traditional congressional legislation and oversight. That Congress and the executive branch play different roles throughout a total policy process that includes policy planning, legislative drafting, resource allocation, implementation, oversight, evaluation, and representation is taken as a given. Accordingly, each case study examines a full range of congressional-executive relations, including, as relevant to the case, the dynamics of policy making and policy implementation and management, informal communications, and traditional oversight hearings and investigations.

Second, the case studies concentrate on a particular kind of congressional behavior (that is, direct and detailed involvement in policy and program development and implementation) rather than *all* possible forms of congressional behavior. Instances in which Congress was never much involved in the details are not represented. However, most of the cases studied describe periods of time in which Congress had not yet become—or later ceased to be—integrally involved.

Although it is unlikely that any truly "representative" cases could be identified, the objective from the first was to select cases that would be "illustrative" of a variety of intense policy-making relationships between the branches as well as a variety of results in the development of significant or particularly revealing policies and programs during the past decade. The cases presented here were selected from well over a hundred "nominations" received during initial interviews with more than fifty legislative, executive, and nongovernmental specialists from six broad policy areas: transportation, environment, health, energy, defense, and foreign affairs.

After preliminary investigation of each recommended case, screening by the National Academy of Public Administration's Congress and Executive Panel, and further research and consideration by all of the contributors to this volume, the ten cases that follow were selected as those thought best to illustrate a variety of important (though not necessarily the most newsworthy) policy issues and patterns of Congress-executive involvement in diverse policy-making and program-management settings.

The two transportation cases presented first, the Federal Aviation Administration's *Traffic Alert and Collision Avoidance System* and the Department of Transportation's *Highway Demonstration Projects* could hardly be more different—in congressional motivation for involvement, tactics, administrative response, and programmatic results—even though both are located in the same executive department. The next two cases, development of the Department of Energy's *High-Level Nuclear Waste Disposal* policy and the Environmental Protection Agency's *Hazardous Waste Disposal* program, appear to be even more similar in policy type. But here again, the patterns and results of the Congress-executive relationship in these cases are remarkably different. The *Defense Nuclear Weapons Complex Cleanup* case spans domestic (environmental and energy) and defense policy in an extreme case of mismanagement and neglect by both branches, finally brought to a new, more active and expensive phase by belated congressional intervention and administrative response. The case of the *Prospective Payment System,* affecting hospitals under the Medicare program, provides an inside look at the complex world of the budget reconciliation process, where interbranch fiscal politics outranks program function in importance.

The two defense cases of this volume, Air Force acquisition of the *Advanced Medium-Range Air-to-Air Missile (AMRAAM)* and the *Goldwater-Nichols Reorganization of the Department of Defense,* are both studies in interbranch antagonism, yet their scopes are vastly different. The case of AMRAAM represents a midlevel weapons development program with many of the problems that appear to have become endemic to such programs: mismanagement, delays, cost escalation, weapons system unreliability, overoptimism, disinformation, and outright deceit. Congressional participants intervened in reaction to executive difficulties; however, the interplay remained confined to the program at hand with little reference to programmatic alternatives and seismic changes in the structure of external threats and international power. The *Goldwater-Nichols Defense Reorganization* case, on the other hand, identifies Congress, uncharacteristically, as a broad-scale initiator of major organizational change, with the executive branch defending the difficult and ultimately untenable terrain of a parochial status quo.

The *Foreign Aid and Human Rights* case describes the means of congressional micromanagement used effectively toward the end of policy change in a reluctant State Department bureaucracy. In the *Foreign Military Arms Sales* case, congressional action responded more to articulate constituency interests than to broad-scale policy concerns; nonetheless, direct and specific legislative intervention has fabricated a consultative process between the branches, tempering both policy outcomes and arbitrary executive action.

From the outset of the research effort to develop these cases, it was clear that the studies presented here would cover a range of diverse and complex subject areas. The study team therefore developed a common framework for case study research and presentation. This enabled subsequent comparisons across settings and types of detailed congressional intervention in policy making, and provided the means to identify cross-case patterns and conclusions. Without such a framework, findings from such diverse cases would not be comparable.

For each case, the following concepts are described: (1) the policy context; (2) key events between the branches during a specific time period, with an emphasis on the role of Congress in developing and directing the specifics of policies and programs; and (3) effects of congressional intervention and executive response as perceived by participants and by the principal investigators of each case.

Notes

1. E.S. Corwin, H.W. Chase, and C.R. Ducat, *The Constitution and What It Means Today* (Princeton: Princeton University Press, 1978). Also see Roger H. Davidson, "An Invitation to Struggle: An Overview of Legislative-Executive Relations," *Annals, AAPSS* 499 (September 1988): 9–21.

2. James L. Sundquist, "Congress as Public Administrator," in *A Centennial History of the American Administrative State,* ed. Ralph Clark Chandler (New York: Free Press, 1987), 263.

3. John A. Rohr, *To Run a Constitution: The Legitimacy of the American Administrative State* (Lawrence: University of Kansas Press, 1986), 26.

4. Leonard D. White, *The Federalists* (New York: Macmillan, 1948), 118.

· 5. Louis Fisher, "Micromanagement by Congress: Reality and Mythology," in *The Fettered Presidency: Legal Constraints on the Executive Branch,* ed. L. Gordon Crovitz and Jeremy A. Rabkin (Washington, D.C.: American Enterprise Institute, 1989), 141.

6. Louis Fisher, *The Politics of Shared Power: Congress and the Executive,* 2d ed. (Washington, D.C.: Congressional Quarterly Press, 1987), 74.

7. Woodrow Wilson, *Congressional Government: A Study in American Politics* (Baltimore: Johns Hopkins University Press, 1981; originally published 1885), 49.

8. Wilson, *Congressional Government,* 50.

9. James L. Sundquist, *The Decline and Resurgence of Congress* (Washington, D.C.: Brookings, 1981); Allen Schick, "Congress and the Details of Administration," *Public Administration Review* (September/October 1976), 516–28.

10. President Nixon's substantial cancellations ("impoundments") of appropriated expenditures provided an additional congressional incentive for passage of the Congressional Budget and Impoundment Control Act. Public perceptions were widespread that Nixon's actions were improper, if not illegal, and Congress clearly did not want him to prevail. Allen Schick, *Congress and Money* (Washington, D.C.: Urban Institute, 1980), 46–48; Aaron Wildavsky, *The New Politics of the Budgetary Process* (Glenview, Ill.: Scott, Foresman, 1987), 135–36.

11. See Barbara Hinkson Craig, *The Legislative Veto: Congressional Control of Regulation* (Boulder, Colo.: Westview Press, 1983).

12. See Theodore Lowi, *The End of Liberalism: The Second Republic of the United States,* 2d ed. (New York: Norton, 1979).

13. Harold H. Bruff and Ernest Gelhorn, "Congressional Control of Administrative Regulations: A Study of Legislative Vetoes," *Harvard Law Review* 90 (1976): 1369; Craig, *The Legislative Veto.*

14. Morris S. Ogul and Bert A. Rockman, "Overseeing Oversight: New Departures and Old Problems," *Legislative Studies Quarterly* 15 (February 1990): 5–24; Bert A. Rockman, "Legislative-Executive Relations and Legislative Oversight," *Legislative Studies Quarterly* 9 (1985): 387–440.

15. National Academy of Public Administration, *Watergate: Its Implications for Responsible Government* (Washington, D.C., March 1974); and *Congressional Oversight of Regulatory Agencies: The Need to Strike a Balance and Focus on Performance* (Washington, D.C., September 1988).

16. Morris Ogul, *Congress Oversees the Bureaucracy: Studies in Legislative Supervision* (Pittsburgh: University of Pittsburgh Press, 1976), 181.

17. Mathew D. McCubbins and Thomas Schwartz, "Congressional Oversight Overlooked: Police Patrols Versus Fire Alarms," *American Journal of Political Science* 28 (February 1984): 165–79. A recent opposing view is that of Joel D. Aberbach, who finds that at least formal oversight hearings have increased dramatically since the early 1970s. See *Keeping a Watchful Eye: The Politics of Congressional Oversight* (Washington, D.C.: Brookings, 1990).

18. Quotation from David Kirkpatrick, "It's Simply Not Working," *Fortune,* 19 November 1990, 181.

19. Mark L. Goldstein, "Our Myopic Legislature," *Government Executive* (January 1991): 10–15, 56, and "Hollow Government," *Government Executive* (October 1989): 12–22.

20. For example, National Academy of Public Administration, *Senior Policy Makers on Congress and Public Management* (Washington, D.C., 7 February 1989); Pamela Fessler, "Complaints Are Stacking Up As Hill Piles On Reports," *Congressional Quarterly*, 7 September 1991, 2562–66; Gordon S. Jones and John A. Marini, *The Imperial Congress* (New York: Pharos Books [Heritage Foundation and Claremont Institute], 1988); Crovitz and Rabkin, *The Fettered Presidency*; Susan M. Davies, "Congressional Encroachment on Executive Branch Communications," *University of Chicago Law Review* 57 (Fall 1990): 1297–1321; Goldstein, "Our Myopic Legislature," 10–15, 56; National Academy of Public Administration, *Revitalizing Federal Management* (Washington, D.C., 1983).

21. Fisher, "Micromanagement by Congress," 139–40.

22. James Q. Wilson, *Bureaucracy: What Government Agencies Do and Why They Do It* (New York: Basic Books, 1989), 241–42.

23. National Academy of Public Administration, *Senior Policy Makers on Congress and Public Management*, 5.

Part One

Domestic Issues: Transportation, Energy, Environment, Health

2

Accelerating Implementation: The Traffic Alert and Collision Avoidance System

Diana Evans

Background and Overview

The Federal Aviation Administration (FAA) initiated its current aircra[ft col]lision-avoidance program, known as the Traffic Alert and Collision [Avoid]ance System (TCAS), in 1981, when newly appointed FAA Adminis[trator] Lynn Helms laid out its specifications. Research and developmen[t] shifted from a partially ground-based collision avoidance system [to an] airborne system. Aircraft would detect and respond to signals f[rom equip]ment operating on other aircraft, a system that would be ind[epen]d[ent of] ground equipment. Helms was convinced the new system wo[uld] major problems that had plagued its predecessor, Beacon Co[llision-Avoid]ance System (BCAS), which had been in development for at le[ast]

Helms came to the FAA with what was in his view a [man]date from the Reagan administration to renew U.S. leadership [in aviation.] The eventual product of that mandate was the Nationa[l Airspace] (NAS) plan.[1] The first task in the development of the [collision-avoidance] determine the characteristics of the collision-avoidance [system] program would have required a major support syst[em] computers and towers. An airborne system consider[ably reduced those re]quirements in the NAS plan. The decision to remove [collision-avoidance] sion-avoidance systems from direct FAA control [generated some] opposition within the FAA, as did Helms's insisten[ce that the system be de]signed and built in the private sector, subject to th[e FAA's requirements and] specifications.

Since at least 1957 Congress has made cle[ar] [at the executive branch] must solve the problem of midair collisions. T[he 1958 statute that created] the FAA was prompted by a collision between [two major air carriers] over the Grand Canyon. For many years ther[e was no air traffic control sys] tem was the primary collision-avoidance system, but also in the 1950s, the industry began developing a dedicated collision-avoidance system. By the early 1970s, several systems had been developed. Although the FAA had monitored and supported those efforts, not until congressional hearings on midair collisions in 1971 did the FAA itself become actively involved in developing and evaluating collision-avoidance systems.[2]

Through the years Congress refrained from imposing a schedule for the development and installation of collision-avoidance systems by the FAA, but congressional interest, concern, and in the case of some members, exasperation were again aroused in the mid-1970s by the FAA's decision to abandon its previous commitment to an airborne system and move to a ground-based beacon system (BCAS). The event leading to the more concentrated congressional attention of the 1980s was the midair collision on 28 September 1978 over San Diego between a Pacific Southwest Airlines plane and a general aviation aircraft, an accident in which 144 people died, including 7 on the ground. At that point, congressional pressure on the FAA began to build, but official action did not go beyond oversight hearings and report language (lacking the force of law) directing the agency to take certain actions to advance the program.

The midair collision over Cerritos, California, in August 1986 between AeroMexico airliner and a private aircraft that took eighty-two lives mpted a more pointed response. Both the Appropriations and authoriz- ommittees reported out bills that would force the FAA to proceed to plementation of the system. In the airport reauthorization legislation , Congress mandated a schedule for the completion and installation n-avoidance equipment. The FAA and the airlines did not meet the in and through a roundabout process persuaded Congress to loosen es and restore some discretion to the FAA—which Congress did

ping Patterns of Congressional-Executive
Relations

The 1987 T
In 1979 three and Mode C Requirements
the House Appr committees held hearings on collision avoidance, and
FY 80 expressed ions Committee report on the DOT funding bill for
standard for a colli mmittee's desire for the FAA to develop a national
Los Angeles airspace voidance system, directing the FAA to test BCAS in
the agency's R&D fro une 1981 J. Lynn Helms announced a switch in
airborne system, design e partially ground-based BCAS to a completely
System; initially designated TCAS (Traffic Alert and Collision Avoidance
precursor to the broad-base hreat Alert CAS). This announcement was the
National Airspace System Plan, announced in

December. The FAA told the House Science and Technology Committee in 1981 that TCAS would be ready for installation on airliners by 1984 or 1985.

TCAS was not ready by 1985. Explanations varied from one participant to another. Several felt that Helms's timetable had been unrealistic from the start. Many thought that for want of a hard push from policymakers, FAA engineers simply continued to work on the system. As one respondent said, "In engineering, better is the enemy of good enough." A number of people both on the Hill and at the FAA believed that Helms's initial decision not to require TCAS but simply to develop and test it was in part responsible for the slow pace and for the apparent feeling among the technical staff that closure was not an imperative.

No one thought, moreover, that the airlines were particularly eager to acquire what would be an expensive new system. One participant's comment: "The airlines don't ever want to spend a dollar on anything new; they have had to be dragged kicking and screaming to new technology." Additionally, the Air Line Pilots Association stressed the need for system reliability. Pilot confidence in it would have to be so high that it would be used rather than turned off: "The pilots wanted perfection from day one." Hence, during the early to mid-1980s there was little impetus toward expeditiousness.

A spate of midair collisions and near-collisions in the mid-1980s, particularly the August 1986 collision over Cerritos, California, engendered an atmosphere of crisis. A congressional staffer remarked, "Midair collisions are rare, but the air traffic control system 'permitted' them every so often." The system was "permitting" near-collisions as well: 589 in 1984, 839 in 1986. At least as alarming was the fact that the proportion involving commercial airliners increased from 32 percent in 1985 to 40 percent in 1986.[3] Over Cerritos, a general aviation aircraft had collided with an AeroMexico airliner on its landing approach to Los Angeles. The small plane had not been noticed by air traffic control. During the National Transportation Safety Board investigation, the controller said that he "did not remember seeing radar returns of the Piper," whose pilot had intruded into the terminal control area without permission. However, even if the controller had seen it, he could not have determined its exact location because the Piper did not carry a Mode C transponder, a device that transmits altitude in addition to location.[4]

Two other midair collisions, each involving commuter airliners and general aviation aircraft, and the dramatic increase in the number of near-collisions in the mid-1980s provided further impetus for congressional action. According to then-Administrator Donald Engen, the FAA had already been prompted to begin work on a proposed TCAS requirement by a lack of industry initiative in developing and installing TCAS; the Cerritos collision added to the sense of urgency at FAA.[5] The collision also energized Congress to become directly involved in the implementation of the aircraft collision-avoidance program.

In particular, the Cerritos collision raised the issue of Mode C altitude encoding and reporting transponders for the majority of the general aviation fleet, which still did not carry them. Although Mode C is an integral part of TCAS, used alone, it constitutes a ground-based system. Mode C transponders enable air traffic controllers to alert pilots to collision hazards. At the time of the Cerritos collision, Mode C transponders were required for all aircraft flying above 12,500 feet and in a limited number of terminal areas.

TCAS, designed primarily for airliners, independently receives information on the proximity of another aircraft from the second craft's Mode C transponder. All versions of TCAS provide the pilot with alerts on potential "conflicts" with other aircraft. TCAS II and III, unlike TCAS I, also provide the pilot with avoidance maneuvers: TCAS II provides climb and descend instructions; TCAS III, when its development is completed, will additionally provide horizontal avoidance instructions.

Within a month of the Cerritos collision, the House Appropriations Committee reported a continuing appropriations resolution that required the FAA to initiate rule-making to require altitude encoding and reporting (Mode C) transponders in aircraft flying in all terminal airspace where the FAA provides radar coverage, and in all airspace above an altitude to be determined by the FAA; to implement such a rule as soon as possible; and to report quarterly to the Appropriations committees on the agency's adherence to its recommended schedule.[6]

In late 1987, also in response to the Cerritos collision, the House Public Works and Transportation Committee and the House Science and Technology Committee reported, and the House passed nearly unanimously, a bill requiring the FAA to move on TCAS II and Mode C transponders in line with precise timetables specified in the legislation. According to the report of H.R. 1517 by the Public Works and Transportation Committee, "[I]f airline aircraft are equipped with TCAS-II equipment the statistical probability of mid-air collisions involving airline aircraft would decrease from once every several years to once every several hundred years. In other words, TCAS-II would virtually eliminate mid-air collisions involving airliner aircraft."[7]

Specifically, H.R. 1517 required the FAA to complete certification and operational approval of TCAS II within eighteen months, and to develop, within eighteen months, regulations to require its installation on all aircraft with more than thirty seats within thirty months of certification. The committee intended that TCAS II be installed on all such airliners by the end of 1991. With respect to Mode C, H.R. 1517 required the FAA to promulgate regulations to require all other aircraft flying in high-density traffic areas to have Mode C altitude encoding transponders.

According to one participant, the Mode C requirement was deliberately vague. The Public Works and Transportation Committee had been pressured by the interest group representing general aviation pilots, the Aircraft Owners and Pilots Association (AOPA), which, according to one respondent, "tried to forestall efforts to legislate Mode C requirements." The committee was sympathetic to the AOPA's complaint that the FAA had been heavy-handed in its regulation of general aviation pilots, and although committee members felt compelled to respond to the Cerritos collision with some reference to a stricter Mode C requirement, they "fuzzed it over," in the words of one staff member. Specifically, the bill did not define the high-density traffic areas in which Mode C was to be required; thus it was not clear exactly how much the committee wanted the FAA to expand the requirement.

On the other hand, the Senate Commerce, Science, and Transportation Committee was particularly concerned with Mode C transponders. It did not hold hearings on TCAS or Mode C; instead, Chairman Ernest Hollings (D-S.C.), and Senators Pete Wilson (R-Calif.), John Danforth (R-Mo.), and Robert Byrd (D-W.V.), offered a floor amendment to the bill reauthorizing the airport and airway system that included essentially the same language as the House bill on TCAS II and III, although it required TCAS II on all aircraft with more than twenty, rather than thirty, seats. In addition, the Hollings amendment imposed a much more specific and quite strict requirement for altitude-encoding transponders; specifically, the FAA was to promulgate a rule within six months that all aircraft operating in terminal airspace controlled by radar be equipped with and use the transponders within two years of enactment.[8] AOPA was much less successful with the Senate committee than it had been with the House committee. In fact, general aviation representatives admitted privately to the Senate committee that half their members liked the idea of a Mode C requirement; the committee used the admission to hold AOPA demands at bay.

Why did the Senate committee want to thwart the wishes of such an active and reputedly influential group? Staff interviews indicate that strong personal commitments of the active senators were instrumental. For Wilson, in particular, who had been mayor of San Diego at the time of the 1978 midair collision there, the Cerritos collision was the last straw; he asked for and received a waiver of Senate rules that limit committee membership so that he could sit on the Commerce, Science, and Transportation Committee in 1986 and participate in its response.

In the House-Senate conference on the airport and airway reauthorization, to which the TCAS and Mode C requirements had now been added, the TCAS II schedule was not controversial. And the Senate prevailed on its stricter Mode C requirement, agreeing only to push back the deadline from two years to three, despite House conferees' misgivings about the interests of general aviation pilots. One participant described the disagreement between the author of the House measure and Hollings: "[Congressman Ron] Packard [R-Calif.] was doubtful about Hollings' Mode C requirement, but Hollings was overpowering."

Why did Congress establish dates certain for implementation of a requirement for highly technical and complex aviation equipment? Congressional staff unanimously said that the crisis atmosphere created by several midair collisions and hundreds of near-collisions each year obliged Congress to be seen by the public as taking action. Indeed, the motivation was so strong that the Air Transport Association, the airline industry group, was not able politically to oppose the legislation, despite its private assertion that its members would not be able to meet the schedule.

If external crisis were the only explanation for congressional action, however, the Pacific Southwest Airlines (PSA) midair collision in 1978 also would have generated more than hearings, which it had not. The crisis of the mid-1980s occurred in the context of FAA promises throughout the early 1980s that a workable system was just around the corner and its concurrent failure to complete development of the system and see to its use. In the words of two participants: "Congress was frustrated [with FAA] because the development of the technology never seemed to cross the goal line," and "[This bill] was the culmination of all the Hill's frustrations over thirty years; there was always something better down the road." Thus, Congress was doubly exasperated. It was convinced by the protracted development of collision-avoidance technology and the public's perception of increased risks of air travel that the FAA had to hear a more forceful message.[9]

The FAA was at that time in the process of moving toward a proposed rule requiring TCAS II. As the House Public Works Committee was fashioning its legislation, the FAA was preparing a Notice of Proposed Rule-Making (NPRM). Within two weeks of the committee's report of its bill mandating implementation by the end of 1991, the FAA issued its NPRM 87–8, which proposed that installation of TCAS II be completed by 1992 or 1993.[10] Packard, the southern California Republican who was the original sponsor of the House legislation, drafted the bill with an eighteen-month deadline for TCAS II installation but, according to congressional staffers, had been persuaded by the FAA and the airline industry to extend the deadline somewhat, although not to the FAA's preferred deadline. As a result of the legislation, the FAA was forced to modify its proposed rule to conform to the legislative language. The final rule was issued in January 1989.[11]

In the meantime, changes in attitude had taken place at the FAA. When Administrator Helms announced the switch in 1981 from a ground-based to an airborne system, according to one participant at the FAA, "there was disappointment within FAA about separating the system from the ground; there was also some doubt about whether it could be done." Specifically, some wondered if the system's technical problems could be solved to allow it to operate effectively in high-density terminal areas without triggering false alarms in its equipment. Ultimately, however, TCAS was accepted at the FAA, and because by 1987 the agency was going forward with its own NPRM, it did not believe that the Packard bill was necessary. The FAA supported the bill nevertheless; in the political climate of the time, it could not do otherwise. Associate Administrator for Flight Standards Anthony Broderick said then, "The public and Congress are very concerned ... [they] will not tolerate anything less than a very aggressive program."[12]

The airlines did not oppose the legislation actively for at least two reasons. First, they knew that congressional action was inevitable and did not want to take a public position against a safety measure. Second, according to a congressional staff member, they feared that the alternative was much more stringent regulation from the FAA, such as broad traffic restrictions, which the National Transportation Safety Board had already recommended. TCAS was clearly preferable. Hence, instead of opposing the legislation, both the FAA and the ATA worked with Packard to extend his original deadlines.

The Mode C Flap
The drive to mandate TCAS in the Senate was related, more strongly than in the House, technically and politically to the drive for Mode C transponders. As noted earlier, the House Public Works Committee, including Aviation Subcommittee Chair Norman Mineta (D-Calif.), were more sympathetic to the concerns of general aviation pilots than was the Senate Commerce Committee, particularly its leadership. The House bill gave the FAA the discretion to determine the definition of the "high-density traffic areas" in which Mode C would be required, giving the AOPA an opportunity to lobby the FAA for a regulation the interest group could live with. Hollings and his cosponsors, on the other hand, explicitly did not want to allow that discretion to the FAA.

Although the airlines and the FAA had doubts about the feasibility of the TCAS schedule mandated in the 1987 legislation, that portion of the collision-avoidance requirements was much less controversial than the extension of Mode C requirements to more airports. Because most midair collisions involve general aviation aircraft, supporters of TCAS argued that a broad Mode C requirement was necessary to provide maximum protection to airliners. The FAA did not move publicly to propose a rule until enactment of the legislation. Six weeks after the TCAS and Mode C requirements became law, the FAA issued its Mode C NPRM. The battle for which the AOPA had reserved its ammunition was joined.

Perceptions vary among participants as to the stringency of the proposed rule compared with Congress's intent. Several congressional staffers felt that the FAA had interpreted the legislation very literally; some thought—as did the AOPA—they had gone overboard. On the other hand, a respondent at the FAA argued that although the agency might indeed have overreacted, the proposed rule was *less* stringent than the law required, in that both the Appropriations Committee and the authorizing committee mandates directed the FAA to require Mode C in all terminal airspace where radar service is provided, which includes nearly every terminal in the United States.

If the FAA did in fact overreach in its proposed rule, it was in reaction to the Cerritos collision as well as to the congressional mandate. The controversial proposed rule required Mode C altitude-encoding transponders at and above 6000 feet (the previous floor was 12,500 feet) and within a forty-nautical-mile radius of any airport with radar approach-control service, which includes approximately 254 airports. The airlines, the Air Transport Association (ATA), and Hollings all supported the rule, although, as one participant said, "Hollings thought every general aviation plane should have Mode C." The general aviation community most emphatically did not support the proposed rule, however. The AOPA generated 70,000 letters to Congress and the FAA in opposition to the rule, pressure that did not go unnoticed.

Ten members of the House Public Works Committee, including the chairs and ranking minority members of both the full committee and the Aviation Subcommittee, wrote in April 1988 to FAA Administrator T. Allan McArtor asking for an extension of the public comment period. More to the point, they said that the proposed rule went "well beyond" the goals of the legislative mandate. They argued that the forty-mile radius would include relatively small airports that need not be included, and requested that the radius, or Mode C "veil," be reduced, without specifying an alternative distance. They also asked that aircraft with a limited ability to install Mode C be exempted, particularly gliders. The FAA responded that the final regulation would be "reasonable," so the demurrers would not have to legislate their desired changes.

The key senators, on the other hand, essentially approved of the proposed rule and made no official attempts to modify it. Other senators did, albeit unsuccessfully, in the face of opposition from the leadership of the committee of jurisdiction.

As an FAA manager noted, final rules must fall within the boundaries of proposed rules, and the final Mode C rule did indeed reduce the Mode C requirement somewhat. In fact, the final rule issued on 21 June 1988 essentially granted all that the House Public Works Committee letter had requested. It specified that Mode C would be required within a thirty-nautical-mile radius of all Terminal Control Areas (or TCAs, the 23 busiest areas), and within the actual boundaries of the 109 Airport Radar Service Areas emplaning more than 200,000 passengers a year. The floor above which Mode C was to be required was raised from the proposed 6000 feet to 10,000 feet. It exempted balloons, gliders, and aircraft built without electrical systems.[13]

The 1989 Deadline Extension

The Air Transport Association and the FAA believed from the beginning that the TCAS II schedule mandated in the 1987 legislation would be impossible to meet both technologically and economically. As noted earlier, they did not actively oppose the legislation, once they had persuaded Packard to loosen his original bill somewhat, because the political climate made unacceptable even the appearance of foot-dragging by the airlines or the FAA. Nevertheless, the ATA and FAA continued to discuss the matter, and within seven months of final enactment of the 1987 legislative requirement, the ATA asked Wendell H. Ford (D-Ky.), chair of the Senate Commerce Committee's Aviation Subcommittee, to request a report from the Office of Technology Assessment (OTA) on the ability of the airlines to meet the mandated schedule for TCAS II.[14]

In September 1988 Ford complied with the request. At about the same time the House Public Works Committee also began exploring the issue, writing in December to the FAA administrator for the FAA's views on the difficulties entailed in meeting the 1987 schedule. Congressman James Oberstar (D-Minn.), the new chair of the Aviation Subcommittee, had not, according to some participants, been deeply involved in the 1987 legislation. Moreover, as one said, Oberstar "had a personal problem" with Congress's mandating deadlines for the executive branch and was inclined to restrict Congress's role to overall policy guidance and oversight. "Packard wanted a firm deadline, but Oberstar wanted to give FAA a further out, so he pressed for up to a two-year extension with FAA having further power to extend [the deadline]."

The airlines, for their part, wanted enough time to fit TCAS installation into their regular maintenance schedules rather than having to take aircraft out of service for a number of days to install the new equipment. Moreover, because they were to be required to install windshear warning and flight-path guidance systems as well, they wanted a schedule that would permit installation of all systems at once. They also argued that they lacked enough mechanics and enough maintenance bays to complete the installations by the deadline. Indeed, one FAA respondent asserted that 90 percent of the reason for requesting the extension was economic; 10 percent was technical: "They could have met the '91 deadline, but it would have been incredibly expensive for the manufacturers and the airlines."

One of the ATA's technical arguments for the extension was that further testing, with TCAS installed on many aircraft at once, was essential to ensure pilot confidence in the system because the use of TCAS on many planes at once in a given airspace could cause unanticipated malfunctions. The FAA also wanted to maximize pilot confidence to ensure use of the system; that concern was lent validity by the airline pilots' assertion that only TCAS III, which unlike TCAS II provides vertical as well as horizontal avoidance directives, met their desiderata.

As the FAA and ATA had hoped, the OTA report legitimated their concerns. Edith Page, who was in charge of the OTA project, was widely cited on all sides in interviews as being highly respected and credible. In preparing the report, she held a workshop to which all participants were invited and at which disagreements were thrashed out. And as a congressional staffer noted, the report "gave Congress political cover" by justifying the extension.[15]

Ultimately, the legislation authorizing phased implementation was relatively uncontroversial. The House version of H.R. 2151, sponsored again initially by Packard, provided for a yearlong operational evaluation of TCAS II beginning 30 December 1990, and authorized extension of the installation deadline for up to two years beyond the December 1991 deadline if the FAA administrator deemed it necessary to ensure a "safe and orderly transition" to TCAS or for other safety reasons. It also permitted the administrator to extend the deadline further if necessary for safety reasons, with a ninety-day advance notification of the committees of jurisdiction.[16] Thus, what had been a strict schedule in the House was considerably loosened. At most, it told the FAA that the committee would be closely watching its progress.

The Senate Commerce Committee did not hold hearings on the legislation but reported it favorably. When it reached the floor in the closing hours of the 101st Congress, Howard Metzenbaum (D-Ohio), who reputedly keeps a close eye on all last-minute legislation, insisted on taking out the indefinite deadline extensions in the House bill, agreeing only to the initial extension. As one staffer said, then "the bill just bounced back and forth [between House and Senate] in the middle of the night; finally there was no time for another bounce," and the House accepted the Senate amendment.

Effects of Congressional Intervention and Executive Response

The Problems

Congress had been led to its initial specification of deadlines by frustration with FAA delay on TCAS, frustration that was evident in hearings throughout the 1980s, and the sense of crisis fostered by the Cerritos collision and a spate of highly publicized near-collisions around that time. Several respondents said that the FAA does not like to be told what to do—which is not surprising—but that given the political climate, FAA could negotiate privately with Packard to loosen his initial deadlines provided it supported the bill publicly. The FAA and the airline industry, with which it worked closely on the issue, succeeded in getting Congress to ease up, with the help of a major clientele group of the authorizing committees, the ATA.

On the Mode C requirement, the FAA reacted as much as Congress to the crisis atmosphere, and proposed an extremely strict rule. Perhaps not by accident, that rule provoked such an outcry from an important constituency group of the House committee that the committee exerted pressure on the FAA to soften it.

From the perspective of most participants, the central problem in this case was the FAA's delay in developing and requiring TCAS. There are at least two mutually compatible views of the reasons for the delay. First, Administrator Helms's initial decision to develop TCAS was accompanied by a decision not to require airlines to install the system but to allow the market to produce incentives for the airlines to do it on their own. If the incentives existed at all, they developed too slowly for Congress. As one participant noted, without an imminent requirement, the market for TCAS simply did not exist in the first half of the decade; hence, private development of the devices was slow.

The second view, according to another participant, rested on the organization and operation of the FAA. According to this participant, the FAA's functioning had been impeded by poor horizontal communication among divisions that should have been working together on program and systems development. In the case of TCAS, there was little coordination among the three sectors of the FAA that were or should have been working on or concerned with the system: research and development, regulation and certification, and air traffic control.[17] The needed coordination came about largely as a result of the widespread sense of crisis engendered by the increase in midair collisions and near-collisions.

Results for Policy

With the exception of one respondent at the FAA, everyone interviewed agreed that congressional intervention in the TCAS program probably sped implementation, despite the fact that Congress had to back down essentially to the deadlines that the FAA proposed in its original NPRM. Some congressional staffers believed that without the legislation, the FAA would not have promulgated a rule. One staffer who gave the FAA less favorable reviews than other staffers said, "The FAA tends to lurch from one crisis to another. Cerritos was fading, and the airlines had an economic disincentive to do TCAS, so manufacturers had no incentive to produce the systems and get the cost down." Another argued that "a tight deadline is better than none," although the need for the 1989 legislative extension of the deadlines "illustrates the pitfalls" of trying to specify an exact schedule. Most participants thought that the legislative mandate helped to focus FAA attention on the program and raise its priority for the agency.

One FAA manager pointed out that a proposed rule on TCAS II was under development even as the House Public Works Committee considered Packard's first bill. He said that the FAA was obviously going to require TCAS and would have established a deadline within a year or two of the congressional deadline anyway. Still, the majority view was that the legislation produced a faster result.

Executive branch respondents argued that the congressional intervention actually made the FAA's job easier on the collision-avoidance system, because the agency did not have to argue with the industry over deadlines, as it would have had to do in a usual NPRM proceeding. In other words,

Congress, by attending to its own and constituents' concerns about aviation safety, broke through customary subgovernment constraints, and in doing so took the FAA off the political hook.

The FAA later aligned itself with the ATA in persuading Congress to roll back the deadline and to give the FAA discretion in implementing the program. Both Congress and the agency responded flexibly to interest groups, cooperating when it helped to achieve their own policy or political goals and resisting when it was to their advantage. This case also suggests that when the issue is salient to a large number of constituents, Congress is in a position to resist interest group requests, as the Senate's support of Mode C requirements in the face of AOPA opposition indicates.[18]

This case illustrates the use of one technique in two vehicles for affecting policy implementation: legislative mandates in authorization and appropriations bills. As the timeline indicates, the appropriations committees, especially in the House, took a continuing interest in collision avoidance throughout the 1980s. The NPRM on Mode C was prompted by both the FY 87 Continuing Resolution and the 1987 Airport and Airway Reauthorization. Results are mixed.

It is impossible to ascertain whether without the legislative mandate, the FAA would have gone forward as soon as it did with rule making, although the majority of inteviewees thought it would not. It is certain, though, that its timetable for TCAS II would have been longer than Congress's original one. Whatever might have been, the congressional mandate on TCAS II was only partially successful, in that the FAA clearly did not attempt to force the airlines to implement Congress's schedule. Indeed, it held a number of discussions with the airline industry on how to get Congress to change the schedule.

Ultimately, the strategy worked; thanks to the OTA report on TCAS implementation, all participants agreed that the 1989 extension was good public policy. On the other hand, in assessing the success of the legislative mandate as a strategy, congressional staffers point to the twenty- to thirty-year history (depending on how one counts FAA involvement) of collision-avoidance-system development and argue that the FAA could have gone on in an unending pursuit of the perfect system. Instead, TCAS II was being installed on airliners in the early 1990s.

With respect to the Mode C requirement, the legislative mandate was imposed as the FAA was working on tighter rules. As the FAA was formulating the final rule, the general aviation community exerted intense pressure extending from political appointees through midlevel career civil servants. Thus, it is possible that Congress's mandate stiffened the FAA's resolve to write a restrictive requirement and provided it with political cover to do so. The FAA did in fact write a proposed rule that some considered a very literal interpretation of the strict congressional requirement and then was able to back off from that, reducing somewhat the force of the AOPA argument that it was being unreasonable on Mode C. That strategy did not deter the AOPA from working for a relaxation of the rule, albeit unsuccessfully. However, the FAA agreed after issuing the final rule to relax the deadlines for transition from one type of transponder to a more advanced version. The AOPA, in turn, "wisely recognizes that Mode C transponders" provide protection for both airliners and general aviation planes.[19]

Thus, in the case of Congress's Mode C requirement, which appeared in both appropriations and authorization language, the legislative mandate technique seems to have been more successful because the FAA did, on the whole, comply with congressional intent. The final rule conformed to the House Public Works Committee's request as expressed in the letter cited earlier, and although Hollings in particular wanted a broader requirement, the Senate was not dissatisfied with the final rule.

The question raised by use of an explicit legislative mandate technique rather than the more common informal intervention techniques is whether the more heavy-handed legislative technique produces results closer to congressional intent than less formal techniques. One case cannot answer that question, but interviews did suggest at least one condition under which nonlegislative requests, including report language, can raise the priority of an issue in the executive branch. Specifically, the prospect that a committee will take up legislation to limit an agency's discretion may give the agency an incentive to try to discover and adhere to congressional intent in order to forestall formal legislative action.[20]

If that is so, why did Congress find it necessary to act legislatively rather than more informally? The answer appears to lie at least partly in the crisis atmosphere that was created by the Cerritos collision and the two smaller midair collisions involving commuter airlines, as well as the highly publicized increase in the rate of near-collisions. For Congress, it was politically necessary to take highly public, formal action rather than the less formal but perhaps equally effective action that is possible when the issue is less salient to constituents. Moreover, one congressional staffer noted that occasionally the FAA ignored report language directing it to take an action. On the other hand, the negative side of formal legislative action in the TCAS case is the time and energy devoted by key actors to justifying extension of the schedule.

Results for Management

Within the FAA there was the feeling that before Congress intervened, TCAS was not really an overall "FAA program" in the sense that only R&D was working on it. The 1987 mandate not only focused the attention of R&D but also brought into the program parts of the agency that previously had not been involved, and got the FAA as a whole vitally concerned with the program's implementation. One respondent thought that the FAA had learned from this the value of "linking arms early" in the life of a program within the FAA and is now doing that more often. In the same vein, another participant said that partly as a result of its experience with TCAS, the FAA in recent years has engaged in more efforts at coordination among divisions on particular programs.

With respect to the impact of the interactions on the discretion of political appointees at the FAA, clearly the 1987 legislation was intended to reduce their ability to implement the program at their preferred pace. Had that legislation stood unchanged, it would have done just that, unless the FAA had simply defied the mandate. As it happened, the FAA sought and eventually received legislation that restored a good deal of its discretion: the 1989 legislation gave the administrator the authority to extend the installation deadline for up to two years beyond the original deadline.

Congressional intervention can assist program managers and political appointees in implementing program goals. In the case of Congress and the FAA, the perception existed within the committees and among some at the FAA that in the office of the secretary of DOT during the Reagan years, there was little commitment to air safety, despite public statements to the contrary. Although many people at the FAA were unhappy about the nature of congressional intervention in the TCAS case, one congressional staffer offered the opinion that oversight pressure from Congress on safety issues often gave the FAA a way to overcome high-level DOT resistance to safety measures, or even legislatively to reverse high-level DOT decisions on such issues as staffing of safety programs. At times, congressional intervention can serve the policy and management goals of both Congress and the agency.

Results for Interbranch Relations

Assessments of the impact of congressional-executive interactions on interbranch relations were mixed. There was considerable agreement that in the early to mid-1980s, relations between Congress and the FAA were not particularly good, due in large part to the perception in key congressional committees that the FAA had not moved quickly enough either with the National Airspace System Plan, announced at the end of 1981, or on a variety of other safety measures, including seat strength, flammability, and overall cabin safety. One respondent described a series of interactions between Chairman Mineta of the House Public Works Aviation Subcommittee and the FAA over cabin-safety issues in 1984. A number of bills intended to force the FAA's hand had been introduced, and the FAA, which already had regulatory initiatives in the works, wanted to head off possible legislative mandates. Mineta agreed not to legislate if the FAA proceeded quickly; in return he asked the FAA to commit to implementation dates and to report monthly on progress to the committee. The committee believed that the arrangement had raised the priority of these issues at the FAA and was generally satisfied with the result.

Furthermore, the same interactions with the committee worked in the interests of the FAA in its ongoing conflict with the top leadership at the Department of Transportation. The monthly progress reports that the committee required of the FAA on cabin safety allowed the committee to pinpoint sources of delay, which sometimes were located not in the FAA but higher up in the DOT. One participant remarked, "The committee could [then] proclaim that [Secretary Elizabeth] Dole was sitting on safety regulations. There was a conspiracy of sorts between the committee and FAA."

As a result of the FAA's perceived cooperation on these issues and during and after legislative action on TCAS, the majority of those interviewed believed that relations had improved, although reviews were mixed. The FAA was perceived to have become less resistant to adoption of an airborne collision-avoidance system and more receptive to establishing standards that the industry would implement in its own way, the strategy preferred by Congress, especially by the appropriations committees. That flexibility and the FAA's general cooperation once it became clear that Congress was determined to pass legislation on TCAS earned congressional praise. Nevertheless, a number of respondents believed that the interactions on TCAS had left bad feeling at the FAA, especially at the professional and civil service levels. If that perception is accurate, it is unclear how that has affected subsequent relations. However, FAA dissatisfaction with Congress's 1987 TCAS schedule accounts for the agency's discussions with the ATA concerning strategies for persuading Congress that the schedule was unrealistic.

The relationship between the FAA and Congress on the 1987 legislation cannot be thought of as particularly favorable. The FAA was not happy about congressional intervention but was resigned to its inevitability and did not actively oppose it; indeed, the FAA publicly supported the legislation. This investigator deems the relations unsuccessful because there was no mechanism in place for genuine consensus building on a realistic schedule. Relations on the 1989 deadline extension were much more effectual because the new legislation emerged from a consensus developed largely by the OTA study of the problems of implementation, a study that was universally accepted and praised as careful and objective.

Conclusions

The cumulative results of Congress's involvement in the collision-avoidance program are generally looked upon as positive. To summarize:

- Congressional intervention probably sped program implementation because it focused FAA attention on the program and raised its priority.
- Congress temporarily took the FAA off the hook with general aviation pilots, who were hostile to the Mode C requirement, by allowing the FAA to

write a stricter requirement than it could have done without a congressional mandate.

- Congress then returned discretion to the FAA for the schedule of implementation of TCAS after mandating an excessively tight schedule in 1987.
- Congressional involvement gave the FAA a way to overcome high-level DOT resistance to safety measures.
- Most participants believed that congressional-FAA relations had improved, although a few participants held that bad feelings lingered at the professional and civil service levels of the FAA.

Both the printed record and the comments of participants in this case make it clear that mistrust was a serious impediment to constructive cooperation between Congress and the FAA on TCAS. One congressional staffer faulted the FAA for its lack of public relations; another argued that it had been particularly heavy-handed with general aviation. But the larger problem was program-based: Congress believed that the FAA had delayed unnecessarily on crucial safety programs. Although congressional intervention in the program was prompted by the "fire alarms"[21] of two midair collisions in eight years, it is manifest that Congress in this case engaged in more than mere crisis-based oversight. Since the 1978 San Diego collision Congress has paid fairly regular attention to FAA implementation of the collision-avoidance program. Another crisis prompted more aggressive congressional involvement, to be sure, but throughout the 1980s, Congress monitored the program fairly actively and was prepared to take strong action when it became obvious that it was necessary. Congress's involvement has been characterized not by sporadic oversight but by ongoing monitoring and periodic active intervention.[22]

Congressional intervention in the development and implementation of this program conforms to some conceptions of Congress's role in the policy process and deviates from others. If this case is seen strictly as an oversight issue, congressional intervention to some degree conforms to a "fire-alarm" model of oversight in which Congress initiates oversight of executive branch programs in response to a crisis or other acute indications from outside actors that something is amiss.[23] In this case, a major midair collision in 1978 and another in 1986 each produced a flurry of congressional activity in the succeeding months and years that subsided after a time but, significantly, did not disappear (see the Timeline of Events).

This pattern of crisis and congressional response is consistent with that found by John Kingdon in his study of governmental agendas and policy making. In transportation policy in particular, Kingdon found that a disaster such as an airliner crash may serve as an early warning of a serious underlying problem, as did the 1978 midair collision over San Diego. Additionally, such a crisis event may reinforce a perception that a problem exists, especially if it occurs along with a number of similar events, as did the 1986 midair collision over Cerritos and a rash of near-collisions in midair. Such events tend to place the perceived problem on the governmental agenda.[24]

These disasters raised the importance of collision avoidance for Congress, but Congress previously had demonstrated an ongoing, if irregular, interest in the FAA's collision-avoidance procedures, an interest dating back to the establishment of the Federal Aviation Agency (later Administration) in 1958 in response to a midair collision between two airliners over the Grand Canyon. Although it would be an exaggeration to characterize Congress's oversight of the program as the systematic search for information that Joel Aberbach argues characterizes much of congressional oversight,[25] it is also the case that oversight of the program is not purely episodic and crisis-driven. It appears that in this case the committees of jurisdiction engage in more oversight than some scholars deem likely.[26] A frequently stated view of the incentive of members of Congress to engage in oversight of administration appears in a textbook: "There is little political payoff either in Washington or at home for senators and representatives who are aggressive overseers."[27]

Other scholars have long noted a tendency for Congress to become deeply involved in program administration, especially but not exclusively through the appropriations process. For example, as early as 1943 Arthur MacMahon observed a high level of supervision of administration by the Appropriations committees. In 1964 Joseph Harris noted that legislative control of administration was increasingly common not only because of the growing complexity of legislation but also because of greater staff and organizational capacity; indeed, he asserted that Congress interfered too much in administrative decisions.[28]

This case reflects a congressional interest in FAA administration of the aircraft collision-avoidance policy that spanned more than a decade. Not surprisingly, much of the day-to-day congressional work was done by subcommittee staffers. Although the time frame of this study does not predate the expansion of staff produced by the various committee reforms of the mid-1970s, it is clear that subcommittee staff contributed to the ability and possibly the inclination of Congress to participate more actively than some scholars expected in the administration of public policy.

This case also illustrates that subsystem politics does not always dominate decision making, despite Lawrence C. Dodd and Richard L. Schott's pessimistic analysis of the crippling impact of clientele groups on congressional control of the executive branch in the decentralized Congress.[29] The crisis atmosphere in which the decisions on the collision-avoidance program were made enabled at least one of the committees (the Senate Commerce, Science, and Transportation Committee) as well as the FAA to overcome strong pressure for weak regulation from the Aircraft Owners and Pilots Association (AOPA), long considered one of the two most influential aviation interest groups.[30] In this case, although the AOPA was influential in the

House Public Works and Transportation Committee, the Senate Commerce Committee was notably unsympathetic to its arguments. Moreover, the legislative requirement that the FAA promulgate certain rules gave the agency the cover it needed to resist the demands of the AOPA and the estimated 70,000 general aviation pilots who lobbied the FAA during its rule-making proceeding.

Thus, a perceived crisis in air safety and the attendant high public visibility of the issue led Congress to engage in three years of intensive supervision of the FAA following a much longer period of lower-level scrutiny and more informal supervision. In the case of the Mode C transponder requirement, a powerful clientele group was thwarted successfully in the process. As a result, congressional intervention sped the implementation of a program to which Congress had for decades been committed.

Timeline of Major Events in the Traffic Alert and Collision Avoidance System Case

28 September 1978	Midair collision over San Diego between PSA and general aviation aircraft.
27 October 1978	House Commerce Committee hearings on aviation safety.
21 February 1979	House Science and Technology Committee hearing on FAA R&D authorization; included discussion of collision-avoidance technology.
26 November 1979	House Ways and Means Committee hearing on midair aviation safety.
6 December 1979	House Public Works and Transportation Committee hearing on the safety of the air traffic control system, including consideration of collision-avoidance systems.
7–8 December 1979	House Government Operations Committee hearings on the collision avoidance-program.
13 June 1979	House Appropriations Committee report on FY 80 DOT appropriations stated the committee's desire for the FAA to develop a national standard for a collision-avoidance system. Report directed the FAA to test trimodal BCAS in Los Angeles. Senate DOT appropriations report concurred.
31 March 1981	House Committee on Science and Technology hearings on collision-avoidance systems.

23 June 1981	New FAA Administrator J. Lynn Helms announced a switch in FAA R&D from ground-based BCAS to TCAS, an airborne system. Projected date for TCAS to be operational: mid-1985.
19 August 1982	House Appropriations Committee report on DOT funding bill directed the FAA to continue to insist that TCAS standards be expressed as performance objectives and not to specify the hardware to be used.
September 1982	House Committee on Science and Technology hearings on collision-avoidance systems.
June 1984	The FAA published the Final National Standard for TCAS II, to be used by large airliners, which completed engineering and technical development.
August 1984	Midair collision over San Luis Obispo, California, between Wings West Airlines and general aviation aircraft.
23 November 1985	House Science and Technology Committee, Subcommittee on Investigation and Oversight hearing on TCAS and microwave landing systems in San Diego.
April 1986	TCAS II prototype installed and evaluated on a Piedmont Airlines aircraft.
18 July and 19 August 1986	House and Senate Appropriations committees recommended $3 million over the budget request for TCAS III Limited Installation Program (LIP) for FY 87. House directed the FAA to report to the committee on the LIP by 1 January 1987.
August 1986	Midair collision over Cerritos, California, between AeroMexico and general aviation aircraft.
17 September 1986	House Appropriations Committee reported a continuing appropriations resolution for FY 87 (H.J. Res 730) that required the FAA to initiate rule making to consider requiring Mode C transponders in all terminal airspace where radar service is required and above a minimum altitude to be determined by the FAA, to be effective as early as possible. Would increase the number of terminal areas where Mode C is required from 9 to approximately 180, and could lower the minimum altitude from the current 12,500 feet. (Included in final legislation.)
25 September 1986	House Public Works Committee, Subcommittee on Investigations and Oversight held hearings on the status of the FAA TCAS R&D program.
10 October 1986	House Science and Technology Committee, Subcommittee on Investigation and Oversight report based on November 1985 hearing. Did not propose legis-

	lation but recommended that the FAA minimize delays in the TCAS II program and issue a rule requiring altitude encoding transponders in general aviation aircraft operating under instrument flight rules.
January 1987	Midair collision near Salt Lake City between Sky West Airlines and general aviation aircraft.
29–30 January and May 1987	Senate Commerce Committee, Subcommittee on Transportation held oversight hearing on safety of air traffic control system.
Summer 1987	LIP began, with installation of TCAS II on fourteen aircraft belonging to United, Piedmont, and Northwest airlines.
7 July and 8 October 1987	House and Senate Appropriations Committee reports on DOT FY 88 funding recommended $6 million over the budget request for the TCAS III LIP.
7 August 1987	House Public Works Committee reported H.R. 1517 to require the FAA to complete within eighteen months certification and operational approval of TCAS II, and to develop within eighteen months regulations to require TCAS II on all aircraft with more than thirty seats within thirty months of certification (or by the end of 1991). The bill would also have required the FAA to issue regulations to require all other aircraft flying in high-density traffic areas to have Mode C altitude-encoding transponders.
26 August 1987	TCAS II NPRM issued by FAA. The rule would have required all commercial and corporate aircraft to be equipped with TCAS II by the early 1990s. It proposed finalizing the rule by October 1988 and completion of installation by 1992 or 1993.
9 September 1987	House Science, Space, and Technology Committee, Transportation Subcommittee hearings on status of FAA TCAS R&D program; considered H.R. 1517 briefly.
6 October 1987	House Science, Space, and Technology Committee reported H.R. 1517 with the same language as in the Public Works Committee report.
28 October 1987	Senate adopted on a voice vote an amendment by Hollings to the airport and airway reauthorization (see entry for 15 December 1987) to require the FAA to promulgate a rule requiring Mode C transponders in nearly all terminal airspace where radar is provided within two years of enactment, and to require TCAS II on all airliners with more than twenty seats.
3 November 1987	House passed H.R. 1517, 405–4 (see 7 August 1987 entry).

15 December 1987	Conference committee reported airport and airway reauthorization, H.R. 2310; report included a compromise on the TCAF and Mode C requirements of H.R. 1517 and the more stringent requirements adopted by the Senate on 28 October 1987.
30 December 1987	P.L. 100-223, Airport and Airway Safety and Capacity Expansion Act of 1987, directed the FAA to require installation of TCAS II on aircraft with more than thirty seats by the end of 1991, and to require altitude-encoding transponders within three years.
12 February 1988	The FAA promulgated NPRM to require Mode C transponders with encoding altimeters on all aircraft flying at or above 6000 feet and all aircraft flying within forty nautical miles of any airport with radar approach-control service. The rule would cover 254 airports.
21 June 1988	Final rule on Mode C issued by the FAA (*Federal Register*, 23356–74); required Mode C within thirty nautical miles of 23 TCA airports and in ARSAs emplaning more than 200,000 per year (approximately 120 airports), and above 10,000 feet everywhere by 1 July 1989.
19 September 1988	Wendell H. Ford, chair of the Aviation Subcommittee of the Senate Commerce Committee, requested a report from OTA on the ability of airlines to meet the congressionally mandated schedule for TCAS II.
21 December 1988	Letter to FAA administrator from Public Works Committee and Aviation Subcommittee chairs and other committee members asking for the FAA's views on the difficulties entailed in meeting the TCAS schedule mandated in the 1987 legislation.
10 January 1989	The FAA issued the Final Rule requiring TCAS II on all aircraft with more than thirty seats by 30 December 1991.
February 1989	Submission by OTA to Senate Commerce Committee of special report, "Safer Skies with TCAS," which recommended extension of deadlines for installation of TCAS II.
4 May 1989	House Public Works Committee, Aviation Subcommittee hearing on airlines' problems meeting mandated schedule for installing TCAS II.
26 July 1989	House Public Works Committee reported H.R. 2151, to extend for up to two years (until 30 December 1993) the deadline for installation of TCAS II, pending an operational evaluation beginning by 30 December 1990.

18 September 1989   Senate Commerce Committee reported in favor of
                       H.R. 2151.
15 December 1989   P.L. 101-236, extending the TCAS installation sched-
                       ule, signed by the president.

Notes

1. U.S. Department of Transportation, Federal Aviation Administration, *National Airspace System Plan* (Washington, D.C.: Government Printing Office, December 1981).

2. U.S. General Accounting Office, *Air Safety: FAA's Traffic Alert and Collision Avoidance System,* GAO/RCED-88-66 BR (February 1988), 8–9; U.S. Congress, Office of Technology Assessment, *Safer Skies with TCAS: A Special Report,* OTA-SET-431 (Washington, D.C.: Government Printing Office, February 1989), 4.

3. House Committee on Public Works and Transportation, *Aircraft Collision Avoidance Act of 1987,* H. Rpt. 100-286 (Washington, D.C.: Government Printing Office, 7 August 1987, 3.

4. Keith F. Mordoff, "NTSB Study of DC-9 Crash Shows Piper in Area without Clearance," *Aviation Week and Space Technology,* 8 September 1986, 45–51.

5. "FAA to Require TCAS-2 on Jet Transports," *Aviation Week and Space Technology,* 29 September 1986, 34.

6. House Committee on Appropriations, *Continuing Appropriations, 1987,* H. Rpt. 99-831 (Washington, D.C.: Government Printing Office, 1987), Y1.1/8: 99–831.

7. House Committee on Public Works and Transportation, *Aircraft Collision Avoidance Act of 1987,* H. Rpt. 100-286/pt.1 (Washington, D.C.: Government Printing Office, 1987), 3.

8. "Collision Avoidance Systems," *Congressional Record,* vol. 133, 28 October 1987, S15255.

9. Congressional staffers suggested an additional, more personal motive. They observed that both members of Congress and staff are "frequent flyers" and have as large a personal interest as anyone in safe skies. The Cerritos collision thus may have awakened awareness of a forgotten danger.

10. 52 *Federal Register* 32268–77 (26 August 1987).

11. 54 *Federal Register* 944 (10 January 1989).

12. Philip J. Klass, "Carriers Question U.S. Timetable for Mandatory TCAS Operation," *Aviation Week and Space Technology,* 21 December 1987, 42.

13. 53 *Federal Register* 23356–74 (21 June 1988).

14. An earlier study of TCAS by the OTA, according to respondents, led both the ATA and FAA to believe that an investigation and report by the OTA would support their case for further testing and a phased installation schedule.

15. U.S. Congress, Office of Technology Assessment, *Safer Skies with TCAS—A Special Report.*

16. House Committee on Public Works and Transportation, *Schedule for Installation of the TCAS-II Collision Avoidance System,* H. Rpt. 101-174 (Washington, D.C.: Government Printing Office, 1989), Y1.1/8:101–74.

17. Because TCAS is an airborne system, the role of air traffic control in its implementation is minimal. Nevertheless, as this respondent noted, there was a need for air traffic control to be involved in deciding what would happen in case of a conflict between instructions issued to pilots by air traffic control and the on-board TCAS. Under standard procedures at the time, failure of a pilot to follow air traffic control instructions triggered an investigation; thus, some accommodation to TCAS involving air traffic control at the FAA was needed.

18. David E. Price, "Policy Making in Congressional Committees: The Impact of Environmental Factors," *American Political Science Review* 72 (June 1978): 548–74.

19. Philip J. Klass, "TCAS Comes of Age," *Aviation Week and Space Technology,* 11 January 1988, 9.

20. Morris S. Ogul, *Congress Oversees the Bureaucracy* (Pittsburgh: University of Pittsburgh Press, 1976), 161; Christopher H. Foreman, *Signals from the Hill* (New Haven: Yale University Press).

21. Mathew D. McCubbins and Thomas Schwartz, "Congressional Oversight Overlooked: Police Patrols versus Fire Alarms," *American Journal of Political Science* 28 (February 1984): 165–79.

22. For evidence that such a pattern is widespread, see Joel D. Aberbach, *Keeping a Watchful Eye: The Politics of Congressional Oversight* (Washington, D.C.: Brookings, 1990).

23. McCubbins and Schwartz, "Congressional Oversight Overlooked."

24. John W. Kingdon, *Agendas, Alternatives, and Public Policies* (Boston: Little, Brown, 1984), 103–5.

25. Aberbach, *Keeping a Watchful Eye,* 98.

26. Ogul, *Congress Oversees the Bureaucracy;* Seymour Scher, "Conditions for Legislative Control," *Journal of Politics* 28 (1963): 526–55.

27. Randall B. Ripley, *Congress: Process and Policy* (New York: Norton, 1988), 360.

28. Arthur W. MacMahon, "Congressional Oversight of the Administration: The Power of the Purse–II," *Political Science Quarterly* 58 (1943): 380–414; Joseph P. Harris, *Congressional Control of Administration* (Westport, Conn.: Greenwood Press, 1964), 8–10, 19–21, 88–90.

29. Lawrence C. Dodd and Richard L. Schott, *Congress and the Administrative State* (New York: Wiley, 1979), 175.

30. Steven E. Rhoads, *Policy Analysis in the Federal Aviation Administration* (Lexington, Mass.: Lexington Books, 1974), 39.

3

Reconciling Pork-Barrel Politics and National Transportation Policy: Highway Demonstration Projects

Diana Evans

Background and Overview

The 152 highway demonstration projects mandated by the Surface Transportation and Uniform Relocation Assistance Act of 1987 were among the most highly contended provisions of that major reauthorization of the nation's highway and mass transit programs. They were named by President Reagan as a chief reason for his veto, subsequently overridden. Disagreement over them had contributed to the demise of the 1986 House-Senate conference on the bill at the end of the 99th Congress, which in turn produced a five-month gap in program spending authority for states.

The conflict was due not to the existence of demonstration projects per se but to the tremendous growth in their number between the previous program reauthorization, in 1982, and the 1987 reauthorization. The Surface Transportation Assistance Act of 1982 contained ten demonstration projects, which were primarily for key committee and chamber leaders; the 1987 legislation contained 152.

Demonstration projects are specially designated projects for the districts of individual members of Congress. They range from "a preliminary engineering study to plan and design alternatives to the Ferry Street Bridge in Eugene, Oregon" to "a new route from Los Alamos, New Mexico, to Santa Fe, New Mexico." Some project descriptions, like the preceding, do not refer to demonstrations of any kind. Others do, as in a project in San Bernadino, California, "for the purpose of demonstrating methods of improving highway access to an airport which is projected to incur a substantial increase in air service."[1]

Demonstration projects were initially included in the 1987 bill by the House Public Works and Transportation Committee, the committee of jurisdiction.[2] The projects were desirable to the legislators who received them for obvious constituency-service reasons. For the committee's leadership, they served the additional purpose of helping to construct a coalition that would pass the bill with the leaders' policy goals intact, including the 55-mph speed limit and adequate funding for urban mass transit.

The Senate Environment and Public Works Committee initially opposed the inclusion of demonstration projects, because they entailed extra spending above state allocations and would build projects that were of low priority to states. Additionally, the size of senators' constituencies made such relatively small-scale projects less profitable in an electoral sense than they were for House members. Nevertheless, soon after the beginning of the 100th Congress, the second conference committee worked out a compromise by which the Senate agreed to allow demonstration projects with certain provisions to make them less costly to the Highway Trust Fund. Once it was a foregone conclusion that the projects would be in the bill, Senate conferees added fifty or so projects of their own to the approximately one hundred House projects already in the bill.

Although the president and the Department of Transportation (DOT) vigorously opposed demonstration projects, the congressional negotiators essentially took little account of their stance. Congressional staffers criticized the DOT for refusing to bargain and for waving the veto threat. Political appointees and career managers at the Federal Highway Administration (FHWA) and the DOT were (and still are) unalterably against the projects on the grounds that they distort state priorities and undermine the integrity of what had been an exemplary national system of integrated highways.

Members of Congress who requested the projects did so precisely because they were unhappy with state priorities. Congressional staffers offered somewhat mixed evaluations of the effects of demonstration projects. Those from the House argued that all of the projects met program criteria; hence, members' assessments of their districts' needs were likely to be at least as valid as those of administrators. Moreover, they deemed relatively insignificant the projects' share (just under 2 percent) of the total spending authorized for the program. On the other hand, they conceded that it might not be wise to displace state priorities with low-priority projects, especially in an era of growing budget constraints, a view with which the Senate concurred.

Although there are various perspectives on the highway demonstration project issue, there does appear to be agreement on several general observations. First, as the interstate highway construction program reaches completion, there are fewer new highways for which members of Congress can take partial credit; further, many projects that are of high priority to the localities in which they would be located have not been built, and are so low on the states' priority lists that it will be years before work on them begins—if ever. Increased funding constraints on the states further reduce the probability of those projects' being built under normal procedures. Still, members of Congress can gain credit for seeing to it that those roads are built if they can get them mandated in the legislation. The inclusion of some demonstration projects in the 1982 legislation as well as the earmarking of Highway Trust Fund money for urban mass transit for the first time in 1982 seems to have sent a signal that the House Public Works Committee was receptive to requests for the projects. The committee, in turn, found acceding to the requests helpful in putting together a winning coalition on the legislation.

The impetus for requesting demonstration projects in the next bill certainly exists. Still, there appears to be a sense within both the House and Senate committees that the process needs to be brought under control.

The Demonstration Project Issue

In late March of 1987, President Ronald Reagan vetoed the Surface Transportation and Uniform Relocation Assistance Act of 1987, which authorized $88 billion for federal-aid highway and mass transit programs. It was the first reauthorization of the widely supported thirty-year-old highway program since 1982. By the time Congress overrode the veto on 2 April, the previous five-year authorization had expired and a five-month funding hiatus had begun.

Why did the president veto an ongoing program that he and his secretary of transportation mostly supported, that had passed both houses of Congress almost unanimously? Ironically, a key provision of the bill helped produce both the large margin of victory in Congress and the presidential veto: highway demonstration projects.[3] Variously condemned as pork and praised as lifesavers and economic boons, most of the demonstration projects in the 1987 act mandated construction, but some authorized only the performance of site selection and environmental studies or design and engineering projects. The 1987 act contained 152 demonstration projects at a five-year cost of $1.4 billion out of a total program authorization of $88 billion.[4] Of the $1.4 billion, $890 million was drawn from the Highway Trust Fund; the remainder came from DOT discretionary funds.[5]

Most of the funding in the act went to long-standing formula programs, such as construction of the remainder of the interstate highway system, construction and repair of other federal-aid highways and bridges, "Interstate 4-R" or rehabilitation and reconstruction of outmoded and deteriorated interstates, highway safety, capital and operating assistance for mass transit systems, and relocation assistance for individuals and businesses displaced by the program. Demonstration projects constituted less than 2 percent of the dollars authorized yet accounted for much of the conflict over the bill, being partly responsible for the failure the 1986 House-Senate conference on the bill in the last weeks of the 99th Congress.[6] One calculation of the ultimate cost of the demonstration projects in the 1986 version exceeded $8 billion, assuming that all projects contemplated therein came to fruition.

The House committee hotly disputed that figure, but the Office of Management and Budget (OMB) recommended the presidential veto partly because it believed that for most of the projects, the five-year authorization of $890 million would be only the beginning of a much larger commitment.

Despite the clear constituency benefits of demonstration projects for members of Congress, and despite the dominance of some other program areas by particularistic benefits, until the 1980s the highway program had been remarkably free of such considerations.[7] According to data supplied by the FHWA, the 1973 reauthorization contained only 14 demonstration projects;[8] the 1978 act, 8; and the 1982 act, 10. Most of the projects were for leaders, chairs of key committees, and members of the authorizing committees. The 1987 act's 152 projects were distributed among thirty-six states and the District of Columbia, among the districts of leaders and nonleaders, members and nonmembers of the committees of jurisdiction alike. In the past, according to one DOT respondent, "There were more real demonstration projects, like pavement studies; they were supported by the states, Congress, and the Department. In the '87 bill, there isn't a single real demo."

In early 1987, at the beginning of the 100th Congress, both houses passed the bill again, this time as H.R. 2. During the conference, Senate negotiators dropped their previous opposition and agreed to allow demonstration projects, adding more than fifty of their own. For its part, the House agreed to include a 20 percent match for states to meet (as opposed to the previous practice of providing 100 percent federal funding), and to allow a vote on raising the speed limit to 65 mph. The compromise overwhelmingly passed both houses. The presidential veto was easily overridden by the House, but the override carried by just one vote in the Senate, and then only on reconsideration of a vote the day before to uphold the veto, a situation highly publicized in the media.[9]

In his 27 March veto message, the president criticized demonstration projects, among other things, arguing that state highway priorities should be determined by the states themselves, not by Congress. It is clear, therefore, that the proliferation of demonstration projects injected into surface transportation politics a new element of contention between the legislative and executive branches, as well as between the House, which initiated the projects, and the Senate, which initially opposed them.

Developing Patterns of Congressional-Executive Relations in Negotiating Demonstration Projects

The View from Congress

Although House Public Works Committee staffers maintained that some demonstration projects really do demonstrate substantive technological advances, the primary and most obvious motivation of members of Congress for requesting such projects in the program reauthorization was to enhance their chances for reelection through constituency service. Initially this motive appeared to be stronger for House members than for senators. As one respondent said, "Anyone would concede that what they're demonstrating is how a member of Congress can come to the Public Works Committee, get a project, and go home and put out a press release."

The stated purpose of most of the demonstration projects substantiates that view. For example, the legislation authorizes several projects as follows:

- ... to demonstrate the benefits of enhancing safety and improving economic vitality of a depressed area.
- [to] demonstrate the effectiveness of construction of parking facilities in relieving on-street parking congestion and unsafe parking practices.
- [to demonstrate] methods of improving economic development and diversification, and eliminating traffic and highway safety hazards....[10]

In the Senate there was more resistance to the projects. As one staffer said, "House members take a more parochial view. It's harder for a senator to help a state this way; they can't meet the potential demand." That is, senators would need many more projects than House members to make a real difference to their reelection chances, and the demand especially in the larger states might become unmanageable once the door was opened. Moreover, senators have greater access to the media for personal publicity and position-taking purposes. House members, less visible, need more tangible ways, like district benefits, to gain constituent attention.[11]

The House Public Works Committee leaders used demonstration projects to build a supportive coalition that would allow them both to write the bill with a freer hand and to produce a bill that would be veto-proof. The political science literature gives much attention to logrolling as a device that enables passage of narrow special-interest bills, but logrolling has not been generally recognized as a device used by committee leaders to assemble enough votes to pass broad general-purpose legislation.[12] In this case, although there was no explicit quid pro quo, it was understood that the Public Works Committee leaders expected that members who received demonstration projects would support the leaders' version of the bill. One staffer said, "It's like the godfather: 'You came to me, but once I do you a favor, you have to be loyal.' The committee doesn't go out and say it's having a sale of demos; *you* go to the committee; it says, 'Jump through these hoops, and you get it.' Six months later, maybe even on another bill, they call in their chits."

If demonstration projects are so useful to members and the committee, why have they not always been abundant in program reauthorizations? Why the growth in the number of projects by over 1500 percent from 1982 to 1987? Interviews with congressional staffers suggested several possibilities. In the late 1970s states began spending up to their obligation ceilings, and there was insufficient money to do their own high-priority projects, much less those of members of Congress. Then in the 1980s construction costs spiraled. Accordingly, demonstration projects are attractive because they come into being with extra money exempt from obligation ceilings.

Additionally, states are less cooperative now with members of Congress because states have mostly completed the interstate system and would rather spend on the rehabilitation of existing roads than on new highways. And, although the states' share of total highway funding has remained relatively constant, the federal share has declined over the years, and the county and municipal share increased from 22 percent to 29 percent between 1977 and 1987.[13] It is to local government that members of the House in particular are most responsive. One staffer observed, "With inflation, highway needs have grown faster than the funds available. The states couldn't do everything they wanted, and this was even more true for the localities, which started lobbying their congressional delegations for specific projects."

So it happened, then, that the 1982 bill, with its ten demonstration projects, opened the eyes of members of Congress to a solution to declining highway construction in their states and districts. And a committee whose leaders sought a coalition accommodated many of their requests.

Requirements and Negotiations. — The contentious House-Senate conference on H.R. 2 produced a compromise on the number and funding of demonstration projects. The conference version authorized 152 projects; for each project, 50 percent of the funding was to come from the Highway Trust Fund, exempt from state obligation limits; 30 percent was to be from the transportation secretary's discretionary funds; and 20 percent was to come from state sources. For most states, the federal money was extra funding; it was not to come out of their regular allocations. The House and Senate overwhelmingly accepted the conference bill.

Prior to the conference, the House and Senate had been far apart on demonstration projects. The House version of the bill had been much more generous, providing as in the past 100 percent federal funding exempt from obligation limits; as in the conference compromise, the money would not have come out of the state's allocation.[14] The Senate version included no demonstration projects; instead, a less costly alternative, "priority projects," would come out of a state's normal funding allocation and would be built only if the state requested. States would be given the flexibility to move extra money from other categories to build the projects, an option they normally would not have.[15]

Separate negotiations were conducted in the House and Senate, in the two House-Senate conference committees, and between the administration and the Senate on the veto-override vote. House members who wanted projects went directly to the Public Works Committee leaders, not the typical

pattern for the committee. Staffers are generally credited with great technical expertise and power,[16] and lobbyists normally would go to them first
concerning specific provisions. Demonstration projects were different. One
staffer remarked, "Some made the mistake of going to the staff first, but the
staff liked their jobs, so they sent them to the members [of the committee]."
In other words, the power to give out demonstration projects was a prerogative not taken lightly.

Requesters were expected to justify projects with facts and figures; a
staff member explained, "You needed to be able to say how many people
died on that curve." The committee kept a record of these data for purposes
of defense on the floor. Chairman James Howard (D-N.J.) expected in return for granting a request that the recipient would support the committee
leadership's position on the bill (and perhaps on other bills as well), and denied projects to requesters who had opposed the committee on key votes
and even members who had asked the Appropriations Committee for projects in its DOT appropriations bill. According to one staffer, "They kept a
list of those who voted against the committee with black dots next to their
names. Those people did not get demonstration projects." Among Howard's
own policy commitments, which he furthered by including demonstration
projects in the legislation, were a strong mass transit program and the
55-mph speed limit.

The Senate Environment and Public Works Committee initially accommodated those who came asking for projects in the form of priority projects, largely because of an individual senator's ability to hold up legislation
on the floor. Although split internally, the committee held the line against
the more expensive and restrictive (for states) House approach. Thus, the
stage was set for conflict between the House and Senate over their respective
versions of the bill: demonstration projects were a major bone of contention. The first House-Senate conference failed during the closing days of the
99th Congress; the Senate negotiators' hostility to full federal funding of
demonstration projects was key among several reasons for the failure to
reach agreement, as was the House's desire to preserve the 55-mph speed
limit.[17]

At least partly in anticipation of the conference, the House Public
Works Committee designed a formula change for Interstate 4-R, the interstate rehabilitation program, that would hurt sparsely populated western
states. As a House staffer commented, "The Senate's pork was in the form
of formulas anyway." The Senate correctly perceived the formula change as
a bargaining tool to force it to agree to demonstration projects; the House
eventually did drop the change in conference as partial payment for the Senate's capitulation.

During the second conference, in the early weeks of the 100th Congress, the Senate successfully insisted on a funding change for demonstration
projects: a 20 percent local share rather than full federal funding. Senate ne-

gotiators additionally proposed that 30 percent of the funds come from a state's regular apportionment; the House agreed instead to allow 30 percent to come from the secretary's discretionary funds. The Senate conceded that the remaining 50 percent would not be subject to obligation limits and would not come from a state's regular allocation but would be new money from the Highway Trust Fund.

Once it became clear that demonstration projects would survive the conference, the Senate added approximately fifty projects of its own, including the conversion of some priority projects to demonstration projects, in addition to the House's hundred or so projects. Funding was more or less equally divided between House and Senate projects. According to a House staff member, some of the Senate's demonstration projects were among those that had been rejected by the House; the requesting House members had taken them to their counterparts in the Senate. Other projects were requests from state transportation departments, some of which had been in senators' files for some time.

In a major concession to the Senate by the House committee chair, Howard, the House conferees agreed to allow a separate House vote on a 65-mph speed limit on rural interstates. The speed limit and demonstration projects had been two of the major sticking points of the failed previous conference. Now, in the 1987 conference, they had been resolved.

With respect to negotiations between Congress and the executive, the Department of Transportation was viewed by Congress as unwilling to engage in give-and-take on the bill and its demonstration projects. Indeed, Congress believed the administration's sole bargaining tactic to be the veto threat. A Senate staffer recollected, "We consulted with them and they made their position clear: no demos and no priority projects." And a House staffer noted, "The biggest opponent of demos was the administration. Yet the Hill had given them discretionary programs, which are the same thing; it's just a question of who gets to choose where the project is." Because of the administration's perceived intransigence and its tardiness in producing its own highway bill (it delayed until there were already at least two versions before Congress), it was not seen as a major force in the negotiations. Federal Highway Administrator Ray Barnhart and some of his people spent a good deal of time on the Hill even so, trying to persuade the committee's leaders and other members to drop the demonstration projects.

On 27 March Reagan vetoed the reauthorization act, citing its demonstration projects as a major reason. The House easily overrode the veto, but on 1 April the Senate sustained it by two votes, one of which was cast by Majority Leader Robert Byrd (D-W.V.) in order to entitle him to move to reconsider the vote. During the twenty-four hours between the first and second votes, intense pressure was applied to the thirteen Republicans who had voted to override the veto. One staffer recalled, "The President himself came to the Hill, which he almost never did, to change one vote; and the big

'Eagle' [campaign] contributors called about ten senators. The press also put on the pressure by calling an override a major defeat for the President." A press report confirmed that account:

> Senators who met with the President today said he had begged for their support in an extremely uncomfortable session. But his pleas failed and, in the opinion of some there, perhaps even backfired. Not a vote was changed.
>
> Other Republicans expressed regret that Mr. Reagan, already weakened by the Iran affair, chose to stake his prestige on opposition to a bill that passed the House by a vote of 407 to 17 and the Senate by a vote of 79 to 17.[18]

A House staffer said that to aid its effort, the administration used discretionary DOT funds to "bribe" senators to uphold the veto. No Republicans changed their votes, and freshman Senator Terry Sanford (N.C.), the lone pro-veto Democrat, switched the following day to a vote in favor of the override. The bill became law.

The most controversial aspect of the veto fight and the one that left lasting bad feeling in Congress, was the distribution by Minority Leader Robert Dole (R-Kan.) of a table purporting to show that forty-one states would receive less money under the conference version of the bill than under the Senate-passed version (which did not contain demonstration projects). It eventually was widely agreed in the Senate that both the numbers and conclusions were false; it was also generally assumed, at least initially, that they had come from Administrator Barnhart's office. Once the dust settled, it became clear that the numbers had come from the "political people" in Transportation Secretary Elizabeth Dole's office. According to a staffer: "The administration took the demo money and 'spent it out' under formula to show that states would get more under the Administration bill, but they cooked the numbers. The career people in Federal Highways refused to participate; this came from the Secretary's office." In a hearing held in late April by Daniel Moynihan (D-N.Y.), chair of the Senate Environment and Public Works Committee's transportation subcommittee, the FHWA's Barnhart disavowed the figures and called them inaccurate and misleading.[19]

Some bitterness remained in Congress, particularly in the Senate. True to classic subsystem politics, the bitterness did not extend to the FHWA, despite the fact that the administrator is a political appointee who reports to the secretary.

Appropriations Committees' Demonstration Projects.—The vast majority of ongoing highway demonstration projects were provided in the 1987 program reauthorization. In the past few years, however, the appropriations committees have become much more involved in giving out their own demonstration projects in the annual DOT Appropriations bill.

The upward trend in Appropriations committees' highway demonstration projects, although less steep than for the authorization process, shows approximately the same tendency. That is, before 1987, the year in which the highway authorization bill set a new standard for demonstration projects, DOT appropriations bills rarely contained more than three new projects and continued funding for a few others. However, in the FY 87 legislation, 7 new projects were funded, all at full federal funding, unlike other highway programs, which require at least a 10 percent state share. In FY 88, 8 new projects and 14 continuing projects were funded; in FY 89, 18 new and 22 continuing projects; and in FY 90, 10 new and 25 continuing projects. In FY 91, 12 new and 26 continuing projects were funded and the conference report named an additional 54 new projects that the committees wanted built. A career manager at FHWA had this to say: If the agency "wants to enjoy good relations with Congress," it will see to it that those named in the conference report also are built. In 1988, 1989, and 1991, the majority of new projects required a 20 percent state share (like the authorization demonstration projects), but for FY 90, half of the new projects were funded at 100 percent.

A staff member explained the process by which the appropriations subcommittees on transportation decide to fund demonstration projects: "We operate under a [Section] 302(b) [spending] restraint. We have to fund FAA, the National Transportation Safety Board, mass transit, and so on. We look at each program and go through a lot of iterations. What is available for demos is determined by what we have to give the other programs. But we look at the projects, who asks [for them], and how adamant they are." The Senate subcommittee sends the requests to the FHWA for evaluation. The FHWA, which usually knows something about each proposed project, may find another way to fund some of them. The above respondent observed that most of the projects are legitimate, but far down the states' priority lists.

The growth in the number of demonstration projects in the House appropriations bills has generated turf battles between the Public Works and Appropriations committees. Members who go to one committee for a project may be penalized in the other committee. The Public Works Committee, in particular, considers Appropriations demonstration projects an illegitimate incursion into its policy domain. However, the temptation for members to go to Appropriations is strong because that committee produces a bill every year and authorizations are done only every five years. A staffer of the House Public Works Committee described the situation: "We resist members going to them [Appropriations] and we fight them. But when there's an authorization only every few years, some members may have to go to them." According to several staffers, when members go to Appropriations for favors or side with that committee on floor votes, Public Works may see to it that they lose projects in authorizing legislation or amendments to help district interests. Likewise, it costs members Appropriations projects when they go against that committee on floor amendments or "side with Public Works on the squabbles between the two committees." It is clear that demonstration projects are used both as currency to purchase votes and as broad-spectrum weapons in jurisdictional infighting.

A truce of sorts was worked out between the two committees in 1987 or 1988. Appropriations agreed to clear (or to have project requesters clear) demonstration projects with Public Works first; to fund projects from general revenues and not the Highway Trust Fund; and to require a 20 percent state share. The truce seems unstable because many Appropriations projects receive 100 percent federal funding, and the committee has sometimes violated the agreement that projects first be cleared with Public Works.

There appears to be little competition between the two relevant Senate committees on demonstration projects, largely because overlapping membership precludes turf battles.

The View from the Executive

Within the Department of Transportation, both political and career people agreed that demonstration projects, in the words of one career manager, "demonstrate the ability of members to bring home the pork." Another said, "They don't demonstrate anything except how to get an extra dip in the public till." Staffers universally denied that the projects in the 1987 bill demonstrated technological advances in methods of highway construction, safety, reduction of traffic congestion, or any of the other purposes stated in project authorizations. Nevertheless, one respondent felt considerable sympathy for the political situation of members of Congress: "Members run under terribly trying circumstances with their constituents. They tell the members, 'If you don't get it for us, we'll elect somebody who will.'"

Like the congressional respondents, DOT people agreed that from Congress's point of view, demonstration projects help the House committee construct winning coalitions not only on highway legislation but also on other bills. There is considerable potential benefit to the House Public Works Committee, for example, from inserting projects for Congressman Dan Rostenkowski (D-Ill.), chairman of the Ways and Means Committee, because that committee has jurisdiction over the gas tax, which largely funds the highway program.

With respect to the executive branch's motives for opposing demonstration projects, the most public was budget constraints, but the most prevalent in the responses of those interviewed was the effect of the projects on the highway program. In explaining his veto of the highway bill, Reagan called it a "budget-buster," and placed much of the blame on demonstration projects. Unlike the OMB, which focused on projected long-term costs, some in the DOT discounted the dollar impact of projects because they constituted less than 2 percent of the five-year authorization. Instead, they emphasized that the integrity of the highway program, as the national program it was intended to be, was compromised by what some termed "special interest projects." The DOT's motives for opposing the program, in other words, tended to be largely programmatic (see section on effects for fuller discussion).

One respondent in the FHWA did point out that demonstration projects put the secretary in a politically untenable position, in the following sense: the federal-aid highway program is based on funding formulas that, in theory, treat states equitably. By accepting demonstration projects for some members, therefore, the secretary effectively says that some states' projects are better than others just because some got into the bill and some did not—a position that the secretary does not want to take, even implicitly.

When asked about the explosion in demonstration projects between the 1982 and 1987 reauthorizations, one respondent from the FHWA suggested two major reasons: First, as the Interstate Highway system came near completion and the national goals of the program were essentially accomplished, members of Congress began to see that there were billions of dollars in the Highway Trust Fund that could now be spent on individual projects [as opposed to other purposes], if only they were authorized. Second, in the 1982 Act, the gas tax was increased by 5 cents per gallon. One penny of that increase was for the first time dedicated to urban mass transit, funds that effectively went to 18 big cities. This earmarking for cities helped to fuel the demand for earmarking for specific highway projects as well. Another respondent offered a similar perspective: "During the heyday of interstate construction under normal formula programs, members of Congress had more opportunity to appear at ribbon-cuttings of new roads. Since most of the construction is completed, demonstration projects provide the only opportunities to take credit for highway construction projects."

Requirements and Negotiations.—Although the executive branch monolithically opposed demonstration projects, the FHWA is bound when requested to provide technical assistance to individual members of Congress and the committees in the evaluation of the feasibility of proposed demonstration projects "no matter how big a turkey a project is." The requests are handled by the appropriate technical office, which may accompany its recommendations with suggested draft language for the project; if the project is built, the FHWA feels that the suggested language makes it as workable as possible so that it will accomplish what the member wants. And most of the time, officials said, Congress does take the technical advice about how to build a project, if not the political advice about whether to build it.

Although the top political people in the secretary's office and the FHWA tried to talk the House committee and then the conference committee out of including demonstration projects in the 1987 bill, there is no evidence that anyone was listening. As one Public Works Committee staffer observed, the DOT kept telling members that the projects were displacing state priorities, but "what [the DOT] never quite understood was that was what members wanted to do."

Indeed, there was nothing the administration could have done to keep demonstration projects out of the bill. As the interviews in Congress indicated, the veto threat was a major but ineffective bargaining tool. Although the FHWA publicly supported the presidential veto, there was private dissension within the DOT over its political advisability once the House and Senate passed their compromise version overwhelmingly, making it unlikely that a veto could be sustained.

The View from the States

The major interest group representing state governments on demonstration projects is the American Association of State Highway and Transportation Officials. The AASHTO officially opposes demonstration projects on the same grounds as the executive: they displace state priorities and disrupt the planning process. Despite that position, however, the organization has kept a low public profile on the issue, restricting opposition to testimony in hearings for two reasons. First, states are dependent especially on the House Public Works Committee for the highway program, and probably seek not to antagonize it. Second, some states actively attempt to get demonstration projects through their congressional delegations, so there is some difference of opinion within the organization on the projects' desirability.

The National Association of Counties was somewhat more equivocal. In its 1985–86 American County Platform, the NACO called not for elimination but for limitation of demonstration projects to a small percentage of highway program spending. It also called for standards that would restrict funding to genuine innovations and unusual needs.

Effects of Congressional Detailing of Demonstration Projects

The View from Congress

Assessments by committee staffs of the effects of demonstration projects ranged from positive to negative. On the House side, where the projects are most valued, evaluations were somewhat ambivalent. House staffers argued defensively that although the projects override states' priorities, there is no *a priori* reason to think that states' priorities are superior to member priorities. One staffer declared, "The political considerations in the state capital may be different from members', but the state priority process isn't pure either." Similarly, another staffer declared that if members of Congress can justify their projects, their priorities should prevail over those of "unelected administrators." Still another said that the projects often provide seed money for projects supported by local governments and constituents that simply may be too far down on the state's list to be funded any time soon. All argued that by and large the projects are meritorious and eligible for funding under program regulations.

Reflecting on the use to which demonstration projects are put by committee leaders, one staffer further defended them as bargaining chips that allow the committee to "do the greater good," helping it to form coalitions to enact needed policy changes in the highway and mass transit programs. About the 1982 reauthorization, one staffer mused, "Demos may have increased the gas tax from 4 to 9 cents; who's to say?"

Despite the perceived political benefits of the demonstration projects to members of Congress and to the House Public Works Committee, House staffers conceded that the projects may have negative effects. For example, some said that the projects may distort state priorities, making more difficult the achievement of short- and long-term planning goals. Additionally, because the national program is shrinking in relative terms and the interstate highway system is in increasing need of rehabilitation and modernization, it is hard to justify funding the projects.

Senate staffers echoed strongly the negative assessments of demonstration projects. Their major criticism was that particularly in a time of budget constraints, it is a mistake to take money from established programs to fund low-priority projects, some of them of questionable value. Although they granted that some of the projects were developed by members of Congress in consultation with state DOTs and thus were probably justified in a policy sense, they maintained that overall the program effects were negative because states build their high-priority projects without earmarked funding. One staffer said, "Some of the projects were a state's priority if there was a lot of consultation [with the member of Congress]. Some were good, others probably never would have been done otherwise. Some probably never will start, but are tying up money anyway. They also undermine a little the relationship between states and locals, which need to work out a coordinated program."

Congressional staff assessments of the impact of demonstration projects on the administration of the highway program were mixed. Some thought the projects created an "administrative headache" because each is a separate program category, which adds well over one hundred categories to the twelve usual program categories. Others believed the administrative effects were negligible, despite the extra categories that had to be created for accounting purposes.

The View from the Executive

Officials at the DOT and the FHWA were unanimous in negatively evaluating the programmatic effects of demonstration projects. One official asserted that the projects subvert the process of selection of highway projects;

state departments of transportation have sophisticated rules governing the establishment of state priorities, to which demonstration projects are not subject. For the FHWA, the fact that 30 percent of the money for each project comes out of the agency's discretionary funds means that it, too, must set aside some higher-priority projects. It deems the projects detrimental to the integrated national transportation system that has been built under normal procedures. The traditional federal-state partnership has created a strong national system, and special-interest considerations should not enter into project selection, forcing states to build what are often low-priority projects.

One FHWA official was a bit gentler in his criticism, but the conclusion was the same: "I don't think they're boondoggles; they are desirable projects, but they're not top priority." The injection of parochial considerations into an integrated national system, he argued, tends to discredit the highway program.

As for the effects of demonstration projects on program administration by the FHWA, officials differed somewhat. One thought that the projects did not pose special administrative problems; even the annual reports on each project required in the legislation were not viewed as onerous because of their brevity. However, another argued that the projects are burdensome in that they make it more difficult for administrators to plan their own work if they have to do studies for members of Congress. In general, however, DOT officials did not think that the projects entailed much in a purely administrative sense. Once authorized, they constitute a small percentage of the total number of highway projects: "When you're dealing with hundreds of thousands of projects, it doesn't make doodly-squat." Their objection to the projects is based on policy considerations and on the limitation of executive discretion that results from such congressional mandates.

Conclusions

Summary Evaluations
The evaluations of the impact of demonstration projects on the national highway program, administration, and interbranch relation are summarized below.

Impact on the Program
1. Demonstration projects often provide seed money for good projects that are supported by local governments and constituents, and that are too far down a state's priority list to be funded in the foreseeable future.
2. Demonstration projects are used by committee leaders as bargaining chips that help them to form coalitions to enact policy changes in the highway and mass transit programs.

3. Demonstration projects distort state priorities, which makes more difficult the achievement of short- and long-term planning goals and sidetracks projects that are more crucial to the state as a whole.
4. Demonstration projects are detrimental to the integrated national transportation system that has been built under normal procedures.

Impact on Administration
Opinions are mixed, but overall opinion in both Congress and the DOT is that the burden is not excessive.

Impact on Interbranch Relations
Although the demonstration project issue was "a vehicle for rancorous discussion" between the branches, it had no lasting negative effect on the relations between Congress and the FHWA.

Effectiveness of the Pattern of Congressional-Executive Interactions for Reaching Agreement on Policy Outcomes
Given the lack of negotiations between the branches on the desirability of demonstration projects, the interactions that did occur must be termed unsuccessful from the perspective of the executive and successful from the perspective of Congress.

Proposals and Prospects for Change

In 1991, when Congress passed and President Bush signed a six-year reauthorization of the highway and mass transit programs, the Surface Transportation Efficiency Act of 1991, those programs were at a turning point. The interstate highway construction program was virtually complete, and all key players in the subsystem worked with the realization that they were reshaping the system in the most important reauthorization since the creation of the Interstate Highway System in 1956. As expected, the new legislation (P.L. 102–240) put interstate highway maintenance and rehabilitation near the top of the list of federal funding priorities. Among many other provisions, it also created a new National Highway System composed of the interstate network and primary highways, reflecting a proposal that had been under discussion within the subsystem for a number of years. Among the biggest changes in the program was unprecedented flexibility for states to shift federal funds among previously sacrosanct categories of spending, particularly between highways and mass transit. The new legislation gave urban areas much more discretion as well.

Prior to the shaping of this legislation, staff members on both House and Senate committees talked about possible mechanisms to control the growth of demonstration projects. Opponents of the projects were heartened by the designation of Norman Mineta (D-Calif.) as chair of the House Public Works Committee's Surface Transportation Subcommittee, because

Mineta had refused, as chair of the Aviation Subcommittee, to grant demonstration projects in that subcommittee's bills. However, Robert Roe's (D-N.J.) defeat of Mineta for the chairmanship of the full committee following the Democratic caucus's ouster in December 1990 of Chairman Glenn Anderson led some to predict continued support for demonstration projects at the top of the committee.[20]

With passage of the 1991 reauthorization, the worst fears of the opponents of demonstration projects were realized. The legislation designated 539 projects, a 350 percent increase over the 152 authorized in 1987, at a cost of $6.2 billion, or 4 percent of the total authorization. The political heat in 1987 had apparently inflicted some lasting burns in one sense, however; Chairman Roe refused to call them "demonstration projects," preferring instead to label them "Congressional projects of national significance,"[21] a designation that perhaps understandably has not achieved broad currency.

Once again, the projects were included despite the stated desire of the administration to hold the line against what it considered politically motivated highway projects. Career managers at the DOT would have preferred restriction of such projects to those that truly demonstrated technological advances in transportation, as several respondents argued had been the case in the past. Examples of such projects were included in the 1991 legislation, especially the funding for magnetic levitation trains and intelligent highway and vehicle projects. However, the special projects in the 1991 bill overwhelmingly resembled those in the 1987 legislation. Clearly, the pressures for traditional district projects proved impossible to resist.

The 1991 reauthorization was like the process in 1987 in that inclusion of district-oriented projects was most beneficial for House members. Thus, the projects proved useful to the leaders of the House Public Works and Transportation Committee, particularly in 1987, as those leaders crafted legislation that reflected their own policy preferences, giving out demonstration projects as inducements for member support for the committee bill. For senators, on the other hand, the formulas used to determine the states' total funding were far more critical than demonstration projects—in 1987 and again in 1991.[22]

Timeline of Major Events in the
Demonstration Projects Case

1973	Highway reauthorization legislation contained 14 demonstration projects.
1978	Highway reauthorization legislation contained 8 demonstration projects.
1982	Highway reauthorization legislation contained 10 demonstration projects.
October 1984	H.R. 5504, an interim bill to approve interstate cost estimates died in conference, partly due to House-Senate dispute over demonstration projects. House version of 5504 had 52; Senate version, 16.
October 1986	H.R. 3129 died in conference at the end of the 99th Congress; a major reason was failure to resolve the House-Senate dispute over demonstration projects.
21 January 1987	House passed H.R. 2, virtually identical to H.R. 3129, 401–20.
4 February 1987	Senate passed H.R. 2, 96–2.
February–March 1987	House-Senate conference resolved the impasse on the bill when House Public Works Committee Chairman James Howard agreed to allow the House to vote on a 65-mph speed limit and to require a state match of 20 percent on demonstration projects (rather than 100 percent federal funding). The Senate, in return, after adding projects of its own, agreed to accept demonstration projects.
27 March 1987	President Reagan vetoed H.R. 2, citing demonstration projects as a major reason.
2 April 1987	Following the House override vote, the Senate narrowly overrode the veto, and H.R. 2 became law containing 152 demonstration projects.

Notes

1. "Surface Transportation and Uniform Relocation Assistance Act of 1987," P.L. 100-17, 2 April 1987.

2. House Committee on Public Works, *Surface Transportation and Uniform Relocation Assistance Act of 1986,* H. Rpt. 99-665 (Washington, D.C.: Government Printing Office, 2 July 1986).

3. Reagan's other reasons for the veto included the total cost of the bill and the earmarking of funds for mass transit from the general fund. Linda Greenhouse, "Senate, for Now, Upholds the Veto of Roads Measure," *New York Times,* 2 April 1987. Office of Management and Budget sources have suggested

that demonstration projects were actually a minor reason for the veto despite their prominence in White House public criticism of the bill.

4. At the end of 1987, five more demonstration projects were added as technical amendments to the authorization legislation in P.L. 100-202, the FY 88 DOT Appropriations Act. The five projects constituted a reallocation of 1987 funding for several projects in that authorization; thus, no new funding was authorized for them.

5. "Surface Transportation and Uniform Relocation Assistance Act of 1987," P.L. 100-17, 181–201.

6. "Highway Reauthorization Dies Amid Disputes," *1986 CQ Almanac* (Washington, D.C.: Congressional Quarterly, 1987), 284.

7. For just two of many examples of studies of such benefit programs, see Arthur Maass, *Muddy Waters* (Cambridge: Harvard University Press, 1951); John A. Ferejohn, *Pork Barrel Politics: Rivers and Harbors Legislation, 1947–1968* (Stanford: Stanford University Press, 1974).

8. As with the 1987 authorization legislation, 14 demonstration projects were authorized in the original legislation; amendments to that legislation passed in each year from 1974 through 1977 authorized a total of 7 more.

9. The critical vote in the Senate was cast by freshman Terry Sanford (D-N.C.), the only Democrat to support the veto. His vote provided the president with victory on the override. Following some savvy parliamentary maneuvering by Robert Byrd (D-W.V.) and behind-the-scenes pressure, a new vote was taken, Sanford changed his vote, and the veto was overridden. Greenhouse, "Senate, for Now"; Linda Greenhouse, "Senate Rejects Reagan Plea and Votes 67–33 to Override His Veto of Highway Funds," *New York Times,* 3 April 1987.

10. "Surface Transportation and Uniform Relocation Assistance Act of 1987," P.L. 100-17, sec. 149.

11. David Mayhew, *Congress: The Electoral Connection* (New Haven: Yale University Press, 1974), 73.

12. For a seminal theoretical treatment, see James M. Buchanan and Gordon Tullock, *The Calculus of Consent* (Ann Arbor: University of Michigan Press, 1962), 131–45. For empirical investigations of logrolling, see Thomas Stratmann, "The Effects of Logrolling on Congressional Voting," *American Economic Review* (forthcoming); J.B. Kau and P.H. Rubin, "Self Interest, Ideology and Logrolling in Congressional Voting," *Journal of Law and Economics* 22 (October 1979): 365–84. However, Arnold argues that bureaucrats use awards of district projects in a way similar to that found here: to reduce congressional members' opposition to their programs. See R. Douglas Arnold, *Congress and the Bureaucracy* (New Haven: Yale University Press, 1979), 56–57.

13. Mike Mills, "Skinner Steers Federal U-Turn As Interstate Dead Ends," *CQ Weekly Report,* 15 December 1990, 4137.

14. House Committee on Public Works, *Surface Transportation and Uniform Relocation Assistance Act of 1986,* 39.

15. Senate Committee on Environment and Public Works, *Federal-Aid*

Highway Act of 1987, Rpt. 100-4 (Washington, D.C.: Government Printing Office, 27 January 1987), 22–23, 35; *Federal-Aid Highway Act of 1986*, Rpt. 99-369 (Washington, D.C.: Government Printing Office, 5 August 1986), 19, 35.

16. Burt Solomon, "Staff at Work," *National Journal,* 16 May 1987, 1174–76.

17. "Highway Reauthorization Dies amid Disputes," *1986 CQ Almanac* (Washington, D.C.: Congressional Quarterly, 1987), 284.

18. Greenhouse, "Senate Rejects Reagan Plea."

19. Senate Committee on Environment and Public Works, Subcommittee on Water Resources, Transportation, and Infrastructure, *Accuracy of Information Supplied by the Department of Transportation Hearing.* S. Hrg. 100-66, 28 April 1987.

20. Mike Mills, "Roe Wins Job He's Waited For: Ascent on Public Works," *CQ Weekly Report,* 8 December 1990, 4062.

21. "Highways, Mass Transit Funded," *1991 CQ Almanac* (Washington, D.C.: Congressional Quarterly, 1992).

22. Mike Mills, "Highway Bill Debate Becomes War Between the States," *CQ Weekly Report,* 8 June 1991, 1487–89.

4

"Not in My Back Yard": High-Level Nuclear Waste Policy

James A. Thurber

Background and Overview

The Nuclear Waste Policy Act of 1982 (NWPA) (P.L. 97-425) and the subsequent Nuclear Waste Policy Amendments Act of 1987 (NWPAA) (Title V of P.L. 100-203 and P.L. 100-507) provide the legislative framework for the Department of Energy's (DOE) Office of Civilian Radioactive Waste Management (OCRWM) program to find a long-term means for storing high-level civilian nuclear waste in the United States.

In 1987 Congress directed the DOE through the NWPAA to study ("characterize") the Yucca Mountain, Nevada, site for suitability as a national nuclear waste geologic repository, while at the same time prohibiting the search for a second repository site. The selection of Yucca Mountain was the geographic expression of congressional agendas that reflected the power structure within Congress and well-entrenched political-economic relationships in the nuclear power arena.

The passage of the NWPAA was a direct result of the policy adopted in the Nuclear Waste Policy Act of 1982. The NWPA had enjoined the Department of Energy to hold hearings wherever site characterization studies were conducted in order to identify the public's concerns and calm citizens in affected areas by educating them about the repository site selection process. DOE, politically weak and convinced that public liaison was unnecessary and irrelevant, only halfheartedly attempted to implement the public comment portion of the 1982 policy. As the program neared collapse in 1987, Congress reacted with new legislation—the NWPA Amendments.

This case shows that decision-making processes concerning the disposal of high-level civilian nuclear waste evolved through several policy-making subsystems. From 1956 until 1979, the subsystem was dominant, exhibiting stable relations among a small group of decision makers. After the Three

Mile Island accident in 1979, however, a large number of new participants entered the decision-making process and conflict over the goals of civilian nuclear waste policy emerged. These changes enabled a competitive subsystem to arise that shaped and passed the Nuclear Waste Policy Act in 1982. However, competitive subsystems exhibit coalitions that are short-lived due to competition for resources and information. Public dissatisfaction with the 1982 policy and the DOE's implementation of the hearings process led to the breakdown of the policy. As the political cost of remaining in the decision-making process rose, most actors left the subsystem. This caused a new, micropolitical system to emerge that molded and guided passage of the Nuclear Waste Policy Amendments Act in 1987, and has governed implementation of the policy ever since.

Using interviews with congressional, executive branch, and private-sector respondents, and an analysis of primary source documents, this chapter analyzes the nature of decision making through the lens of subsystems theory.[1] The study concludes that the subsystem that made decisions regarding the long-term storage of civilian high-level nuclear waste began as a dominant (closed and low-profile) decision-making system in the 1950s and evolved into a more open, conflictual, and competitive system of actors in the 1980s and 1990s.

Congressional-Executive Relations and the Implementation of Nuclear Waste Policy

Congressional-executive relations associated with nuclear waste policy have evolved through three stages. In the first stage, a closed and dominant policy-making system typified by congressional-executive cooperation in the research and development of waste management isolation technologies operated with a high level of executive branch secrecy and discretion from 1956 until 1979. The second, competitive stage existed between 1979 and 1986. In this stage, the system became more open to participation by other actors. This encouraged congressional-executive conflict and witnessed the passage, implementation, oversight, and ultimate revision of the NWPA. As the DOE focused on specific sites, the politics of the nuclear waste problem entered a third, or micropolicy, stage lasting from the latter half of 1986 until passage of the NWPA Amendments in early 1987. In a fourth period, co-management between Congress and the DOE of the funding and implementation of the nuclear waste policy acts, which is common, informal, and limited to a few actors, is again dominant. This fourth period has extended from 1987 to the present.

Disposal of high-level radioactive waste is one of the most enduring controversies about commercial nuclear power facing the American people.[2] From the beginning, the development of long-term waste repositories has been the responsibility of the federal government. The goal of the current program is to establish a permanent deep geologic repository for highly radioactive spent nuclear fuel and other high-level nuclear waste. It is a first-of-its-kind program in the world.

High-level nuclear waste from commercial power plants accumulates daily on-site. The DOE estimates that all currently operating nuclear power plants will produce approximately 87,000 metric tons of spent nuclear fuel during their lifetimes.[3] Most high-level nuclear waste is being stored in temporary, near-surface facilities at the sites where it is generated, sites that cannot contain the waste for the 10,000 years specified in federal regulations.[4]

Between 1956 and 1979, a policy-making subsystem existed that was wrapped in secrecy, included only a few key actors, and dominated political activity concerning nuclear power. In 1954, as a direct result of President Eisenhower's "Atoms for Peace" initiative, Congress demilitarized nuclear energy and created the Atomic Energy Commission (AEC) to regulate and promote civilian nuclear power. The actors in the dominant subsystem that arose were dedicated to making atomic energy economically viable. These actors included the Atomic Energy Commission (later it was broken into two agencies: the Nuclear Regulatory Commission and the Department of Energy), the Joint Committee on Atomic Energy (JCAE) in Congress, utilities engaged in nuclear power production, and a few private organizations with expertise in the nuclear power field.

The stated goal of the AEC was the development of a long-term storage option that would last literally thousands of years. On-site storage was accepted as the short-term solution to the waste storage problem, but the AEC publicly argued that long-term storage solutions could be developed by 1970 (approximately fifteen years after the development of civilian nuclear power).[5] The geologic repository concept became the most commonly accepted repository option after the National Academy of Sciences endorsed it at a conference held at Princeton University in September 1955.[6] Beginning in the mid-1960s, the Oak Ridge National Laboratory began to look at salt domes as a promising medium.[7] Testing the suitability of salt domes as repositories was eventually conducted at Lyons, Kansas, during the 1960s, and basalt formations at the Hanford site in Washington were analyzed beginning in 1968. The Kansas site was later abandoned and a new site in New Mexico studied.

But work on a long-term storage option progressed slowly during this period. A salt dome repository program was initiated by the DOE in the early 1970s, and a program to develop a waste processing center was announced in 1976. The slow pace of implementation of the geologic repository program has been explained in a number of ways. Rigorous site characterization naturally takes many years and billions of dollars to complete, but some critics have argued that this does not account for the two decades of delay in starting that process.[8] The reasons most often cited as responsible for the repository program's slow development are a preoccupation with reactor development; a belief that waste repository technology was too expensive and that costs would decline proportionately as commercial nuclear power came into its own; a scientifically weak program; a belief that breeder reactor or reprocessing technology would take care of the problem; uncertainty about whether the commercial nuclear power industry would generate enough waste to require a deep geologic repository; and a belief that temporary storage technology was sufficiently long-lived so that there was no need to rush development of a repository.[9]

These beliefs and actions often remained unchallenged because of the closed and dominant nature of the nuclear power subsystem during this period. Some historical observers note that the JCAE-AEC relationship was designed to be closed to public scrutiny for national security reasons; deference to the JCAE was high due to the strong rights given to it by statute and the technical nature of the committees' jurisdiction; and problems with nuclear power (such as long-term waste disposal) were often dealt with by the AEC and JCAE in closed or off-the-record sessions of the committee.[10] Major decision makers in the commercial nuclear power subsystem were largely restricted to the AEC's director of reactor development, his staff, the AEC general manager, the five AEC commissioners, and the members and staff of the JCAE.[11] In addition, the AEC was accused of suppressing documents that criticized its waste management activities, and firing or reassigning scientists working for the agency who urged alternative policies.[12] Del Sesto found that citizen participation in AEC hearings was restricted to a "ritual form."[13] Although the AEC and JCAE often clashed on the appropriate means to promote commercial nuclear power, Clarke concluded that "the policy changes that were imposed on the AEC by the JCAE were not so radical that the AEC changed its [fundamental] goals."[14]

Since no major incidents had occurred at nuclear power plants and information about the safety and environmental issues associated with nuclear power was not widely known outside the dominant subsystem, the public did not pressure the AEC to enforce its regulations rigorously and find a solution to the nuclear waste problem.

During this period, the JCAE held few hearings concerning nuclear power or waste storage. The closed nature of the decision-making process meant that agreement on policy was easy to maintain, and the various actors in the political subsystem agreed that problems should be worked out privately between participants in the subsystem. Well informed about the AEC's goals and in agreement with them, the JCAE did not develop independent expertise about nuclear power. Rather, members of the JCAE deferred to experts who worked for private industry and the AEC, rarely questioning the AEC's requests for more time to study the issue or its arguments that on-site storage was safe.

During this period, an "engineering culture" grew up within the AEC.[15]

The civilian production of nuclear energy had been seen primarily as an engineering issue, and engineers rose to positions of authority within the AEC. To these individuals, the production of nuclear energy was a problem in engineering, and engineering was considered the only approach capable of identifying, addressing, and solving problems (such as waste storage). This "culture of engineering" specified that the decision-making processes and rules of mathematics and physics, rational thought, and engineering principles govern decision making in the AEC. Holding hearings or addressing public concerns did not solve problems that, the professionals at the AEC believed, engineering could not solve better.

Several events in the 1960s and 1970s—some of them directly associated with nuclear power and some of them not—opened this political subsystem to input from other actors. The new actors did not share in the engineering culture of the AEC, and many believed in open (not closed and dominant) decision-making systems.

During the 1960s and 1970s, both long-term and short-term changes occurred that led to the breakup of the dominant subsystem. The public was increasingly conscious of and worried about environmental and worker-safety issues, a long-term trend that led to passage of the National Environmental Protection Act and the Occupational Safety and Health Act in the early 1970s. Concern over these issues increasingly affected the nuclear power industry, too.

Short-term trends, however, were more important in encouraging new actors to participate in the decision-making subsystem and challenge the emphasis on economic viability and production that the dominant subsystem had maintained. Often, however, these changes were unrelated to problems with nuclear energy. For instance, the AEC was broken up in 1974 in order to promote nuclear power more readily in the wake of the first OPEC oil embargo. The AEC's regulatory duties were given to the newly created Nuclear Regulatory Commission (NRC), and its responsibility to promote nuclear energy transferred to the Energy Research and Development Administration (ERDA).

In 1976 the JCAE was abolished and its oversight duties scattered among several House and Senate committees. The dissolution of the JCAE occurred largely because members of the Senate and House wanted to simplify the operation of the chamber and provide more opportunities for substantive participation. Several of the members of Congress who now participated in the new subsystem came from districts or states where anti-nuclear-power sentiment was abundant. These electoral realities encouraged some members of Congress to dig for embarrassing incidents and cover-ups, and to open the subsystem to other political actors, like environmental groups. As a result, the subsystem became less secretive about its decision-making process and decisions.

The energy crisis of the late 1970s also indirectly affected the old subsystem. As nuclear energy came to be seen as the solution to the energy crisis, more people became aware of the industry's problems. Nuclear advocates sought to investigate and deal preemptively with the storage issue so it would not become a problem later. Antinuclear groups, concerned with the radioactive waste nuclear power produced, sought to dispel the myth that nuclear energy was a "clean" technology by conducting research that exposed the contamination, safety, and health problems associated with on-site, long-term storage of nuclear wastes. The growing problems of the nuclear power industry and the continuing energy crisis soon created even more institutional change. In 1977 the ERDA was transformed into the Department of Energy (DOE), a move that persons and groups both for and against nuclear power believed would help resolve the nuclear waste storage issue.

The near-meltdown at the Three Mile Island nuclear power plant in Pennsylvania in the fall of 1979 mobilized a large, aggressive, vocal anti-nuclear-power lobby that took advantage of the weakened position of the dominant subsystem. The anti-nuclear-power lobby was assisted by a dramatic increase in the public's awareness of nuclear waste issues. Figure 4.1 documents these changes. There was a marked increase in the number of articles about nuclear waste during passage of the NWPA in 1982–83: an average of ten articles per quarter compared with an average of five articles per quarter in the 1980–81 period. However, although the number of articles appearing dropped to an average of eight articles per quarter after passage of the NWPA, the level was far above the 1980–81 average. This demonstrates the public's concern with the DOE's implementation of the nuclear waste policy. The number of articles dropped significantly to an average of three articles per quarter after Senator J. Bennett Johnston (D-La.) introduced his NWPA Amendments in September of 1986. This lends credence to the argument that a micropolicy system had arisen to govern the nuclear waste policy arena. Implementation of the 1987 legislation and the additional concern generated by the Chernobyl accident led to an increase in the average number of articles per quarter during 1987 and 1988, but this was still below the average produced during the summer 1983–fall 1986 period.[16]

Problems with on-site storage were soon uncovered by participants in the new, open, and competitive subsystem. First, much of the waste was found to be poorly housed. At a few sites, widespread contamination of the water supply and soil had occurred. The contamination was due to three factors. First, much of the waste produced prior to 1970 had been stored when the scientific community and the AEC knew little about how nuclear wastes spread radioactive contamination, how quickly and how severely contamination could spread, or how bad the health effects of this contamination could be. Second, enforcement of post-1970 regulations had been inadequately enforced by the AEC and NRC. Third, industry demands that

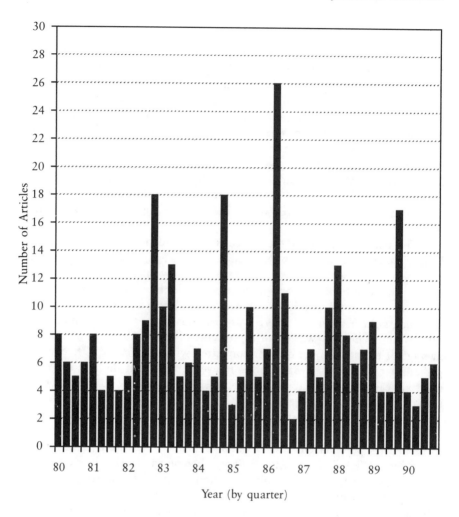

FIGURE 4.1
NUMBER OF ARTICLES IN POPULAR MAGAZINES AND NEWSPAPERS
ON HIGH-LEVEL NUCLEAR WASTE, BY QUARTER, 1980-90

SOURCES: *New York Times Index, Washington Post Index,* and *Reader's Guide to Periodical Literature.* Articles that referred to low-level nuclear waste disposal or to technical or scientific issues were not counted. Articles that appeared before 1983 are not necessarily specific to the Yucca Mountain siting decision. Key terms used included, for the *Times Index, atomic energy* and *radioactive waste disposal;* for the *Post Index, radioactive waste disposal;* and for the *Reader's Guide, radioactive waste disposal* and *United States–Department of Energy.* Key words differ because different indexes may use different rubrics as subject headings; however, key words used here are comparable. Also, an index may use different key words for the same subject over time, or use many key words to cover one subject.

the AEC and NRC protect the nuclear power industry had often led to cover-ups of spills, accidents, and contamination.

The second problem with on-site storage was that anti-nuclear-power groups demanded immediate action on development of a long-term solution. These groups rejected on-site storage as unworkable, arguing that industry domination of the DOE or the NRC would soon reassert itself, bringing weak storage rules, lax enforcement of regulations, and more cover-ups. The anti-nuclear-power lobby also demanded immediate action on locating a geologic repository, condemning more delay in the name of science as stall tactics.

As the AEC's most politically visible successor, the Department of Energy was the choice of most groups to develop the long-term storage option. Prodded by the Carter administration's Interagency Review Group on Radioactive Waste, the DOE issued several studies in the early 1980s that documented the probable environmental effects a repository would create, and even characterized several possible sites. This seemed so similar to the old tactics of study and delay, however, that many constituents pressured Congress to "do something." In April 1982 the Office of Technology Assessment, an arm of Congress, published a report outlining the major policy issues facing the nation. It set the agenda for a Congress ready to act. Congress soon took discretion concerning the long-term storage program out of the executive branch's hands.

In 1982 Congress enacted the Nuclear Waste Policy Act (NWPA) to provide a legislative framework for evaluating potential sites for geologic disposal of civilian high-level nuclear waste. Prior to the NWPA, consideration of a particular site for characterization had generated considerable opposition. Citizens living close to such sites quickly fell prey to the NIMBY (or "not-in-my-back-yard") syndrome. Although most people recognized the need for a national nuclear waste repository, most also found various excuses to justify why such a repository should not be built near *their* homes. During the 1970s the AEC and the DOE had studied only one site at a time, which concentrated NIMBY pressures in one or two congressional districts and one state and prevented widespread public unrest.

Congress attempted to structure the NWPA to avoid NIMBY pressures.[17] Allowing the DOE to study one site at a time would have led to long delays and angered the anti-nuclear-power groups. Therefore, an electorally minded Congress created a multisite selection process. This process, however, would have led to a great deal of NIMBY pressure. Anticipating this, Congress decided to "spread the pain" and defuse NIMBY pressure by mandating that there be two regional repositories: one in the eastern/midwestern region and one in the western region of the United States.[18] This was a carefully crafted compromise by congressmen who wanted to assure constituents that one particular region would not receive all the nuclear waste. The act's schedule required the DOE to begin disposing of waste at one of the repositories no later than 31 January 1998. The Nuclear Waste Fund (NWF) and tax on utilities generating electricity from commercial nuclear power plants was established to pay for the burial sites.

It also appears that Congress deliberately cast the DOE as the source of public information, comfort, and persuasion. Traditionally, Congress has taken the role of educator in many policy debates, but some members now worried that if Congress itself tried to educate the public about the repository site, Congress would appear to be the project's "champion" and voters who disliked the nuclear waste policy would retaliate against incumbents at election time. Therefore, the DOE was given the mandate to play the role Congress traditionally did. The NWPA mandated that the DOE hold public hearings in areas under study for site characterization, listen to constituents' concerns and worries, address the issues raised, and distribute information in such a way as to calm the public and persuade it that the nuclear waste repository would be environmentally sound. Some in Congress felt that this approach epitomized the way democratic government was supposed to operate. But for most, the public liaison policy was only an electoral cover.

The 1982 act also required the DOE to comply with regulations issued by other federal agencies. Congress created the Office of Civilian Radioactive Waste Management (OCRWM) within the DOE to manage the nuclear waste program.[19] However, by requiring the DOE to adhere to standards issued by other agencies, Congress felt that the utilities' hold on the DOE could be broken. Therefore, the DOE now had to comply with regulations published by the Environmental Protection Agency (EPA)[20] and the Nuclear Regulatory Commission (NRC).[21]

Congress also authorized the DOE, through the NWPA, to site, construct, and operate a monitored retrievable storage (MRS) facility for the short-term storage of high-level radioactive waste. This "grandfathered" DOE's ongoing search for an MRS facility into the NWPA.

Passage of the NWPA was evidence that a different decision-making subsystem had arisen. This subsystem may be called competitive. In the competitive subsystem, decisions and the decision-making process were more open to public view, and the number of actors in the subsystem was larger. However, disagreement among the participants was common, and coalitional behavior was often displayed in lawmaking and in the application of pressure tactics.

Effects of Congressional Intervention in Nuclear Waste Policy

The passage of the Nuclear Waste Policy Act of 1982 failed to resolve many of the issues that concerned the public, and each element of the NWPA raised new issues of significant concern to Congress, state and local governments, and citizens. Members of Congress and their constituents became more interested in DOE nuclear waste policy as potential states were identified for site characterization. As constituent pressure against the siting of the nuclear waste sites increased, so did congressional oversight and the number of committees and subcommittees having a stake in radioactive waste management.

Figure 4.2 illustrates the trends in hearings on the nuclear waste storage issue. Hearings were frequent and regular during the 1980–83 period as the competitive subsystem built the coalition that passed the NWPA. But in the 1984–87 period, hearings became even more frequent, indicating the public dissatisfaction that existed with the NWPA's implementation. More important, expert and executive branch witnesses appearing at each hearing showed dramatic trends upward in both frequency and numbers after passage of the NWPA in late 1982 (see figure 4.3). This indicates that hearings became much more substantive during the NWPA's implementation than before its passage or after the NWPA Amendments in 1987. These data indicate that the scope of conflict over the nuclear waste issue also expanded as NIMBY sentiment spread. The wider the conflict, the less influence the congressional nuclear power advocacy committees and the DOE had over the outcome of nuclear waste policy.

The DOE's handling of the public hearings process worsened the situation. DOE personnel believed in an organizational culture and norms that ignored politics, and refused to discuss issues except in the technical jargon of the engineering profession. These cultural norms made it difficult for the DOE to believe that the "politicking" Congress had mandated under the NWPA would solve the problem of which site to pick. To the DOE, site selection was not political but technical. The DOE held hearings as mandated by the NWPA, but its attitude toward the hearings and the ways in which it responded to the public made its political problems worse.[22]

Soon, members of Congress, their constituents, and state government officials began to doubt the DOE's ability to implement the new policy successfully. DOE scientific credibility suffered, and the agency lost a high degree of institutional legitimacy. Members of Congress, state governments, opposition interest groups, and many citizens thought the DOE might cut scientific and technical corners simply to expedite decision making. DOE managers feared that states might seek to block waste management activities within their borders, no matter what assurances were provided.

Other political pressures not associated with the NWPA implementation also encouraged the DOE to avoid a faithful implementation of the NWPA. The Reagan administration had taken office in 1981 asking Congress to abolish the DOE, and was pressing hard during the end of its first term to abolish the agency. The DOE's primary constituents and supporters—the energy utilities—were weakened by the energy crisis. With many critics and few strong supporters, officials at the DOE reasoned that the

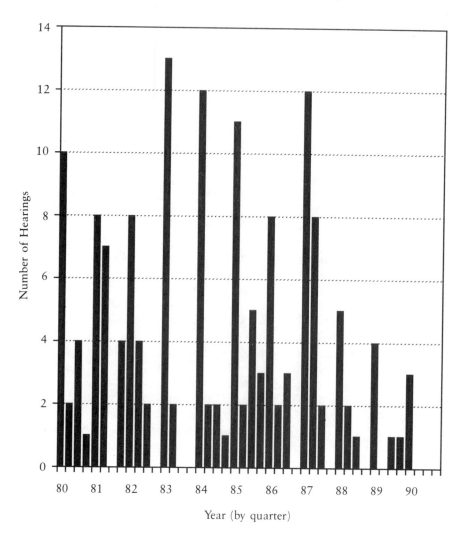

FIGURE 4.2
NUMBER OF CONGRESSIONAL HEARINGS ON HIGH-LEVEL NUCLEAR WASTE,
BY QUARTER, 1980-90

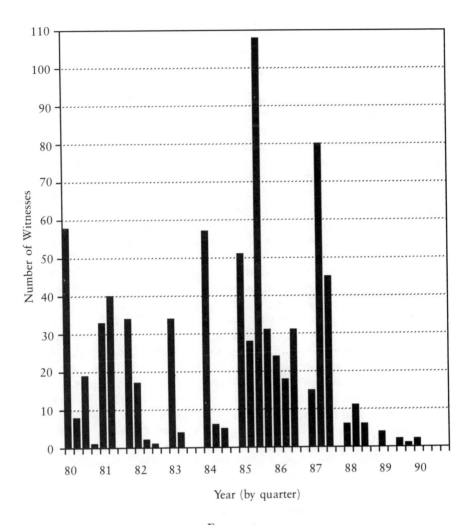

FIGURE 4.3
NUMBER OF WITNESSES AT CONGRESSIONAL HIGH-LEVEL NUCLEAR WASTE
HEARINGS, BY QUARTER, 1980-90

agency could not survive if it became the public's scapegoat over the nuclear waste repository siting issue. In a sense, the DOE purposefully refused to implement the NWPA as Congress demanded in order to force Congress to reappraise the NWPA and find a way to calm an angry public.

In this atmosphere of deepening distrust, the DOE's actions exacerbated NIMBY sentiment. The DOE formally identified nine potentially acceptable sites in February 1983: one in Louisiana, two in Mississippi, one in Nevada, two in Texas, two in Utah, and one in Washington. In January 1986 the DOE identified twelve sites in the eastern and midwestern states as potential candidates for the second nuclear waste repository.

Strong criticism from the public, interest groups, congressional committees and subcommittees, and members of Congress regarding the eastern and midwestern sites led the DOE to insulate itself from this pressure and throw the issue back into the lap of Congress.[23] In May 1986 the DOE "indefinitely postponed" the search for a second repository in the Midwest and East, thus breaking a carefully developed agreement between western and eastern members of Congress. At the same time, the DOE formally selected the Nevada, Texas, and Washington sites for site characterization. The DOE appeared to have chosen these sites not only because they met the NWPA's criteria but because they were politically feasible. The site in Washington state was already host to a nuclear weapons production facility run by the DOE, and political support for the repository was evident there. The Texas site was economically depressed, and would welcome the repository.

The Nevada site was chosen for much different reasons. Nevada had a weak congressional delegation that could not prevent a repository from being imposed on the state by Congress. Forcing Nevada to accept a repository would not anger large numbers of the population, either. The federal government also owned over 80 percent of Nevada's land area, further weakening the state's position.

Narrowing the potential sites to three ignited citizen and congressional opposition to a nuclear waste repository anywhere in the United States. Western members of Congress were outraged by the DOE's decision to drop—without warning—the eastern/midwestern repository. The intense constituent pressure and display of NIMBY attitudes engendered even greater distrust of the DOE in Congress.

Congress tried to save the NWPA policy by holding hearings, but it quickly found that people with NIMBY attitudes were not responsive to attempts at persuasion. The NIMBY syndrome fundamentally exaggerates the perception of risks to one's own life and health. Whether the NIMBY syndrome is a rational response to risk or not, its premises are particularly resistant to information that challenges the beliefs. Congress soon found that its role as an information broker and "friendly ear" was not changing opinions about the repository site selection process. As NIMBY pressures mounted, members of Congress responded by enacting new legislation.

By 1986 few members of Congress were willing to tackle the politically hot repository issue. The NIMBY outcry was so loud that for many in Congress opposition to the DOE's search for a repository site had become a political necessity, and few legislators were willing to risk their careers by advocating a new policy until the public's views on how to respond to the growing nuclear waste crisis became clearer.

The political pressure was particularly acute in Louisiana. Senator Johnston and his constituents were convinced that Louisiana (which had been a prime candidate for a repository earlier on) would become home to the new nuclear repository. Johnston, because of political pressure and a belief that the DOE might actually reconsider Louisiana, took the point in making sure that legislation and executive policy guaranteed that Louisiana would not house the repository. His position as chairman of the Environment and Public Works Committee and the Appropriations Subcommittee on Energy and Water Development helped him to forge a new compromise with a Congress unwilling to tackle the issue again.

Johnston recognized the political quandary the DOE found itself in, and realized that the agency would refuse to carry out any "take-the-heat" mandate. Johnston and the staffs under his control worked behind the scenes with DOE personnel to craft a bill that would take the political heat off the agency while still forcing it to take a more proactive role than it had in the 1960s and 1970s in finding a permanent storage site.

In September 1986 Johnston unveiled a "two-track" approach to siting the nuclear repository. Under the two-track proposal, site characterization was restricted to the Yucca Mountain site in Nevada, and the search for the eastern/midwestern repository was put off until 2007. Almost no other members of Congress were involved in shaping Johnston's legislation. The bill was inserted into omnibus budget legislation at the end of the 1986 session during a House-Senate conference committee, and the amendments were never discussed in committee or on the floor. Lodged as it was in the huge reconciliation legislation, most in Congress were barely aware of the changes that Johnston's bill made in the NWPA policy. This legislation became known as the Nuclear Waste Policy Amendments Act of 1987.

The Nuclear Waste Policy Amendments Act of 1987 directed the DOE to conduct site characterization studies at Nevada's Yucca Mountain, thereby terminating site-specific studies at all other sites. It prohibited any site-specific and generic studies regarding a second repository, terminated research on crystalline rock as a means of storing waste on-site, and pushed to between 2007 and 2010 a DOE report to Congress on the need for a second repository. Yucca Mountain did not automatically become the site of the permanent disposal repository. Rather, it became the sole "candidate site" to be "characterized" to determine whether or not it met the requirements set forth in law and regulations for the long-term disposal of high-level nuclear waste.

The Yucca Mountain siting decision was a major turning point in relations between Congress and the DOE. Congress narrowed the discretion of DOE managers, but by making the technical and scientific decision for the DOE, Congress also took the political heat off the agency and gave the DOE a much stronger mandate to proceed.

The NWPA Amendments changed the way oversight of the DOE was conducted by embedding the agency in an oversight "spiderweb." No longer would Congress have the sole responsibility to oversee the DOE. Several executive branch agencies were charged with insuring that the DOE met the regulations they had written. A three-member Monitored Retrievable Storage (MRS) Review Commission was created to advise the DOE concerning the siting, construction, and operation of an MRS facility. The commission was to report to Congress on the facility's advantages, disadvantages, and technical utility. Congress nullified sites previously identified by the DOE for an MRS facility and deferred site selection until the commission's report.

Congress also established the Nuclear Waste Technical Review Board (TRB) as an oversight body independent of the DOE to evaluate the technical and scientific validity of activities undertaken by the DOE in site characterization and the packaging and transportation of spent fuel. Its eleven members are nominated by the National Academy of Sciences and appointed by the president of the United States. The board must report to Congress and the DOE at least twice a year until disposal begins in a permanent repository.

Congress also tried to smooth site selection in two other ways in the NWPAA. First, it authorized payment to Nevada of $10 million per year during siting and construction of the Yucca Mountain repository, and $20 million per year during operation, but in order to receive the funds the state had to give up its right to veto the site. Second, Congress created the Office of the Nuclear Waste Negotiator. The negotiator, appointed by the president with the advice and consent of the Senate, was charged with seeking a state or Indian tribe willing to host a repository or MRS facility at a qualified site on reasonable terms. If the negotiator found a willing site, Congress would be expected to approve it. The negotiator was, however, to be responsible to Congress, not the executive branch.[24]

Conclusions

Relations between the DOE and Congress since passage of the NWPAA in 1987 have been cooperative and informal. The subsystem has lapsed into a dominant mode again. There are relatively few actors involved in decision making concerning Yucca Mountain, and although conflict with the state is relatively high, the scope of the conflict is quite limited. Discussion between actors is active and free-flowing, and largely informal.

The cooperative atmosphere has been marred by studies questioning the DOE's ability to manage the site characterization. An investigation by the General Accounting Office (GAO) found that quality control over data collection was so bad that it could derail site characterization. The DOE pointed to its quality assurance plans, but GAO said little was being done at that time to assure their proper implementation.[25] The Nuclear Regulatory Commission and the National Research Council's Advisory Committee on Nuclear Waste also questioned the DOE's ability to manage site characterization. A team of hydrologists from the U.S. Geological Survey charged that technical problems at the Yucca Mountain site could make it "scientifically indefensible." Finally, the National Research Council criticized the DOE's analysis of groundwater problems at the site.[26]

GAO was also critical of the DOE's suppression of negative information about potential repository sites. GAO concluded that "DOE might never have publicly released the information if the NRC, through its on-site representative, had not identified and pursued the issue."[27] A report by a DOE geologist that cast doubt on the faulting, seismic, and volcanic-activity analysis at the Yucca Mountain site was not released until after the NWPAA passed. The geologist said that his opinions about the geologic problems at the site, which could make the site unlicensable, had been delivered to the DOE more than a year before passage of the 1987 amendments, leaving plenty of time for internal peer review. Another DOE report that was ignored concluded that the Yucca Mountain site had a probability of volcanic activity one hundred times greater than DOE estimates. Still other analyses took issue with the DOE's plans to locate the repository's shaft openings in a floodplain.[28] These and other questions have been included in subsequent site characterization plans, but no resolution of these issues will be possible until years of study have been completed.

Despite these revelations, Senator Johnston and Congress have refused to back away from the NWPAA legislation. However, Congress seems to show its disapproval of the DOE's shortcomings by consistently reducing funding requests for site characterization. The administration's requests for Fiscal Years 1987 and 1988 were roughly halved, and outlays have consistently outpaced appropriations since 1987 (see table 4.1). In FY 91 and FY 92, however, funding requests have been more limited, and congressionally mandated cuts have been less severe.[29] However, Johnston and his staff have proceeded to work closely with the DOE in an attempt to compensate for site deficiencies. This close cooperation, or co-management, has been made possible by the weakening of the anti-nuclear-power movement and the direction of the nation's attention to other problems.

DOE respondents feel that there are currently no serious problems with micromanagement (unreasonable intervention in DOE programmatic details) by Congress. When the amendments to designate Yucca Mountain as the sole site to be characterized passed Congress, one respondent said, "It

TABLE 4.1.
ADMINISTRATION REQUEST, ENACTED FUNDING, AND OUTLAYS
FOR THE FIRST CIVILIAN HIGH-LEVEL NUCLEAR
WASTE REPOSITORY, FY 83–FY 93
(IN MILLIONS OF DOLLARS)

Fiscal year	Request	Enacted	Outlay
1983[a]	—	192.5	157.4
1984	279.8	246.5	209.5
1985	247.1	235.2	221.2
1986	436.8	386.0	292.5
1987	541.8	296.0	383.8
1988	525.0	256.0	304.5
1989	289.7	223.7	236.4
1990	338.6	176.1	204.5
1991	193.2	155.2	188.7
1992	172.2	165.6	323.1
1993	248.3	375.0[b]	— [c]

SOURCES: Marc S. Hollander, chief, Budget Branch, Office of Program and Resources Management, Office of Civilian Radioactive Waste Management, U.S. Department of Energy, 12 March 1992; U.S. Department of Energy, *Congressional Budget Request,* Fiscal Years 1984-1993; Gary Huettl, chief, Budget Branch, Office of Program and Resources Management, Office of Civilian Radioactive Waste Management, U.S. Department of Energy, 12 January 1993.

NOTE: For FY 83–FY 86, figures are for all sites (salt, basalt, granite, and tuff) under study; for FY 87, figures are for the Hanford, Deaf Smith, and Yucca Mountain sites only; and for FY 88–FY 93, figures are for the Yucca Mountain site only.

a. No budget request was made for FY 83 because the program had been enacted only in January 1983.

b. Congress appropriated only $275 million for the repository program from the Nuclear Waste Fund. However, it shifted $100 million from other DOE programs to the repository program as a means of paying the Department of Defense's "share" of storing defense-related nuclear waste in the repository.

c. Final outlays for FY 93 not yet available.

was 98 to 2 time in the Senate, which solved a major political problem for us [DOE]." Several respondents in Congress and the DOE concluded that "everyone wanted the repository to be somewhere else," and that Nevada had "a great deal of public land and two relatively weak Senators" who could not prevent the site from being put there. The NWPAA decisions made Congress, in effect, a "co-manager" of site characterization and freed the DOE from making comparisons of the relative effectiveness of different geological formations and sites for nuclear waste isolation. As one observer said, "Any semblance of regional equity in the original site selection process was scrapped in what became known as the 'Screw Nevada Bill.' For years, various utilities had called the characterization of three sites too expensive and a waste of time. They got their wish."[30]

Since the Yucca Mountain decision in 1987, the subsystem has returned to its dominant stage. Congress is again inactive, waiting for information to come in about the nuclear waste program. There is a preference for informal contacts with administrators by members of Congress and their staffs. Congressional and DOE functional specialists are working closely together in the site characterization process. Post–Yucca Mountain, there has been limited use of formal oversight mechanisms like hearings. Congress is relying upon the TRB, the MRS Commission (now disbanded), NRC, and EPA to oversee and check the progress of the DOE in the management of the nuclear waste program.

The interaction between the two branches can best be explained by the reelection incentives facing members of Congress. Reelection-seeking senators and representatives have spent their time on the nuclear waste issue making sure that the repository is not located in their states or districts. Currently, the perception is that Yucca Mountain will be the repository site, so few members of Congress have focused on the program. Only members from the Nevada congressional delegation, the DOE, the Technical Review Board, the Nuclear Waste Negotiator, nuclear utilities, rate-payer groups, interested clientele groups, environmental groups, DOE contractors, scientists, and the chairs of the committees with primary jurisdiction over the issue have been active in the nuclear waste policy subsystem. The state of Nevada is considered the outsider, a nonplayer inside the subsystem. Thus, Nevada is using the courts to pursue its policy objective of stopping site characterization at Yucca Mountain. Generally, the post-NWPAA decision-making system structured around nuclear waste policy has again evolved into a dominant policy subsystem that is relatively closed, cooperative, and dominated by experts and functional representation.

Timeline of Major Events in the High-Level
Nuclear Waste Disposal Program

1954	Atomic Energy Act of 1954 passes Congress, establishing the Atomic Energy Commission.
1957	National Academy of Sciences panel recommends salt deposits as possible repository sites.
1963–67	Tests conducted in salt deposits at Lyons, Kansas.
1968	Evaluation of sites in the basalt formation at Hanford, Washington, begins.
1972	Lyons, Kansas, site withdrawn; search shifted to salt formations in New Mexico.
1974	Waste Isolation Pilot Plant (WIPP) facility proposed for New Mexico.
1976	National Waste Terminal Storage program announced.
1979	Interagency Review Group on Radioactive Waste Management publishes its report. Studies in progress at WIPP, the Nevada Test Site, Hanford, and four salt basins (including Utah and the Gulf Coast).
1980	Final environmental impact statement, "Management of Commercially Generated Radioactive Wastes," is issued by DOE.
1981	DOE program policy modified to focus on intensive site investigations and accelerated construction of a facility.
April 1982	OTA report entitled *Managing Commercial High-Level Radioactive Waste* presents major policy issues and key elements of a comprehensive waste management policy.
20 December 1982 and 3 January 1983	House and Senate pass the Nuclear Waste Policy Act of 1982; legislation grandfathers 1983 previously studied sites into a new site selection process conducted by DOE.
February 1983	DOE identifies nine sites in three geologic media as potentially acceptable for the first repository.
January 1986	DOE selects twelve sites in the eastern/midwestern region of the country to undergo site characterization for the second repository.
May 1986	DOE postpones selection of second repository site. DOE recommends Yucca Mountain, Nevada; Deaf Smith County, Texas; and Hanford, Washington, as the final three sites to be characterized under NWPA.
March 1987	DOE proposes siting the Monitored Retrievable Storage facility in Oak Ridge, Tennessee.
14–21 December 1987	House and Senate conferees discuss amendments to NWPA, and insert the NWPA Amendments into the

	omnibus budget reconciliation bill.
January 1988	Nuclear Waste Policy Amendments Act of 1987 becomes law.
November 1989	Nevada legislature passes resolutions declaring that Nevada disapproves of the Yucca Mountain site according to the procedures of NWPA.
September 1990	U.S. Court of Appeals for the Ninth Circuit, ruling in a case brought by DOE, declares the Nevada resolutions of 1989 invalid because final site selection has not occurred.
May 1992	GAO report entitled *Nuclear Waste: DOE's Repository Site Investigations, A Long and Difficult Task* criticizes DOE for mismanaging the Yucca Mountain site characterization process, and absolves Nevada of purposefully slowing the characterization process.

SOURCES: James A. Thurber, "Congressional Oversight of High-Level Nuclear Waste Disposal Policy: Yucca Mountain and the DOE Weapons Complex Clean-up" (Paper presented at the 1991 American Political Science Association Annual Meeting, Washington, D.C., 31 August–2 September 1991), "Congressional-Executive Interaction and the Nuclear Waste Site Selection Process," Appendix A; Gerald Jacob, *Site Unseen: The Politics of Siting a Nuclear Waste Repository* (Pittsburgh: University of Pittsburgh Press, 1990), 46.

Acknowledgments

I would like to thank the numerous present and former congressional and executive branch staff and private-sector respondents who gave freely of their time and knowledge about high-level nuclear waste isolation policy. This study would not have been possible without their cooperation and careful recollection of the key events surrounding passage and implementation the 1982 and 1987 nuclear waste acts.

I would also like to thank Samantha Durst, Ph.D. candidate at the American University, for her excellent assistance with the interviews and her careful notes from the lengthy sessions with the key actors in this case. Thank you to Tim Evanson, Ph.D. candidate at the American University, who assisted in preparation of the timeline, development of the bibliography, collection of budget data, and careful editing of this manuscript.

Notes

1. For a general discussion of the theoretical underpinnings of subsystem theory and its details, see James A. Thurber, "Dynamics of Policy Subsystems in

American Politics," in *Interest Group Politics,* 3d ed., ed. Allan J. Cigler and Burdett A. Loomis (Washington, D.C.: CQ Press, 1991), 318–43.

2. For brevity and to reflect accurately the concepts used by the respondents in this case study, the terms *nuclear waste, radioactive waste,* and *waste* are used to mean both spent nuclear fuel from commercial nuclear power plants and high-level radioactive waste. *High-level nuclear waste* refers only to spent fuel rods and other highly radioactive materials produced by fission in commercial nuclear power reactors; it does not refer to military high-level or transuranic wastes, or to commercial low-level wastes. Policies governing military wastes and low-level waste disposal have different origins and histories (see the case study of DOE's attempt to manage high-level defense nuclear waste in James A. Thurber and Timothy C. Evanson, "Subsystem Politics and the Nuclear Weapons Complex: Congressional Oversight of DOE's Environmental Restoration Program," in *Problems and Prospects for Nuclear Waste Disposal Policy,* ed. Eric B. Herzik and Kevin H. Mushkatel (Westport, Conn.: Greenwood, 1993).

3. *Commercial Nuclear Power 1989,* DOE/EIA-0438 (Washington, D.C.: U.S. Department of Energy, Energy Information Administration, 1989), ix.

4. 10 CFR [Code of Federal Regulations] 60. The 10,000-year figure is based on the average half-life of spent commercial nuclear fuel. "Half-life" is the amount of time it takes for half of any quantity of a given radioactive isotope to disintegrate.

5. See Daniel Metlay, "History and Interpretation of Radioactive Waste Management in the U.S.," in *Essays on Issues Relevant to the Regulation of Radioactive Waste,* ed. W. Bishop et al. (Washington, D.C.: U.S. Nuclear Regulatory Commission, 1978).

6. National Academy of Sciences, "Disposal of Radioactive Waste on Land," report of the Committee on Waste Disposal of the Division of Earth Sciences, appendix B, "Proceedings of the Princeton Conference," NAS-NRC publ. 519 (Washington, D.C., September 1957).

7. Luther J. Carter, *Nuclear Imperatives and the Public Trust* (Washington, D.C.: Resources for the Future, 1987), 56.

8. Ibid., 36–38.

9. Carrol Wilson, "Nuclear Energy: What Went Wrong?" *Bulletin of the Atomic Scientists* 35 (June 1979): 13–17; James R. Temples, "The Politics of Nuclear Power: A Subgovernment in Transition," *Political Science Quarterly* 95 (Summer 1980), 242; George T. Mazuzan and Samuel J. Walker, *Controlling the Atom: The Beginnings of Nuclear Regulation, 1946–62* (Berkeley: University of California Press, 1984), 347–49; Eugene A. Rosa and William R. Freudenburg, "Nuclear Power at the Crossroads," in *Public Reaction to Nuclear Power,* ed. William R. Freudenburg and Eugene A. Rosa (Boulder, Colo.: Westview Press, 1984), 22; Carter, *Nuclear Imperatives and the Public Trust,* 38–39, 56, 62. See also Edward J. Woodhouse, "The Politics of Nuclear Waste Management," in *Too Hot to Handle?* ed. Charles A. Walker et al. (New Haven: Yale University Press, 1983), 165–66.

10. Harold B. Green, "The Peculiar Politics of Nuclear Power," *Bulletin of the Atomic Scientists* 38 (December 1982): 59–62; Temples, "The Politics of Nuclear Power," 241, 243; Mazuzan and Walker, *Controlling the Atom,* 12, 25–26, 211.

11. Joseph G. Morone and Edward G. Woodhouse, *The Demise of Nuclear Energy?* (New Haven: Yale University Press, 1989), 45.

12. Woodhouse, "The Politics of Nuclear Waste Management," 165; H. Peter Metzger, *The Atomic Establishment* (New York: Simon and Schuster, 1972); Philip Boffey, *The Brain Bank of America* (New York: McGraw-Hill, 1975); Temples, "The Politics of Nuclear Power," 241.

13. Steven L. Del Sesto, *Science, Politics and Controversy: Civilian Nuclear Power in the United States, 1946–1974* (Boulder, Colo.: Westview Press, 1979), 220; Morone and Woodhouse, *The Demise of Nuclear Energy,* 6–7, 6 n. 19.

14. Lee Clarke, "The Origins of Nuclear Power: A Case of Institutional Conflict," *Social Problems* 32 (June 1985): 481, 483; Green, "The Politics of Nuclear Waste Management," 59–62; Harold P. Green and Allen Rosenthal, *Government of the Atom* (New York: Atherton Press, 1963); Temples, "The Politics of Nuclear Power," 241, 242; Richard G. Hewlett and Jack M. Holl, *Atoms for Peace and War, 1953–1961* (Berkeley: University of California Press, 1989), 341–44, 351–74, 489–506.

15. For a discussion of how organizational culture can affect an agency and "engineering culture" specifically, see Charles Pruitt, "People Doing What They Do Best: Professional Engineers and NHTSA," *Public Administration Review* 29 (July/August 1979): 363–71.

16. The average number of articles per quarter during the summer 1987–winter 1990 period (when the NWPA Amendments were being implemented) is 7.2, higher than the baseline average of 5.1 produced during the spring 1980–winter 1981 period (during which a competitive subsystem existed but NWPA had yet to be introduced). However, after controlling for the abnormal increase in the number of articles in the winter of 1989, the average number of articles per quarter drops to 5.6, which more closely approximates the baseline. This evidence also suggests that a micropolicy system has existed since 1989. Since the summer of 1989, the average number of articles per quarter (after controlling for the abnormal increase in the winter of 1989) has hovered near 3.6, far below even the baseline spring 1980–winter 1981 period.

17. John Gervers, "The NIMBY Syndrome: Is It Inevitable?" *Environment* 29 (October 1987), 43.

18. Many commentators have asserted that NWPA mandates that one repository be built in the East/Midwest and another repository in the western region of the country. However, the East-West arrangement was not explicitly written into law. NWPA only instructs DOE to consider "the advantages of regional distribution in the siting of repositories," and the Nuclear Waste Policy Act of 1982 states that "geologic conditions" of potential sites are to be the "primary criteria" for selection of an appropriate nuclear waste site. But enough

western members of Congress assumed that one repository would be in the East/Midwest to ensure passage of the 1982 legislation. See Joseph A. Davis, "Nuclear Waste: An Issue That Won't Stay Buried," *CQ Weekly Report* 45 (14 March 1987), 452.

19. OCRWM has guided the repository site selection process through regulations published at 10 CFR 960, "General Guidelines for the Recommendation of Sites for Nuclear Waste Repositories."

20. 40 CFR 191, "Environmental Radiation Protection Standards for Management and Disposal of Spent Nuclear Fuel, High-Level and Transuranic Radioactive Wastes."

21. 10 CFR 60, "Disposal of High-Level Radioactive Wastes in Geologic Repositories."

22. Agencies with scientific professionals as the core staff often behave this way under pressure. See Marissa M. Golden, "Exit, Voice, Loyalty and Neglect: Bureaucratic Responses to Presidential Control During the Reagan Administration," *Journal of Public Administration Research and Theory* 2 (January 1992): 28–62.

23. This is a common strategy for agencies under fire. See B. Romzek and M. Dubnick, "Accountability in the Public Sector: Lessons from the *Challenger* Tragedy," *Public Administration Review* 47 (May/June 1987): 227–38.

24. The president refused to have the Office of the Nuclear Waste Negotiator in the Executive Office of the President (EOP). It is now freestanding, directly responsible to the president and Congress but not part of EOP or DOE (see P.L. 100-507).

25. U.S. General Accounting Office, *Nuclear Waste: DOE's Repository Site Investigations, A Long and Difficult Task,* GAO/RCED-92-73 (Washington, D.C.: Government Printing Office, 1992).

26. *Nuclear Waste News,* 28 April 1988, 135–36; 29 September 1988, 308; 17 November 1988, 368; 13 July 1989, 249–50; and Nuclear Regulatory Commission, *News Releases,* 11 July 1989 (NUREG/BR-0032, vol. 9, no. 28).

27. U.S. General Accounting Office, *Nuclear Waste: DOE's Handling of Hanford Iodine Information,* GAO/RCED-88-158 (Washington, D.C., 1988).

28. Gerald Jacob, *Site Unseen: The Politics of Siting a Nuclear Waste Repository* (Pittsburgh: University of Pittsburgh Press, 1990), 174.

29. The reductions in funding requests are largely due to work stoppages in Nevada. Nevada has delayed licensing of several work and environmental impact permits in an attempt to hinder the repository siting process (surface work at Yucca Mountain, for instance, ceased in 1986 and resumed only in March 1992, after Nevada issued three drilling and water permits). However, funding requests have also been smaller recently as DOE has improved its forecasting work and R&D has lowered costs, and as congressionally mandated changes in the NWPAA legislation have become fewer.

30. Jacob, *Site Unseen,* 169.

5

Hazardous Waste Disposal: The Double-Edged Sword of the RCRA Land-Ban Hammers

ALEXIS A. HALLEY

Background and Overview

U.S. public policy regarding the management of hazardous waste addresses a problem of enormous magnitude: how to dispose safely of the huge volumes of municipal and industrial solid waste (hazardous and nonhazardous) generated nationwide. Much of the waste makes its way into the environment, where it can pose a serious threat to ecological systems and public health.

There was a time when the amount of waste produced was small and its impact on the environment relatively minor—when it was supposed that a river could purify itself every ten miles. But by the end of World War II, U.S. industry was generating roughly 500,000 metric tons of hazardous waste per year. In 1974 the Environmental Protection Agency (EPA) estimated the amount to be 8.9 million metric tons; in 1985, 264 million metric tons. Since 1950 over 6 billion tons of hazardous waste have been disposed of on land. Unfortunately, the phenomenal growth in the production of waste has not always been mirrored by growth in the field of waste management.

In the past decade the Resource Conservation and Recovery Act (RCRA) has revolutionized the management of hazardous waste. Its impact on the nation and on protecting human health and the environment has been undeniable. This case is the story of the design and implementation of the "land-ban hammers" or land-ban restrictions in the 1984 Hazardous and Solid Waste Amendments (HSWA) to RCRA. Congressional "hammers" are a special case of the more general use of legislative deadlines as mechanisms to force compliance with statutory mandates. In basic form, the hammers examined in this case impose a legislated regulation (that is, Congress's judgment) if the agency fails to adopt alternative regulations by the deadline.[1] The land-ban hammers were the centerpiece of the HSWA legislation and marked a conceptual and institutional turning point in waste management and in the role and force of Congress in the EPA's implementation of the RCRA program.[2] According to Marcia Williams, former director of the agency's Office of Solid Waste:

> No other hammer is of as much significance as the land-ban set. Most other hammers are self-implementing. For example, to figure out how to implement the Loss of Interim Status hammer, EPA just had to get the guidance out—not a big deal. And the same was true for the hammer on retrofitting surface impoundments. But the land-ban hammers required massive technical analysis, a huge burden on the EPA; they were draconian. Wastes absolutely could not go into the ground without treatment. The land-ban hammers absolutely could not fall. Other hammers could fall and were intended to fall. But not the land bans.

Critical provisions affecting the land-ban restrictions are codified in one act, the 1984 Hazardous and Solid Waste Amendments to RCRA, and in a series of regulations promulgated by the Office of Solid Waste and Emergency Response (OSW) of the EPA. Although the agency must issue the regulations, it is industry (those who generate, transport, treat, and dispose of hazardous waste) that bears the greater financial burden of the requirements. This case examines congressional intervention in the EPA's implementation of the land-ban restrictions from 1982 to 1990.

Evolution and Revolution in Hazardous Waste Policy

Change, in the form of evolution and revolution, is a regular feature of environmental policy. Hazardous waste policy is no exception. Major reforms in the substance and the politics of the hazardous waste system have occurred in at least three areas over the past fifty years. The behavior of Congress and the executive branch in implementing the 1984 RCRA land-ban hammers must be seen in the context of these broader changes, which set the stage and drive much of the action between those institutions during the period examined.

Eras of Waste Management

The view of the federal government toward waste management has evolved from pollution control regulation, to managing the disposal of hazardous waste, to preventing significant contamination from occurring in the future, to proposals for minimizing or eliminating all risks from hazardous waste. Prior to 1984 most hazardous wastes were untreated and disposed of on land in a "bury and forget it" or "out of sight, out of mind" mentality. In 1965 Congress passed the Solid Waste Disposal Act, the first federal law that required environmentally sound methods for the disposal of household, commercial, and industrial refuse. In 1970 Congress amended the 1965 act when it passed the Resource Recovery Act. That same year, President Nixon created the Environmental Protection Agency (EPA) by executive order.

As the complexity and breadth of the waste management problem grew, the federal government saw a need for a comprehensive program geared to *preventing* significant contamination problems. To address those needs, Congress enacted the 1976 Resource Conservation and Recovery Act. RCRA was the first federal effort to regulate the disposal of hazardous waste, and came before the extent and danger of hazardous waste disposal problems became widely known. Subtitle C of RCRA required the EPA to develop a comprehensive regulatory program to control the generation, transportation, storage, and disposal of hazardous waste. Under RCRA, the EPA was initially given complete responsibility to determine the technology appropriate for the disposal of particular wastes. At the time most hazardous wastes were deposited on land. The act itself did little to move the nation away from that primary means of management.

For decades industry had simply disposed of chemical and other wastes in the ground, with minimal protections for the environment. Congressional action during the 1970s, an era that came to be called the environmental decade, included several statutes intended to narrow the range of acceptable disposal options (for example, the Federal Water Pollution Control Act or the Clean Water Act, the Clean Air Act of 1970, the Toxic Substances Control Act of 1976, the 1974 Safe Water Drinking Act, and the 1972 Federal Insecticide, Fungicide and Rodenticide Act). Yet, as the requirements of these and other pollution control statutes were gradually implemented, the industrial sector's pursuit of the most economical method of waste disposal led it to rely even more heavily on land disposal.[3]

In October 1984, Senator John Chafee (R-R.I.) told the Senate:

> The continued use of some methods of land disposal of some hazardous wastes presents an unwarranted and unnecessary risk to human health and the environment. Land disposal is extremely cheap when compared with the available alternatives such as incineration or chemical-physical treatment. Therefore, we should not be surprised to find that land disposal and treatment in land disposal facilities such as surface impoundments are being utilized much more frequently than the newer high tech options.... [A] classic example of the inability of the free marketplace to provide for the public good."[4]

The same concerns were voiced by Republicans and Democrats alike in the House of Representatives. Congressman Norman Lent (R-N.Y.) told the House, "For too many years in this country, we have permitted the practice of dumping hazardous wastes in the land to go virtually unchecked."

In the 1984 Hazardous and Solid Waste Amendments to RCRA, Congress rewrote the book on hazardous waste management.[5] HSWA mandated a move away from land disposal as the primary means of hazardous waste management by requiring treatment of wastes before final disposal. The findings-and-objectives section of the law reflected this: "Land disposal, particularly landfill and surface impoundment, should be the least favored method for managing waste."[6]

HSWA ranked desirable waste management options, starting with source reduction and recycling, then treatment, and as a last resort, land disposal. In perhaps the boldest and strongest thrust of the 1984 amendments, Congress required movement away from the land disposal of untreated hazardous waste.[7] The provisions, which came to be known as the land-ban restrictions or land-ban hammers, established a four-year time frame in which the EPA was required to promulgate regulations identifying the best demonstrated available technology (BDAT) that could be used to treat a hazardous waste before its land disposal. The provisions are the focus of this case study.

From a policy perspective, HSWA launched a new phase for the Subtitle C of the RCRA program. The statute was extremely detailed and comprehensive; it fundamentally redirected the RCRA program and the EPA's management of it. HSWA closed numerous regulatory loopholes, encouraged waste management practices that prevent or minimize environmental releases, and sought to ensure stringent regulation and clean up of releases when they do occur.[8]

> A massive change in this country's disposal practices. That is, away from land disposal and toward appropriate recycling, waste reduction, and treatment. (James J. Florio [D-N.J.], chair, House Commerce, Transportation, and Tourism Subcommittee)

> HSWA was like a bomb went off in hazardous waste management. (executive observer)

> HSWA was a radical policy change—a dramatic departure from how waste was managed in the past. (executive observer)

HSWA greatly expanded the magnitude of waste types and waste management facilities requiring regulation. The RCRA-regulated universe today consists of 4700 hazardous waste treatment, storage, and disposal facilities (including approximately 81,000 waste management units, most of which have received hazardous waste and from which contamination may have spread to the soil and groundwater) and 211,000 facilities that generate hazardous waste. The number of generators covered by RCRA has increased almost ninefold over the past ten years, with the largest increase resulting from the EPA's regulation of small-quantity generators in 1985. Similarly, the universe of treatment, storage, and disposal facilities requiring a permit and/or a closure plan increased by approximately 1000 from 1980 to 1990.[9]

The RCRA authorizing legislation has thus evolved through cycles of enactment (1965–76), implementation (1977–82, 1985–90), and reauthorization (1980, 1982–84), beginning with the Solid Waste Disposal Act of 1965. The Hazardous and Solid Waste Amendments of 1984 are the second major reauthorization of the 1976 RCRA. HSWA reauthorized RCRA to FY 88. The RCRA program was funded in 1989 without a reauthorization bill, and in 1990 reauthorization was postponed for development and consideration to 1991.[10]

Changing Role of Congress

A second area of radical change in hazardous waste management has been the role of Congress and the nature of congressional directives and involvement with the executive branch. In the 1970s Congress established an environmental protection regulatory system by passing laws that, like many preceding regulatory statutes, set relatively broad goals and timetables and left substantial discretion to the implementing agency on how best to achieve those goals. For example, in the 1976 RCRA, Congress identified in relatively broad terms what the EPA was to achieve and by when. The agency was directed to develop standards within eighteen months for facilities disposing of hazardous waste and to include provisions for recordkeeping; treatment, storage, and disposal methods; contingency plans for accidents; and financial responsibility requirements.[11] The principal substantive direction was that the EPA regulations "protect health and the environment."[12]

All that changed with passage of the 1984 Hazardous and Solid Waste Amendments. In HSWA, Congress not only adopted what many would regard as a revolutionary policy change but also assumed the role of regulator and rule maker, making some of the detailed technical and administrative determinations typically left to the implementing agency. As Congressman Florio explained:

> Between 1887, when the Interstate Commerce Commission was established, and 1980, the congressional paradigm for coping with regulatory problems remained largely unchanged. Congress established regulatory agencies, issued rather general guidelines for agency decision making, and delegated to agencies discretion over the details of rules and implementation tactics. Indeed, the relatively broad mandates of the 1976 RCRA are similar to those established in 1887 in the Interstate Commerce Act.... But in the area of hazardous waste regulation during the 1980s, the traditional reliance on delegated responsibility has collapsed ... and Congress began making specific policy and implementation decisions traditionally in the domain of the agency.[13]

Perhaps nowhere in the legislation was this role change more explicit than in the land-ban restrictions. There, Congress wrote into law its desired level of environmental protection, which would go into effect unless the executive branch could define alternatives by a certain date—a series of so-called land-ban hammers. As one executive observer put it, "The land-ban program is the hallmark of the tension between the technical administrative agency defining how best to accomplish the goals of science and uncertainty, and Congress substituting its judgment."

Starting at least with the 1970 Clean Air Act, Congress has established numerous specific deadlines in environmental laws. Congressional deadlines are certainly not unique to environmental programs; however, Congress has made increasing use of statutory deadlines to oversee the EPA. Moreover, environmental organizations and associations use statutory deadlines as a way to hold the EPA accountable to congressional directives. The latter is reflected in a growing body of so-called deadlines litigation, which can result in court-ordered schedules of implementation. The 1984 RCRA amendments (HSWA), carry seventy-six statutory deadlines, including eight with hammer provisions. Congress also enacted other mandates that did not contain deadlines.

> As part of the toughness, the new (HSWA) amendments signed into law by President Reagan last November include an array of provocative "hammers" designed to make the EPA and the Executive Branch (and the Office of Management and Budget) make specified go or no-go decisions by dates certain, or else the actions take effect immediately. Even the law's defenders acknowledge that it will pose Brobdingnagian management challenges for the EPA, especially in a budget-tight and resource constrained environment.[14]

Hammer provisions were not common before the 1984 amendments, but the unique design of the land-ban hammers was such that whether or not the EPA was able to act in a timely manner, the continued disposal of untreated waste would stop.

Changing Roles of Governments

A third area of change in hazardous waste management is in the roles and relationships among levels of government. Beginning in 1965 with the Solid Waste Disposal Act, Congress shifted waste management from a state and local to a federal responsibility. The EPA was designated as the lead federal agency in the implementation of the 1976 Resource Conservation and Recovery Act; however, both the EPA and Congress envisioned that a successful national hazardous waste management program would be put in place only through joint state and federal action. The statute made clear that Congress intended the states to assume primary implementation of the program. However, the statute also reserved some specific program implementation responsibilities for the federal government.

According to the EPA, the state-federal relationship in hazardous waste management has followed a cyclical pattern.[15] In the early developmental stages of the program, the relationship between the agency and the states was flexible, but this situation changed dramatically with the advent of the 1984 Hazardous and Solid Waste Amendments. The EPA's focus on meeting HSWA's prescriptive mandates and deadlines led to reduced flexibility in its relationship with the states.

Developing Patterns of Congressional-Executive Relations

Seeds of Distrust

The land-ban provisions were part of the RCRA reauthorization deliberations that took place over three years, starting in 1982. The context in which these provisions were enacted had political, institutional, and environmental policy dimensions.

By the early 1980s evidence of the seriousness and scope of the hazardous waste problem had mounted. Congress had access to a wealth of information not available in 1976. Literally hundreds of in-depth studies and analyses had been performed by a broad range of interests. For example, an EPA study conducted by Arthur D. Little, Inc., calculated that industry generated over 33.8 million metric tons of hazardous waste each year. Another EPA study set the figure at closer to 41 million metric tons. Then a study by Westat, Inc., commissioned by the EPA estimated closer to 264 million metric tons. And even that figure did not provide a full picture because it excluded hazardous wastes not regulated under RCRA.

By the early 1980s Congress was also frustrated with the EPA's slow implementation of the hazardous waste program.[16] The 1976 RCRA statute had contemplated a two-year start-up period to put the statutory requirements into effect, allowing the EPA eighteen months to promulgate all basic regulations and an additional six months for companies to submit their permit applications.

Unbeknownst to Congress or the EPA in 1976, however, was that the problem was far more complex than had been assumed. Subsequently, the agency discovered it lacked sufficient data and the scientific understanding necessary to construct reliable regulations and a workable program. What started as an eighteen-month task grew into a six-year odyssey during which the hazardous waste rules from the 1976 RCRA were promulgated in three phases: in May 1980, January 1981, and July 1982. By 1982 the patience of the public and Congress had worn thin.[17] Further, as a result of the controversy surrounding the management of the Superfund program, waste management program issues also became a source of considerable friction with Congress.[18]

Congress also distrusted the EPA's commitment to the effective future implementation of the program. The Paperwork Reduction Act of 1980 and Executive Order 12291, issued in 1981, reflected a government-wide emphasis on reducing industry's paperwork burden and costs associated with complying with federal regulations. The executive order authorized the Office of Management and Budget to review proposed or final regulations for these purposes. Because of the regulatory climate, RCRA rule making continued only slowly, and the EPA revised, suspended, or deferred a number of requirements. The agency was accused of consistently ignoring important technical information whenever the information appeared to lead to additional environmental regulation, and thus increased costs to industry. For example, the EPA "clung doggedly to the belief that land disposal was an environmentally sound policy and was preferable to other disposal methods, despite evidence that land disposal caused serious environmental hazards and despite widespread recognition that effective and available treatment alternatives existed."[19]

Further fueling the flames of public and congressional anxiety were some well-known "horror stories" involving the disposal of hazardous waste that prompted congressional action on hazardous waste amendments at a time when other pollution control legislation was stalled on Capitol Hill.[20] For instance, Love Canal in New York, where residents were forced to abandon their homes through a government salvage sale rather than face future health risks from exposure to highly toxic chemicals. Or Times Beach, Missouri, where the casual spraying of tens of thousands of gallons of contaminated used oil to suppress dust on several miles of unpaved roads once again led to the abandonment of an entire residential area and another hazardous waste site "fire sale."

The administration did not offer its own bill for RCRA reauthorization, which prevented the EPA from proposing its vision for the RCRA program as HSWA was being debated. The agency's relations with the Hill were strained, in part because OMB distrusted the EPA's representation of the position of the administration. The overall negotiations were largely senior-staff driven, with principal leadership from the House Energy and Commerce Committee and the Senate Environment and Public Works Committee. Congressional staffers recall seeking technical assistance from the EPA regarding the impact and feasibility of their proposals. According to recollections from both sides, much time was spent at the staff level talking things out.

Eventually, in a bipartisan, bicameral, and virtually unanimous manner, Congress reached the conclusion that the overall RCRA program was seriously deficient: implementation had been slow and unfocused; existing regulations were weak and contained too many loopholes; enforcement needed improvement; the creation of new Superfund sites needed to be prevented; and much hazardous waste was still not being managed in an environmentally acceptable manner.[21]

Deliberations Surrounding the Land-Ban Restrictions

Congressional deliberations with respect to the land-ban provisions were similar to the overall context; Congress had the lead with respect to their substance. Congressional staffers, in particular, played a key role. They had significant authority and crafted the architecture and language of the restrictions. This left the administration in a reactive posture, focused more on timetables and less on substantive policy alternatives.

The House and Senate worked independently on versions of the land-ban restrictions. The fact that the EPA was aligned with the Senate, and that it began implementation in accord with the Senate version, which ultimately did not pass, would have important later consequences. The differences between the versions centered on the basis the agency would use to define treatment standards.[22] Under both versions the "hammer nature" of the policy would have been present, but other differences were scientific and politically symbolic.

The Senate's approach to treatment standards was *health-based:* waste was to be treated to the point that it posed no problem to human health and the environment. The political symbolism of this strategy was that it granted considerable discretion and control of uncertainty to the agency, particularly in the form of the assumptions that would have driven the final regulatory decisions. The House version, not supported by the EPA, based treatment standards on the *best demonstrated available technology (BDAT),* a strategy perceived to be scientifically and symbolically more objective and more stringent, and granting far less or at least different discretion to the agency.

When HSWA passed, the House version of the land-ban treatment standards prevailed. It should be noted, however, that although the two approaches are framed as being different, they are also subtly interconnected. Both are concerned with decreasing the risks to human health and environment. The issue is whether that risk is minimized (health-based treatment standards) or eliminated (best demonstrated available technology-based standards). Further, whatever approach to treatment standards is used, it is also connected to other provisions of the RCRA program (for example, delisting).

The administration was consulted and played an active role in developing a timetable for the land-ban restrictions. Congressional observers recalled that Lee Thomas (the EPA administrator) had a seat at the table to provide technical assistance and comments. In putting together the time frames for the land-ban program, they recall asking him whether each deadline was workable, and if not, what would be. Several also stated that when congressional staff meetings were held between conference sessions, very often EPA staffers were there as well. Congressional observers characterized these efforts as "thrashing a consensus timetable out with the executive branch, and after that procedure felt comfortable holding them to it." "The schedule we came up with—the executive branch said, 'It's ambitious, but we can do it.' After the fact, they came back later and said, 'Well, we were looking at things in isolation when we said that.'" The argument after the fact was that the deliberations did not address how the land-ban timetable fit into all of the other timetables that were being negotiated.

Observers from both branches recalled a disconnect between the RCRA program and its relationship to other environmental statutes, with the exception of CERCLA, or Superfund. The discovery of additional Superfund sites was a major impetus for the character of this RCRA reauthorization, as well as for the land-ban restrictions, and there was some thought given to linking the passage of HSWA to Superfund. That was fended off, however, because "it would have meant HSWA would never have passed."

The land-ban restrictions were characterized by gaps between goals and resources, of which most parties seemed to be aware. Some of those interviewed suggested that the EPA requested additional resources, but the request was not granted by the OMB. Others pointed to the fact that the president's budget request did not reflect a perceivable increase to implement the land-ban restrictions. Yet, nearly all commented that the land-ban restrictions alone were an exceedingly ambitious task for the EPA; when the restrictions were viewed in the context of all the other EPA requirements, expectations clearly exceeded resources.

> OMB was concerned about the cost of the hammers. There were sentiments that they were "mindless, across the board edicts," that the provisions in general "ignored local conditions and nuances and could cost between $10 and $40 billion depending on how the EPA wrote the regulations. (former OMB staffer)

> There was a disconnect between goals and resources: the president's budget request did not request additional resources to implement the land-ban provisions. With the land-bans, they were staring a loaded revolver in the face—yet they failed to request additional resources. So the appropriations committee, which had limited $ to play with to add resources, saw little attraction to add to the land-ban program. If the administration had not asked for extra dollars, why would we? We saw soft spots in other areas of program implementation—e.g., permitting, enforcement, inspections. (congressional staffer)

In sum, no single event could account for the character of the final land-ban restrictions. The context was socially and politically volatile (for example, hazardous waste horror stories such as Love Canal, post-Watergate distrust of government, the EPA's delayed implementation of RCRA in direct contradiction to congressional mandates). Congressional "strategy," carefully crafted by congressional staffers and members, was a complex of intentions fundamentally and forcefully to redirect policy in a legislative design that would guarantee an end to the status quo. Congress was also motivated to offset the role of the courts and to fend off OMB's efforts to stall implementation of radical and potentially costly change. For all these reasons, comity between the branches during the development of the land-ban policy was lacking. Instead, the seeds of deep institutional distrust were sown, producing the kind of detailed stipulation that often appears when parties lack trust and are addressing highly technically complex and controversial issues.

An Ingenious Detailed Congressional Intervention

> An ingenious way to make it happen—put a gun to the agency's head to get it done and out on time. (executive observer)

Congress expressed the land-ban restrictions to the executive branch in a decision framework that included a tightly interwoven and highly detailed policy framework, an implementation schedule of deadlines, and congressional regulations in the form of penalties that would take effect if the EPA failed to meet the schedule.

Policy Framework of the Land-Ban Hammers.—Figure 5.1 shows the decision framework of the land-ban hammers. Before HSWA, there were no barriers to the disposal of hazardous waste on the land. With the land-ban restrictions, Congress defined a set of decision rules that had to be applied before land disposal. The objective was to make land disposal the least-preferred option.

The first part of the framework was an outright ban of land disposal of the RCRA hazardous wastes *unless* (a) the generator treated the waste in accordance with standards defined by the EPA, or (b) the generator petitioned the agency to exempt the specific waste. The authority reserved to the EPA was to override (via regulation) the ban for specific wastes where it believed the prohibition would not be required (for example, due to pretreatment).[23] The EPA's definition of a treatment standard for a particular waste would determine the conditions under which the waste could safely be disposed of on land. The presumption that a waste was banned unless the specified conditions (treatment or petition) were met is the substantive aspect of the land-ban hammer provisions.

Implementation Schedule and Congressional Regulations.—The second part of the land-ban hammer provisions is time or deadlines coupled with con-

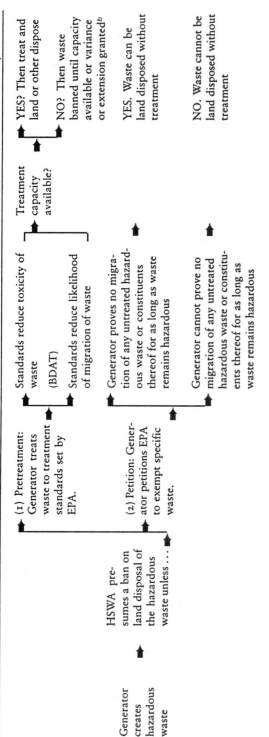

FIGURE 5.1

THE STATUTORY DECISION FRAMEWORK IN THE HSWA LAND BAN HAMMERS

NOTE: Although the statute presumptively prohibits the land disposal of virtually all hazardous wastes, the presumption can be overcome in one of two ways: (1) by pretreatment that substantially diminishes the toxicity or substantially reduces the likelihood of migration or (2) by a waste-specific petition that demonstrates that there will be no migration for as long as the waste remains hazardous.

a. "Hazardous waste" actually refers to a classification scheme, set up in 1980, of complex matrices and decision rules that define hazardous wastes as, for example, those that are listed and those that are characteristic.

b. EPA may grant variances or case-by-case extension for up to two years.

gressional regulations. The deadlines framed the delegation even more precisely: if the EPA failed to make a decision within the allotted time frames, the congressional regulations would take effect, namely, the wastes would be automatically prohibited from land disposal (table 5.1).

Congress identified what would happen, and when it would happen, if the EPA did not comply. Congress defined the relevant universe of hazardous waste in the following five categories: (1) dioxins and solvents, (2) the California list wastes, (3) the first third of listed and characteristic wastes, (4) the second third of listed and characteristic wastes, and (5) the remaining third of listed and characteristic wastes.[24]

Congress, by virtue of the deadlines, instructed the EPA administrator regarding the order in which particular evaluations were to take place over the next four and a half years. The instructions resulted in distinctions known as "hard" and "soft" hammers. For dioxins and solvents, California list wastes, and eventually all the wastes listed and identified on the schedule, the hammers were "hard"; if the administrator failed to issue the regulations by the date specified, then the relevant wastes would be banned from land disposal—period (see table 5.1, columns B through F).

Congress provided some interim flexibility by including two so-called soft hammers applicable to the first third and second third of listed and characteristic wastes (see table 5.1, columns D, E). If the administrator failed to issue regulations by the dates specified for any wastes on these lists, the soft hammers temporarily delayed the fall of the hard hammer by allowing their continued land disposal under certain minimal provisions. However, if the administrator still had not promulgated regulations for any of these wastes by the time of the third third (sixty-six months), the hard hammer would fall and land disposal would be prohibited.

Additional Restrictions and Discretions.—A few other aspects of the land-ban delegation that prescribed the conditions for implementation should be noted.

- The EPA was to issue within twenty-four months a plan that identified in much greater detail which third of the listed and characteristic wastes would be evaluated in each segment (that is, at forty-five, fifty-five, and sixty-six months; no formal hammer was attached (table 5.1, column A). The EPA plan was to be exempt from the Administrative Procedure Act, the Paperwork Reduction Act, and judicial review.
- A "rolling" requirement was that as the agency identified new hazardous wastes, decisions on land disposal must be made within six months of identification (table 5.1, column G).
- A statutory requirement for early consultation with Congress was carried forward from RCRA [sec. 1008 (b)]: the EPA must notify committees within a "reasonable time before publishing any . . . proposed regulations" of their content.

TABLE 5.1
HIGHLIGHTS OF THE IMPLEMENTATION SCHEDULE . . .

	A	B	C
Congressional deadlines	8 Nov. 1986 (24 months)	8 Nov. 1986 (24 months)	8 July 1987 (32 months)
Types of wastes[a]	EPA must issue a plan identifying how particular hazardous wastes will fall into this schedule.	Dioxins and Solvents	California List Wastes
	NO HAMMER	HARD HAMMERS[b]	
Consequences of failure by EPA to make required determinations by date specified	Exempted from Administrative Procedure Act, Paperwork Reduction Act, and judicial review. (This column only.)	Land disposal of these wastes will be prohibited by statute unless the EPA administrator determines that the prohibition is not required in order to protect human health and the environment for as long as the waste remains hazardous, taking into account the criteria specified by Congress.	

a. The five sets of wastes that the EPA administrator must first evaluate with respect to the acceptability of continuing to dispose of them on land and for the disposal of which the administrator must then issue regulations.

b. Prohibitions take effect by statute.

TABLE 5.1. — *Continued*
... SPECIFIED BY CONGRESS TO EPA

D	E	F	G
8 Aug. 1988 (45 months)	8 June 1989 (55 months)	8 May 1990 (66 months)	Rolling (six months after the date of listing)
First Third of Listed and Characteristic Wastes	Second Third of Listed and Characteristic Wastes	Third Third of Listed and Characteristic Wastes	Newly Listed Hazardous Wastes

(temporary) SOFT HAMMERS		HARD HAMMER[b]	NO HAMMER
If the administrator fails to issue regulations by the specified dates, the wastes on these lists can continue to be disposed of in a landfill or surface impoundment until 8 May 1990 or until the administrator issues regulations, whichever comes first, if and only if the following minimum regulatory controls are placed in effect: a. the impoundments and landfills fully comply with the dual-liner and other containment requirements applicable to new facilities; and b. prior to such disposal, the generator of the hazardous waste has certified to the administrator that the generator has investigated treatment capacity and has determined that the use of landfill or surface impoundment is the only practical alternative to treatment currently available to the generator.		All wastes listed and identified on the schedule, including those scheduled for prohibition at 66 months for which a determination has not been made, are prohibited from all forms of land disposal if the administrator fails to issue regulations by specified date.	

- EPA regulations implementing the land bans (defining treatment standards) were to be effective upon promulgation, although the EPA could grant some postponements and exceptions. For example, it could set the effective date of a prohibition for up to two years beyond the statutory date if alternative treatment and processing capacity was not available. It could also grant exceptions to individual facilities for up to one year and renew them for an additional year.

Origins of the Land-Ban Hammers

HSWA was the first legislation in which hammer provisions appeared on such a wide scale. Where did the notion of a congressional hammer in this policy arena originate and why? Some think it was born "through sheer frustration with the EPA's lack of implementation." Others equated the device with a fail-safe mechanism, tracing it "to the Endangered Species Act. As one congressional staffer explained, "It's an outgrowth of an approach that says this is what will happen unless the Executive Branch decides it should be some other way—it's more an evolving device." But the proximate origin, especially of the land-ban application, is more likely the original RCRA reauthorization bill from 1982, H.R. 6307 (97th Cong., 2d sess.), a discrete bill with a range of specific provisions that dealt in a general way with the land-disposal bans.

Under then-existing RCRA regulations, small-quantity generators were exempted so that the EPA could concentrate on regulating the larger generators. Small-quantity generators—facilities generating less than 1000 kilograms per month of hazardous wastes—could therefore dispose of their wastes at sanitary landfills. According to a former congressional staffer, "Even though small quantity generators were exempt, the EPA had authority to regulate them, but it chose not to do so." H.R. 6307 provided for a two-tiered set of standards: standards for generators in the 100–1000-kilogram range, and standards for generators who produced more than 1000 kilograms.[25] According to Richard Fortuna, then staff toxicologist to the House Energy and Commerce Committee, the standards were accompanied by "a garden variety of directives to the administrator" but no hammers.

About three weeks after the bill passed committee, a philosophy at the EPA of "doing more with less" was prominent.[26] This refers to the Reagan administration's policies of selecting the least expensive means to dispose of hazardous waste, even if doing so ran counter to a statutory prescription for the regulatory system to protect the environment; for example, the agency reversed suspension of a ban on dumping liquid toxins in landfills. Simultaneously, the House committee got calls from numerous representatives of small-quantity generators (SQGs) who were vehemently opposed to coming under the authority of RCRA. House staffers met numerous times with these SQGs, but, according to Fortuna, it became clear that "no matter what we did, they weren't going to deal with the environmental issue."

Congressional staffers believed that if they were getting this kind of pressure from the industry, EPA staffers were as well. Fortuna noted, "Bureaucracies buckle to eleventh-hour pleas for clemency and they need some excuse to fend off such pleas." That insight, combined with happenings at EPA, led to revision of the bill: A new SQG provision would automatically impose existing RCRA regulations for large generators on most small-quantity generators if the EPA failed to promulgate small-generator rules by a certain deadline.[27] That is, the provision was restructured as a hammer; it would be self-implementing in the event of agency inaction.

House staffers had one last meeting with SQG representatives and extended the proposed time frames. During that meeting, one of the representatives metaphorically labeled the provisions "a hammer." Fortuna recalled: "They hated the provisions, but we argued it flipped the dynamic and pushed the industry to push the EPA—it was a new vehicle for enforcing congressional will, but it was a very discrete application."

H.R. 6307 did not become law and the RCRA reauthorization process continued through 1984. But the concept of a fail-safe mechanism with the twin objectives of greatly increasing the likelihood of EPA implementation with strong support from the industry had taken coherent form, at least in the minds of a few key congressional staffers as well as members debating the merits of the proposals.

Norms of Distrust During Implementation

Administratively and scientifically, implementing the land-ban restrictions was construed then and is construed now to be a daunting if not draconian undertaking. For two to three years, the land-ban program consumed a third of the resources of the Office of Solid Waste and Emergency Response (OSW). An RCRA implementation task force was set up in the EPA in response to the HSWA provisions; however, the matrix structure within OSW for the land-ban provisions was in place before final passage of HSWA. Today, the land-ban deadlines are considered to have been met because all of the required regulations were promulgated in timely fashion.

An Overt Clash over Congressional Intent.—The EPA began to implement the land-ban restrictions during the 1983–84 RCRA reauthorizations. In developing an implementation framework, the agency had assumed and preferred that the Senate version, favoring a health-based approach to defining treatment standards, would be adopted. "The agency was going down one path with the hammers in mind,"[28] and "there were no meetings or discussions held between EPA and the Hill until well into the development of the land-ban program."[29] "Legally, the agency is required to consult with the Congress—to give prior notice—before putting a rule out, but we forgot to do it on the first land-ban rule."[30] Reflecting on conditions at that time, Marcia E. Williams, former director of the Office of Solid Waste, said:

I don't think anyone could visualize the entire system. People were focused on the first hammer—dioxins—rather than the total system (i.e., the complex regulatory system laid out in the 1980 regulations to which the landban provisions would apply, the matrices of infinite possible interactions among wastes, and the prospect of having to come up with treatment standards for each). No one asked the what-if questions. By the time I realized what was happening, it was too late.

The 164-page implementation framework was published in the *Federal Register*, 13 January 1986. Congress was formally notified one day earlier. To that point, the EPA had "spent $8 million on the computer model." There was "a firestorm" in Congress; it "went berserk." Environmentalists "went wild." Hearings on the proposed rule were held on both sides of the Hill, and are recalled by all as significantly bitter and unpleasant. In part, the interchange between the branches went as follows:

> Senator Chafee: We try to give the agency some discretion, but we didn't give you an awful lot of discretion in the RCRA amendments in 1984. We strapped you down pretty tight. I am not sure that that is the best way to go, but certainly it will be the attitude of the conferees in Superfund, that if you give EPA any discretion, or you don't give them discretion, they still assume it. So it is not a strong argument for mutual confidence and respect, and trust, if you would, between the two groups, between us and you.
> Dr. Porter (Assistant Administrator for Solid Waste and Emergency Response, EPA): Senator, we simply feel that the way we proposed is legal and can be a good technical way to proceed.... I wish we could have had more dialog earlier on the subject.
> Senator Chafee: Yes, but you have heard the argument ... the lack of dialog came because you didn't tell anybody up here that you were coming out with your proposed regulations. We will be having more dialog on it. I don't want confrontations between us and you. I don't look on this committee as a committee solely here to be an antagonistic, confrontational system with EPA. I look on it as a committee ... designed to assist us in reaching our mutual goals. Oversight hearings are necessary and we will have those, but I far prefer to spend my time on constructive efforts, moving ahead on something we are both seeking.
> Dr. Porter: I understand your comments, and we will certainly take them into strong consideration.[31]

EPA Administrator Lee Thomas received a classic eight-page, single-spaced, bipartisan, bicameral letter from eleven members of Congress on 4 March 1986.[32] Two excerpts follow:

> Congress has been criticized by you and others for the degree of specificity

that we included in the HSWA. However, we now find that even with the extraordinary degree of specificity that was included in the HSWA, the agency is determined to ignore clear congressional intent and statutory requirements and to invent its own approach to the problem of hazardous waste land disposal. It is hard to imagine how we could have more clearly expressed our intent.

EPA's proposal to cap treatment standards with a health based threshold erroneously construes this requirement to minimize threats to human health and the environment as a requirement to reduce such threats to an acceptable level. It is precisely this type of subjective analysis that we were seeking to avoid.

Then Michael Burns, a policy analyst with OSW entered the controversy. He pronounced the proposed implementation framework "fundamentally flawed," and offered his critique in a lengthy letter to Congressman Florio, chair of the Subcommittee on Commerce, Transportation, and Tourism of the House Energy and Commerce Committee, who released it to the press on 12 March 1986.[33]

People differ on why these events occurred. Some attributed congressional fury to the treatment industry lobby. An executive observer recalled, "The treatment lobby was very powerful and influential and able to affect the legislators." Another attributed the volatility and fury to a small number of influential congressional staffers: "A lot of the clash was staff-driven. Congress dissolved into 1 or 2 staff people who were offended. It came down to a few people who felt very paternalistic about the bill. A lot of the time, when you hear 'the Hill' it means 'one staff person says,'" an executive political appointee said. Still others suggested that Congress viewed the EPA's proposed approach as a tool of the Reagan administration: Congress distrusted the science and believed it allowed the EPA too much manipulation. Still others argued that the clash was purely policy-driven; in their view, the law is not unambiguous and the science is not always clear. "We pretend the science says more than it does" (executive staffer). And "the agency had written treatment levels that would have eaten through the liner systems" (congressional staffer).

The most visible result of the controversy was that the EPA changed its proposed approach, although not everyone would agree that the shift was real. Some people saw it as a straightforward acquiescence to Congress: "Congress caused EPA to reverse its position in spite of the fact Congress at that point had no more legal authority over implementation than anyone else" (executive staffer), and "We ultimately changed our approach and went with a straight technology-based approach" (executive staffer). Others were more guarded and detected a change that might have been more symbolic than real: "Although EPA changed, they ended up still using a health-based model to make technology-based decisions—and that shows up in the third third controversy. The decisions aren't just best demonstrated available technology [BDAT], they are BDAT as it affects risks to health and human environment. This is contrary to intent" (congressional staffer).

The confrontation between the branches was complex and subtle, and the statute, for all its specificity, could still be construed as ambiguous. Simple generalizations are risky, in no small part due to the technical intricacies of the issues (for example, health-based versus technology-based treatment standards).

> On matters of policy, the legislature is not nearly as clear—there is always room for interpretation. In the final analysis, though, I did not have as much flexibility as I thought I had. There was no question about the hammers and the deadlines—those are clear. The issue was what kind of treatment and how much. We had developed a model to treat to level x; Congress opposed our approach. (executive political appointee)

> Congress slammed the door on the use of risk assessment in land restrictions. But you can get out of RCRA through the delisting process. And when risk assessment was abandoned in land, it went over to delisting and could have become another way to circumvent congressional intent. It didn't work out that way, however. (congressional staffer)

> EPA needed to be more aggressive to force industry to develop treatment capacity. I was disappointed with the rigor with which they went about checking BDAT. For example, informally, EPA would ask whether Congress wanted the very, very best technology that may not be widely available or the second best that was. I made it clear second best was ok as long as the gap was not dramatic. (congressional staffer)

The EPA was sued, and the controversy became even more complex. The court ruled, after the agency had changed directions, that it had the discretion to choose either a health-based or a technology-based approach in promulgating the first land-ban regulation.[34] "The courts said that both technology-based and health-based approaches were reasonable, but the fact that the agency chose a technology-based approach needed to be justified on a basis other than a letter from Congress. So EPA revised their rationale" (congressional staffer).

Irrespective of whether EPA really did acquiesce to Congress, observers were unanimous that the net effect of the confrontation was "an add-on to existing interbranch distrust," and "a controversy that carries forward to this day."

The executive branch was surprised at Congress's reaction: "Their reaction was a surprise to me and those above me."[35] Moreover, the program became infinitely more complex to manage. For example, a former special assistant in the Office of Solid Waste commented in hindsight:

> Using the health-based approach, we had a relatively small staff and the logic was straightforward: check the levels necessary to protect human health and environment first, then see how technology responds. For example, if the protective level was 2, and incinerators yielded 1, then we were done. But using technology-based standards, the process became much more complex, requiring EPA to look waste by waste at the whole array of technologies to see which one does the best job.

Others interviewed agreed that the implementation approach EPA chose was incredibly complex and cumbersome. For example, just the testing and recordkeeping alone were immense undertakings.

In addition to implementation complexity, many believed the EPA had lost a flexibility essential to implementation:

> The end result? We accommodated to the direction Congress wanted. They took away our flexibility to determine what was reasonable. (executive staffer)

> The hearing signaled to many of us that the Hill did not want us to exercise discretion, and placed us between the Hill, OMB, and the industry who want what's cost effective and reasonable. How to do the right thing, in a reasonable time, offending the fewest people. (executive political appointee)

> The agency becomes jerked in a kangaroo court by one or two members' reading of the statute. They do tend to paralyze people. (executive political appointee)

Two principal lessons were learned from the results of these confrontations: (1) the critical importance of executive communication and consultation with Congress, and (2) the mistakes that can be made under a time frame that allows virtually no room for error. Lee Thomas suggested, "I should have spent much more time communicating directly with members. I could have gotten more of them to agree with me—or at least I could have known in advance that they disagreed." A former senior EPA section director, concluded:

> A serious mistake was made when we did not go to the Hill and communicate what we were doing. After the negative reaction to the proposed rule from the Hill, a small middle-management group formed and engaged in discussions with Hill staff. But the bottom line was that the Hill did not

trust modeling results—the validity of the data. From their point of view, the only legitimate approach was pure technology.

And a former director of the Office of Solid Waste, observed:

> Very few people understood the whole issue and the amount of money that was being expended or needed to be expended at EPA. Despite EPA's best efforts, the statutory hammers and time frames in the 1984 HSWA did not give EPA the necessary time to fully think through the various options it had. Moreover, once EPA chose to go down a given path, due to the extremely tight time frames, there was great reluctance due to the sunk-cost problem to change directions. Finally, the 1980 regulations and the 1984 requirements are incompatible and this makes it virtually impossible to come up with a rational way to implement the land-ban until the basic definitional structure is fixed.

Members Challenge Technology-Based Standards.—Before HSWA, the oil industry spread petroleum-refining wastes on land and let "oil bugs" break it up, arguing that such treatment rendered them no longer hazardous. The practice was called land farming or land treatment. In HSWA, Congress defined land disposal to include, but not be limited to, land treatment. One executive observer said, "the American Petroleum Institute (API) was asleep when this one went through." In setting treatment standards for the relevant waste streams (petroleum/mining, furnace dust, and waste water treatment sludge), the EPA wiped out a favorite practice of the petroleum industry.

In informal discussions of the regulations, EPA staffers told API, "Don't talk to us, talk to your congressmen. This is not a matter where we have a lot of discretion—it's in the law." API did go to the Hill. In fact, perceptions are that the "oil industry had an all-out attempt at lobbying and asked Congress to write letters to EPA and say that land treatment is not land disposal." This was followed by a huge flurry of letters and phone calls from Congress to the EPA asking whether land treatment would meet the no-migration standard. One executive observer commented:

> So first we change to best-technology standards from health-based standards after hearings on both sides of the Hill. Then we come out with standards that meet best technology. Then Congress sees the potential impact in their home states, and the same people who came after us to change to pure technology standards are now saying, "How could you possibly do this?" And this despite the fact that they had specifically banned land treatment.

The EPA did not reverse its decision, a stand upheld in subsequent litigation. Perceived results of these congressional-executive interactions ranged from "not a lot of impact" to "a nuisance" to "this is the only place other than the 1986 controversy where Congress came close to intervening." Another result, however, is that the issue may surface during reauthorization in the form of a proposal to undo the requirement that says land treatment is land disposal. At the time of this writing, the EPA had taken no position on the matter.

Controversy over the Final (Third Third) Land-Ban Rule.—The next controversy between the branches concerned treatment levels for characteristic wastes involved in the final (third third) land-ban rule. Highly simplified for present purposes, the question, in part, is whether the EPA can justify setting treatment standards for characteristic wastes on a basis other than the best demonstrated available technology (BDAT). At the time of most of the interviews, the case was in litigation and people were reluctant to comment. Nevertheless, four aspects emerged as important to understanding the transactions that took place in the context of this study: (1) EPA's shift of approach between the notice of proposed rule making (NPRM) and the issuance of the final rule, (2) the exchange of letters between Congress and the EPA, (3) the court ruling upholding the agency, and (4) comments on the controversy, especially responses as to whether these events were similar to those in 1986.

SHIFT OF APPROACH AFTER NPRM. In its proposal, the EPA said it would require that characteristic wastes be treated with BDAT, even if that meant control below levels where they would no longer be considered hazardous. After issuing its proposal, the EPA began considering allowing treatments to be capped at the level the waste loses its hazardous characteristic (the characteristic level) rather than the BDAT level.[36] Such a method would be less costly than the EPA's proposed version and would digress from its BDAT standards for other wastes in the land-ban program. The shift of approach occurred after the NPRM was issued.

EXCHANGE OF LETTERS BETWEEN THE BRANCHES. On 29 September 1989, Senators Chafee, Quentin Burdick (D-N. Dak.), and Max Baucus (D-Mont.) notified EPA Administrator William Reilly by letter that contemplated EPA actions to implement the third third series of the land-ban provisions "either contradict statutory mandates or otherwise fail to implement the spirit and intent of the law in a timely manner."[37] The specific issues raised by the senators concerned land-ban treatment standards for characteristic wastes, transforming the no-migration variance into a no-harm standard, and other pending issues or long-delayed regulations. Of note are three aspects of the letter:

- Its technical specificity: "The constituent profiles for listed and characteristic solvents are virtually identical. Deactivating characteristic ignitable solvent wastes merely by adding sand does not decrease the toxicity or mobility of the hazardous constituents that remain.

- An attachment, the 4 March 1986 bipartisan, bicameral letter: "We understand the agency is proposing to resurrect an interpretation of the no migration variance. [T]his approach was originally proposed in 1986. We urge you to review the relevant portions of the (attached) letter and to refrain from repeating errors of the past."
- A request for staff-to-staff communication: "To promote a closer working relationship, we urge that you make appropriate arrangements for the Office of Solid Waste staff to meet with the staff of the Environment and Public Works Committee as soon as possible to provide us with a status report on these regulations and to clarify any misunderstandings that may have occurred either in the agency's interpretation of the law or our reading of the agency's proposals."

On 30 April 1990, Chafee and Burdick wrote to Reilly again, "reiterating our earlier position and alerting you to our serious concern over reports that your agency is preparing to publish a regulation that contradicts our position, is inconsistent with the agency's previous pronouncements, will seriously undercut the effectiveness of the land-ban program, and is unlawful."[38] Of particular note, "If the creation of facility specific exceptions is not possible, the agency should propose legislative solutions and prepare to work with the Congress to correct the perceived problem in the course of pending legislative action to reauthorize RCRA."[39]

The final rule was signed on 8 May 1990. Reilly responded to the earlier congressional communications on 27 August 1990.[40] Selected items in his letter are these:

- Equivocal statutory language: "EPA has aggressively defended its authority to establish treatment standards based on BDAT in the face of somewhat equivocal statutory language."
- Conceptual and practical problems: "Applying the land disposal prohibitions to characteristic wastes at the point of their generation means that the prohibitions will apply to nonhazardous waste management. This creates enormous conceptual and practical problems."
- Conflicting goals and policies within and among statutes: "Congress provided no specific answers to these types of questions in the land disposal prohibitions legislation, although RCRA does command ... that EPA integrate the provisions of Subtitle C with other provisions of RCRA and with other statutes that EPA administers. Under these circumstances, standard administrative law principles accord EPA great leeway to balance these conflicting goals and policies committed to EPA by statute."
- Give us a call: "If you have any questions or comments about the third-third final rule, please feel free to have your staff contact Don R. Clay, the Assistant Administrator for the Office of Solid Waste and Emergency Response."

COURT RULING. The U.S. Court of Appeals, District of Columbia Circuit, on 29 June 1990, upheld the EPA's less stringent standard, and agreed that the agency has discretion to interpret as it did the ambiguous statutory language of the Hazardous and Solid Waste Amendments of 1984.[41] In a sixteen-page dissent Chief Judge Patricia Wald argued that the standard required in the law is the far stricter one, not the one adopted.[42] The case is on appeal.

As in 1986 and throughout implementation, people differ about why these events occurred. Some suggested that the congressional-executive controversy over the third third rule illustrates what happens when the EPA fails to consult with Congress. A congressional staffer declared, "The real issue? It's the failure of the agency to consult with us when they make these critical decisions. They may notify us right before the decision, but that is not the same as consulting with us at key points during the decision process. The level of contact between the branches is pitiful." Others pointed out that Congress did not really intervene in the third third controversy; only three or four members had written to the EPA administrator, compared to eleven members in 1984. Still others noted that, once again, a federal court had upheld the EPA's actions. Those of the last persuasion argued that the strong likelihood of such judicial support provides yet another motivation for Congress to be even more specific in its statutes. A congressional staffer suggested, "The judiciary finds opportunities to read ambiguity into the law that was not intended."

Is the third third controversy like the 1986 implementation framework controversy that followed passage of HSWA? It seems that there are significant similarities and differences. On the one hand, there is some realization that whereas the 1986 controversy was philosophical and dealt with the broad implementation framework for the land-ban program, the 1990 controversy is technical and the EPA more clearly has discretion. On the other hand, the sense is that the agency "pulled a fast one" by making the change after issuing the proposed rule.

The Same
- "It's the same issue as in '86: treatment for treatment's sake. Congress is skeptical—there is still a lot of frustration, but not nearly as harsh a reaction. Partly this has to do with the waste involved." (congressional staffer)

Different
- "It has elements of 1986, but there is a difference. There is a sense among some of us that in '86, decisions were being made on a purely philosophical basis. Then, based on obstinacy, EPA did not want to change course. Now, EPA is making a more conscious decision based on their assessment of what's doable ... so even though we may be uncomfortable with the decision, I feel less comfortable arguing the specifics.... Now we are at a level of technical detail that is the agency's prerogative." (congressional staffer)

- "1990 is more subtle and the impacts are potentially as bad. EPA made the change after issuing the proposed rule—so that's the source of the sense they pulled a fast one—they remembered what happened in '86 and this time went their own way in the eleventh hour." (congressional staffer)
- "EPA has the discretion on this one. In 1986, it was a 50–50 call. In 1990, it's a 90–10 call. There are far fewer actors in Congress who are opposed." (executive observer)

Summing up a sentiment shared by both sides, an outside observer commented, "These clashes are in the end very unhelpful to creating a good program or an effective use of resources." In the same breath, however, came the gleeful remark that "this one was a procedural victory for EPA."

RCRA Reauthorization.—The last significant interaction between the branches has a present and future orientation: reauthorization of RCRA. In keeping with a tradition in environmental legislation, emphasis at the next reauthorization is expected to shift away from hazardous waste management to another aspect of waste management, that of (nonhazardous) solid waste. Few expect Congress to do much with respect to hazardous waste, although one executive observer thought there was a "wait-and-see attitude on how much the hazardous waste issue would be opened up." Another suggested that the upcoming reauthorization may "be a new world—moving away from the RCRA mecca of command/control and possibly coming up with economic incentives." Still others suggested that the next few months offered an opportunity for both branches to reflect on the lessons suggested by the past years.

At least two documents should be noted as potentially significant to setting the stage for interbranch deliberations during the forthcoming reauthorization, not only for their content but also for what they symbolize.

The 19 July 1988 GAO report *Hazardous Waste: New Approach Needed to Manage the Resource Conservation and Recovery Act* is the culmination of GAO's work in the RCRA area for the prior five years and draws on approximately thirty reports in reaching overall conclusions about the agency's management of RCRA. GAO believes that (1) the EPA could strengthen its relationship with Congress and improve RCRA implementation by establishing specific, measurable goals for its major RCRA efforts and by developing a long-term strategy for achieving the goals; (2) the EPA's accountability could be maintained through periodic reporting to Congress, outlining progress in attaining the goals; and (3) Congress may wish to amend RCRA to require the EPA to establish, in consultation with Congress, measurable goals for priority areas and a long-term strategy to achieve the goals.

In July 1990 EPA-OSW released the RCRA implementation study, *The Nation's Hazardous Waste Management at a Crossroads,* which evaluates the cumulative progress of the RCRA hazardous waste program and the key issues affecting the program as it enters the 1990s. Some of the principal findings included the following:

- RCRA is plagued by too many high priorities, many of which are conflicting and unrealistic; priorities need to be clarified.
- The roles of involved parties—EPA headquarters and regional offices, the states, the Office of Management and Budget, the courts, Congress, and the public—are unclear.
- Communications between external groups and the EPA and within the agency need improvement.
- Human resources need invigorating.
- Better measures are desirable for judging the program's performance and for setting realistic goals.
- The program should be steered in a direction that will encourage innovation in hazardous waste management and cleanup.

Both congressional and executive observers believed that the RCRA implementation study is significant, though a few thought it was too soon to comment, and one criticized the report for lacking an action plan.

> This may be the most significant event. What they're saying is what critics have been encouraging them to do.... This is a whole new approach to working with the Congress. (congressional staffer)

> This sets the agenda for RCRA for the next ten years. It could be another major turning point in the program or just another report. (congressional staffer)

Effects of Congressional Intervention and Executive Response

Virtually every participant contacted expressed the sentiment that hammers of the type used in the land-ban restrictions are a "double-edged sword." The instrument—or weapon—was invented at one point in the long history of cycles and continually shifting relations of comity, trust, and distrust between Congress and the executive branch. Appreciating the three eras of congressional intervention with the executive suggested in table 5.2 provides an important context for interpreting the significance of the results of this kind of congressional intervention.

Results for Congress

For Congress, the land-ban hammers symbolize institutional leadership and offer a mechanism to set priorities, allocate resources, and have greater assurance that implementation will be achieved. "I see the setting of hammers

TABLE 5.2
CONGRESSIONAL INTERVENTION IN RCRA LAND BANS

Traditional Cooperation and Conflict	Congress as Regulator	Possible Crossroads
1960s to early 1980s Seeds of Distrust	Mid to late 1980s Norms of Distrust	Early 1990s Beyond Distrust?
• Horror stories (Love Canal, Times Beach, Missouri) • Slow and unfocused program development and implementation • Executive Order 12291 and the Paperwork Reduction Act of 1981 • Reagan appointees revise, suspend, or defer regulations that may protect the environment but that increase costs or burden industry • Industrial lobbies apply tremendous pressure to Congress, OMB, EPA • Hammer invented in H.R. 6307 • Broad goals and deadlines in legislation	• Congress writes regulations into HSWA as penalties that will take effect unless EPA meets deadlines • EPA begins implementation of land-ban restrictions before HSWA passed • 1985–86 controversy over first rule promulgated by EPA • 1987-88 congressional challenge to land-treatment/land-farming regulations • 1988-90 congressional challenge over third-third rule • No substantive legislative changes to HSWA from 1984 to 1990 (pertaining to land restrictions)	• Environmental issues rise again in national prominence, but hazardous waste issues are not prominent on the public agenda • EPA issues RCRA implementation study • EPA achieves implementation of the land-ban restrictions . . . on time • Next major RCRA reauthorization due

as largely a congressional prerogative—that is, without much executive involvement. It's Congress saying this is what we want done—we're fed up and we're not going to take that anymore. It's not strictly adversarial though —it's also a way to be sure a project gets funded" (congressional staffer).

Hammers, in the context of HSWA, also reflect a congressional emphasis in environmental policy weighted more toward the structuring of statutes than toward subsequent oversight of implementation.

> Congress puts less effort into oversight and much more effort into initial statute writing. (executive observer)

> Congress, in structuring a statute like this, is admitting its oversight is inadequate. The implication to the authorizing committees is they've got only one bite. The institution can't keep up with it through oversight. That's bad. (executive observer)

> Leaving EPA almost completely alone during implementation is too far in the other direction. If you have oversight hearings, they can be very instructive to members to learn about an issue, for example, why corrective action is a problem. They can be useful in getting members up to speed. Failing to do that hurts Congress's ability to effectively strengthen the program. The agency has no one formally breathing down their neck. (congressional staffer)

As environmental legislation has evolved, the communicative force of legislative language has changed considerably. It is no longer sufficient for Congress to say simply, "The administrator shall do x." Rather, what the hammers and accompanying technical details and deadlines show is that for Congress to be confident that the law will be implemented, Congress believes it must create a different and more compelling structure of language. That said, hammers, especially as they were framed in the land-ban restrictions, contradict the history of administrative law and place Congress in the role of rule making. One observer suggested that the land-ban restrictions also "resemble some of the provisions in the War Powers Act."

People also believe that hammers, especially the land-ban hammers, are "budget busters" that result in altered relations among authorizing and appropriating committees. Hammers, according to this view, are more the result of a game of one-upmanship among the authorizing committees, vying for resources from appropriations committees.

Finally, irrespective of the rationale and need, more than a few congressional observers were disturbed at the institutional implications of Congress's taking on the traditionally executive role of regulator. Some argued that Congress has no business getting so specific. Several congressional staffers strongly asserted that the tendency of Congress to write regulations is not a good trend. But others noted that although it is unfortunate that Congress has to go to such lengths to get bureaucratic attention, "aside from public hanging, that's about what it takes." In their view, Congress should not start down this road, but when Congress does, it is because the executive branch "forces it upon Congress."

Results for Executive Management

The land-ban hammers had positive and negative consequences for executive management in three areas: strategic, administrative process, and organizational capacity (see table 5.3). On the positive side, it is clear that the hammers significantly changed administrative dynamics within the executive branch such that traditional fields of tension were fundamentally realigned: the OMB and the EPA were forced to cooperate (the alternative of no action was unthinkable); industry was forced to work with the EPA (they shared a goal—to avoid the hammer); priorities were clear to all; and EPA managers had the resources and were rewarded for goal achievement. One executive observer noted an interesting twist: The EPA itself has recently begun selective use of the hammer approach in writing regulations.

The positive features were offset, however, by assertions of faulty conceptualization (for example, of the environmental problem and analysis of alternatives), so that today some argue that the land-ban program and environmental results are dysfunctional and contradictory, take a heavy toll on human resources, and exemplify implementation for the sake of implementation or some mindless "pursuit of deadlines for the sake of deadlines."

> If EPA had started from scratch after the 1984 amendments had been passed, it is highly unlikely that they would have used (the approach they did) to implement the land-ban restrictions. The approach was extremely time consuming to implement and required a large number of dollars to collect constituent specific data for each waste stream by each technology.... The much more obvious approach to have taken to implement the final language of the statute would have been to identify technologies that were appropriate for various types of waste streams.[43]

EPA observers in particular reported that implementing the land-ban restrictions took a heavy toll on human resources: people burned out, were afraid, and to this day feel a lack of credit for accomplishing an incredibly complex task under great duress.

Results for Institutional Relations and Processes

The double-edged sword of the hammer is nowhere more apparent than in its effects on branch relations, in particular, congressional-executive relations. On the positive side, some observers argue the hammer provisions have paradoxically created (or forced) a clear foundation of shared priority goals between the branches. Hammers flag certain parts of the program as more important. In that sense, they build a foundation where two sides can understand each other better in terms of setting priorities. Depending on how onerous the consequences associated with imposition of the congressional penalty, they apparently also increase the likelihood of resource allocations on both sides.

TABLE 5.3.
DOUBLE-EDGED SWORD OF THE HAMMER ON EXECUTIVE MANAGEMENT

	Strategic	Administrative process	Organizational capacity
Positive	Forced action/set priorities Gave management significant leverage Set the bottom line for OMB	Improved information base for decision making by changing relationship between EPA and industry	
Negative	Resulted in some mindless pursuit of meeting deadlines and being pulled in all directions Constrained long-term flexibility and capacity Opened the door for citizen lawsuits	Treatment standards were based on very little real data Required resource intensive implementation Resulted in fragmented, incremental implementation of a complex system—some conceptualization errors and reinforcement of verticalness of problem solving	Created fear Created mixed esprit de corps Burnout Contributed to lack of positive congressional feedback to the agency—never a "job well done"
Mixed		Significantly affected the process of issuing regulations in terms of • timing (down to the wire) • overall process • institutionalizing an EPA strategy for dealing with OMB • complex, more costly regulations • EPA using hammers in its own regulations	

Others paint a more negative portrait. They argue that hammers are not an instrument of interbranch cooperation. They breed mistrust, widen the gap between goals and rational consequences, and are perceived differently on both sides in terms of accountability (that is, who the hammers are "on"—the EPA or industry).

And some observers say the land-ban hammers have simultaneous positive and negative results for relations between the branches:

> The land-ban hammers got the agency to focus and got them on track. But their success depends on whether you take the long- or short-term view. The cost was a lot of trust and missed opportunities. (congressional staffer)

> Congress wants the agency to take action and uses hammers to convey that intent. But Congress doesn't always think of the consequences in a rational framework. (executive observer)

The land-ban hammers are symbolic of a new order of congressional-executive relations. Basically, although they may contradict the history of administrative law in the sense that they place Congress in the role of regulator, they also reflect Congress's realization that the bureaucracy needs backup if it is to achieve its goals. They may have been spawned by the Reagan era, but they appear to have evolved into an approach that will be maintained of necessity. The institutional issue is the manner in which they ought to be used effectively:

> For what most people thought war powers and the Boland Amendment were about—that's as close to where Congress can be said to interfere. While foreign affairs is different from what we are talking about, the same concept is at play in domestic policy. That is, it [land-ban hammers] identifies the practical concern of Congress and its staff implementing the law and making the kind of administrative decisions that appropriately should be left to executive agencies, whose existence depends on their greater expertise in carrying out these legislative grants of authority. Recall the attempts in the 1930s to set up regulatory agencies, except that the rationale for their eventual creation was finally their greater expertise. Hammer provisions run counter to that philosophy, but I don't think they interfere with the president's constitutional prerogative to faithfully execute the law. I don't think we are at that point yet. (executive political appointee)

> I see Congress's role as the allocation of uncertainty—and in turn structuring administrative discretion to conduct this allocation. The most fundamental questions to be answered include who bears the burden if we are wrong, who decides, and when. (congressional staffer)

We're never going back to the days of unstructured executive discretion. That's in part due to distrust, in part to the recognition of the inherent passivity of bureaucracy, and in part to the need to back up industry. These issues cut across political lines. (congressional staffer)

The judiciary plays an important role in environmental decision making and therefore affects legislative-executive relations in the environmental arena. Observers pointed out that the philosophical clash going on in the courts, especially at the appellate level, concerning how literally bureaucracies should read statutes, is beginning to visit itself on congressional-executive relations. Indeed, this issue has played out in this case in the ruling on the third third litigation that upheld the EPA's discretion. It is important to note this dynamic when discussing legislative-executive relations. "Conceptually, it does make sense for Congress to say here's what we want if the agency can't do the job, rather than having the courts say it. I'd much rather have Congress specify standards than the courts—and hammers are that—Congress specifying the default setting" (executive observer).

Results for Policy

Even from the vantage of policy (substance and context), the land-ban hammers produced polar or simultaneously positive and negative consequences. The hammers got the attention of industry, who in turn made it clear to the EPA and OMB that it would be a disaster if the deadlines were not met. They created certainty for industry and thus enabled the eventual increase in treatment capacity. They provided an incentive to industry to provide data to the agency, often at industry's own expense, for the purpose of conducting treatment studies. It should also be noted that some small businesses disappeared as a consequence of the regulations.

The land-ban hammers gave the EPA an incentive to prioritize promulgation of the required rules. Many believed that though the hammers might have been "a little too brute force," they were an essential element to progress and improvement in hazardous waste management—probably "a net positive impact on the environment that will go some ways toward not having future Superfund sites." A congressional staffer summed up the multiple benefits: "Congress has achieved what it wanted: regulations out in specified time frames; a marked change in how industry disposes of waste; a tightening of the system of disposal."

Hammers are today viewed as a powerful congressional device for leveraging scarce resources toward congressional priorities—which may or may not coincide with executive priorities.

Now, the hammer is a resource issue—it directs where the agency will put resources. What you see currently is a program that is significantly understaffed in terms of full-time equivalents (FTEs) and an agency that puts the resources where there are hammers. So if you don't put hammers, they won't allocate resources. The hierarchy—in order of most likely resource allocation and highest priority given to implementation—is hammers, court-ordered deadlines, statutory deadlines, no deadlines. (congressional staffer)

There are, however, at least three significant limitations to the perceived success of the land-ban hammers from a policy perspective. First, the hammers exacerbate fragmentation (for instance, between policy expectations and available resources, among competing programs, between tight deadlines and human resources, and between desirable policy goals and costs to society).

There's a real disconnect between the number of requirements and the resources the executive has sought or provided. That is, even if you agree on policy, how will the program be carried out? On one side, deadlines are not met and interest groups figure out more ways to lobby Congress and litigate. On the other, the agency is in a squeeze between Congress and OMB with respect to the allocation of manpower. Yet, you never see the agency saying, "We don't have the resources to do that." It's always easier for them to say they can meet the deadline. As a result, there is a statute filled with deadlines, but the resources don't match. (congressional staffer)

The land-ban hammers were an expensive requirement that took away from other programs, took a heavy toll on people, and had an impact on the environment, although they were most appropriate for the really hazardous, large-volume wastes. (executive observer)

The land-ban program met the policy goals but at a cost of management efficiency and a greater cost to society. (executive observer)

A second limitation is that the land-ban hammers have probably been a factor in compromising the quality and coherence of the regulations eventually promulgated: "Hammers done like the land-bans lead to bad rule making. The Hill seemed not to understand the time and dollars it takes to put these out and to have them stand up in court. Substantive quality was compromised—in fact, the only way the regulations have held up is due to the way the law is structured, which almost precludes EPA from losing" (executive observer).

And a third limitation of the land-ban hammers is that they contributed to a program complexity that is widely regarded as outstripping the capacity of most to comprehend—let alone implement and enforce.

The land-ban program illustrates the complexity of RCRA. RCRA is so complicated and so broken that only a few people understand it and thousands of people are trying to. Something is wrong—we haven't achieved our intent, which is environmental protection. (executive observer)

The land-ban hammers layered in requirements onto prior legislation, creating contradiction and possible incompatibilities. (executive observer)

Conclusion

Whether the hammer device will be put to effective future use in both Congress and the executive branch is a critical question. Certainly, the experience and reflections of those involved in the invention and implementation of the land-ban hammers can be an important resource for deriving criteria that might guide practice. An initial framework might include guidelines regarding when to use hammer provisions, when not to use them, and how to craft them when they are used.

Hammers like those in the land-ban restrictions can signal with absolute clarity that the status quo cannot persist beyond a date certain, communicate highly significant priorities, and provide certainty to industry. Crafted somewhat differently, hammers can also be positive and effective on straightforward requirements where EPA need take no action to implement (that is, having the hammer fall is actually desired). This occurred, for example, with a provision regarding loss of interim status where EPA wanted the hammer to fall and had to do very little implementation.

Draconian hammers applied to areas of high technical complexity and involving extraordinary rule making are clearly risky. Setting separate implementation schedules with hammer deadlines under all the environmental statutes, or even within the same statute, can make it impossible for the executive agency to set priorities in a rational way. Writing hammers without enabling the agency to make "smart balancing" trade-offs between costs and benefits can backfire. However, that kind of discretion assumes a high level of congressional trust toward the Office of Management and Budget and the EPA and their ability to withstand numerous external demands (for example, from industry).

Hammers—and even more clever inventions that redefine traditional institutional roles and implementation processes—will be much more likely to emerge in a context of high distrust among Congress, OMB, and the executive agencies. Any sword can be a weapon of destruction or a force of salvation. Skillful use of a double-edged sword—like the hammers in the land-ban restrictions—requires overcoming opposing forces to create both the symbol and the substance of positive institutional authority.

Timeline of Major Events in the RCRA
Land-Ban Hammers Case

1981   California Office of Appropriate Technology landmark
                    study states that over 75 percent of waste generated
                    in state should be restricted or prohibited from land-
                    fill disposal (*Alternatives to Land Disposal of Haz-
                    ardous Wastes*).

1981   Office of Technology Assessment and the National
                    Academy of Sciences reports confirm desirability of
                    substantial reductions in the use of land disposal
                    (OTA: *Technologies and Management Strategies for
                    Hazardous Waste Control;* NAS: *Management of
                    Hazardous Industrial Wastes*).

5 February 1981   Early drafts of land-disposal regulations, *Federal Reg-
                    ister.*

28 July 1981   Letter from EPA administrator Anne Gorsuch to Con-
                    gressman John J. LaFace: "Landfilling represents the
                    lowest risk option currently available for dealing
                    with the large quantities of hazardous waste gener-
                    ated each year."

1982–84   Reauthorization of 1976 RCRA: 1984 Hazardous and
                    Solid Waste Amendments. Some informal staff-to-
                    staff consultations on land-ban deadlines.

January 1982   H.R. 6307 begins the HSWA reauthorization process;
                    contains forerunner of the land-ban hammer provi-
                    sions in terms of the concept of the hammer, and
                    lays groundwork for 1984 HSWA, including land-
                    disposal restrictions.

31 March 1982   House hearings on RCRA Reauthorization.

16 December 1982   EPA Assistant Administrator for Solid Waste and
                    Emergency Response Rita Lavelle testifies before
                    House committee that "we believe most wastes can
                    be satisfactorily managed in the land and that it can
                    be done with a reasonable margin of safety more
                    cheaply in this manner."

22 March 1983   House hearings on the Hazardous Waste Control and
                    Enforcement Act of 1983.

30 March 1983   House hearings on environmental problems associated
                    with landfill disposal.

8–9 June 1983   Senate hearing on the 1983 Solid Waste Disposal Act
                    Amendments.

3 May 1983   House hearings on environmental problems associated
                    with landfill disposal.

December 1983   EPA reports more than 180,000 surface impound-
                    ments used for management of wastes; more than
                    30,000 of which were for the management of indus-

trial wastes. Of the latter 70 percent had no liner or retention systems and 39 percent had high potential to contaminate groundwater. Other studies confirm that more than 30 percent of current Superfund sites were caused by leaking lagoons.

April 1984	EPA's comprehensive survey of waste generation and management practices (Westat Report) reveals magnitude of hazardous waste generation and mismanagement.
1982–84	Numerous studies (e.g., by U.S. Department of Interior, Hazardous Waste Treatment Council, Louisiana Office of Conservation) indicate scope of hazardous waste problems.
3 May 1984	Largest hazardous waste fine in history ($10 million) levied at an Ohio site for release of an estimated 45 million gallons of hazardous waste from deep-well and surface impoundment operations.
31 August 1984	Alvin Alm, EPA deputy administrator, approves strategy to govern development of agency's first rule to implement the presumed forthcoming land-ban provisions, clearing way for OSW to prepare a proposed rule outlining the schedule and decision rule(s) EPA intends to follow for deciding whether land disposal would be restricted or prohibited for specific wastes. Strategy is a health-based approach to setting treatment standards, corresponding to Senate version of the land-ban provisions.
9 November 1984	Reagan signs HSWA into law.
1985	Congressional hearings confirm Jay Winston Porter as assistant administrator of solid waste and emergency response.
1985	EPA strategy for land-ban implementation framework (first rule) developed and finalized under Porter and Marcia Williams (director of the Office of Solid Waste).
31 May 1985	EPA proposes a schedule determination of all remaining listed and identified wastes that are not solvents, dioxins, or on the California list.
November 1985	995 of 1538 land-disposal-facility owners or operators decide to cease operating rather than certify their facilities comply with regulatory requirements.
14 January 1986	EPA proposes first land-ban rule and implementation framework for land-ban restrictions, *Federal Register*.
7 February 1986	James Florio seeks details from EPA analyst Mike Burns of events at EPA that led to land-ban pro-

posal; Burns had called proposal fundamentally flawed.

19 February 1986	House hearing on adequacy of EPA restrictions on the disposal of hazardous wastes under 1984 HSWA.
24 February 1986	Senate hearing reviewing EPA implementation of hazardous waste disposal programs under 1984 HSWA, including the land-disposal ban proposal.
4 March 1986	Letter to EPA Administrator Lee Thomas from eleven members of Congress.
6 March 1986	Response to Florio letter of 7 February from Burns.
12 March 1986	Congress releases letter from Burns.
24 September 1986	House hearing on EPA hazardous waste management programs under 1976 RCRA and on hazardous waste volume estimates and potential disposal capacity problems.
28 May 1986	EPA changes strategy; Final Rule (land disposal determinations schedule), *Federal Register.*
7 November 1986	Solvents and dioxins treatment standards issued.
14 April and 5 June 1987	Senate hearing on EPA solid waste and hazardous waste disposal regulatory and enforcement programs under RCRA; focuses on implementation of land disposal restrictions of hazardous wastes; twenty-three witnesses.
8 July 1987	California List wastes: EPA sets treatment standards for some of the California list, but it extends the deadline for most types of halogenated organic compounds to July 1989 because of a lack of treatment capacity.
15 December 1987	GAO testimony on the closure status of RCRA hazardous waste land disposal facilities.
1987	Litigation on first land-ban rule: *Hazardous Waste Treatment Council* v. *EPA,* U.S. Court of Appeals, District of Columbia Circuit, No. 86-1677; decided 15 September 1989).
1988	Little additional treatment capacity built. GAO, *Hazardous Waste: Future Availability and Need of Treatment,* argues consideration of extending deadlines on treatment capacity premature; future availability and need for treatment capacity are issues.
January 1988	EPA issues report on current hazardous waste management practices in the United States.
19 July 1988	GAO, *New Approach Needed to Manage RCRA,* addresses deadlines and hammers.
17 August 1988	First third rule, *Federal Register.* Oil industry complaints to Hill about regulations banning land treat-

	ment result in letters and phone calls to EPA from about 250 members of Congress.
February 1989	Office of Solid Waste issues *Agenda for Action.*
23 June 1989	Second third rule, *Federal Register.* Land disposal determinations, newly listed wastes, *Federal Register.*
9 August 1989	House hearing on hazardous waste landfills.
29 September 1989	Letter to EPA administrator from Senators Chafee, Burdick, and Baucus on third third rule; 4 March 1986 letter attached.
November 1989	Proposal for third third rule.
1990	RCRA reauthorization delayed to 1991.
1990	Oil industry granted six-month capacity variance for refining wastes by EPA; shortened to one year after objections from Hazardous Waste Treatment Council.
January 1990	Proposal on third third is out.
1 January 1990	Land disposal determinations, newly listed wastes, *Federal Register.*
30 April 1990	Second letter to EPA administrator from Senators Chafee and Burdick on third third rule.
2 May 1990	EPA considers less stringent treatment standards for characteristic wastes than proposed in November 1989.
8 May 1990	EPA issues final third third rule and grants a three-month extension for more than 350 untreated hazardous wastes.
10 May 1990	Groups ask overturn of third third land-ban rule (*Natural Resources Defense Council* v. *EPA,* U.S. Court of Appeals, District of Columbia); case on appeal.
29 June 1990	Court upholds EPA's third third rule.
July 1990	OSW study on RCRA implementation issued.
Summer 1990	House and Senate RCRA reauthorization bills.
27 August 1990	EPA administrator replies to earlier letters from senators with respect to third third rule. Treatment capacity asserted by EPA to be 88 percent available.

Acknowledgments

Many people contributed to the development of this case study, but I would like to express particular gratitude to Bob Gilmour, Karen Koster, Jim McCarthy, Marcia Williams, Howard Messner, and George Alapas.

Notes

1. Other hammer provisions were included in the 1984 Hazardous and Solid Waste Amendments, including one on the identification of hazardous wastes (delisting); one on standards for small-quantity generators; and four terminating interim status and referred to as LOIS (loss of interim status). The most intricate and discernibly coherent *system* of hammer provisions, however, was the set articulated in the land-ban provisions.

2. John Skinner, "Banning Wastes from Land Disposal," in "Papers Presented by EPA Office of Solid Waste and Emergency Response at the First Public Briefing on the 1984 Amendments to the Resource Conservation and Recovery Act" (video teleconference, 11 December 1984, Washington, D.C.); Marcia Williams, "The HSWA Land Ban: Is It Fulfilling Its Potential?" (unpublished manuscript, 1990); Richard Fortuna and David Lennett, *Hazardous Waste Regulation: The New Era* (New York: McGraw-Hill, 1987); Marc Landy, Marc Roberts, and Stephen Thomas, *The Environmental Protection Agency: Asking the Wrong Questions* (New York: Oxford University Press, 1990).

3. Christopher Harris, William L. Want, and Morris A. Ward, *Hazardous Waste: Confronting the Challenge* (New York: Quorum Books, 1987).

4. John Chafee, 5 October 1984, quoted in Harris et al., *Hazardous Waste,* 12.

5. According to William Rodgers, evolution is a central concept in environmental law, with evolutionary change regularly taking place at both the legislative and administrative levels. Cited in Robert F. Blomquist, "Beyond the EPA and OTA Reports: Toward a Comprehensive Theory and Approach to Hazardous Waste Reduction in America," *Environmental Law* 18 (Summer 1988): 818.

6. House of Representatives, *Conference Report on the Hazardous and Solid Waste Amendments of 1984 (to accompany H.R. 2867),* 98th Cong., 2d sess., 3 October 1984, H. Conf. Rept. 98-1133, 5.

7. Williams, "The HSWA Land Ban."

8. Fortuna and Lennett, *Hazardous Waste Regulation.*

9. EPA, *The Nation's Hazardous Waste Management Program at a Crossroads: The RCRA Implementation Study* (Washington, D.C.: Office of Solid Waste and Emergency Response, July 1990), 7.

10. In 1992 the House and Senate engaged in reauthorizing RCRA. On 20 May 1992, the Senate Environment and Public Works Committee approved, 12-5, a reauthorization of RCRA that set new standards for recycling, the disposal of municipal garbage, and the growing interstate commerce in waste. The

bill's sponsor, Max Baucus (D-Mont.) refers to it as "a landfill law," a relatively modest proposal to deal with the explosive problem of a nation that churns out 180 million tons of garbage a year and is trying to fit all of it into an ever-smaller number of landfills (Phillip A. Davis, "Senate Panel Trims RCRA Bill, Approves Landfill Law," *Congressional Quarterly*, 23 May 1992, 1442.) Events later than 1990–91 are outside the scope of the case research.

11. James J. Florio, "Congress as Reluctant Regulator: Hazardous Waste Policy in the 1980s," *Yale Journal on Regulation* 3 (Spring 1986): 351–82, at 354.

12. Ibid.

13. Ibid., 375.

14. "Understanding the New RCRA: Landfills and Surface Impoundments the Least Favored Methods," *Environmental Forum* (January 1985): 21–22.

15. EPA, *The Nation's Hazardous Waste Management Program at a Crossroads.*

16. Ibid.

17. Gary N. Dietrich, "Information Burdens and Difficulties in Conceptualizing the Crisis: A Reappraisal," in *Beyond Dumping: New Strategies for Controlling Toxic Contamination,* ed. Bruce Piasecki (Westport, Conn.: Quorum Books, 1984).

18. "Superfund" refers to the Comprehensive Environmental Response, Compensation and Liability Act (CERCLA), passed in December 1980 with the intent of providing $1.6 billion to correct pollution problems at hundreds of toxic waste sites. At the time there was limited appreciation for the fact that unless hazardous waste management practices complemented CERCLA, an endless supply of new Superfund sites would continue to be created. Harris et al., *Hazardous Waste,* 9.

19. Florio, "Congress as Reluctant Regulator."

20. Harris et al., *Hazardous Waste.*

21. John H. Chafee, quoted in Fortuna and Lennett, *Hazardous Waste Regulation,* v, vi. The remarks are corroborated in the interviews conducted to develop this case, as well as in the practical and scholarly literature.

22. Interviews; and Williams, "The HSWA Land Ban."

23. Fortuna and Lennett, *Hazardous Waste Regulation,* 202.

24. Parenthetically, it should be noted that in other sections of HSWA, Congress included additional provisions related to land disposal, such as requirements pertaining to groundwater monitoring and exposure assessments, corrective action, minimum design standards, and general permitting and other operating requirements. These are excluded from the scope of this case.

25. House debate on H.R. 6307, *Congressional Record* H6747, 97th Cong., 2d sess., 8 September 1982, 221–72.

26. EPA Administrator Anne Gorsuch, *Newsweek,* 7 March 1983: 21.

27. House Committee on Energy and Commerce, Subcommittee on Commerce, Transportation, and Tourism, *Hearings: Hazardous Waste Control and*

Enforcement Act of 1983, 98th Cong., 1st sess., 22 and 24 March 1983, Serial No. 98-32.

28. Executive observer interviewed for this case.

29. Ibid.

30. Ibid.

31. Senate Committee on Environment and Public Works, Subcommittee on Environmental Pollution, *Hearing on H.R. 3917 (an act to extend the period allowed for compliance with certain financial responsibility requirements applicable to land disposal facilities under the Solid Waste Disposal Act) and Resource Conservation and Recovery Act Amendments of 1984 Oversight*, 99th Cong., 2d sess., 24 February 1986, S. Hrg. 99-549.

32. Letter to Lee M. Thomas from John D. Dingell, John H. Chafee, James J. Florio, Robert T. Stafford, George J. Mitchell, Billy Tauzin, Barbara A. Mikulski, Frank R. Lautenberg, Dennis E. Eckart, John Breaux, and Wayne Dowdy, 4 March 1986.

33. "EPA Analyst Calls Agency's Proposal on Land Disposal Ban Fundamentally Flawed," *Environment Reporter*, 21 March 1986, 2090; letter from James J. Florio to Michael Burns requesting a detailed description of the events at EPA that led to the proposal, 7 Februrary 1986; letter to James J. Florio from Michael Burns (twenty-seven single-spaced pages), 6 March 1986.

34. *Hazardous Waste Treatment Council, Petitioners* v. *U.S. Environmental Protection Agency, Respondent,* with Edison Electric Institute, Chemical Manufacturing Association, et al. as Intervenors, and consolidated cases Nos. 86-1677, 87-1016, and 87-1057, U.S. Court of Appeals, District of Columbia Circuit, No. 86-1657, decided 15 September 1989.

35. Executive observer interviewed for this case.

36. "Less Stringent Waste Treatment Standard Considered by EPA under Third-Third Rule," *Environment Reporter*, 4 May 1990.

37. Letter from Senators Burdick, Chafee, and Baucus to William K. Reilly, 29 September 1989.

38. Senate Committee on Environment and Public Works, letter from Senators Chafee and Burdick to William K. Reilly, 30 April 1990.

39. Ibid.

40. Letter to Senator John Chafee from William K. Reilly, 27 August 1990.

41. *Natural Resources Defense Council, Inc.* v. *U.S. Environmental Protection Agency,* with American Iron and Steel Institute, Rubicon, Inc., E.I. DuPont de Nemours and Company, Texstor, Institute for Chemical Waste Management, and American Petroleum Institute as Intervenors, No. 88-1657, U.S. Court of Appeals, District of Columbia Circuit.

42. Also see Patricia Wald, "The Sizzling Sleeper: The Use of Legislative History in Construing Statutes in the 1988–89 Term of the United States Supreme Court," *American University Law Review* 39 (Winter 1990): 277.

43. Williams, "The HSWA Land Ban."

6

Making Up for Lost Time: The Defense Nuclear Weapons Complex Cleanup

Jᴀᴍᴇs A. Tʜᴜʀʙᴇʀ

Background and Overview

For nearly fifty years nuclear weapons have been produced at fourteen facilities operated by the U.S. Department of Energy (DOE) and its predecessor agencies that together constitute the nuclear weapons complex.[1] The facilities have generated vast amounts of chemically toxic and highly radioactive waste and have released large amounts of radionuclides and hazardous chemicals into the environment. As early as August 1947 a team of specialists in environmental health and safety matters from the newly created Atomic Energy Commission (AEC) warned the agency about the effects of radioactive and toxic materials on the people building nuclear weapons and the communities surrounding the bomb-making facilities. They found that "the whole problem of the disposal of radioactive and toxic wastes needs immediate laboratory and field study. The disposal of contaminated waste ... if continued for decades, presents the gravest of problems. This is one of the areas of research that cannot be indefinitely postponed."[2] The extent and complexity of the environmental pollution and nuclear waste throughout the complex that have built up since the report in 1947 present major challenges for DOE, other federal agencies, the states, and Congress in the post–Cold War 1990s.

Since the 1940s the nuclear waste produced by the weapons complex has been processed, stored, or disposed of in ways that do not meet today's environmental standards. Spills and leakages at inactive waste sites have contaminated the soil and groundwater in several locations, and there are hundreds of contaminated, empty buildings within the complex. Until recently, the health and environmental risks posed by this situation were hidden from the public behind the veil of national security.

Since the mid-1980s, however, the risks have been widely discussed and

debated by an attentive public and key congressional committees. For example, twenty-seven congressional committees and subcommittees have
shown some interest in the cleanup, interest that ranges from passing new
laws to holding oversight hearings. The decision-making framework for implementation of the cleanup policy has evolved into a highly combative political arena compared with the experience of the previous forty years. The
old policy-making system was low-profile and "captured" by the nuclear-
bomb-making industry, the U.S. Department of Energy (and its predecessors), the eight national energy laboratories, other weapons complex contractors, and a few key congressional actors (mainly the Joint Committee on
Atomic Energy). The new policy-making system surrounding the weapons
complex is rife with conflict and accusations of fraud, waste, abuse, and
careless disregard for the health and safety of the weapons complex workers
and the public.

Developing Patterns of Congressional-Executive Relations

Cooperation and conflict between Congress and executive branch agencies
during the management of the nuclear weapons complex cleanup have
evolved through two distinct stages spanning almost fifty years. From the
mid-1940s to 1976 congressional-executive relations were cooperative, secretive, and closed to "outsiders." A relatively closed policy-making system
consisting primarily of the Joint Committee on Atomic Energy (JCAE), the
Atomic Energy Commission, the national energy laboratories, the managers
and nuclear scientists at the weapons complex sites, and the weapons complex contractors was dominant.[3] There was little public worry about the environmental effects of the bomb-making activity.

   The second stage, from 1976 (the year the JCAE was abolished) to the
present, is characterized by more intricate, open, and conflictual relationships between Congress and the DOE. The relationships among the dozen
congressional committees and subcommittees, DOE, the weapons complex
managers and contractors, environmentalists, state and local government officials in the affected states, citizen groups, and the specialized media exhibit
more variety in this second stage. The conflict and decision making have
been open and vary from highly visible confrontations to quiet cooperation.[4]
DOE's weapons production complex became the focus of intense congressional and public scrutiny in the late 1970s.[5] The accidents at Three Mile Island in 1979 and Chernobyl in 1986 energized public concern and forced
the issues of health and safety effects of the DOE complex into the open.
Extensive environmental and health problems revealed in the late 1980s
generated further strong public demands for Congress and DOE to shut
down and clean up the facilities. Concern about the safety of nuclear weapons facilities also increased as the Reagan administration accelerated production of atomic warheads. Even conservative members of Congress were

investigating the weapons plants in order to identify problems and to advocate fixes before the problems became political liabilities in their local communities and states. Liberals also sought to expose the problems in order to clean up the mess and to justify a shutdown of nuclear weapons production. Numerous congressional investigations and General Accounting Office reports soon uncovered major safety, environmental, and management problems in the DOE weapons complex.

Today, most of the DOE nuclear weapons facilities are virtually shut down because of serious environmental, safety, and management problems. These problems include deterioration of equipment; noncompliance with environmental, safety, and health standards; vast amounts of radioactive and chemical wastes that have been improperly buried and stored for decades; and contaminated groundwater, surface water, sediments, and soil. In 1990 the General Accounting Office (GAO) estimated that the cost of addressing these problems may be as high as $155 billion.[6] Though the cost estimates for the cleanup of the weapons complex are varied and highly unreliable, in 1992 they were close to $200 billion and still climbing.[7]

This case study relies on interviews with current and former members of Congress, DOE officials, contractors, congressional staff, lobbyists, and state regulators. These more than fifty face-to-face, in-depth elite interviews, as well as studies of congressional and DOE documents and congressional oversight hearings, have shown that opposition to DOE cleanup efforts has developed into advocacy coalitions within the policy-making system surrounding the cleanup. Coalitions based on concerns about health, safety, and the environment have engendered distrust of DOE. Broad coalitions of anti-nuclear-weapons activists, environmentalists, and not-in-my-back-yard (NIMBY)—or not-in-my-state—advocates are joined in opposition to the department, and many members of Congress have been responsive to them. However, many political actors support current DOE cleanup efforts. They believe that nuclear power is relatively safe; that nuclear weapons are needed for national security; that DOE is doing the best that it can in using known technology to clean up nuclear and toxic waste in the complex; and that DOE is being delayed by unnecessary legal actions and restrictive environmental laws. These political actors also are championed by some of the congressional actors in the system.

Controversies in Cleaning Up the Weapons Complex

DOE's ability to clean up the weapons complex to the satisfaction of the public and Congress has been challenged by key congressional committees since the late 1980s. The feasibility of DOE's goal of cleaning up all sites within thirty years has been met with growing public and congressional skepticism.[8] The Waste Isolation Pilot Plant (WIPP), a repository intended for the storage of certain types of radioactive waste, is not yet open and toxic and radioactive wastes continue to back up at DOE facilities.[9] Most of the waste awaiting permanent disposal, as well as future waste, will most likely remain at the sites of generation for many years to come. Progress in cleaning up the pollution and nuclear waste is hampered by the lack of ready technical solutions, qualified personnel, and data about the problem.

During the past decade Congress and its support agencies, especially the General Accounting Office and the Office of Technology Assessment (OTA), have documented and expressed concern over hundreds of continuing environmental, safety, and management problems at the weapons complex.[10] The problems have included DOE's emphasis on production over environmental, safety, and health matters; shortcomings of DOE's oversight; contractor performance; mistrust of DOE on the part of the public and some members of Congress; lack of a technically qualified staff, resulting in heavy reliance on contractors; and inadequate data analysis, research on solutions, and plans for addressing the problems of the weapons complex. Over the past decade, GAO reports have found problems with uncontrolled costs associated with the cleanup, lax standards for evaluating DOE contractors, excessive overhead, managerial incompetence, contract fraud, and contractor "coddling" by DOE.

Recently, with detailed administrative direction and reporting requirements in legislation and in congressional committee reports, DOE has taken steps to solve its weapons complex problems. The initiatives, which were seen as a direct result of congressional intervention, include the following: (1) management and oversight restructuring inside the department; (2) issuance of strategic plans concerning environmental restoration and waste management; (3) assessment of facilities to determine whether they meet federal, state, and local safety, environmental, and health requirements; and (4) tougher oversight to make contractors more accountable for environmental and health matters at the facilities. Congress required DOE to issue a second *Five-Year Plan* in 1990. The plan outlines a $30 billion, five-year effort—FY 91 through FY 96—to bring facilities into compliance with environmental laws, to begin cleaning up environmental contamination at DOE sites, and to begin improving management of a wide variety of radioactive and hazardous wastes that DOE facilities generate.

Although Congress has increased its oversight and involvement in DOE's cleanup effort, the problems are still critical. There is little consensus among the major political actors (DOE, Congress, scientists, national laboratories, contractors, interest groups, and state and local governments) on how the cleanup should proceed or where to dispose of the chemical and nuclear waste produced, and how quickly new technologies can be researched, developed, and tested in order to clean up the sites. There continue to be major problems of waste, inefficiency, and even corruption in the cleanup of the nuclear weapons production facilities.

Congressional Intervention and Executive Response in the Management of the Nuclear Weapons Complex Cleanup

The nuclear weapons complex has been the focus of intense public and congressional scrutiny during the past six years. Contaminated groundwater, radioactive air emissions, leaking nuclear waste tanks, and improper chemical waste disposal are among the environmental problems acknowledged by DOE. Before the complex achieved its current prominence on the congressional and public agenda, DOE had fostered a secretive climate in which environmental and safety considerations were brushed aside if they interfered with weapons production. The situation was compounded during the nuclear arms buildup of the early 1980s, when DOE was required to boost production sharply, with minimal upgrading of aging facilities.

The 1986 explosion and graphite fire at the Soviet Union's Chernobyl nuclear power plant escalated public concern about the safety of DOE reactors that produce nuclear materials, particularly the graphite-moderated N reactor at the Hanford site. Subsequent safety studies brought about by press accounts and congressional directives led to the indefinite shutdown of that facility. A series of highly publicized safety incidents at DOE's Savannah River reactors in 1988 also prompted a torrent of news articles and dozens of congressional hearings and government reports examining every aspect of the nuclear weapons complex. With the occurrence of these accidents and shutdowns, the health and environmental risks posed by conditions at the complex suddenly began to receive widespread attention.

Since the 1940s the production of nuclear material and nuclear weapons has generated large quantities of radioactive and chemical waste. This "defense waste" was often processed, stored, or disposed of on-site and in ways that were not environmentally sound. Unlike commercial nuclear waste, the management of defense radioactive waste had not been subject to regulation and oversight by the Nuclear Regulatory Commission, the Environmental Protection Agency, or any other outside agency.[11] The management and cleanup of hazardous and mixed waste, however, is subject to regulation by EPA.

At least seven federal environmental statutes contain explicit provisions covering DOE facilities. Most contain language that makes federal executive agencies and employees subject to administrative and judicial environmental enforcement at the federal, state, and local levels. The federal laws and regulations that apply directly to the DOE cleanup program include the National Environmental Policy Act of 1969 (NEPA), which requires that an Environmental Impact Statement (EIS) be filed for each major federal construction project; the 1976 Resource Conservation and Recovery Act (RCRA) and the Hazardous and Solid Waste Amendments of 1984, which require that disposal of hazardous wastes meet EPA treatment standards;

the Comprehensive Environmental Response, Compensation, and Liability Act of 1980 (CERCLA, or "Superfund"), which provides guidelines and priority-setting requirements for the handling of hazardous and mixed chemical and radioactive wastes at DOE facilities; the Nuclear Waste Policy Act of 1982 (NWPA) and the Nuclear Waste Policy Act Amendments of 1987 (NWPAA); the Clean Air Act of 1990; the Clean Water Act; and DOE's environmental restoration and waste management guidelines in the *Five-Year Plan.*

Several congressional committees have argued that DOE has consistently failed to meet the requirements of these laws. Compliance with the National Environmental Policy Act of 1969, which requires federal agencies to consider the environmental effects of major actions that they are planning, has been a long-standing problem for DOE. DOE and its predecessor agencies repeatedly have been accused of failing to prepare the Environmental Assessments and EISs required by law, and of inadequately considering environmental factors when making major decisions. These federal laws and their state-enacted counterparts bring together a mix of political actors in the cleanup policy-making system.[12]

Some of the most difficult technical problems at DOE weapons facilities involve waste generated, stored, or disposed of prior to 1970. Much of that waste is buried and its precise location and composition are unknown, and all of the inactive waste sites from that period have yet to be identified and located. There is more information about the post-1970 waste. Most is stored at known locations and has been identified and monitored. Both types of waste have become of intense concern to dozens of members of Congress and their staffs, who want it cleaned up immediately. As the number of contaminated inactive sites and buildings identified by DOE has increased, organized constituencies have pressured members of Congress and committees with jurisdiction to see that decontamination takes place and to intervene in DOE's management of the environmental restoration.

Widespread public and congressional concern about defense waste and contamination did not develop until more information about the nuclear waste problem became available during the past decade. Accounts, for example, of health and safety problems at Hanford, Savannah River, Rocky Flats in Colorado, and the Feed Materials Production Center in Ohio have heightened worries over potential hazards from federal defense facilities. In recent years, John Glenn (D-Ohio), chair of the Senate Committee on Governmental Affairs, has pushed DOE to correct those conditions in a timely fashion. Glenn's hearings have intensified state and public demands for immediate action by DOE.

More recently, Congress has expressed concern about the cost of the cleanup. Projected funding levels ranging from $70 to $150 billion for environmental restoration and additional tens of billions for waste management have raised eyebrows. Members of Congress express surprise that the problem appears to be so much bigger and the proposed solutions so much more expensive than before imagined. Further, DOE's past efforts to respond to congressional requests for plans and funding estimates have generated much criticism. DOE Secretary James D. Watkins promised Congress that DOE would work with EPA, the states, and the National Academy of Sciences to develop future *Five-Year Plans* and to design technology development initiatives that could eventually result in lower costs.

The defense waste backlog includes many types of high-level, transuranic, and low-level radioactive wastes.[13] Because of congressional committee directives during the 1980s, DOE has published inventories of waste at the weapons complex, but the department acknowledges that the data are inaccurate and incomplete. (Most respondents in this study confirm that data accuracy has become a major area of conflict between Congress and DOE.) In addition, most of the waste has been buried with nonradioactive, chemically hazardous substances and is thus considered "mixed waste." Although congressional committees have requested that DOE publish inventories of mixed waste at the various sites, DOE has not done so because it does not know the extent to which mixing has occurred, how much mixed waste there is, or where it is located.

In most cases, DOE has just begun to determine the extent of contamination and the precise substances involved. The job is extremely difficult and costly because little is known about the location and content of the toxic and radioactive hazards at many of the oldest disposal sites. After direction from Congress, DOE in 1983 issued *Defense Byproducts and Waste Management*, a plan that laid the groundwork for handling these problems. It promised to "reverse the open-ended 'interim' storage approach which has been in effect for decades."[14] The plan called for construction of waste treatment and disposal facilities, construction of new storage facilities, and a revised transportation system for nuclear waste. Much of the plan was subsequently included in DOE's 1990 *Five-Year Plan*. Several of the large and controversial storage facilities, such as the Waste Isolation Pilot Plant near Carlsbad, New Mexico, and the Defense Waste Processing Facility (DWPF) at Savannah River, are nearly complete.[15]

Under pressure from House and Senate committees in the late 1980s, DOE reorganized its environmental programs around three major activities: environmental restoration, corrective activities, and waste management. Dozens of congressional committees and subcommittees have jurisdiction over parts of DOE's cleanup activities, and they held more than sixty-five hearings between January 1980 and December 1992, resulting in a variety of congressional directives and intense oversight.

Extensive congressional pressure came from a variety of actions. For example, with congressional direction, funding for the nuclear weapons complex cleanup was dramatically increased from $1.7 billion in FY 89 to nearly $6 billion in FY 92, thus forcing the department to shift its focus from production to environmental restoration. Congress also placed great reliance on the General Accounting Office for audits about the management of the cleanup effort that have become essential to the monitoring and redirection of DOE. The GAO produced some sixty reports of environmental, health, financial, and managerial problems at the production facilities.

The Office of Technology Assessment also played a significant role in helping congressional committees redirect the DOE with publication of its multiyear study, *Complex Cleanup: The Environmental Legacy of Nuclear Weapons Production* (1991). OTA's analysis called for major policy initiatives to improve DOE's cleanup program. The report found that Congress could increase its oversight of DOE, EPA, and other federal agencies to develop and implement improved programs to strengthen agency personnel, improve plans for safe waste storage, improve technology development, coordinate and accelerate standards-setting relevant to the cleanup, and strengthen site monitoring programs. The report called as well for Congress to establish a new and separate health assessment office, health "Tiger Teams" of experts to conduct exposure and assessments at each site, and a national independent environmental health commission. Congress has acted on all of these ideas. For example, in 1992, against the objections of DOE, the U.S. Department of Human and Health Services was given the responsibility to monitor the health of the weapons complex workers. OTA recommended that Congress establish advisory boards with technical staff at each site and a national coordinating and advisory board to provide public participation in key cleanup policy and technical decisions. With congressional urging, DOE reacted quickly to this suggestion and has established local advisory boards at each site. The OTA report also called for Congress to authorize an institution to regulate those aspects of radioactive waste management activities now subject exclusively to DOE's authority. OTA suggested that these functions be given to a new national body or an existing body such as the Nuclear Regulatory Commission or EPA. The idea is popular with many House members and has been actively debated at various congressional hearings.

Senator J. Bennett Johnston (D-La.), as chair of both the appropriations subcommittee and the authorization committee with prime jurisdiction over nuclear waste policy, has given pivotal leadership to redefine the DOE's mandate and authority for the environmental restoration of the weapons complex. Johnston and his staff on the Energy and Natural Resources Committee have intervened to limit DOE management discretion and provided more funding or reallocated funding for the cleanup effort. Johnston's congressional hearings have focused on uncontrolled costs, mismanagement, and unrealistic schedules for the cleanup, which have been a major incentive for DOE to redirect the cleanup policy.

House and Senate committees have also required DOE to provide plans and budgets to address the defense waste contamination problem. As a result of congressional intervention, DOE has been required to prepare periodic reports covering present conditions, proposed approaches, and cost estimates, of which *Environmental Restoration and Waste Management: Five Year Plan* is the most important. DOE has acknowledged that its cost estimates are driven by budget considerations and are not based on a definitive assessment of needs. In response, congressional hearings on DOE proposals have stressed the necessity of both a clear definition of the problems in the weapons complex and a rational process for arriving at solutions.

House Energy and Commerce Committee hearings have discovered that DOE managers have been incapable of assessing contractor management performance, thus forcing Congress to require the GAO to do quarterly management assessments of the cleanup program. In 1989 Congress also forced DOE to base contractor fees not on the number of weapons produced but on the extent of compliance with environmental safety and health rules. This was an attempt to redirect the agency from a culture of production to one of concern for health and environment.

In response to these and other congressional directions, the former secretary of energy, Admiral Watkins, promised to reverse the department's poor environmental record. After taking office in March 1989, he required stricter environmental compliance by contractors (who operate virtually all DOE facilities), issued the *Five-Year Plan* for beginning the cleanup, and established the Office of Environmental Restoration and Waste Management to implement the plan. At the urging of congressional committees, DOE requests for cleanup funding escalated from $1.3 billion in FY 89 to $3.8 billion in FY 91 to nearly $4.3 billion in FY 92. The total estimated cleanup budget for FY 91–FY 96 is $30 billion. The stepped-up congressional oversight and mandated new philosophy for DOE may not solve the mismanagement problems in the short run. Leo Duffy, the DOE's head of the cleanup effort, has acknowledged that waste and inefficiency will continue to eat up as much as forty cents of every dollar spent. He recently concluded that "we're in the 60 to 65 percent efficiency range." At some sites, he said, "You're down in the range of 25 to 30 percent efficiency." Congressional redirection of DOE and allocation of new funds for the cleanup have changed the department, but mismanagement seems to continue.

Environmental enforcement efforts to date have relied primarily on "federal facilities compliance agreements" negotiated by EPA, state regulators, and DOE. The agreements, enforceable through the courts, generally establish site-specific deadlines and schedules for correcting problems. Meeting the terms of the agreements is expected to entail steady increases in funding, and budgetary shortfalls could eventually conflict with the agreement demands. The likely conflict is a major concern for DOE and congressional players in the cleanup decision-making system.

After questioning from congressional critics, Secretary Watkins admitted that DOE has made little progress in the cleanup. "I am certainly not proud or pleased with what I have seen over my first few months in office," he declared in June 1989 in announcing his own ten-point cleanup plan, released in response to congressional hearings. DOE foot-dragging is not generally believed to be a problem, though. According to a recent OTA report:

> At a few sites, some simple containment and stabilization activities have been performed by "capping," or by removing contaminated soil and storing it elsewhere in a more controlled form. Technologies that would effectively remediate certain sites are not available or cannot be applied with the resources now contemplated. It may be impossible with current technology to remove contaminants from certain groundwater plumes and deeply buried soil or, even if possible, it may be extremely expensive or require prolonged periods of operation.[16]

Instead, increasing public pressure on members of Congress to clean up the sites, regardless of the problems involved, has contributed to the disagreements between DOE and Congress.

Watkins's plan included establishment of "Tiger Teams" (teams of outside nationally known specialists) to examine sites, establishment of distinct environmental responsibilities for program managers, increased incentives for environmental compliance, and greater environmental funding. Implementation of most of those early initiatives has been completed, including new performance criteria for the contractors who operate most DOE facilities. Under the new rules forced on DOE by Congress, a contractor's unsatisfactory performance carries the risk of the loss of all potential bonuses, or "award fees." In the first round of bonus awards under the new system (spring 1990), DOE withheld more than three-quarters of Rockwell International's potential $8 million in fees because of environmental and safety problems at the warhead component production plant at Rocky Flats, Colorado. However, the DOE field offices have been slow to comply with the change and some have taken steps to circumvent it. According to GAO and committee reports, several DOE field offices have paid contractors roughly what they would have been paid under the old system, even if they have received low safety and pollution scores from outside regulators. For example, DOE's inspector general found that the DOE's Nevada field office increased fees awarded to contractor EG&G by more than $1 million to compensate for the increased costs required by its compliance with new congressional environmental and safety standards.

After extensive congressional intervention and committee-set deadlines, DOE in 1990 completed the revised *Five-Year Plan,* which outlines how the department will tackle its environmental problems. Most had been identified under former Secretary of Energy John S. Herrington. The first *Five-Year Plan* (31 August 1989) called for DOE to complete the cleanup and achieve full compliance with all environmental requirements within thirty years. The first annual update, for FY 92–FY 96, was completed in June 1990. Implementation and annual updates of the *Five-Year Plan* are reviewed by congressional committees and carried out by the Office of Environmental Restoration and Waste Management. Established 1 November 1989, the office consolidates environmental projects and programs previously implemented by offices with other major responsibilities—primarily the Defense Programs office, the Nuclear Energy office, and the Office of Energy Research.

Cost estimates for the total DOE environmental compliance effort, such as the widely cited $155 billion figure, are highly speculative at this point. Comptroller General Charles A. Bowsher noted in February 1989 testimony before Congress that uncertainty still exists not only regarding the size of the problems but also regarding the extent to which DOE sites can be cleaned up. In December 1992, one report estimated the cleanup cost at $200 billion over the next thirty years, exceeding the estimate for the government bailout of the savings and loan industry.[17] Watkins had initially assured congressional committees that DOE could develop new technologies to keep cleanup costs below estimates by making research and development a key component of the *Five-Year Plan*. However, annual costs in the latest version of the plan are nearly double 1989 levels. DOE is no longer attempting to estimate a total cost for the thirty-year effort, and OTA now questions DOE's ability to meet the primary goal of cleaning up all weapons sites within the time set: "DOE's stated goal—to clean up all weapons sites within 30 years—is unfounded because it is not based on meaningful estimates of work to be done, the level of cleanup to completed, or the availability of technologies to achieve certain cleanup levels. Neither DOE nor any other agency has been able to prepare reliable cost estimates for the total cleanup."[18]

Numerous issues related to DOE approaches and proposals have also been raised over the past few years by congressional committees. Some of the issues have to do with the adequacy of DOE's programs and plans, the selection and availability of technologies to characterize and address problems, the level and pace of funding, and the setting of objectives and priorities for resource allocation. Regulatory and institutional issues regarding defense waste management and environmental restoration have also been raised. Some of the key unresolved issues related to DOE's current approaches and proposals are discussed below.

The aim of DOE's waste management program is to store radioactive and mixed waste in permanent disposal systems planned for each type of waste. Activities under the program include the treatment, storage, transportation, and disposal of waste from current and past production of nuclear weapons. The activities are carried out at various locations in the complex by DOE staff and contractors under the overall management of DOE headquarters in Washington, D.C.

DOE plans to convert high-level waste (HLW) into glasslike forms acceptable for disposal underground in a geologic repository. Major new facilities are planned for this purpose. The Savannah River Plant Waste Processing Facility and the Hanford Waste Vitrification Facility, which are to begin operation in 1999, will vitrify the HLW. The Idaho Waste Immobilization Facility, scheduled to be completed in 2010, will convert the waste contained at the Idaho National Engineering Laboratory (now about 3 percent of all defense HLW) to a solid form and will process future HLW generated at the site. Defense high-level waste is to be permanently isolated in a deep-geologic repository.[19] The suitability of the WIPP site in New Mexico for such a facility is being evaluated. The test placement of approximately 4200 waste canisters was to have begun there in 1991, but placement ceased because of legal challenges and pressure from Congress.

Congressional oversight hearings revealed a number of unresolved issues associated with DOE's HLW program. For example, there is uncertainty regarding the definition of high-level waste, namely, whether it will be defined by source (that is, any waste resulting from spent-fuel processing) or by level of hazard. The source definition, now in effect, would permit more waste to be vitrified and stored in geologic repositories. DOE believes that this course of action will be the more expensive one.

With respect to transuranic (TRU) waste, DOE planned to transport all retrievable waste stored on-site after 1970 to WIPP beginning in 1989. However, geologic and "not-in-my-back-yard" (NIMBY) political problems at the site and other issues with the State of New Mexico—including the licensing of the containers in which the waste would be transported to WIPP, the certification of the waste in order to meet acceptance criteria, and the handling of mixed TRU waste—have delayed matters. Also, because WIPP is designed to hold retrievably stored waste generated between 1970 and 2015, there are unresolved problems of how to deal with the large quantities of pre-1970 TRU waste that were buried. To the extent that TRU waste is mixed, its management is subject to EPA regulation under the Resource Conservation and Recovery Act, adding many more congressional committees and subcommittees with jurisdiction over EPA and the environment to the matrix of decision makers in the cleanup policy-making system. All storage facilities for mixed wastes, therefore, will have to obtain permits under RCRA as well. Some members of Congress and staff members in DOE believe this will cause inordinately long delays. For example, DOE revealed in congressional hearings and reports to Congress that the RCRA process for radioactive mixed waste storage facilities at the Hanford site would not be completed until 1993 at the earliest.

Goals for the cleanup program set by Congress primarily in appropriations bills and committee report language have generally been accepted by DOE: clean up inactive contaminated sites and decontaminate and decommission surplus facilities. DOE and Congress agree that the nuclear weapons complex must be cleaned up safely and quickly, yet members of Congress do not want any waste stored in their states. They want the waste removed to other sites, in essence, not in my back yard. This may not be possible for all DOE surplus facilities, some of which may have to be entombed or placed in protective storage until the radioactivity has decayed to lower levels. Other sites, however, can be cleaned up relatively easily, and processing equipment and buildings may be dismantled and removed so the sites can be used for other activities. DOE and congressional committees have agreed that the environmental restoration activities will have to be tailored to conditions at the individual locations. In most cases, those conditions have not been characterized and assessed; however, congressional committees have had serious questions about cost and cleanup schedule estimates.

Effects of Congressional Intervention on the Funding, Priorities, and External Oversight of the Cleanup Program

With the consolidation of environmental compliance and waste responsibility under a single office, DOE's FY 91 environmental budget request covered the entire department for the first time. Previously, funding for cleanup and waste projects had been divided among several offices.

DOE has acknowledged that its resource estimates beyond FY 94 are not "budget quality." This is largely because as of late 1993, DOE had not developed specific plans, priorities, and schedules for addressing waste problems in the weapons complex. DOE also implies in its 1990 *Five-Year Plan* that the proportion of funding allocated to cleanup at each facility will shift significantly over the next twenty years, but it is not clear just how.

Congressional and DOE respondents in this study indicated that there are many unknown factors that could affect funding needs. DOE and private-sector respondents suggested that new technologies could reduce the costs of cleanup. Others argued that it is possible that developing and implementing new technologies could add substantially to the cost. New technology may also reveal that the problems are more severe than currently estimated. However, congressional hearings and GAO reports have revealed that as characterization techniques become more sophisticated and more information is gathered, the nature and scope of the problems at the weapons complex are more severe than originally thought. Also, the public located by each site is demanding that improved, but more expensive, technologies that have been applied in the commercial sector (for example, for low-level and mixed waste disposal) be applied by DOE to the cleanup. These phenomena create an uncertain technical and political environment that increases the tension between Congress and the DOE.

Congressional hearings have found that current DOE resource estimates may also not reflect all future costs associated with regulatory compliance for hazardous and mixed waste cleanup. For example, DOE is involved with EPA and various state governments in preparing interagency agreements (IAGs) for hazardous and mixed waste cleanup at weapons facilities under applicable statutory provisions. The agreements call for specific measures, including remedial investigation and feasibility studies, and set deadlines for cleanup activities to begin and end. DOE is also preparing Environmental Impact Statements for several sites within the weapons complex. Congressional respondents have noted that previous DOE experience with IAGs and EISs demonstrates that cost estimates are often underestimates.

Congressional hearings have found that one of the most serious issues related to the cleanup program is lack of a system for setting priorities for defense waste management and cleanup. This further affects the reliability of cost estimates. According to several congressional respondents, DOE apparently does not have an effective process for developing waste management and cleanup objectives. For example, many DOE proposals do not state the assumptions made regarding achievable levels of cleanup required at each facility. Ignorance of the nature of the assumptions makes selection of the most effective approaches and technologies and the specification of priorities difficult. Among the questions asked of DOE by congressional actors is whether a particular site can or should be restored to unrestricted public use, should be cleaned up enough to permit only selected uses, or should be deemed inaccessible for public use. The answers are necessarily shaped by the laws and regulations that currently apply, by the public's view regarding acceptable levels of risk to human health and the environment, and by the level of political pressure on members of Congress. Senator Johnston and the staff of the Senate Committee on Energy and Natural Resources are concerned about this and have required numerous reports from DOE and GAO about the goal-setting procedures for the cleanup program.

DOE's method for setting priorities among cleanup needs has not satisfied congressional committees, the states, or citizen groups. Essentially, the DOE approach is to identify the environmental problems, place each problem into one of four categories denoting relative risk to the public, and then to integrate environmental degradation factors into the analysis. The degree of uncertainty concerning the risk-based ranking of each problem is also categorized. This survey-and-ranking method, whereby DOE attempts to assign priorities to environmental hazards at its primary weapons complex locations, has been subject to various criticisms from congressional committees, scientific associations, and citizen groups. For example, DOE's model for generating risk-based rankings (the Multimedia Environmental Pollutant System, or MEPAS) has been criticized by the Natural Resources Defense Council on the grounds that it is too complex and data-intensive, cannot distinguish short-term from long-term risks, cannot identify the most exposed individuals, conflicts with legal obligations, and was developed without public comment. Some congressional delegations and facility operators also do not believe that ranking necessarily reflects the most serious problems. According to House and Senate respondents in this study, preliminary results of the DOE ranking highlight the lack of reliable data, shortcomings in the mathematical model being used, and other deficiencies. Several congressional committees have concluded that although some problems have been identified as matters of serious concern, DOE has not documented the degree and relative severity of risks from these and other conditions within the complex. The Office of Technology Assessment and the Senate Energy and Natural Resources Committee have called for a new structure and process of priority setting for the cleanup to provide public participation in key technical decisions in order to enhance the credibility and quality of those decisions. DOE has responded by holding a series of regular public hearings on cleanup priority setting and other issues at the various cleanup sites.

Congressional critics have also declared that it is not clear whether the priorities list is correlated with DOE's allocation of resources described in the *Five-Year Plan*. With congressional urging and ultimate approval, DOE is developing a "program optimization system" (POS) for allocating environmental restoration funds to inactive hazardous waste sites. The system, which is fairly complex, attempts to account for factors such as health and safety risks, regulatory responsiveness, public concern, and future costs.

DOE's efforts to set priorities are also subject to decisions made by EPA and affected states. DOE facilities are subject to the priority-setting requirements of the Comprehensive Environmental Response, Compensation, and Liability Act (CERCLA) and the Superfund Amendments and Reauthorization Act (CERCLA/SARA), which are implemented by EPA. Pursuant to these laws, EPA has promulgated the revised "National Oil and Hazardous Substance Contingency Plan," which requires DOE to include criteria for determining priorities among releases, or threatened releases, of hazardous substances, pollutants, and contaminants.

With specific direction from Congress, Watkins opened a dialogue with the EPA administrator and the governors of the affected states to arrive at a national priority system for remediation of federal facilities. He also promised Congress that he would work with other executive agencies and the various Native American nations to ensure that their concerns are addressed and that the priorities set are deemed by them to be fair, effective, and timely.

As a general rule, the DOE and other federal agencies are also subject to environmental standards and procedural requirements (such as disposal permits) established by local and state law. Environmental enforcement against federal facilities is made possible by broad waivers of sovereign immunity in most major federal environmental statutes. In practice, however, such enforcement has been hampered by numerous legal uncertainties and interagency disagreements. The nuclear character of most of DOE's defense facilities significantly complicates the environmental regulatory scheme as well. Under the Atomic Energy Act of 1954, the Atomic Energy Commission exercised broad authority over its own nuclear facilities. According to DOE's *Five-Year Plan,* the AEC and its successor agencies, including DOE, have interpreted the language of the act to mean that they are self-regulating with respect to the environment.[20] DOE still establishes and enforces its own requirements for radiological safety and health within the boundaries of its nuclear facilities, including decontamination and decommissioning. Management and disposal of radioactive waste, including the radioactive constituents of mixed waste, are also regulated by the department. The only exceptions to this are the planned, high-level waste storage and disposal sites to be licensed by the Nuclear Regulatory Commission. However, several DOE and private-sector respondents interviewed for this study concluded that environmental statutes, lawsuits, and congressional oversight directives have drastically curtailed DOE's ability to manage its own operations.

A key issue is whether federal facilities can be held responsible for environmental violations if sufficient funding for the necessary cleanup and pollution control is not appropriated. Most major environmental laws requiring federal compliance allow an exemption if Congress does not provide sufficient funding, but such exemptions have never been invoked. The likelihood of a lawsuit is complicated, because interest groups, federal agencies, and the states all may initiate suit against DOE.

To address congressional concerns and respond to members' detailed intervention, Watkins attempted to bring waste management and environmental cleanup activities under the direction of a single individual, Leo Duffy, and took other actions, such as developing the 1989 and annual revisions of the DOE *Five-Year Plan,* to coordinate and consolidate all DOE cleanup activities in an integrated program. He asserted that the *Five-Year Plan* would help reestablish DOE's credibility with Congress, the public, and the states, as well as serve as a baseline for future programs and budget requests. A relatively open and competitive decision-making network involving dozens of congressional committees and subcommittees, DOE, EPA, the laboratories, contractors, environmental groups, citizen groups around each site, local governments, and the states has been set in place to monitor progress in the cleanup of the weapons complex carefully.

Most congressional respondents in this study said that much remains to be done to bring about the transition from a Cold War weapons complex that emphasized production over environmental matters to one that can remedy past environmental problems while continuing to meet the nation's nuclear weapons needs in a post–Cold War era.[21] A workable, cooperative, and credible process involving key congressional actors and the DOE has only begun to emerge.

Congress set strict deadlines in the late 1980s for planning and reports.

It questioned the selection and evaluation of contractors involved in the program. Congressional actors inserted detailed program guidance for DOE in appropriations bills. Congress also established an independent oversight entity, the Defense Nuclear Facilities Safety Board (DNFSB), to monitor safety and environmental issues at the nuclear weapons facilities; created a special House panel to study the cleanup issue; asked GAO to report on cleanup questions more than seventy times; and successfully pressured DOE to create a special office to manage the environmental restoration program.

Additionally, the number of committees and subcommittees with jurisdiction over the cleanup program expanded significantly in the past ten years. In addition to the Senate Energy and Commerce Committee hearings, the House Committee on Energy and Commerce has held dozens of oversight hearings on the DOE cleanup program in the past few years. The Senate and House Appropriations Committees also continue to hold regular hearings with regard to funding the cleanup. The House Government Operations and the Senate Government Affairs Committees have also held numerous hearings on the cleanup.

Generally, House and Senate respondents voiced distrust of DOE's funding estimates, projected deadlines and schedules, management expertise, control of contractors, and technical capabilities. Because members of Congress believe that the cost estimates are often wrong, they frequently rely on a network of "informants" to tell them what the realistic costs might be. GAO and OTA were cited by several congressional respondents as respected and often-used independent sources for estimates.

Regular congressional players in the cleanup decision-making process have often accused DOE of using classified information as an excuse for superficial environmental reviews. DOE's current guidelines allow classified material in an EIS to be placed in a classified appendix or excised altogether. Congressional staff held that classified material should not be eliminated from a report, and argued that stronger guidelines are needed to ensure that environmental reviews of proposed actions and consideration of all reasonable alternative solutions not be hampered by the withholding of information. The early pattern of concealment within the nuclear weapons complex may have been a major contributor to the extreme environmental situation that DOE and Congress must now address. Thus, most of these respondents feel that DOE must work harder to overcome its "cult of secrecy."

Several congressional and environmental interest group players in the cleanup decision-making system also contend that many DOE weapons facilities are operating with outdated Environmental Impact Statements and that supplements are highly desirable; new information about environmental problems at the facilities is cited as evidence. In response to congressional questioning, DOE recently addressed this issue, but an atmosphere of distrust between DOE and key congressional actors over the need for supplemental EISs appears to persist. Although DOE has agreed to prepare programmatic EISs, the range of alternatives to be considered has not yet been determined. Congressional committees and environmental groups are urging DOE to examine alternatives involving rapid cleanup, reductions in the nuclear arsenal, and reductions in production at the sites, but DOE has not yet done so. Many congressional respondents also said that there should be stronger, centralized DOE oversight of compliance with NEPA and other relevant federal statutes.

The number of committees and subcommittees with jurisdiction over the management of the DOE weapons complex is large, and the fragmentation of authority is extensive. This fragmentation, duplication, and decentralization of congressional direction have caused delay and inefficiencies in the management of the cleanup program. A general policy consensus obtains that the weapons complex needs to be cleaned up, but there is little consensus between and within the executive and congressional branches about how clean is clean enough. The president, the political parties, and the leadership of Congress have had little involvement and have given little direction in this policy arena. Most respondents interviewed for this study asserted that Congress must clarify the statutory provisions that apply to the cleanup of the nuclear weapons sites (for example, especially regarding NEPA provisions and other environmental statutes), and Congress must attempt to coordinate the efforts of its committees and subcommittees to create thereby a coherent framework within which DOE can operate.

Congress has used several techniques to help improve management of the program, including informal contacts, agreements, and discussions to apprise DOE of congressional intentions and to gather information. It has required schedules, mission plans, feasibility studies, and quarterly and annual reports on the progress of the program from the three executive branch departments with jurisdiction over the cleanup: the DOE, the NRC, and the EPA. Legislatively ordered reorganizations of DOE and spending requirements in appropriations bills have also helped redirect DOE's implementation efforts. Congress has prodded DOE into action by using nonlegislative bodies as well, as when it created the Defense Nuclear Facilities Safety Board to oversee and report on the progress of the environmental restoration of DOE's nuclear weapons plants.

The three support agencies of Congress have also been extensively involved in overseeing the cleanup. The General Accounting Office publishes regular reports on spending issues and the progress of the cleanup program, and the Office of Technology Assessment and the Congressional Research Service (CRS) also follow the issue. Congressional committees and subcommittees have held a multitude of oversight hearings with respect to the seven major laws that apply to the cleanup. To give guidance to DOE, Congress has held more than sixty hearings on nuclear waste policy in the past ten years. Many of these hearings were prompted by media reports calling attention to problems within the complex, such as the series of *New York*

Times front-page articles in 1987 detailing safety and health problems at the Savannah River plant. Although only a few were called "oversight" hearings, each had an element of oversight. The result of many of the hearings was to give DOE specific policy direction concerning the nuclear weapons complex. Other hearings acted to collect data, and still others allowed the public to express concern about health, environment, and safety problems at nuclear weapons facilities.

Not all congressional policy direction has been helpful. One example occurred when DOE was directed to spend money in a specific manner (some call this micromanagement); House Speaker Thomas Foley set aside $186 million in the energy and water development appropriations bill for a regional office of the U.S. Army Corps of Engineers in Walla Walla, Washington (a city east of the Hanford complex). The bill specified that the corps was to use the money to take the lead role in cleanup activities at Hanford. After a discussion between Watkins and Foley, lead responsibility was returned to DOE, but the funds for the corps to assist in the cleanup stayed in the budget.

Several DOE respondents expressed the feeling that some members of Congress were "having it both ways"—becoming involved in management of the cleanup program only to secure electoral advantages. These members ostensibly take credit for directing DOE policy, then stop its implementation, and then claim even more credit for redirecting it. DOE understands that this type of credit claiming and publicity seeking occurs for reelection purposes, but it is not appreciated.

Conclusions

As a result of growing congressional and public concern about the DOE weapons complex and the cost of the cleanup, as well as a series of highly publicized health and safety incidents and management problems at DOE's Savannah River reactors in South Carolina and the Hanford Nuclear Reservation in Washington State, Congress increased its involvement in the day-to-day management of the cleanup and its oversight of DOE generally in the late 1980s. In the 1980s and 1990s, committees, individual members of Congress, and their staffs have intervened extensively in the administrative details of the DOE environmental restoration program.

The policy-making structure that guides the troubled post–Cold War DOE nuclear weapons complex has evolved into a combative arena over time. Originally a closed (that is, limited to those inside the weapons complex), low-profile decision-making system in the 1940s, it became a highly conflictual system of actors in the late 1970s and early 1980s. The scope of conflict has expanded to include new actors, and the level of conflict within the weapons complex decision-making system has increased rapidly to include the general media and presidents as the public and Congress have learned more about the environmental problems associated with the nuclear weapons plants. The system now includes over a dozen congressional committees and subcommittees, the DOE, the Environmental Protection Agency (EPA), the Nuclear Regulatory Commission (NRC), the Department of Defense (DOD), environmental groups, nuclear weapons laboratories, weapons complex contractors, state grass-roots citizen groups close to nuclear weapons research and production sites, and many state and local governments.

The results of the congressional intervention in DOE's complex cleanup policy as perceived by the respondents in this case study are complex. It took some time for Congress to become interested in the nuclear weapons complex. Congress focused on cleanup of the DOE nuclear weapons sites only after environmental, health, and safety problems brought on a state of crisis. Little knowledge was sought or interest expressed by members of Congress about the weapons complex until there was a breakdown in the management of the production reactors and the waste disposal system. Congressional committees reacted with continued intervention in the program details of the DOE cleanup after GAO investigations, oversight hearings, an OTA report, and media stories became public about the mismanagement of the weapons complex.

Much of the congressional intervention into DOE's policy implementation and details of program management of the weapons complex cleanup has come from congressional hearings. Over a ten-year period, Congress held over sixty-five hearings on the nuclear weapons complex. Most of these hearings called for DOE to undertake a number of detailed initiatives designed to manage better and solve environmental and safety problems within the weapons complex. These interventions severely narrowed DOE's discretion in implementing the cleanup program. For example, Congress established the Defense Nuclear Facilities Safety Board (DNFSB) to provide independent oversight of the cleanup and modernization of the complex. Congress also required DOE to make its contractors more accountable. For example, Congress forced DOE to be more aggressive about pursuing fraud and environmental mismanagement at the warhead component production plant at Rocky Flats, Colorado. Congress also directed DOE to restructure its management and oversight of the weapons complex, and to issue and annually update a five-year strategic plan for the cleanup and modernization of its facilities. Against the opposition of DOE, in 1991 Congress shifted responsibility for monitoring the health of the weapons complex workers from DOE to the Department of Health and Human Services (HHS).

In summary, the variety of congressional tools employed to redirect DOE's cleanup of the weapons complex is illustrated in table 6.1.

Congressional intervention has been both a burden and a strength for DOE administrators. New deadlines, reports, oversight panels, hearings,

TABLE 6.1
TOOLS OF CONGRESSIONAL INTERVENTION IN THE DEPARTMENT
OF ENERGY'S CLEANUP OF DEFENSE
NUCLEAR WEAPONS COMPLEX

Program Direction Tools	Intelligence Tools	Cost-Driven Tools
Informal agreements, telephone calls, staff-to-staff discussions	GAO reports identifying management problems	Increasing environmental funding in appropriations bills
Directions to spend in particular manner in appropriations bill	Requests by committees for data on types of waste at complexes	Consolidation of agency responsibility in legislation
65 hearings between 1980 and 1990 to give specific management and policy direction	Monitoring by OTA, GAO, EPA, NRC, and CRS	
Ordering reorganization in legislation	Informal network of informants that tells Congress realistic costs	
Setting cleanup priorities in legislation	Use of *Five-Year Plans* and OTA and CRS reports to gather and publicize information	
Requiring independent oversight bodies to report cleanup issues		

SOURCE: Revised and adapted from National Academy of Public Administration, *Beyond Distrust: Building Bridges Between Congress and the Executive* (Washington, D.C., 1992), 58.

letters, telephone calls, press conferences, and controls placed on DOE by congressional committees have constituted an extra workload, but the congressional involvement has brought more funding and a stronger programmatic focus to the cleanup effort. With greater congressional involvement has come increased public and media attention to the environmental problems at DOE facilities. New public awareness has generated even more interest by Congress and further congressional directives for DOE. This ever-widening circle of awareness (expansion of the scope of conflict surrounding the cleanup) has therefore aroused more and more interest in DOE's management of the cleanup. The estimated costs of the effort, which are escalating rapidly in an era of budgetary retrenchment, have motivated Congress to increase its focus on cost control and the quality of the DOE financial data.

Intervention by congressional actors has helped to change the overall policy direction of DOE away from Cold War production and toward post–Cold War environmental restoration, professional waste management practices, and safe operations. Controversy and conflict between DOE and Congress continues, nevertheless. Accusations of DOE and contractor waste and fraud abound, prompting further calls for Congress to limit even more drastically DOE's discretion in administering the cleanup program. DOE is responding to congressional concerns more quickly, and is building a supportive coalition within Congress to assure that the necessary resources to clean up the nuclear weapons complex are forthcoming. There is still widespread distrust of DOE technical ability, cost estimates, deadline projections, and schedules, but the current congressional-DOE relationship, although still buffeted by forces that encourage conflict, is temporarily calm as both legislature and executive branch await new direction from President Clinton's energy secretary, Hazel Rollins O'Leary.

Timeline of Major Events in the U.S. Nuclear Weapons Complex Environmental Restoration and Radioactive Waste Management Program

1974	Atomic Energy Commission abolished and the Energy Research and Development Administration established. Waste Isolation Pilot Plant (WIPP) facility proposed for New Mexico by the Department of Energy (DOE).
1976	Joint Committee on Atomic Energy abolished.
1978	Department of Energy established.
January 1980	President Carter signs P.L. 96-164, an energy and water development appropriations bill for the Department of Energy that authorizes construction of the WIPP plant in New Mexico.
January 1983	President Reagan signs P.L. 97-425, the Nuclear Waste Policy Act of 1982. Section 8 permits radioactive waste produced by atomic energy defense activities to be stored in the repository pursuant to a finding by the president. DOE issues *Defense Waste and Byproducts Management: Draft, Program Management Document* (DOE/DP-0010), a preliminary attempt to address environmental, safety, and health issues in its nuclear weapons facilities.

May 1986	The accident at the Soviet nuclear power plant at Chernobyl revives concern over the status of the aging and debilitated U.S. nuclear weapons complex.
January 1988	President Reagan signs P.L. 100-203. Title V, Subtitle A contains the Nuclear Waste Policy Amendments Act of 1987, which selects Yucca Mountain, Nevada, as the sole site to be characterized for nuclear waste from commercial nuclear power plants.
June 1989	Secretary Watkins presents a ten-point plan to improve and accelerate projects conducted under DOE's defense complex environmental restoration plan.
August 1989	DOE's Office of Environmental Restoration and Waste Management issues *Environmental Restoration and Waste Management: Five-Year Plan* (DOE/S-0070), the first of the *Five-Year Plans*.
February 1991	*Complex Cleanup: The Environmental Legacy of Nuclear Weapons Production* (OTA-0-484) is released by the Office of Technology Assessment.

Acknowledgments

I would like to thank the numerous present and former congressional and executive branch staff and private sector respondents who gave freely of their time and knowledge about high-level nuclear waste isolation and cleanup policy. This study would not have been possible without their cooperation and careful recollection of the key events shaping the congressional-executive branch interaction. I would like also to give special thanks to Tim Evanson, a Ph.D. student at the American University, for his editing and research assistance. Thanks also to Stephanie Slocum, Claudia H. Thurber, and Robert S. Gilmour, who reviewed and commented on earlier drafts of this study.

Notes

1. The U.S. Department of Energy weapons complex consists of fourteen primary facilities in thirteen states and more than one hundred secondary sites in thirty-one states and territories. The Energy Department has about 20,000 employees, but the private contractors who operate the primary weapons plants employ over 141,000 people.

2. Atomic Energy Agency report, quoted in "A $200 Billion Scandal," *U.S. News and World Report,* 14 December 1992, 34.

3. See Office of Technology Assessment, *Complex Cleanup: The Environmental Legacy of Nuclear Weapons Production,* OTA-0-484 (Washington, D.C.: Government Printing Office, 1991).

4. From 1980 through 1992 Congress held more than sixty-five hearings on the DOE weapons complex cleanup.

5. From 1948 to 1974, the Atomic Energy Commission was responsible for managing the nation's nuclear weapons production facilities. In 1974 the AEC was abolished; its responsibilities for the nuclear weapons complex were transferred to the Energy Research and Development Administration (ERDA). In 1978 ERDA was assimilated into the newly created Department of Energy.

6. See House Committee on Science, Space, and Technology, Subcommittee on Natural Resources, Agriculture Research, and Environment, *Energy and Water Development Appropriations: FY 91,* 101st Cong., 2d sess., 28 March 1990, statement of Victor S. Rezendes, director, Energy Issues, Resources, Community, and Economic Development Division, General Accounting Office, 1. Of DOE's nearly $19 billion budget for FY 92, nearly $12 billion was earmarked for operating, renovating, and cleaning up the weapons complex.

7. See "A $200 Billion Scandal," *U.S. News and World Report,* 14 December 1992, 34–37, for recent DOE and GAO estimates.

8. See Office of Technology Assessment, *Complex Cleanup,* for a detailed criticism of DOE's ability to clean up the complex within thirty years.

9. For an excellent discussion of the policy process related to the Waste Isolation Pilot Plant (WIPP), see Hank C. Jenkins-Smith, "Alternative Theories of the Policy Process: Reflections on Research Strategy for the Study of Nuclear Waste Policy," *PS: Political Science and Politics* 24 (June 1991): 157–65.

10. OTA's basic function is to help members of Congress anticipate and plan for the impact of technological changes such as the defense nuclear weapons complex problems.

11. In late September 1992 Congress passed legislation subjecting DOE's nuclear weapons facilities to nearly all federal environmental, safety, and health laws, and by extension subjecting them to the agencies enforcing these laws. See the Federal Facility Compliance Act of 1992 (P.L. 102-386).

12. For a more complete discussion of policy subsystems, see James A. Thurber, "Dynamics of Policy Subsystems in American Politics," in *Interest Group Politics,* ed. Allan J. Cigler and Burdett A. Loomis (Washington, D.C.: CQ Press, 1991), 319–40.

13. Transuranic wastes (TRU wastes) contain alpha-emitting transuranium nuclides with half-lives greater than twenty years and concentrations greater than 100 nanocuries per gram of waste.

14. See Department of Energy, *Defense Waste and Byproducts Management: Draft, Program Management Document,* DOE/DP-0010 (Washington, D.C., 1982).

15. The State of New Mexico has resisted completion of the WIPP plant by delaying permits needed for its construction and suing DOE over the way the de-

partment obtained the land used for WIPP. During 1992 Congress moved to end the legal confusion surrounding WIPP, and forced New Mexico to acquiesce to the project for the time being. See the Waste Isolation Pilot Plant Land Withdrawal Act of 1991 (P.L. 102-579).

16. Office of Technology Assessment, *Complex Cleanup*, 1.

17. "A $200 Billion Scandal," *U.S. News and World Report*, 14 December 1992, 34.

18. OTA news release, "OTA Sees a Long, Difficult Road Ahead for Waste Cleanup at Nuclear Weapons Plants," 11 February 1991, 1.

19. For a discussion of commercial high-level nuclear waste disposal issues, see James A. Thurber, " 'Not In My Backyard': High-Level Nuclear Waste Disposal," chapter 4 in this book.

20. See note 11, above.

21. The cleanup issue has been complicated by pressure from the executive branch to keep production of nuclear materials and atomic warheads at a high level. The recent congressional moratorium on nuclear weapons testing will remove part of that pressure as the need for nuclear weapons to replace those used in tests diminishes.

7

Battling for Budgetary Savings: The Prospective Payment System for Hospitals under Medicare

Background and Overview: The Turbulent Environment of Health Policy

Major structural changes have occurred in the nation's health care system during the past fifty years.[1] The delivery system for medical and health care has moved away from physicians' offices into hospitals, nursing homes, outpatient clinics, and other health care arrangements. Who pays for health care and how it is paid for are different now, especially since 1965, when the federal government began to pay for the health care of persons who are medically indigent or over 65.

From 1945 to 1965 the federal government played a principal role in expanding the health care system, especially the number of hospitals. The basic strategy to assure equality of access was to build capacity. The federal government became the banker, distributing seed monies for hospital construction and becoming the major source of funding for research. From the late 1960s to the early 1970s the basic strategy to assure equality of access was to buy health care for the indigent and elderly with the passage of Medicare, Medicaid, and other entitlement programs. Shortly thereafter a different and enduring emphasis emerged: cost containment. In the case of hospital care, cost containment has become the dominant public policy issue.

The 1980s was a decade of revolution in the nation's health care, primarily its financing. One component of the transformation was the 1983 landmark legislation creating the Prospective Payment System (PPS) for Hospitals under Medicare (P.L. 98-21). The Medicare program finances inpatient hospital, skilled nursing facility, home health, and other institutional services (Medicare Part A, Hospital Insurance Trust Fund), and physicians' services and hospital outpatient services (Medicare Part B, Supplementary Medical Insurance Trust Fund) for the elderly and disabled. PPS is the payment methodology for Medicare Part A; it is the formula that defines how the federal government will reimburse hospitals for operating costs they incur providing inpatient care to Medicare beneficiaries.

PPS was one of the regulatory initiatives undertaken to contain hospital costs in the hope of reducing federal outlays reimbursing for portions of those costs. When enacted, it was considered revolutionary: it changed what was paid for, how it was paid for, who determined the price, and why it was offered at all (see table 7.1). PPS is codified in (1) formal legislation ranging from the Social Security Amendments of 1983 to tax, reconciliation, and spending bills enacted throughout the 1980s; and (2) regulations and manuals promulgated by the Health Care Finance Administration (HCFA) of the U.S. Department of Health and Human Services (HHS).

PPS has three distinguishing features: (1) hospital payment rates are set for 474 specific diagnosis-related groups (DRGs),[2] (2) rates are set *before* services are delivered, using formulas defined in the law, and (3) it was designed and intended to operate as a "system" with overall zero-sum features. PPS is thus a means of distributing a federal entitlement: the funds in the Medicare Part A (hospital) insurance trust fund, which is financed by the Social Security payroll tax. Although not the only hospital prospective payment system in operation, the Medicare prospective payment system has had the greatest impact on the health care delivery system because it covers approximately 33.2 million people and accounts for nearly 27 percent of all expenditures on hospital care in the United States.[3]

Federal outlays for Medicare nearly tripled over the decade of the 1980s. Even after lawmakers repeatedly tried to cut back spending, outlays rose from $32.1 billion in FY 80 to $98.1 billion in FY 90. Medicare benefits are expected to grow 41 percent from their FY 90 level to $138.5 billion by FY 94. The rate is such that the executive branch has said that unless policies are adopted to stem growth, soon after the turn of the century outlays for Medicare will exceed outlays for Social Security and defense, two programs that traditionally have held prominent positions in the federal budget.

Millions of Americans cannot afford adequate care; about 31 million lack insurance against acute-care costs, and few are insured against long-term-care costs. This circumstance has prompted proposals—both modest and far-reaching—for changes in the way health care delivery is organized and financed, and in the way payments for care are administered.[4]

The important central fact of the Medicare history is that the basic understanding at the outset was that government agreed to be a cost-plus purchaser without really intervening in how cost was established. When the government decided that its system was driving up not only its own costs but all costs in the system, it tried to undo or at least change the original deal to become a prudent buyer. The effort began in earnest in the mid-seventies, and PPS in the early eighties was its first major achievement. For the

TABLE 7.1.
PPS AS REVOLUTIONARY CHANGE

Retrospective Cost-Based Reimbursement	Prospective Fixed-Rate Reimbursement
Variable Price Retrospective or "after-the-fact" determination of reasonable costs and actual payment to hospitals. Reimbursed hospitals for actual reasonable costs incurred in providing services to Medicare beneficiaries. Costs were determined after the hospital had provided the services and reported its costs to the Medicare program.	➡ *Fixed Price* Prospective or "before-the-fact" determination of fixed per-case revenues while keeping "after-the-fact" distribution of funds. Medicare payments are made at predetermined, specific rates that represent the average cost, nationwide, of treating a Medicare patient according to medical condition.
Costs Driven by the Industry Costs were driven by the individual decisions of physicians and health care professionals.	➡ *Federal Government Sets Price* Under PPS, the federal government prescribes a set price for an entire episode.
Risk-Free Medicare Revenues Hospital Medicare revenues to hospitals were virtually risk free.	➡ *No Guarantee of Medicare Revenues* No guarantee that expenses generated by Medicare beneficiaries will be fully reimbursed.
No Rewards for Constraining Patient Care Costs An assumption that hospitals had no financial incentive to constrain patient care costs.	➡ *Financial Incentives for Constraining Patient Care Costs* An assumption that fixed per-case revenues, prospectively set, would create a financial incentive for hospitals to constrain patient care costs actively.
Zero Is an OK Number No profit intended to be made from providing services to Medicare patients.	➡ *Zero Is Not an OK Number* An assumption that PPS would be an opportunity for hospitals to "profit" from the provision of services to Medicare patients.
No Tool to Reduce Program Outlays The federal government had limited means to reduce program outlays because their amounts were not known in advance.	➡ *A Tool to Reduce Outlays* An assumption that a prospective method would reduce program outlays and preserve the Medicare Part A (hospital) trust fund.

Continued . . .

TABLE 7.1. — *Continued*
PPS as Revolutionary Change

Retrospective Cost-Based Reimbursement	*Prospective Fixed-Rate Reimbursement*
Costs Determined According to Standards	➡ *Prices Determined Using Statistical-Econometric Methods of Estimation*
The federal government relied on a set of American Hospital Association cost principles for determining allowable costs.	The federal government relies on a complex methodological system of regression equations, data bases, and computerized information systems.
No Semblance of a "System"	➡ *The Intent of a "System"*
	Defined by some as "budget-neutral" and "zero-sum" so that in principle whatever one hospital gains, another will lose.

first time, the government had a major voice in pricing, and that was revolutionary.

PPS has evolved through four distinct policy stages: development, 1945 to late 1970s; enactment, 1980 to 1983; transition from a retrospective to the national prospective system, 1983 to 1987; and full implementation, 1988 to the present (see table 7.2). In this case study, PPS is examined as a *system* with respect to the congressional-executive relationship, principally during its enactment, transition, and full implementation.[5]

Developing Patterns of Congressional-Executive Relations

Seeds of Distrust

The conceptual development of PPS was an executive branch initiative, the culmination of at least a decade of leadership committed to addressing hospital cost containment through long-term research and demonstration projects that led to a range of increasingly informed policy proposals. During the process of enacting the original PPS legislation, the stage would be set not only for a radical policy change but also for a new era of congressional-executive relations.

The Movement toward Cost Containment.—In 1978 the Carter administration put forth a cost containment proposal intended to constrain the rate of health care expenditures by the voluntary limitation of revenues. The pack-

TABLE 7.2.
MAJOR LEGISLATIVE HISTORY OF PPS BY POLICY STAGE

Development	Enactment	Transition	Full Implementation
Hill-Burton Hospital Construction Act, 1946	Tax Equity and Fiscal Responsibility Act (TEFRA), 1982	Deficit Reduction Act, 1984	Technical and Miscellaneous Revenue Act, 1988
Medicare Program (Title 18 of Social Security Act), 1965	Social Security Act Amendments, PPS, 1983	Gramm-Rudman-Hollings, 1985	Omnibus Budget Reconciliation Act, 1989
Social Security Amendments, 1972		Emergency Extension Act, 1985	Treasury and Postal Service Spending Bill, 1989
Health Care Finance Administration, created in 1977		Consolidated Omnibus Budget Reconciliation Act, 1985	Omnibus Budget Reconciliation Act, 1990
		Omnibus Budget Reconciliation Act, 1986	
		Balanced Budget and Emergency Deficit Control Reaffirmation Act, 1987	
		Omnibus Budget Reconciliation Act, 1987	

age never succeeded in getting through Congress, but it did lay the ground-work for subsequent debates. By 1979 the Health Care Finance Administration (HCFA) had developed draft regulations to put a reformed payment system into effect and could have done so without the approval of Congress, under authority of section 223 of the 1972 Social Security Amendments. The Carter administration chose not to do this.

In 1980 the Reagan administration took office committed to promoting competition in health care, decreasing the regulatory burden on industry in general, and increasing defense spending. Also in 1980 the administration reorganized the HCFA by creating a layer of political appointees between career administrators/section heads and the HCFA administrator. During this period, the HCFA continued the research it had started in the 1970s and also sponsored a body of demonstration programs and evaluations authorized by section 222 of the 1971 Social Security Amendments.

In 1981 President Reagan issued Executive Order 12291, requiring federal agencies to submit both proposed and final regulations to the Office of Management and Budget (OMB) for review. In 1980–81, escalating hospital costs combined with declining payroll tax revenues threatened imminent exhaustion of the hospital trust fund, and the federal deficit began to expand after passage of the Economic Recovery Tax Act of 1981 (Reagan's tax cut) and the start of a huge increase in defense spending.

In 1981 HCFA Administrator Carolyne Davis appointed a HCFA task force to begin designing a prospective payment system. The Bureau of Program Policy within the HCFA had lead responsibility to develop an options paper on the various methodologies the program could employ to pay hospitals prospectively. After circulation of the paper within HCFA, a meeting was convened of the top policymakers to evaluate the options. Because there was no clear consensus choice, Davis did not send the paper to HHS Secretary Richard S. Schweiker but formed another task force to develop new options. The task force began its work in December 1981, using the original options paper, and was joined in late January 1982 by a work group of five representatives of the hospital industry. The task force refined the issues, disbanded, and the matter was referred back to the HCFA Bureau of Program Policy.

Congress Requires an Executive Policy Proposal.—When the Tax Equity and Fiscal Responsibility Act (TEFRA) was signed into law in August 1982, the basic outlines of what would become PPS had already been developed by the administration. TEFRA was a huge omnibus statute. For Medicare hospitals, it provided that there would be an average per-case reimbursement for particular classes of hospitals and set limits on the amount of the reimbursement. If a hospital came in under the limit, it could keep some of the savings. For cost overruns, a hospital would be penalized and the government would pay only a fraction of the difference. So, TEFRA introduced average costs; limits for particular peer groups of hospitals; caps or annual rates of increase; and percentage incentives.

TEFRA was not intended to last. This was in part indicated by the mandate that by 31 December 1982 the secretary report back to Congress a proposal for prospective reimbursement developed in consultation with the Senate Committee on Finance and the House Committee on Ways and Means. This deadline caused no consternation within the department, because it had been conducting research on alternative systems to control Medicare costs for at least ten years.[6] Thus, PPS was being designed by senior staff and leadership in the HCFA and HHS even as Congress began the process to enact TEFRA. In 1982 work began in earnest by a very small group in HCFA under Patrice Hirsch Feinstein, HCFA associate administrator for policy. By the time TEFRA was signed into law, the basic outlines of what would become the prospective payment system had already been developed, but TEFRA gave the signal that a system of hospital cost containment was imminent.

A *"Bare Bones" Executive Policy Proposal.*—The administration delivered the policy proposal to Congress on time. The report has been characterized as a "bare bones, even harsh proposal" that recommended immediate, across-the-board implementation of the new system. It described the new payment methodology and discussed the ancillary issues but did not contain the actual legislative language, which was still being drafted.

The administration proposed uniform national rates and no gradual phasing in. There was no provision for a prospective payment assessment commission. Among the comparatively few administration people involved, the development of the proposal is recalled as a time of high intellectual challenge, awareness that health policy history was in the making, and certainty that the proposal (or something conceptually similar) would pass. At least within the executive branch, the invention of PPS had all the properties of a revolutionary discovery—akin to the politics and substance of the Watson and Crick discovery of DNA.

A *Masterpiece of Micromanagement.*—Almost as soon as the administration's PPS proposal arrived on Capitol Hill, Congress began to lay the foundation for becoming significantly involved in the details of implementing the system. Four themes capture the mixed views about the character of the legislative process during enactment: (1) the lack of shared policy goals, reflected by the nature and extent of congressional changes to the administration's proposals;[7] (2) the recollection at the staff level of a high spirit of cooperation in drafting the numerous changes; (3) congressional distrust of data or assertions of lack of data to support administration proposals; and (4) the swiftness with which PPS was enacted. These themes are best reflected in the following comments from the interviews:

- *Lack of shared goals.* "Congress saw PPS as an instrument of national health policy; the administration saw PPS as establishing a system of prices that hospitals could take or leave." (congressional observer)
- *Interbranch, bipartisan staff cooperation.* "The acceptance by HCFA of some of the less desirable amendments was made somewhat easier by the fact that HCFA staff was allowed to participate in the drafting of the new version of the bill—a courtesy extended throughout the legislative process. The ground rules were explicit, however—HCFA staff was there for technical assistance only." (outside observer)

   "Drafting PPS was the best experience. Democrats, Republicans, and technicians were there. It was the best example of Congress and the executive working together to design policy. People were open and receptive to other points of view. There was a genuine intent to design the best possible approach." (congressional observer)
- *Seeds of distrust.* "The Prospective Payment Assessment Commission will play a very important role in helping to keep the secretary on track; provides the balance needed between the secretary's concern for holding down Medicare costs and the need to allow some expansion in the rates to accommodate new technologies, medical practices, and other factors; and assures the involvement of all aspects of the health care delivery system in the decision making and evaluation of this new system." (congressional view)

   "Not only was Congress made uneasy by the less than forthcoming attitude of the HCFA with respect to impact data, but the brevity and rigor of the administration proposal made many in Congress sharply aware of the vast amount of delegation that this legislation would entail. The response within Congress was to write a highly prescriptive statute and provide in some detail for the manner in which it would be implemented." (outside observer)
- *Swiftness of enactment.* "When PPS was on the floor, only about one-fourth of the members knew what it was about." (congressional view)

   "PPS was attached to the Social Security Amendments of 1983. If it had been introduced as a stand alone, it is unlikely it would have zipped through Congress as it did." (outside observer)

PPS was enacted in 1983 as part of the Social Security Act Amendments (P.L. 98-21). Observers interviewed for this study characterized the statute, almost admiringly, as a "masterpiece of micromanagement." Viewed apart from the institutional implications, the statute creates an ingenious and artful array of checks and balances between the branches (see table 7.3), including the quasi-independent Prospective Payment Assessment Commission (ProPAC). It also contains a highly detailed implementation structure that defines a period of transition rather than immediate, full-scale implementation; sets out detailed calculation instructions, including numerical amounts and algorithms for decision making; provides for certain discretions granted to the HHS secretary; calls for numerous studies and required reports; and

TABLE 7.3.
ORIGINAL PPS STATUTE AS A MASTERPIECE OF MICRO-
MANAGEMENT: SELECTED HIGHLIGHTS

Detailed Implementation Structure and Checks on the Executive Branch, Examples	*Explicit Grants of Executive Discretion, Examples*
• Defined the basic payment formula and also defined numerous add-ons and exceptions to the formula, with specific instructions on how the calculations are to be carried out.	• "Taking into consideration the recommendations of ProPAC, the Secretary shall determine for each fiscal year (commencing with 1986) the percentage change which will apply as the applicable percentage increase...."
• Set a three-year period of transition for phasing in the PPS system and specified the payment proportions (e.g., in the first cost reporting period, the Medicare payment per discharge will be 25 percent of the regional DRG rate plus 75 percent of the hospital specific rate).	• "The Secretary shall adjust the proportion (as estimated by the Secretary from time to time) of hospitals' costs which are attributable to wages and wage-related costs...."
• "The Secretary shall use an education adjustment factor equal to twice the factor provided under 1983 regulations for hospitals with indirect costs of medical education...."	• "The Secretary shall provide for such exceptions and adjustments to the payment amounts established under this subsection as the Secretary deems appropriate to take into account the special needs of regional and national referral centers (including those hospitals of 500 or more beds located in rural areas) and of public and other hospitals that serve a significantly disproportionate number of patients who have low income or are entitled to benefits under Part A of this title...."
• Structured the payment system to be budget neutral through FY 85 (payments could be no more or less than projected under the earlier TEFRA provisions). After FY 85, the law gave the secretary the responsibility (discretion) to determine the annual increase in DRG rates and to publish his or her recommendation and final annual increase factor in the *Federal Register.*	
• "Capital expenses are excluded from PPS until October 1, 1986...."	• "With respect to sole community hospitals: the Secretary shall provide by regulation for such other exceptions and adjustments to such payment amounts as the Secretary deems appropriate...."
• Administrative and judicial review is permitted except for DRG classification and weights and the level of the	• "At a hospital's request, the Secretary may make additional payments for cases whose costs exceed a fixed

TABLE 7.3. — *Continued*
ORIGINAL PPS STATUTE AS A MASTERPIECE OF MICRO-
MANAGEMENT: SELECTED HIGHLIGHTS

Detailed Implementation Structure and Checks on the Executive Branch, Examples	*Explicit Grants of Executive Discretion, Examples*
payment necessary to maintain budget neutrality in fiscal years 1984 and 1985. • The secretary is required to submit seventeen reports to Congress (on specific topics by specific dates). • Created the Prospective Payment Assessment Commission (ProPAC), a special fifteen-member commission, appointed by the director of the Office of Technology Assessment, to review and provide recommendations to the secretary on DRG recalibrations and to both the secretary and Congress on the amount of the annual increase factor (appropriations will be made from the Medicare Trust Funds to fund the commission's activities).	multiple of the appropriate DRG rate or other fixed amount (outliers) ... the total proportion cannot be less than five percent nor more than six percent of total DRG related payments in any one year...." • "Secretary has the authority to approve Medicare payment under a state cost control system if it meets certain requirements...." • "The Secretary shall establish a classification of inpatient hospital discharges by diagnostic related groups and a methodology for classifying specific hospital discharges within these groups.... For each group, the Secretary shall assign an appropriate weighting factor.... The Secretary shall adjust the classifications and weighting factors in FY 86 and at least every four years thereafter...."

SOURCES: Compiled from P.L. 98-21 (quoted items above) and a legislative summary of it prepared by the Department of Health and Human Services, Office of Legislation and Analysis.

enumerates an array of exceptions and adjustments to account for a wide range of perceived differences throughout the nation.

The statute contains no overarching statement of the goals or intent of the PPS system, although it was clearly enacted in a political environment driven by the need to reduce federal outlays. Yet the procedures for setting prices prospectively are highly specific. One executive observer reflected, "There is a tendency to assume that even with highly specific procedures, congressional intent is clear. That is not always the case." Similarly, a congressional observer noted, "As big a problem as specificity is ambiguity."

The characterization of the statute as a masterpiece of micromanagement is a precise choice of words and conveys the difficulty of simple generalizations about it. Some people support the statute's detailed features; others argue they are symptoms of policy disagreement and fundamental distrust. The truth likely comprehends both.

Three arguments are offered in support of the statute's features: (1) the legislation gave discretion to the HHS secretary in certain areas and left many specific implementation issues to be resolved at the discretion of the department; (2) the administration desired specificity from Congress in regard to a regulatory process; and (3) the administration resisted congressional attempts to provide for discretion to the secretary, according to some observers. These arguments must be counterposed to the level of distrust that was emerging between the branches with respect to data supporting the policy proposals. The example most often cited is the creation of ProPAC, a novel entity intended to "buffer PPS from interest group politics and mediate between the congressional committees and HCFA."[8] That is, ProPAC came into being largely because Congress did not believe that the executive branch would provide accurate information about implementation. The commission's seventeen members are appointed under the supervision of the Office of Technology Assessment and include physicians, registered nurses, employers, third-party payers, individuals with expertise in biomedical and economic research, and those with expertise in technologic and scientific advances in health care.[9] David Smith summarizes the congressional-executive tensions in the statute:

> Inevitably, a vast amount of discretion remains with "the Secretary," which is to say with the bureau directors, program analysts and regulations writers, and the technical advisory committees and consultants who help determine the content of the implementation regulations. The statute shows a cognizance on the part of Congress of this need for extensive delegation: for instance, leaving the annual update of the overall DRG rate of increase to the Secretary. At the same time, the legislation showed the ambivalence in the collective mind of Congress: a hope that the Secretary would administer PPS in a spirit acceptable to the Congress, and a substantial fear that he or she would not.[10]

In a remarkably prescient observation at the time of enactment, a congressional participant said, "Do you realize what you've done? You've created a system where any dissatisfied hospital can go to Congress arguing unfair treatment." The checks and balances and exceptions for particular constituencies that were built into the statute guaranteed that Congress would be involved throughout implementation of PPS, but few foresaw how. In 1983 there was a sense that a revolution was about to begin.[11]

Norms of Distrust during Battles for Budget Savings

The HCFA published the first regulations implementing PPS, on time, in the *Federal Register* in September 1983. The final version was published in January 1984. The initial delicate balance between the branches in 1983 changed dramatically between 1985 and 1989.

New Rules of Policy Making and Budgeting: Who Gets Credit for Savings?
—During the period 1983 to 1989, the pace of change rapidly overwhelmed both Congress and the executive branch. The year 1985 was a major turning point. It was then that President Reagan issued Executive Order 12498, which required the OMB to approve analyses accompanying all major regulations. Agencies had to demonstrate that proposed regulations satisfied the administration's regulatory principles, unless an agency is prohibited from making such determinations by its enabling statutes. The period 1984–85 was also the first two transition years for implementing PPS. Distrust between the branches solidified as some hospitals received higher payments than intended and the administration "stonewalled" certain aspects of implementation.

Some hospitals received higher payments than intended for three reasons. First, when PPS was enacted, the data on which the original prices were based were unaudited and reflected what hospitals reported under retrospective payment procedures. Second, PPS required hospitals to change what they reported to the federal government about each case. As hospitals began to report the clinical characteristics of cases in much more detail and far more accurately, the case-mix index jumped through the roof and federal payments were too high compared to operating costs per case. Third, for teaching hospitals, Congress had doubled the payment rate originally proposed. Some observers argue this resulted in such hospitals being overpaid. The overpayments radically undercut arguments that Congress or the OMB should exercise forbearance, and indicated that PPS needed drastic tightening.[12]

The Reagan administration intended to make the government a prudent buyer of care. Defense was taking more and more of appropriations, and the government was perceived to be overcommitted to domestic programs, especially entitlements. One objective was to hold down Medicare Part A, even though it has limited net impact on the budget because it is funded entirely by payroll taxes. So, during these first two years, when there was much to be done in PPS implementation, and there were clearly problems with overpayments and a beginning distribution of winners and losers, the general perception is that the administration basically either did nothing or stonewalled on implementation. This did not sit well with Congress.

Passage of the Balanced Budget and Emergency Deficit Control Act (in short, Gramm-Rudman) was a major turning point in the PPS congressional-executive relationship. It reduced Medicare payments to hospitals for

FY 86 and, more broadly, reflected a major procedural change in the budget process.[13] Gramm-Rudman essentially required five yearly sequential across-the-board reductions in federal spending until the deficit reached zero—if prior agreement on reductions was not forthcoming.[14]

Gramm-Rudman was amended and weakened by the Omnibus Budget Reconciliation Act (OBRA) of 1987. Then Gramm-Rudman was suspended, for the time being, by the five-year deficit reduction pact and discretionary caps instituted by OBRA 1990.[15] But for PPS, Gramm-Rudman and the accompanying reconciliation process institutionalized the relationship between the branches as a game of who gets credit for savings. Indeed, many observers characterize significant PPS events subsequent to Gramm-Rudman as simply "everything after Gramm-Rudman." In essence, the game is that if the administration proposes a change through regulation, it will get credit for a saving; if Congress proposes a change through reconciliation, it will get credit.

Congress Opens the Door for PPS Pork-barreling.—Fiscal year 1985 was the second transition year of PPS implementation. Under the original PPS legislation, national DRG (diagnostic related groups) payment rates were to be phased in over a three-year span, during which time a hospital's payment rate was to be based on a declining portion of its historical costs and an increasing portion of the PPS methodology (regional and national DRG rates). After three years, all hospital payments would be determined under a wholly national DRG payment rate.

The Consolidated Omnibus Budget Reconciliation Act of 1985 (COBRA 1985) extended the transition period for one year *for all hospitals except those in Oregon.* It turned out that Oregon would benefit financially from moving forward as planned; this is the "Packwood amendment." Observers suggest it came about as a result of routine member trading. Congressman Dan Rostenkowski (D-Ill.) wanted to slow the PPS transition because hospitals in Chicago were going to "get it in the neck," while Senator Bob Packwood (R-Ore.) wanted the transition to proceed on schedule. The upshot of their discussions was a delay of PPS transition for all hospitals except Oregon's. One congressional observer suggested that when some other members discovered this, they were displeased because the states they represented would have benefited from an exception too. But the Oregon exemption opened the door to pork-barreling—"up until then, no one had done anything quite that blatant" (congressional observer).

Retrieving Executive Discretion.—OBRA 1986 was the first time Congress intervened in responsibility it had assigned to the executive branch in the original 1983 PPS legislation. Observers speculate that it was the result of the administration's stonewalling. Congress was saying, "Here is what you are going to do and how you're going to do it." Their specific example is the update factor, the percentage by which the rate of payment per case increases.[16]

During 1986 there was a protracted congressional-executive argument, especially over the update factor. Congress had intended the percentage to be set by the secretary, but during the first two years of PPS, the amount was an empirical decision in that the rate had to be budget neutral with respect to the limits set in TEFRA. After that the rate of increase was variable, and the battle over credit for savings was joined.

The secretary made a recommendation, in 1986, regarding the rate of increase, but Congress was unwilling to accept it, primarily because it meant that Congress could not get credit for savings. Starting with FY 87, Congress postponed the secretary's authority to set the update; that year and thereafter, Congress has set the update factor and received credit for the savings. Because of this, one congressional observer has suggested, "The update factor is now not the most important element in operating the program."

Virtually every piece of reconciliation legislation since OBRA 1986 contains PPS provisions. The overall process is described by several observers as follows. Each year, the Senate Finance and House Ways and Means committees are instructed that they must report "×" savings in Medicare. This has two effects. First, a foregone conclusion that there will be a reduction in the update factor that is below current law. That is, the law sets the update factor at the hospital market basket (an index of hospital inputs similar to the Consumer Price Index), but to realize the required savings, Congress will set it below market basket. Second, a foregone conclusion that it will be set one year at a time. Congress always knows it will have to do this, so it writes the law to achieve the savings one year at a time. This has occurred since Gramm-Rudman.

- "The biggest change in PPS is the greater inclination of Congress to administer the program—passing more and more prescriptive language in the law." (outside observer)
- "The biggest impact has been the whole idea of the PPS policy as being budget-driven and the chicanery we've gone through to preserve savings." (congressional view)
- "Two things forever changed the congressional-executive relationship. The first was Congress's unwillingness to accept the Secretary's recommendation on what the rate of increase should be (update factor). The second was the ridiculous definition of disproportionate share produced by the executive. Things have never been the same. They intervene in everything." (executive view)
- "The way PPS is implemented has put the administration in control. We intervene primarily to set rates and to say, 'You can't' to other reforms. . . ." (congressional view)
- "Today, you won't see people from the two branches working together as

they did during PPS enactment—there's too much mistrust." (congressional view)

The 1991 *Green Book* issued by the House Committee on Ways and Means reports that changes in policy during the 1980s in committee entitlement programs resulted in budgetary savings of more than $100 billion for one fiscal year—1993.[17] For example, the committee declares that the Medicare program was reduced by $61.5 billion, primarily because of Medicare provider reductions of $51.1 billion.

The Wide Reach of Distrust

The Prospective Payment System can be described as having three parts: (1) elements within the PPS methodology, namely, the basic PPS formula and add-ons and exceptions to the basic formula; (2) elements outside PPS but inside Medicare or hospital Medicare reimbursements that still occur on the basis of reasonable costs; and (3) units involved in administering or otherwise implementing PPS (see table 7.4, pp. 168–69). The distrust between Congress and the executive branch surfaced in virtually all components of the system (see table 7.5, p. 170, for examples) during the period examined.

Most persons interviewed suggested that although Congress clearly intervenes throughout PPS, it is less inclined to address the more-strictly-medical aspects (such as specific drugs or medical technologies). These themes are illustrated in the following comments:

- "Congress is involved in virtually every aspect of the system." (Congress, executive)
- "I'd say in almost every specific policy." (Congress)
- "Local issues are the biggest noise in the system." (executive)
- "On local issues (e.g., riders on bills, special criteria and carve outs, certain hospitals' defining services like regional referral centers)." (executive)
- "A lot of the instructions are nitty gritty (e.g., telling the secretary to go collect data on the wage index)." (Congress)
- "In a lot of little stuff that illustrates policy and definitional differences (e.g., transition period, whether we can have an urban-rural split, how we define regional referral centers, distances between counties for boundary purposes, and so on)." (Congress)
- "A lot of one member trading with another member for specific provisions and exceptions." (Congress)
- "There are some areas where Congress has never interfered. These tend to be very technical and specific (e.g., a new drug for heart attack patients)." (Congress)

Whether the issue involved the basic payment formula, add-ons and exceptions to the formula, or administration, a general pattern was fairly common. Over the six years examined, Congress made numerous, detailed changes annually to PPS through the budget reconciliation process. Congress relied heavily on estimates and analyses from committee staff, the Congressional Budget Office (CBO), Congressional Research Service (CRS), General Accounting Office (GAO), and especially ProPAC. The general thrust of these congressional communications, over time and for different motivations, was to withdraw or constrict any executive discretion that could result in the executive's being given credit for savings. The OMB also played a significant formal role within the executive and in Congress, and was cited as delaying the issuance of regulations by passing back to the secretary recommended figures for further reductions in budget estimates before their submission to Congress, and by negotiating adjustments.[18] During the period examined, HHS political leadership appeared to have limited, visible involvement in this formal interbranch dynamic.

Informally, interbranch relations are more paradoxical. On one hand, there is a staff-to-staff competition in analysis between the branches. On the other, there is a great deal of informal staff-to-staff communication to solve specific technical problems, to accommodate the need to respond to special interests while preserving policy integrity, and to negotiate specific provisions. During the period examined, ProPAC was described as mediating between the branches, and many viewed it as an agent independent of Congress.

Most of the situations cited during the interviews as being illustrative of how the branches have interacted can be classified under five issue rubrics (see table 7.6, p. 171).[19] These issue types cut across the elements of PPS (e.g., the basic payment formula, add-ons and exceptions, administration).

Showing Savings or Scoring Points.—Congress makes yearly adjustments to PPS and withdraws or otherwise constrains executive discretion when its objective is to score points for savings. The congressional prohibition on regulations, the DRG recalibration, and the varied use of the secretary's general exception and adjustment authority are three additional examples.

PROHIBITION ON ISSUING REGULATIONS. In addition to the update factor described above, another example occurred in OBRA 1987 and in each OBRA since. OBRA 1987 contained a provision prohibiting the secretary from authorizing any regulation, instruction, or other policy estimated by the secretary to result in a net reduction in expenditures under Title XVIII of the Social Security Act of more than $50 million. Congressional observers suggest this was motivated by distrust of the administration, a need to take credit for savings, and a desire to prevent the secretary from taking all hospitals off periodic interim payments. Executive observers see it primarily as a budget issue.

DRG RECALIBRATION. The secretary is authorized to adjust (recalibrate) DRG (diagnostic related group) weights on the basis of cost data. In 1989 the department determined the weights to be too high and reduced

TABLE 7.4.
ELEMENTS OF THE PROSPECTIVE PAYMENT SYSTEM

Elements within the DRG Methodology	
Basic PPS Payment Formula	*Add-Ons and Exceptions to the Basic PPS Payment Formula*
Payment Rate for each DRG (diagnostic related group)	*Add-Ons*
=	*Outlier Payment* (allowance for sicker patients)
National Base DRG Payment Amount	*Indirect Medical Education Payment* (allowance for teaching hospitals)
(An average standardized amount with exceptions and adjustments for particular hospitals and regions—urban and rural, regional and national:	*Disproportionate Share Hospitals* (allowance for hospitals treating significant number of low-income or Medicare patients)
Wage Index is used to adjust base payment amount for area differences in hospital wage levels. *Regional Floor* extended transition provision for certain hospitals. Base payment amount is updated each year by use of an *Update Factor*.)	*Exceptions*
✕	*Sole Community Hospitals* (hospitals that are the sole source of inpatient services reasonably available in a geographic area)
Relative DRG Weighting Factor	*Regional Referral Centers* (hospitals meeting these criteria are paid according to payment rates for "other" urban areas rather than rural rates)
(Varies only by DRGs; constant across hospitals. DRG recalibration and amendment process addresses periodic changes in the DRG weights and redefinition of the substance of a DRG.)	*Hospitals in Rural Counties Treated as Urban Counties* (legislation changing the standards for defining urban and rural boundaries)
	Excluded Hospitals (Medicare payments made to certain hospitals or parts of hospitals through systems other than PPS—states with cost control systems and certain specific kinds of hospitals)

TABLE 7.4. — *Continued*
ELEMENTS OF THE PROSPECTIVE PAYMENT SYSTEM

Elements outside PPS	*Elements of Administration*
Hospital Medicare Reimbursements on the Basis of Reasonable Costs	*Key Units Involved in Administration/Implementation*

Direct medical education costs	*Congress*
Capital-related costs	House Ways and Means Committee Senate Finance Committee
Bad debts of Medicare beneficiaries	Prospective Payment Assessment Commission
Kidney acquisition costs	CRS, CBO, GAO Issue caucuses Individual members
Anesthesia services of hospital-employed nonphysician anesthetists	*Executive*
	HCFA/HHS Geographical Review Board Fiscal intermediaries EOMB
	Other
	Review activities (peer review organizations) Administrative and judicial review Hospital associations

TABLE 7.5.
CONGRESSIONAL INTERVENTION BY PPS ELEMENT, EXAMPLES

Element of PPS	Issue Where Congress Intervened	Kind of Congressional-Executive Action/Reaction
Basic payment formula	1. DRG recalibration	Congress taking back executive authority: games of who gets credit for savings
Administration	2. Congressional prohibition on issuing regulations	Ditto
Add-ons and exceptions	3. Disproportionate share hospitals	Congress taking away the secretary's discretion and then invoking the secretary's general exception and adjustment authority
Add-ons and exceptions	4. Hospital boundary moves	Congress responding to special interests—then partially moving operational decisions back to the executive
Administration	5. Prospective Payment Assessment Commission	Congress creating a quasi-independent source of advice

them by a constant (1.22 percent) in regulations.[20] At the same time, the department proposed that Congress legislate the market basket at 1.5 percent. From the perspective of HCFA, this was a purely technical action, but key players in Congress interpreted it as an executive attempt to save money: "They would have saved $500 million by that correction." Congress legislated an update factor to achieve the same effect and removed the secretary's authority ever to take a similar action. Perceived results by the executive branch: "We used to be able to administer the system; now we can't take the 'DRG creep' out"; "Congress took the credit—but they required subsequent changes to be budget neutral. We're all still trying to figure out what that means." And a significant comment: "We all [executive, industry, Congress] think this was undesirable."

TABLE 7.6.
DISTRUST AND DISAGREEMENT BETWEEN THE BRANCHES —
ILLUSTRATIVE ISSUES

Type of Issue	*Specific Examples in PPS*
1. Solving technical policy issues: issues relating to the need to clarify, correct, adapt, and further develop technical aspects of a prospective system	• Resolving overpayment to hospitals during the early years • Conducting studies on urban/rural differentials • Defining disproportionate share hospitals
2. Showing savings or scoring points: decisions or actions that enable one side or the other to show a saving, pretty much set in motion by Gramm-Rudman and the increasing federal deficit	• Update factor • DRG recalibration • Congressional prohibition on issuing regulations • General exception and adjustment authority • Perceived administration stonewalling on disproportionate share • Source of funding dispute for disproportionate share • OMB approving regulatory analyses
3. Responding to pressures from the hospital industry: individual hospitals or groups of hospitals arguing for exceptions to particular provisions	• Hospital geographical boundary moves • Creation of the Geographical Review Board • Packwood amendment exempting Oregon hospitals from delayed transition
4. Generating "trusted" data on which to base decisions: issues where the need is to separate trust in the data and accompanying methodology from decisions made from the data	• Emergence of the Prospective Payment Assessment Commission (ProPAC)
5. Solving systemic health policy problems: issues linking PPS to all of Medicare as well as issues concerning PPS, the entire health care industry, and quality of care	• Discovering next steps in PPS—addressing constraints on PPS policy

NOTE: David Smith characterizes key PPS implementation issues as setting the annual update, DRG amendment and recalibration, monitoring the system and proposing amendments to improve it, and unresolved issues, including old and new mandates from Congress. Unpublished manuscript, 1990.

SECRETARY'S GENERAL EXCEPTION AND ADJUSTMENT AUTHORITY AND
DISPROPORTIONATE SHARE. Presumably to save dollars, some executive responses to congressional mandates have provoked a chain of events resulting,
first, in withdrawal of executive discretion and, then, in Congress's invoking the
secretary's general exception and adjustment authority. The disproportionate-
share "tug-of-war" is an example of this complex dynamic.

The Medicare disproportionate-share adjustment is a program payment
add-on for hospitals that serve a disproportionate share of certain patients.
In the 1983 PPS legislation, Congress directed the secretary to take into account the needs of such hospitals. The secretary chose not to implement that
directive during the first and second years of PPS (1984–85). Congress responded in the Deficit Reduction Act of 1984 (DEFRA) by directing the secretary to define a disproportionate-share hospital and to present a list of
qualifying facilities. Several hospitals, contending they had higher operating
costs because of such patients, sued the secretary and won. The administration had argued it was not the responsibility of Medicare to cover bad debts
hospitals incur from non-Medicare patients. HHS demurred on setting
guidelines under which hospitals would qualify for an adjustment and simply produced a list of disproportionate-share hospitals. The health community reacted with scorn.

ProPAC conducted a study and recommended a definition to both the
administration and Congress. The administration rejected it; Congress
adopted it in COBRA 1985 by inserting an explicit disproportionate-share
adjustment, thereby eliminating the secretary's discretion on the issue.

- "The definition we produced in the *Federal Register* was a joke with respect to what Congress asked for. Basically the people inside the administration did not want to spend the dollars. So we came up with a definition
  that allowed only ninety-nine hospitals to qualify. We did not have a good
  definition, but the one we eventually published was the worst. Things [be-
  tween the branches] have never been the same." (executive view)
- "OMB may have prevented action on the part of the administration."
  (congressional view)
- "Congress is using PPS to go beyond its original intent to create a payment
  system for Medicare. Disproportionate share is being used to provide financial support to hospitals—paying some greater amounts than what it
  costs the hospital to treat patients." (outside observer)

The secretary, under the enabling legislation, holds a "general exception
and adjustment authority" that has been rarely invoked because of the cost
implications. But when Congress, in OBRA 1989, adjusted the disproportionate share index upward, a dispute erupted between Congress and the administration regarding the source of funding for the increase. The HHS
drafted rules to implement the increase on a budget-neutral basis; hospital
officials and Congress countered that this was contrary to congressional in-

tent. The HCFA administrator requested written clarification from Congress; Congress responded that the HCFA should invoke the general exception and adjustment authority and implement the provision on a budget-neutral basis. HCFA did. The general exception and adjustment authority is thus not a unilateral device.

Responding to Pressures from the Hospital Industry.—In response to pressures from hospitals, Congress has moved the geographic (census) boundaries of hospitals, which affect whether a hospital is considered urban or rural for PPS purposes. However, in 1989 Congress shifted boundary decisions to the Geographical Review Board, which it located, at least nominally, in the executive branch.

Exceptions for specific hospitals began with the Packwood amendment in COBRA 1985, which extended the PPS transition period for one year to all hospitals but those in Oregon. Congress and the HCFA experienced strong pressure from certain hospitals to redesignate their status from rural to urban for PPS purposes. The typical response from the HCFA over the years has been that "urban is urban and rural is rural." Thus denied, the hospitals took their cases to Congress, and over the years legislation has included a number of ad hoc provisions to redesignate boundaries and use one or another algorithm to have the same effect.

In OBRA 1989 Congress recognized this ad hoc approach was unfair and wanted decisions made in a more systematic way. At that time, a number of members had proposed provisions for individual counties, but they agreed to table their requests in favor of creating the Geographical Review Board. The GRB is limited to PPS and considers appeals by hospitals for a change in classification from rural to urban or from one urban area to another urban area. This marks a recognition by Congress that such decisions rightly belong in the executive branch. Observers commented, however, that congressional distrust of the executive branch is still evident in the way Congress structured the GRB.

The GRB has five members named by the secretary, with one member being a ProPAC member. Decisions by the GRB are final unless the applicant appeals to the secretary within fifteen days after the board renders its decision. Only at that point can the secretary issue a decision on the change in a hospital's geographic classification; the decision of the secretary is final and not subject to judicial review. The secretary can also dismiss board members.

- "The GRB was an awful thing to have done to HCFA." (congressional view)
- "It adds another layer of complexity and makes it even more difficult to understand how decisions are made." (congressional view)
- "If the GRB is controlled through regulations, it may be all right. Otherwise, it could be a loose cannon." (executive view)

Generating Trusted Data on Which to Base Decisions.—Data on costs drive political and administrative decision making on the PPS. But in a political environment where numbers mean a win or a lose for either Congress or the executive branch, accurate, reliable, and trusted information will be a valued and probably scarce commodity. In PPS the novel solution is ProPAC (the Prospective Payment Assessment Commission) and an accompanying increase in the analytic capacity of Congress.

Observers' perceptions as to why ProPAC was created generally converge around five motivations: (1) lack of trust in the administration, (2) lack of administrative responsiveness to Congress, (3) need for Congress to have an independent view of technical matters, (4) need for a broker and for check and balance between the branches, and (5) need for Congress to have a greater role in implementation.

ProPAC's major roles are perceived to be advising both branches; providing a systematic forum for the policy input of industry views; conducting research; and helping to craft legislation.[21] At least that was the perception until 1990, when there was controversy over—or at least ambiguity in—the institutional location (quasi-executive, quasi-legislative) of ProPAC. An effect of OBRA 1990 was to make ProPAC, like the Physician Payment Review Commission (PPRC), a congressional agency.

Perceptions are mixed concerning the effects of ProPAC. On one hand, it is thought to have resulted in (1) better policy decisions, in part by separating trusted data from decisions made from the data, (2) improved interbranch relations, and (3) the offering of a truly independent source of advice. On the other hand, ProPAC is perceived to have played a major role in weakening executive analytic capability, increasing congressional analytic capability, and confusing interbranch relations. According to David Smith,

> [T]he Commission [appears to] supply some of the "neutral competence" that executive agencies such as the Office of Management and Budget once did. Further, its recommendations fit so nicely, both temporally and by virtue of their scope and substance, with the budget reconciliation process. They give Congress many of the proposals and alternatives that it needs at a time and in the form that it needs them.... [Thus] ProPAC is essential to prevent crude favoritism and corruption of PPS and yet, perforce, [it is] an accomplice in showing Congress how to "fix" it so as to benefit constituents.[22]

Addressing Broad Health Policy Problems.—By the fifth year of PPS, some of its limits were becoming increasingly clear to the members and staff of ProPAC, especially to Chairman Stuart Altman and Executive Director Donald Young.[23] The two problems at issue were the need for fresh challenges and the need to think beyond the regulatory limits of the policy. The health industry environment by this time had changed dramatically from what it was at the inception of PPS, characterized, for example by a steady movement of procedures out of hospitals; PPS payments controlling less and less of the total variance in hospital costs; and hospitals increasingly less able to control their own destinies because of an influx of patients with AIDS, uninsured patients, and so on.

ProPAC began incrementally shifting its mission in 1988, seeking to broaden its jurisdiction and establish a larger role with respect to Congress. The commission "both responded to discerned trends and anticipated future ones; accepted and sought out new congressional mandates." Specifically, ProPAC has (1) sought to increase its own resources and capabilities to meet the need for analytical justification and strengthen features of PPS; (2) pushed for additional and more timely data, for the merger of Medicare Part A and Part B data files, and for retention and increased use of the Medicare Cost Report; (3) endorsed the efforts of the HCFA to enhance DRG performance and incorporate capital into PPS; (4) explored the possibilities of closer collaboration between ProPAC and the Physician Payment Review Commission to coordinate regulation of A and B expenditures; and (5) vastly expanded its role in surveying and commenting on the entire health care industry and quality of care, shifting its attention from PPS to the health care environment as a whole, of which PPS is a part but not necessarily the cause.[24]

Effects of Congressional Intervention and Executive Response

Virtually every participant contacted expressed concern over the cumulative effects of congressional-executive relations illustrated in PPS.[25] PPS vividly exemplifies the long history of cycles and shifting comity, trust, and distrust between Congress and the executive branch. The three eras of congressional involvement with the executive suggested in table 7.7 provide an important context for comprehending the results for policy and institutional relations and processes.

Results for Policy.—With respect to policy, direct effects of congressional involvement in the details of administration were suggested for intent and policy goals, decision-making processes, and hospitals and quality of care.

INTENT AND GOALS. Most of those interviewed believed that the intent of PPS has changed as a consequence of congressional-executive interaction. For example, they suggested that PPS has (1) moved from being an interim to permanent solution, from being a dynamic to an ossified system; (2) moved from not supporting insolvent institutions to subsidizing institutions that were intended to go under; (3) moved from being health policy

Table 7.7.
Congressional Involvement in PPS by Era

Traditional Cooperation and Conflict 1970s to early 1980s Seeds of Distrust	Protracted Conflict over Savings Credits Mid to late 1980s Norms of Distrust	Possible Crossroads Late 1980s, early 1990s Beyond Distrust?
• Medicare trust fund crisis	• Crisis of the federal deficit	• Crisis of federal deficit, rising hospital costs, and overall crisis of health care system
• Pattern of executive proposes; Congress disposes (e.g., draft regulations for reformed payment system in 1979 not implemented by Carter; PPS proposal to Congress)	• Enactment of Gramm-Rudman • OMB must approve regulatory analyses accompanying all major regulations	• Continuation of savings-for-credit games • Appointment of new, highly respected HCFA administrator
• Executive branch reorganizations (HCFA political appointee layer; OMB regulatory reviews)	• Perceptions of administration stonewalling on PPS implementation	• A few signs of mixed flexibility noted (e.g., creation by Congress of Agency for Health Care Policy and Research;
• Seeds of distrust become prominent during design of PPS	• Packwood amendment opens door for hospital exceptions and pork-barreling (e.g., Congress moving some hospital urban-rural boundaries to achieve greater payment rates for individual hospitals)	movement of hospital boundary decisions to the HHS)
	• Entrenched "credit-for-savings" game	

(changing the incentive structure for hospitals) to being budget policy (using PPS as a budget-cutting device); (4) moved from a primary focus on cost containment to a focus on equity; and (5) failed at many of the goals that marked its creation. A widely held view is that PPS has fundamentally turned Medicare entitlement into a distributional game no longer operating under a monolithic set of rules.

There were also a few comments indicating there has been no change of purpose from 1983 to 1990 as a consequence of congressional intervention—that is, that the basic PPS framework remains intact despite congressional detailing. Others suggested that although Congress has achieved its goals, hospitals have not achieved theirs. Still others asserted that because of its actions, Congress is getting what it wanted: to slow the rate of growth in federal hospital spending. Larry Oday and Allen Dobson, formerly of the HCFA, write:

> PPS policy has changed behavior in fundamental, anticipated and perhaps unanticipated ways. The system is credited with dramatic decreases in length of hospital stays and increases in out-patient care; and with reducing federal Medicare outlays to hospitals from what they would have been under retrospective cost reimbursement, without negatively affecting quality of care. But many of the actual consequences, particularly those financial in nature, have been unintended and unanticipated, running counter to the incentives built into PPS.[26]

Substantively, PPS is at a critical crossroad. Future payments per case are predicted by some to be less than operating costs per case. Hence, hospitals will have to find ways to reduce operating costs without negative impacts on quality of care. The justification for adjustments on technical grounds is diminishing as precision of prediction increases. These are policy tensions that will continue to be the subject of much friction between the branches and the industry.

The cumulative and broader effect may be that so much attention to PPS has diverted attention from other health issues, especially health policy in general. Concern was expressed that as a nation we are doing something wrong in a major way in health policy in general, but the primary cause may not be PPS or the congressional-executive relationship.

DECISION MAKING. Perhaps the most significant policy effects of congressional intervention and the congressional-executive interaction in general are those concerned with the quality of the policy-decision process. Four effects were identified as concerns; a fifth was more qualified. Decision making is characterized as follows: (1) there is decreased flexibility in making policy changes; (2) decisions on technical issues have become politicized in both branches; (3) technical adjustments and political responsiveness have become equally important; and (4) the system is now characterized by a new nightmare of unintended consequences—it is highly complex administratively and a paper layer of regulations more than an inch high is added each year. Observers also noted that the effects on decision making really depend on where one sits. For example, rural hospitals designated as regional referral centers might find the process to be of high quality.

HOSPITALS AND QUALITY OF CARE. Those interviewed were in general agreement that PPS has not adversely affected quality of care, though they acknowledged that quality of care is not easily measured.[27] For hospitals, the process has (1) split the industry into competing groups and specialized associations, (2) created winners and losers, (3) brought into being competition that puts hospitals at risk but without accompanying rewards, and (4) caused hospitals to face excruciating decisions. The diagnosis-related groups (DRGs) and PPS have also changed the location of patient care (from inpatient to outpatient), the management of hospital resources (including cost accounting and patient-reporting practices), and the size of hospital reporting staffs.

Results for Institutional Relations and Processes.—Traditional roles and processes within each branch as well as between the branches have changed dramatically over the past seven years of PPS implementation. Observers identified effects on branch relations, Congress as an institution, and executive management. Most of these effects were negative and a cause of great concern to those interviewed, although a few positive consequences were also identified.

BRANCH RELATIONS. The interface between the branches is formally a battle zone, characterized by profound lack of trust, high tension, incentives to get separate credit for savings, a rising federal deficit, and escalating hospital and health care costs. But the battle lines between the branches are blurred by the emergence of the Prospective Payment Assessment Commission (ProPAC), which is a source of key information for both sides and often plays a positive role of separating information from political decisions made on the basis of that information.

Although ProPAC may indeed be an honest broker of ideas, it is also perceived as providing Congress with the information it needs to substitute its own judgments for those of the executive branch through the political process. ProPAC is increasingly viewed as a neutral arm of Congress; as performing some traditionally executive roles (e.g., emerging as a source of national health policy leadership); and as contributing to the decreased capacity of the HCFA (e.g., assertions that "ProPAC is where one can make a difference on policy"). Accountability for executive and congressional policy leadership and policy results is diffused through ProPAC. Yet observers also point out that ProPAC may be a key mechanism for helping to surface the critical questions that need to be addressed.

Informally, the interface has a high degree of staff-to-staff communication that generally maintains a focus on microlevel details and, at that level, seeks to preserve policy integrity. Congress still does not believe that the executive branch can be trusted to implement its statutes or that the executive branch (the OMB and HCFA) will provide objective analysis and data needed for policy development. There were also signs of distrust within the executive branch (e.g., among the OMB, HHS, and HCFA).

CONGRESS AS AN INSTITUTION. Congress has reclaimed much of the original discretion it granted to the executive branch to administer PPS, and now could be characterized as being a virtual coadministrator. PPS and Congress's role in it may have resulted in increased congressional ability to deal with special interests. Congress has experienced a marked increase in lobbying, and there are few members who understand the issues. The high technicality of PPS, Gramm-Rudman, and the distrust between the branches are all thought to be major factors in the significant increase in the analytic capabilities of Congress at the staff level. In fact, observers suggest that there are three congressional staffers (concerned with PPS) for every one HCFA staffer.

The budget reconciliation process has increased congressional responsiveness, sensitivity and, arguably, budget effectiveness. However, perceptions are that it has also (1) changed who is involved, and when, in congressional decision making, (2) ossified the PPS, (3) created unfair advantages for selected parties, (4) added to the amount and frequency of congressional detailing to the executive, (5) virtually eliminated postaudit congressional oversight, (6) resulted in health policies being overridden by budget policy, (7) increased technical mistakes in legislation, (8) created negative pork, and (9) made it difficult for the executive to govern.

EXECUTIVE MANAGEMENT. Congressional detailing is thought to give better focus to administration. Further, observers pointed out that the HCFA and HHS retain a great deal of administrative discretion in the writing of regulations. Significant concerns were expressed regarding possible harmful effects on executive management that have developed incrementally: (1) HCFA organizational capability has weakened; (2) perceived human resource and morale problems at the HCFA are a consequence of weakened organizational capability;[28] (3) Congress has created an excessive workload for the HCFA, causing missed deadlines; (4) the frequency and detail of legislation have left no time for reflection; and (5) career people are highly distrusted by politically appointed administrators. Observers also pointed out that the executive plays a role in causing some of Congress's behavior, namely, through interactions among the HCFA, HHS, and OMB (i.e., executive seeking credit for savings) and through the politicization of HCFA that took place during the Reagan years.

Conclusions: The High Costs of Confrontation

Four important overall conclusions can be drawn about the congressional-executive interaction in this case. Seven implications are developed from them and the cumulative investigation of PPS in this study.

Overall Conclusions

1. *Relations between the branches to structure PPS implementation were ineffective in identifying and reaching agreement on ultimate policy outcomes, but highly effective in specifying the procedures that were necessary to implement a prospective system.*

In the absence of agreement about broad purpose, the delegation that emerged placed the branches in a delicate "balance": (a) "the Secretary" had detailed procedural instructions from Congress but discretion to implement them in a framework that had no clear goals, and (b) Congress had safeguards to "check and balance" explicit and implied executive discretion through its creation of the Prospective Payment Assessment Commission (ProPAC) as a source of independent advice to both branches, and its specification of a kind of detail in the statute that ensured its involvement throughout implementation.

2. *The initial delicate balance between the branches has changed during implementation.*

The executive has lost much of its original discretion to make critical choices in administering PPS, and its capacity or inclination to produce innovative substantive or fiscal policy initiatives. The losses are due to its own and to congressional actions, and to the effectiveness and adaptability of the initial safeguard Congress provided to the system, that is, ProPAC. Congress has increased its control over PPS by reclaiming much of the original discretion it granted to the executive. Further, Congress appears to be replacing its traditional interaction with the executive branch with a new decision system that largely comprises its own agencies or quasi-agencies—that is, to legislate, Congress is talking mostly to itself, interest groups, and constituents. Congress hears from the executive, specifically the OMB and to a lesser extent the HHS and HCFA, but that interaction is now predictable (deficit reduction tactics, fiscal goals), routine, and nonsubstantive.

3. *Because desired policy outcomes are still in dispute and because of the limits of legislative-administrative channels of communication, the congressional-executive interaction has been ineffective in surfacing the key issues, alternatives, and arguments necessary to monitor and control the total, systemic impact of PPS on the health industry.*

More generally, the congressional-executive interaction as it has evolved in PPS is no longer a sufficient combination to ensure national control over health policy and accompanying fiscal issues (e.g., the federal deficit, rising hospital costs with respect to inpatient and outpatient care). To fill the leadership vacuum, ProPAC, the quasi-legislative commission created to broker between the branches, is taking on national health policy leadership. Its multiple interactions are emerging as the effective ones relative to the criterion of surfacing critical choices. It is open to question whether this is the kind of structural adjustment to our system of governance that is necessary to make a divided-party government work.

4. *All of these conditions can also be viewed as adaptations necessary to enable a divided-party government to function.*

The players on all sides appear fully cognizant of the limits to PPS and to some extent aware of the broader health policy issues. The real questions, for present purposes, are the institutional implications of the interbranch decision system that has eventuated in the contemporary PPS and whether next-generation improvements can be made.

Thus, the critical issue of this case is not a faulty PPS technology; rather, it is the generally unhealthy politics that precludes addressing the larger across-the-board health problems and getting ready to take much needed major new steps to renovate the whole system.[29] Although the case also illustrates a healthy component of systemic adaptation, that too is offset by concerns for the institutional implications. That is, the fact that adaptations have emerged to respond to unmet needs (e.g., absence of systemic leadership) might be construed as healthy, but the content and results of the adaptation could be argued to be unhealthy or at least of institutional concern.

Implications

1. *Conditions between the branches during the development and enactment of major policy change will have a strong and lasting influence on interactions throughout the subsequent implementation period.*

Congress and the executive interacted during the legislative process to create PPS. There was broad agreement surrounding the need for something like a PPS or at least the need to do something different from retrospective cost reimbursement. That agreement broke down when it came time to finalize a legislative package using the proposal from the administration, although not much was made of the breakdown at the time. The seeds of subsequent and increasingly complex distrust were sown during these interactions as Congress came to doubt the data or lack of data provided by the executive. The resulting statute reflected congressional uncertainty and included safeguards that Congress would be involved in implementation. Goals were left ambiguous, ProPAC was created, and executive discretion was limited but certainly not eliminated. These conditions prepared the foundation for how the branches would address issues arising during implementation: with a focus on technical details, continuing avoidance or institutionalization of goal differences, and a reallocation of responsibilities to administer the system.

The original goal differences remain and may be more entrenched today. Congress sees PPS as a means of cost control, protectiveness, and local advantage, so it has made exceptions for specific hospitals, and created add-ons and adjustments to account for regional differences. The OMB sees PPS as a means to reduce federal government outlays, so it continues to propose reductions and to use PPS as a target for achieving them. The HHS and the industry see PPS not as a cost-saving device but as a method of payment less regulative than the former retrospective system and offering better management incentives,[30] so HHS has become largely an issuer of regulations and the industry has organized to lobby Congress extensively.

To this day observers suggest that the multiple, conflicting goals for PPS represent the "lack of a paradigm."[31] The inability to reconcile them plays a large role in keeping actions focused at a technical level. For example, one of the chief emerging conflicts is between so-called health policy (reimbursing hospitals at least to cover average operating costs) versus so-called budget policy (reimbursing hospitals for less than average operating costs because of pressures to reduce the federal deficit and to control rising hospital costs). But another interpretation is that such a tension was in fact desired by the original PPS design: if reimbursements are less than operating costs, there will be an incentive to reduce those costs.

The important point is the collective and recurring nature of these conditions. Parenthetically, the solution may lie outside PPS.

2. *Even with a highly specific implementation framework that reflects lack of agreement on desired policy outcomes, both branches have choices in terms of how they will act and react during implementation. Unless those choices are made with a view toward their impact on institutional prerogatives, the latter may be eroded or significantly changed.*

If retaining the discretion given in the original legislation was an executive goal, it certainly was not achieved during implementation. That is, the price of the way the executive played the game to win credit for savings seems to have been either the loss of the explicit discretion originally granted or new restrictions. This narrowing and blurring of executive discretion to administer the system is due to (1) the deficit-reduction tactics of the OMB and HHS, leading to an open struggle with Congress over the budget that makes PPS a prime and strategic target, (2) implementation delays within the executive, (3) the budget and reconciliation process, and (4) the creation of advisory commissions (e.g., the ProPAC) and decision bodies (e.g., the Geographical Review Board). In the executive, it appears that the environment (short-term budget savings) took priority over institutional considerations (preservation of executive discretion), so if the executive scores a short-term or even cumulative "win" in terms of the budget savings battle, we must ask at what price to its institutional capacity.

The administrative structure for PPS rate setting has indeed been subject to political intervention, with Congress rather than the HCFA controlling the rate-setting process. What choices has Congress made in response to industry and the executive? First, congressional committees and individual members moved the geographical boundaries of some hospitals in the hope of affecting their payment levels. Congress did not have to make this choice. Indeed, this was realized in 1989, when Congress changed the locus of such decisions to a body in the HHS on which it placed controls. Congress could have chosen to spend that time identifying the broader policy questions, anticipating the next system shifts. Second, Congress chose to give the judicial branch a limited role in PPS and created no formal mechanism for hearing and ruling on the unique cases that would predictably arise. Third, Congress has chosen to play the who-gets-credit-for-savings game via the budget and reconciliation process and to counter executive moves to get credit. Were other choices open to Congress? And what is the cumulative price of its choices to its own institutional capacity?

3. *Administrative systems that are primary channels for interbranch communications (e.g., the budget and reconciliation process, the policy and regulatory control process between the OMB and HHS and HCFA) may reach their limits of ineffectiveness when they are used as countermeasures against the other branch.*

By themselves, the budget and reconciliation processes and the OMB regulatory clearance process may have a great deal of integrity and effectiveness, but when they become political channels (e.g., when they are used to counter the other side), the risk is that their inherent weaknesses will be exacerbated. Cries to reform the procedure are thus valid only in part, because it is the procedure coupled with how it is being used that must be reformed or maintained.

The budget reconciliation process is a primary formal channel of communication for substantive PPS legislation between Congress and the executive in PPS. It has become the only place Congress can make policy changes, but it does not mesh well with long-term health needs.[32] It has resulted in a number of "gaming techniques" that are used to achieve required budget savings, to add new spending, and to communicate with the OMB.[33] It has played a major role in fiscalizing congressional-executive debate in PPS, and in maintaining the PPS point-scoring game between the branches.

> The continuing budget deficit makes hospital expenditures and especially excessive hospital margins an attractive target for budget and deficit reduction. A second confounding factor is the strained relations between Congress and the executive branch during the Reagan and Bush administrations. These together have led the executive branch, and especially OMB, to push hard for Reagan-Bush political priorities and for budget savings. They have also given Congress both incentive and excuse to respond in kind, especially with extensive and minute interventions into the implementation of PPS.[34]

Within the executive:

> The practice with a rule of this scope [annual May proposed rule] is for it to go through a number of drafts with extensive comment from various bureaus within the HCFA and an extensive clearance process within HHS that will involve such staff divisions as the Office of General Counsel, the Office

of Management and Budget in HHS, and the Office of the Secretary. A critical step is referring the proposed rule to the Executive Office of Management and Budget that, in recent years, has regularly returned such rules with a "pass back" demand that more budget savings be taken from PPS or a proposed regulation or definition changed, a process that has had much to do with politicizing the PPS update factor.[35]

The HCFA's role in proposing health policy is weakened and unclear, because of, in part, OMB clearance; issuing new regulations on a yearly basis; and the loss of analytic capacity in the HHS. This is a symptom of the inability of the executive branch to offset ideology and central administrative controls with its own executive leadership and management roles. It is also a symptom of an executive branch that appears, at least in health policy, to be as fragmented and politicized as Congress. Hence, whose role is it now to propose health financing policy? The HCFA's? ProPAC's? HHS's? Some not-yet-created structure or group's? Are these effective mechanisms or outcomes?

Looking at the period following the original legislation, both branches seem to use the federal deficit and increased Medicare costs as rationales or perhaps excuses to score points through their respective administrative systems. However, sharing such considerations has not generally translated into "healthy" politics. The limits of ineffectiveness generalization arises because both sides use these administrative processes to play out the same battles year after year; yet they are solving neither the systemic health policy issues nor the federal deficit. They are also perceived to be contributing to apparently unintended consequences, for example, erosion of executive discretion to administer PPS; erosion of national health policy leadership, stemming from the interaction between the branches; and politicization of the environment of advice giving, so that the role of ProPAC has become more important and the role of the secretary less so. And in the midst of such knowledge, the paradox is that these are insufficient incentives for either side to reform the procedures, change the interbranch strategy (politics), or ask higher-level questions.

4. *When the two branches are unable to resolve their discord and when Congress distrusts the executive, novel formal and informal "bridge mechanisms" are likely to appear (e.g., ProPAC; the Geographical Review Board; complex, paradoxical staff-to-staff relationships). These solutions are a double-edged sword: innovative yet symptomatic of the failures of both branches to work out better macrorelationship problems. Over time they may also profoundly alter institutional relations between the branches.*

ProPAC and the Geographical Review Board offer interesting approaches to each of the issue areas they were designed to address: ProPAC to conduct impartial analysis with broad input; the GRB to make decisions on hospital boundary moves. Further, ProPAC is emerging as the source of national health policy leadership because of the existing vacuum. However, both creations are also symptoms of failures of both the executive and Congress to work out better macrorelationship problems, including who exercises the discretion needed to deal with the political heat.

ProPAC was created because Congress did not trust the executive. Although it may be an honest broker of ideas, it is also perceived as "providing Congress with the information it needs to substitute its own judgments for those of the executive branch through the political process."[36] PPS policy cannot operate without a baseline of analytic information, and ProPAC has played the role of separating the data (about which there should be little disagreement assuming appropriate procedure) from the subsequent decisions. But ProPAC is increasingly viewed as a neutral arm of Congress (as opposed to a quasi-legislative body), as performing traditionally executive roles, and as contributing to the decreased capacity of the HCFA.

Because executive policy leadership has not reappeared, ProPAC is now emerging as the source of broad, substantive policy and analytical leadership formerly provided by the HHS, HCFA, and OMB. Institutionally, this a debatable replacement of a capacity traditionally located in the executive branch. Substantively, such a perspective needs to come from somewhere, that is, the policy system needs the function performed.

In part due to discord, lack of strength, or insufficient political adroitness at higher levels, staff-to-staff relationships are another kind of "paradoxical bridge mechanism" between the branches. At these levels, there is a high degree of informal communication accompanied by horizontal career paths among the branches and outside associations. Many players bring multiple perspectives and considerable experience to bear on PPS issues. This is offset, however, by a competition in analysis among the staffs, with partial net effects being that some policy decisions are still made that no one on either side likes and the debate stays pretty much within PPS or Medicare. Individuals and ProPAC are seeking to broaden it, but that is far different from a concerted congressional or executive initiative to do so.

5. *When technical and fiscal problems dominate a "win-lose" discourse between the branches and are not offset by congressional-executive strategic leadership of a policy system, the government may be unable to anticipate the broader next steps and the policy system may enter a period of decline or crisis.*

If PPS is illustrative of health care politics in general, there has been a progressive deterioration of joint congressional-executive strategic leadership of the health care system. The enormous energy and focus on technical aspects of the system coupled with the politics of the federal deficit may be symptoms of the absence of broader policy leadership to guide problem solving and implementation at this level.

Without question, there are vexing technical problems within PPS to which neither side has answers (e.g., variance within diagnosis-related groups [DRGs], urban-rural differences, case-mix index, unexplained variance). Further, a continuing tension—between rational analytic solutions seeking consistent implementation and those based on particularistic values or budget savings—is a given. But when technical problems dominate, they can mask other issues or become ends in themselves.

The issues PPS was designed to address are long-standing. Finding ways to control costs while maintaining quality of care and increasing access have been major concerns for the Medicare and Medicaid programs since shortly after they were enacted. What is relatively new, and has created complex dynamics, is the significant pressure coming from the need to reduce the federal deficit.

As these forces converged into a trend during the 1980s and early 1990s, both Congress and the executive became preoccupied to a high degree with microlevel, technical issues in the context of a shortsighted political game called "who gets credit for savings." There is much evidence in this case that Congress and the executive were doing more monitoring and refining of detailed policy than recognizing the larger across-the-board problems and getting ready to take greatly needed major new steps to renovate the whole system. This makes it exceptionally difficult also to address systemic issues, within the health arena, and also to consider health's relationship to other domestic policies. "Canada is not perfect, but it makes us look like bumbling incompetents in access, in cost control, in dealing with everything from AIDS to infant mortality—and all with no discernible loss of quality."[37]

It may be that no paradigm is possible at this level of analysis (i.e., at the level of PPS). Although tension and conflict are givens in this domain, the real policy problems of PPS may not be at all within PPS. Rather, they may be broader, involving not only Medicare and Medicaid but the whole health industry and how it interfaces with other sectors to produce what results. The shift of the mission of ProPAC to address some of these concerns attests that some of those in the PPS system recognize this.

6. *In a policy system apparently locked into an ineffective congressional-executive interaction, political and career individuals may privately and publicly acknowledge the need for change, yet their actual behavior will maintain the existing system—sometimes with vigor.*

Repeatedly, in interviews, a case council debriefing, and the literature, we were struck by individuals who were deeply concerned about the institutional implications of the present structure of relationships in the PPS health policy system in addition to policy integrity. Perhaps not surprisingly, they were able to articulate these conditions clearly and in almost the same breath reinforce them with vigor and occasional relish. This is perhaps part of the human organizational condition, which demands that participants act out assigned roles within the rules of the existing game. But when the observation is stated more generally and when it is accompanied by the other features of this policy system—specifically, the politics—it may say something about some of the troubling outcomes being observed.

The health policy crisis is well documented; likewise the pressures and limits to PPS as a simultaneous policy solution and budget-savings prize.

7. *A congressional-executive interaction that is ineffective in eventually articulating a coherent national policy but persists in a focus on detailed and frequent procedural changes may create uncertainty for those who must comply (e.g., the regulated community). Such a condition may result in forces that confound systemic problems.*

Because PPS changes are made each year through the budget and reconciliation process, it can be difficult for hospitals to make institutional changes. Equivalently, planning horizons that have a reasonable degree of certainty may be considerably shortened. So it is possible that the perceived consequences of the who-gets-credit-for-savings game in Washington are playing out in a similar dynamic for the industry. It is also possible that the lack of a national policy, the uncertainty from year to year, and the projected tightening of the system below hospital operating costs can combine into forces that actually motivate hospitals and their associations to lobby Congress, and to spend time and dollars that could otherwise be used to discover how to reduce their operating costs and contribute to solving the broader systemic problems.

Timeline of Major Events in Prospective Payment System for Hospitals under Medicare

Development and Enactment, 1946–83

- Congress increasingly involved in health policy, especially hospitals
- Executive taking initiative on "think" work at least ten years prior to PPS enactment (Carter cost containment, HCFA reform initiatives)
- Executive becomes politicized (OMB and HCFA)
- Executive Order 12291 formalizes OMB role in agency regulatory process
- Congress sets cost limits in TEFRA and administration proposes PPS
- Executive proposes the conceptual framework for the system
- Tensions emerge between Congress and executive: PPS as machine versus PPS as flexible machine—PPS enacted
- Foundation laid for Congress to become bureaucratized (ProPAC created; Congress just beginning to realize technical aspects of new system and shifts it will entail)
- Reconciliation process emerging as main vehicle for legislation

Transition, 1984–87

- Margaret Heckler resigns as secretary of HHS; Otis R. Bowen appointed as new secretary; David Stockman of OMB and Carolyne Davis, HCFA administrator, also resign
- HCFA begins to have a decreased organizational capability
- HCFA-HHS-OMB battles; Executive Order 12498 (further OMB regulatory analyses required)
- Increased analytic capability in Congress is in full swing
- Increase in pressure on Congress from hospitals
- Packwood amendment opens door for pork-barreling
- Gramm-Rudman enacted
- Who-gets-credit-for-savings game emerges full force
- Administration narrow interpretation of law; some stonewalling during Reagan era (e.g., disproportionate-share definition)
- Congress takes back authority originally granted to executive when it will result in its getting credit for a savings (e.g., postponing update factor; restriction on issuing regulations resulting in savings of $50 million or more)
- Almost all actions taken by either branch are interpreted in the context of "credit for savings"
- Much informal, interbranch staff-to-staff communication

Implementation, 1988–89

- A highly detailed and technical system has emerged
- The "games" that evolved during transition are now fairly well entrenched
- Congress creates another quasi-independent body: in the executive, the Geographical Review Board, a decision body as opposed to an advisory body

- ProPAC June 1988 report to Congress discusses changes in mission of commission
- Congress takes away secretary's authority to reduce DRG weights by an overall percentage
- Players resigned to current conditions (budget-driven, reconciliation, credit-for-savings game, lack of trust, few shared priorities, and so on)
- Many players concerned with general government implications of current system, especially the quasi-independent commissions, the decreased capacity of HCFA, the role of OMB, the increased analytic capacity of Congress
- Some sense among the players that all of this has resulted in a change of policy intent
- No concrete or cumulative data as to the results of incremental (small at the time) changes to the system
- System may be at next "turning point" (technically as well as procedurally): this time in terms of how decisions are made between branches as well as reflection on the years since enactment and what the future could be

Acknowledgments

Many people contributed to the development of this case study, but I would like to express particular gratitude to Hale Champion, Bob Gilmour, Karen Koster, Bill Morrill, Larry Oday, Julian Pettengill, David Smith, and Don Wortman.

Notes

1. Raymond G. Davis, "Congress and the Emergence of Public Health Policy," *HCM Review* (Winter 1985): 61–73.

2. DRGs indentify the output of hospitals as classes of patients, each class receiving a similar bundle of goods and services in the diagnosis and treatment of the patient's illness. Medicare's PPS uses the product definitions as a basis for payment to hospitals. For each DRG, a rate considered fair payment to the hospital is set for the diagnosis and treatment of the given illness. Robert B. Fetter, "Diagnosis Related Groups: Understanding Hospital Performance, *Interfaces* 21 (January-February 1991): 6–7.

3. Judith R. Lave, "The Impact of the Medicare Prospective Payment System and Recommendations for Change," *Yale Journal on Regulation* 7 (1990): 499.

4. National Academy of Public Administration, *An Agency at Risk: An Evaluation of Human Resource Management at HCFA* (Washington, D.C., June 1991), x.

5. From November 1989 through May 1990, twenty-four current and former congressional, executive, and industry representatives were asked to reflect on PPS as a whole and to suggest specific parts that illustrated the range of decisions, tactics, and countertactics taking place between the branches. On 6 August 1990, twenty-two participants debriefed the results of the interviews in a PPS case council, with a specific focus on analyzing the case for key issues in the congressional-executive relationship and suggesting recommendations for change. This case summary is an analysis of data from these as well as traditional literature sources.

6. Larry Oday, "Development of PPS," unpublished manuscript, 1983.

7. Even though Congress has every right to change administration proposals, the changes in this case were regarded as extraordinary.

8. Smith, unpublished manuscript on PPS and physician payment reform, 1990 (now available as David G. Smith, *Paying for Medicare: The Politics of Reform* [New York: de Gruyter, 1992]).

9. Initially, there were fifteen members, but the commission was expanded to seventeen in 1986 to broaden the base of its representation and expertise.

10. Smith, chapter on PPS implementation, unpublished manuscript, 1990.

11. Oday, "Development of PPS."

12. Smith, chapter on PPS implementation, unpublished manuscript.

13. See Aaron Wildavsky, *The New Politics of the Budgetary Process* (Glenview, Ill.: Scott, Foresman, 1988); Joseph White and Aaron Wildavsky, *The Deficit and the Public Interest* (Berkeley: University of California Press; New York: Russell Sage Foundation, 1989).

14. "Here we have a procedure that almost every member of Congress believes is foolish, if not stupid; that everyone who knows anything about it thinks could be improved upon in five minutes; yet it received majority support in both houses of Congress and was signed by the president. The act, which dramatically affects the future of numerous government programs and congressional budget procedures, was passed without public hearings, without debate by any House or Senate standing committee, and without any substantive debate on the House floor. When everyone says that something is not right, and yet they keep doing it, there is a puzzle that should excite our interest." Wildavsky, *The New Politics of the Budgetary Process*, 236.

15. Smith, chapter on PPS implementation, unpublished manuscript.

16. Actually, the update factor or percentage is by law made up of two parts: (a) the hospital market basket, a figure computed from a number of indexes that takes account of price inflation in the goods and services that hospitals must purchase (largely a technical computation), and (b) a production function that makes allowance for changes in case mix and service delivery (a more discretionary adjustment). Smith, *Paying for Medicare.*

17. House Committee on Ways and Means, *Overview of Entitlement Programs: 1991 Green Book,* WMCP 102–9, (Washington, D.C.: Government Printing Office, 7 May 1991).

18. Smith, chapter on PPS implementation, unpublished manuscript; case study interviews.

19. I am indebted to Professor David Smith, Swarthmore College, for the identification of the fifth issue type by means of his unpublished manuscript.

20. From an interview: "The 1.22 percent reduction last year was caused solely by classifications HCFA made that are supposed to be budget neutral. If HCFA had changed the DRG class rates in FY 88, the payments that year would have been 1.22 percent lower than they turned out to be. So in regulations last year, HCFA said we won't take back the dollars already paid to hospitals to recover that 1.22 percent; instead, when we roll the base forward to FY 90, we will take the 1.22 percent out then. At the same time, we proposed that Congress legislate the market basket at 1.5 percent. We were recalibrating."

21. Interviews conducted for this study.

22. Smith, chapter on PPS implementation, unpublished manuscript, 15.

23. Ibid.

24. A 1984 mandate from the House Appropriations Committee to the commission directed it to review the impact of PPS on the health care industry. This was a part of the commission's work plan each year, pursued in a modest way until 1989, but that year signaled a dramatic change. The commission shifted its attention from PPS to the health care environment as a whole. Smith, chapter on PPS implementation, unpublished manuscript, 48.

25. Interview comments supporting the categories below are available on request to the author. Comments are not attributed to specific individuals.

26. Larry Oday and Allen Dobson, "Paying Hospitals under Medicare's Prospective Payment System: Another Perspective," *Yale Journal on Regulation* 7 (1990): 542.

27. Also see Louise B. Russell, *Medicare's New Prospective Payment System: Is It Working?* (Washington, D.C.: Brookings, 1989).

28. For a somewhat different view, see National Academy of Public Administration, *An Agency at Risk: An Evaluation of Human Resource Management at HCFA* (Washington, D.C., June 1991).

29. Personal communications from Hale Champion, Harvard University, 10 and 13 August 1990.

30. Statement of differing goals from Smith, chapter on PPS implementation, unpublished manuscript.

31. Proceedings of PPS case council, sponsored by the National Academy of Public Administration, 6 August 1990.

32. Henry Waxman, chair, House Energy and Commerce Subcommittee on Health and the Environment, in Julie Rovner, "Reconciliation Dominates Policy-Making Process," *Congressional Quarterly,* 29 April 1989, 964.

33. Rovner, "Reconciliation Dominates Policy-Making Process," 966.

34. Smith, unpublished manuscript, 2.

35. Ibid.

36. Thomas Greaney, "Competitive Reform in Health Care: The Vulnerable Revolution," *Yale Journal on Regulation* 5 (1988): 195.

37. Paragraph drawn from personal communications from Hale Champion, Harvard University, 10 and 13 August 1990.

Part Two
Defense Issues

8

Producing a Reliable Weapons System: The Advanced Medium-Range Air-to-Air Missile (AMRAAM)

Robert S. Gilmour and Eric Minkoff

Background and Overview

Throughout the Vietnam war, U.S. Air Force tactical fighter aircraft relied upon air-to-air missiles that had been developed by the U.S. Navy. As the fruit of that experience, both in Vietnam and in the NATO confrontation of Soviet and Warsaw Pact forces in Europe during the 1970s, internal Air Force demands became increasingly urgent for development of a faster, launch-and-leave-type missile capable of destroying the opposition's jet fighters in a serious dogfight. The Navy's Aim-7 Sparrow (radar-guided) and Sidewinder (infrared, or heat-seeking) missile systems—even if substantially upgraded—were believed by the Air Force to be inadequate for air warfare in the 1980s and 1990s.

By the mid-1970s, the Air Force had developed plans for a smaller, more effective, and less expensive replacement for the radar-guided Sparrow missile system. As described in numerous briefings, the new Advanced Medium-Range Air-to-Air Missile (AMRAAM) would enable jet fighter pilots to launch a lethal strike against multiple enemy aircraft targets at ranges of fifty miles and more (well "beyond visual range" of fifteen to twenty miles). AMRAAM would be, in Pentagon jargon, a "fire-and-forget" weapon. Once launched, AMRAAM's own radar would guide the missile to its target, leaving the pilot free to concentrate on additional targets with the remaining cluster of AMRAAM missiles (from a possible total of six) still in reserve. In essence, the Air Force proposed a powerful "force multiplier" for its jet fighter fleet.

Following a thirteen-month Air Force–Navy "threat" and "operational-requirement" assessment, the Defense Appropriations Act of 1977 (passed by Congress in July 1976) approved the initial development of a new adverse-weather, medium-range air-to-air missile.[1] A subsequent letter to the secretary of defense from congressional committee chairs made it clear that compliance with the Joint Strategic Operating Requirements (JSOR) was expected, that is, that AMRAAM would be a joint Air Force–Navy project.[2] The program was also expected to develop in accord with a "prototyping philosophy," consisting of a three-phase competition among interested development contractors and eventual dual-sourcing (involving at least two companies) for missile production. With the Air Force taking the lead, a Joint Systems Project Office (JSPO) was established at Eglin Air Force Base in Florida.[3]

In the flurry of new-start activity and "sky-is the-limit" financing during the first year of the presidential administration of Ronald Reagan in 1981, the Air Force completed competition for the AMRAAM development contract. In what virtually all observers regard as a fair competition, Hughes Aircraft Company was awarded the contract. But despite widespread agreement that development would require substantially more than four and a half years, a fixed-price, fifty-four-month contract between the Air Force and Hughes Aircraft was agreed to. Jurisdictionally responsible congressional overseers of the Armed Services committees were little involved in and for the most part unaware of this decision. As one close observer put it, "Congress doesn't usually become involved in these things until something goes wrong. . . . Then it's usually too late."

Before passage of a decade, this promising and ambitious project would be well launched but under heavy fire from a variety of critics. Congressional skepticism—focused primarily on missile capabilities, reliability, and cost—would take a variety of forms: member inquiries and media-oriented criticisms, U.S. General Accounting Office (GAO) audits, committee-financed studies, legislatively urged funding for "dual sourcing" of production companies, certifications required from the secretary of defense and the director of the Operational Test and Evaluation unit of the Department of Defense (DOD), and "cost caps" and reports on AMRAAM's development, production, and testing. There can be little doubt that congressionally imposed requirements resulted in far greater Air Force and DOD scrutiny of the program as well as heightened external visibility.

Congressionally imposed limits also markedly slowed the transition of the AMRAAM acquisition process from full-scale development to full-rate production. In February 1990 the future of the program appeared altogether bleak. At that point the Air Force itself suspended contractors' delivery of further AMRAAM missiles, citing design flaws that created reliability problems when attached to their primary launch vehicle, the F-15 jet fighter. Moreover, as the Cold War melted amidst soaring federal budget deficits, the urgency of the move to full-rate production had been reduced. After an additional year's effort to resolve these problems, the Defense Acquisitions Board (DAB) again refused to approve full-rate production until AMRAAM could meet "all" its requirements.[4] Nonetheless, limited deliveries of the missile had been resumed in the summer of 1990.

Virtually every participant contacted who had been directly involved in the AMRAAM case expressed the view that the Air Force, and to some extent AMRAAM contractors, had been unrealistic (or worse) in their estimation of costs and technical hurdles to be overcome, and that this was damaging to Air Force credibility. Congressional involvement with AMRAAM —in specifying the details of system cost, scheduling, and performance— did focus greater attention on the program but was generally regarded as too imprecise, coming too late in the process to have a very profound impact. Nevertheless, current congressional participants appear largely to see AMRAAM as an example of a weapons acquisitions system "that works," albeit imperfectly. Air Force and DOD participants, particularly those no longer actively involved, are likely to be far more critical of both military and congressional roles in the process and to suggest that significant adjustments are needed. Few of these participants questioned the military's need to replace older air-to-air missiles with AMRAAM, but they did want assurance that the new weapon would be delivered in fully operational condition and at a realistic cost.

Insiders from both branches of government, and outside observers as well, point to serious ethical problems raised by the AMRAAM case, problems that are said to be endemic to the military "culture" in weapons acquisitions and to the parochialism of Congress in defense and in other spending programs as well. Some of the same participants and observers, especially those involved in military program management, also decry congressional parochialism and the "excessive burdens" of "red tape" in the acquisitions process, much of it imposed by congressional involvement.

This case examines congressional-executive relations during the development and acquisition of the AMRAAM system, in the context of a number of defense acquisitions reforms of the 1980s. AMRAAM is viewed in this case as but one example of numerous weapons programs, many of which have been the subjects of other case study reports, and most of which have had a somewhat larger center of inquiry. Here the focus is on the motivations, roles, and specific techniques of congressional involvement in the details of policy development and implementation—also on the motivations and means of administrative reaction to such interventions—with particular concern for the institutional, managerial, and policy results of these interbranch relationships.

Problems in Policy and Program Management

From the first in the AMRAAM case, the Air Force has performed the role of policy initiator and optimistic program advocate. In part the impetus to develop a replacement for the Navy's Sparrow missiles came from Vietnam combat experience. Sparrows worked well enough against large, slow transports but not well at all against faster, more maneuverable MiG fighter jets. Air Force and Navy tacticians alike were determined to develop an effective radar-guided missile for dogfighting. In addition, however, and according to numerous reports, many Air Force officers were also determined, as an institutional matter, that the missile developed be an "Air Force product" to replace the Navy's Sparrow. According to some, this was a "manhood" issue.

The level of institutional and career commitment involved in the AMRAAM program would be difficult to overestimate. "Understand," as one senior official, now retired, put it, "AMRAAM is 'family jewels' for the Air Force. A lot of people have almost gotten fired for questioning AMRAAM." Many careers are tied to the success or failure of weapons-acquisition programs, and in this AMRAAM is no exception. During hearings before the House Armed Services Committee in February 1978, for example, Air Force officials reported that initial AMRAAM development was progressing well and implied that each missile would cost about $68,000, assuming a total buy of 24,000 missiles (17,000 for the Air Force; 7000 for the Navy).[5]

Others not directly involved with the program's development, and particularly those in the DOD's Cost Analysis Improvement Group (CAIG), were less sanguine about the Air Force's projections. Created in response to cost-assessment concerns both within and outside the Pentagon, CAIG was established by the DOD in 1980 to review and evaluate cost estimates of acquisitions programs for the DAB.[6] From the outset the CAIG's civilian and uniformed engineers and cost analysts regarded Air Force estimates and timetables for AMRAAM as "overly optimistic." Individual CAIG analysts argued vigorously for a "more realistic" assessment of projected costs; their views did not prevail.

The Air Force originally estimated that AMRAAM would be ready to fly by 1985. Although a substantial number of tests were completed and declared successful, by late 1991, in the wake of continued (though different) performance failures in operational tests, the missile system had not yet been cleared for full-rate production. Major problems were repeatedly identified as impediments to the program's development; they are discussed below.

Cost Overruns and Confusion

In the mid-1970s rough projections of AMRAAM unit costs in the $50,000 to $60,000 range were reported but not taken seriously. In 1978, however, the Air Force set its baseline cost estimate at $68,000 per copy in current-year dollars.[7] Thus began a saga of AMRAAM cost estimates that would soon fill thousands of pages in hundreds of reports and internal documents of the Air Force and its reviewers.

Cost estimation of high-tech development projects is a difficult and uncertain business at best. It inevitably involves a bewildering array of fast-changing assumptions and design parameters, constant and then-year dollar differentials, and multiple calculations involving rapid tacking from current-year outlays to long-term projected and actual development and production costs. Considerable variations in estimates are to be expected, yet there are a number of data categories and conventions that have become relatively standardized among cost estimators.

Before the decade of the 1980s was out, informed estimates of the final per-copy cost of the AMRAAM missile would be raised more than tenfold by virtually all observers, including those reporting officially for the Air Force. Having disavowed its estimates of the late 1970s, the service revised its initial $68,000-per-copy estimate in its 1982 Selected Acquisitions Report to $169,000 procurement cost per copy in 1978 dollars,[8] and thereafter persistently adjusted official assumptions to stay within arguing range of its 1982 "baseline" number, adjusted for inflation. This entailed dazzling shifts in dollar-year baselines, program acquisition and current procurement breakdowns (with and without "producibility enhancements," "dual-sourcing" assumptions, and so on) to the point that congressional and other observers could only conclude that the service and department were obfuscating, dissembling, or simply confused.[9]

By the beginning of 1990, knowledgeable congressional observers projected AMRAAM procurement costs at over $1,000,000 per missile. Even the Air Force's own estimates in current-year (1989) dollars anticipated a unit cost of $744,000 per copy, assuming a total buy of 18,000 missiles for the Air Force alone. However, such a total buy is regarded by most observers to be unrealistically high, and lower total buys are uniformly supposed to generate higher unit costs. It thus came as no surprise when the department's Selected Acquisitions Report dropped its projection for AMRAAM purchases by 13 percent to a total of 15,450 missiles over the thirteen-year period ending in 1999. The GAO pointed out that as a result of this change, "AMRAAM's unit acquisition cost ... has increased 39 percent, from $612,064 to $848,699, because the lower total acquisition cost is spread over the much lower procurement quantity."[10]

Managerial Discontinuity

The high turnover of AMRAAM program managers during critical development phases of the system coincided with the buildup of cost and technical problems during the early 1980s. From the beginning of 1980 until the end of 1984 the AMRAAM program had five uniformed managers. This "high manager turnover resulted in," the GAO concluded, "at least, a lack of continuity in management of the JSPO [Joint Systems Project Office], i.e., a loss of corporate knowledge and historical perspective."[11] Throughout this period, and to date, the Navy has provided a deputy manager for the program.

Although one Navy deputy was designated program manager for about six weeks while the Air Force selected one of its own officers for the position, little effort was made to accentuate the "jointness" of the enterprise beyond this symbolism.

In July 1984 the Air Force responded to the issue of discontinuity and continued criticism of the program by bringing in Colonel Thomas Ferguson, a former B-52 pilot known for his management savvy. He had previously spent two years salvaging the Air Force's troubled Maverick antitank missile program. Ferguson became the sixth program manager in the program's short history, but he would remain in the position for four years (July 1984 to August 1988). His job, he noted, "was to come up with a plan everyone would accept."[12] Ferguson brought credibility as well as continuity to the AMRAAM program. Since his departure in 1988, Ferguson (by then a three-star general) has been succeeded as program manager by General Charles E. Franklin, who served for over three years, and then in 1991, by Harry Schulte, the first civilian manager of the program.

Technical Difficulties and Schedule Delays

Development of the technology necessary to attain Air Force capability requirements proved to be more difficult and time-consuming than anticipated. Primary difficulties were electronic in character—the incompatibility of a powerful, heat-generating radar unit and sensitive solid-state electronics in the confines of a small missile airframe.

In 1983 Hughes Aircraft Company engineers admitted to the Air Force that they had underestimated the difficulties involved. By the late 1980s most design problems had been resolved. However, significant reliability problems remained, which continued to threaten missile performance in the harsh environments generated by fighter aircraft. Originally estimated to be ready for deployment in 1985, AMRAAM was not yet judged ready for full-rate production by late 1991.

Contract and "Concurrency" Concerns

A continuing debate rages over the type of contract (fixed terms and price versus cost-plus) most appropriate for technology development programs. The fixed-price contract negotiated by the Air Force with the Hughes Aircraft Company for AMRAAM development is estimated to have cost the company a loss of more than $200 million. The price for this shift of burden to the private contractor was prior Air Force agreement to a production decision by an early date, well before satisfactory product design was likely to be complete.

The House Armed Services Committee noted its "great concern over the type of contract used for the development, the details surrounding execution of production options and the associated concurrent schedule....

When the program began to slip and significant data was not available to the Air Force to make a production decision, the Air Force was faced with a difficult choice: either pick up the production option and hope the technical problems were solved in development or defer the option and pick up penalties of $18 million to $93 million." In the committee's judgment, and that of others, "the best interests of the government were compromised by this contracting arrangement."[13] Various critics point out that in view of the unknowns and uncertainties involved in the development of experimental, high-tech weaponry, a cost-plus contract is most appropriate on the front end, followed by competitive-bid, fixed-price contracts for actual production of a known and fully tested system.

Related to cost concerns regarding the type of contract agreed to for AMRAAM's development is the high degree of program development and missile production concurrency that was all but required by the contract's provisions. To simplify, the contractor was required to proceed to the first level of production before the missile was capable of performing its basic mission, let alone fully developed. The unrealistically short development lead time specified by the initial Air Force contract with Hughes Aircraft anticipated production and purchase of missiles before technical difficulties could be worked out and the product fully tested. Concurrency problems placed the Air Force and its oversight and appropriations committees in a state of annual tension over the number of prototype missiles to be purchased, with Congress consistently reducing Air Force requests for budget authority and delivery dates.[14] As one former Air Force official put it, "Any delays will give Congress another opportunity to say that they want to consider canceling the program. So there is a real need to be able to go directly from development into production. If there is a breakdown in the production line, you will end up spending more in the end."

Congressional Action and Administrative Response

Congressional roles in the AMRAAM case were largely reactive in nature, responsive to the technical-development and cost-overrun problems of AMRAAM in "firefighter" fashion.[15] Once congressional staffers became alerted to the "fire," however, their interest and consequently that of their principals was sustained and regularized by the routines of the annual authorization and appropriations cycles. One senior House Armed Services Committee staff professional, a congressman and his personal staff who were unassociated with the primary oversight committees for defense, and the GAO all played notable *investigatory* and *prosecutorial* roles in the case, leaving other members and staff free to develop roles as *program advocates* and *mediators*. Nearly absent were congressional performances of the customary role of *constituency advocate* for parochial interests.

House Staff Inquiry

Almost as soon as the AMRAAM development contractor, Hughes Aircraft, admitted to the Air Force in 1983 that its engineers had underestimated the technical difficulties to be overcome, and that the project was well behind schedule, Anthony Battista of the House Armed Services Committee staff initiated inquiries into the program's prospects. Battista's scientific training and expertise—long-term experience with both the technical end of weapons development as a working engineer and the political end on Capitol Hill as a senior Armed Services staff member—together with his extraordinary network of contacts inside the Pentagon and in the defense contractor community made it possible for him to gather and analyze extensive information on the program's progress. This led him to a tentative conclusion that the program was in deep trouble.

The response of some officials in the Defense Department was to assist Battista by sharing information. As one put it, "I'm proud to be a part of Tony's network." Others referred to "Tony's 'moles'" throughout the military services. Still others sought to discredit him, declaring: "He has a chip on his shoulder"; ". . . always was pro-China Lake [Naval Weapons Center]"; and so forth. But virtually every participant interviewed for this study regarded Battista with considerable, if grudging, respect. "Battista," as one observer puts it, "could have served as prototype for the important but obscure congressional staffer, operating behind the scenes, who exercises power far in excess of his official status. These staff members' influence comes from the expertise they bring to subjects that the elected members lack the time (and sometimes the inclination) to master."[16]

Based on Battista's concerns, the House Armed Services Committee contracted with a small private research company to investigate and evaluate AMRAAM. Although its report in 1984 was not released to the public, informed assessments of its contents concluded that it was "so devastating . . . that even the DOD got scared." In any case, subsequent testimony on its conclusions confirmed Battista's earlier pessimism about the project, particularly with regard to remaining technical problems and escalating costs.[17]

It should be noted, however, that AMRAAM did have advocates on Capitol Hill, most notably on the staff of the Senate Armed Services Committee. Among them, the military need to replace aging Sparrow missiles with AMRAAM was understood as urgent. Had it not been for this countervailing force in the Senate, absent strongly expressed member sentiment, Battista may well have been able to kill the program outright.

Congressman Smith Begins an Independent Review

As AMRAAM's difficulties began to surface in 1984, Representative Denny Smith (R-Ore.), a highly decorated Air Force fighter pilot, began an investigation of his own. Smith had no significant defense interests in his district, nor was he a member of either the Armed Services or Appropriations committees having jurisdiction over AMRAAM. In an effort "to make a difference," as he put it, Smith devoted personal staff resources to his own investigation and eventually initiated several GAO audits of the program.

Smith's initial and fruitless efforts to influence the process through informal telephone calls to contacts in the DOD were abandoned in favor of formal letters and an increasingly successful press conference and media strategy to assure the greater likelihood of a DOD response. Formal congressional letters to the secretary of defense or assistant secretary for acquisitions cannot be treated in the same fashion as informal telephone calls. Letters create a "paper trail," and a written response from the DOD is tantamount to a formal policy statement that must be carefully crafted and "cleared" through the chain of command.

Smith's numerous letters and widely reported statements created a good deal of angst in the AMRAAM program office, and they received careful attention in the Office of the Secretary of the Air Force. Each letter, coming and going, had to be considered as both a policy event and a press event. The Air Force response, in the view of Smith and his staff, was "to stonewall us" then to come forward with apparent "full briefings" on the program only "to omit the critical numbers and test results" when they did so. Smith knew of these omissions both because of his own expertise in the area and because he too had "moles" inside the Pentagon. As often as not, he had the relevant data and answers even before the Air Force briefed him.

General Accounting Office Audits

In response to the requests of Congressman Smith and, in addition, Chairman Les Aspin of the House Armed Services Committee, the GAO conducted a series of audits of AMRAAM program performance and cost. Eventually this led to the maintenance of a continuing GAO audit force on-site at Eglin Air Force Base and the publication of one or two reports specifically on AMRAAM every year since the early 1980s.

GAO reports repeatedly pointed up the technical difficulties involved in AMRAAM's development: lagging schedules, escalating costs, and, more recently, field test failures and reliability problems. The DOD appears generally to take the view that GAO is, as one long-term observer put it, "the enemy." GAO's on-site presence is tolerated, but audit findings are refuted by the DOD, where possible, on a line-by-line basis. Otherwise there is a tendency in the DOD to regard them with derision or studious indifference.

An Approaching "Nunn-McCurdy" Breach

In 1983 AMRAAM was hardly the only military acquisitions program to suffer from serious cost overruns as the result of overly optimistic estimates and technical development problems. In an effort to identify and curb some of the worst of these difficulties, Senator Sam Nunn (D-Ga.) and Congressman Dave McCurdy (D-Okla.) successfully advanced the Unit Cost Reports

("Nunn-McCurdy") amendment to the defense acquisitions statute in 1983.

Under terms of the Nunn-McCurdy amendment, any increase of more than 25 percent in the baseline cost estimate of an acquisitions program requires the secretary of defense to certify to Congress within sixty days that (1) the acquisitions program is essential to national security; (2) there are no equivalent alternatives to the program; (3) new estimates for the program's acquisition unit costs are reasonable; and (4) the management structure of the program is adequate to control unit costs.[18]

The *certification* approach to weapons acquisitions cost containment reflected an increasing congressional realization that unit costs of weapons had escalated in virtually every program. In 1979, for example, the House Government Operations Committee reported:

> Since 1969 the initial (planning) estimate [for weapons systems acquisitions] has turned out to be approximately 100 percent below the actual costs of major systems. The later, more refined, development cost estimate given Congress prior to full-scale development has proven to be approximately 50 percent below actual procurement costs.
>
> The review by the Subcommittee failed to find one example where the Department of Defense accurately estimated or overestimated the cost of any major weapon system. And once initial funds have been provided, it was found that a program is terminated only when the most extreme cost increases have occurred.[19]

On learning of a likely 25 percent increase in the AMRAAM program in late 1983, Secretary of Defense Caspar Weinberger responded, according to various observers: "We are not going to have a Nunn-McCurdy breach." Accordingly, Weinberger ordered three separate "blue-ribbon" committees to conduct a full review of AMRAAM *operational requirements,* all aspects of AMRAAM *design and production,* and *possible alternatives.* Within a month the secretary approved continuation of the project and promised Congress that the missile would meet appropriate cost and performance guidelines. In midsummer 1985 the AMRAAM productivity enhancement program was established, and at that time Assistant Secretary for Research, Development, and Logistics Thomas E. Cooper announced some twenty changes in design that would reduce costs significantly. In addition, the Air Force extended the full-scale development stage from fifty to seventy-nine months.

Operational Test and Evaluation Unit Established

As the defense buildup of the early 1980s began in earnest, congressional interest in weapons quality and effectiveness paralleled concerns about cost containment. Amid numerous reports of often scandalously inadequate preproduction testing of weapons systems, Congress established the Operational Test and Evaluation unit (OT&E) in the DOD, to be headed by a presidential appointee. The director of the OT&E was to prescribe, monitor, coordinate, and analyze all DOD policies and procedures for the conduct of operational tests and evaluations, reporting findings on all major defense acquisitions programs to the secretary of defense and to the House and Senate Armed Services committees. The director was also charged with review and recommendation to the secretary of defense on all budgetary and financial matters relating to operational test and evaluation.

The Office of the Secretary of Defense made an early and reportedly successful effort to co-opt the small OT&E staff into its far larger operation. In the view of a variety of Pentagon observers, the OT&E consequently had "little or no effect" on AMRAAM testing. Congressional observers complained that the OT&E had been "a great disappointment." Nonetheless, by the late 1980s the OT&E was delegated specific test and performance oversight responsibilities for AMRAAM, which could and did delay decisions to increase production.

Competition in Contracting

In 1984 Congress passed the Competition in Contracting Act (CICA; P.L. 98–369) to increase competition among weapons system manufacturers. This, it was believed in many quarters, would increase cost effectiveness and, ultimately, assure the development of better weapons systems. In the AMRAAM case, a commitment to contractor competition for the development contract and dual sourcing of missile production was made by both Congress and the Air Force at the outset of the project. Well before passage of the CICA, much less the completed operational development of AMRAAM, the Air Force had contracted with the Raytheon Company as a coproducer of AMRAAM (along with the developing contractor, Hughes Aircraft Company) on the contention that dual sourcing would reduce overall program costs through competition and associated producibility-enhancement measures. Critics contend, however, that production by only two companies cannot assure "true competition," and that little can be expected in the way of cost containment through this measure.

Certifications Required of the Secretary of Defense

In late 1985 House Armed Services Committee senior staff member Battista successfully challenged DOD projections on Air Force cost, producibility, and reliability projections to the point that the House Committee eliminated AMRAAM from the National Defense Authorization Act for FY 86.[20] Because the Senate Armed Services Committee report continued to support authorization for FY 86,[21] the critical battle over AMRAAM's continued existence centered on the defense authorization conference committee.

What followed there was predominantly a staff-to-staff conference committee struggle over the program's fate; however, Senator Edward Kennedy (D-Mass.) was said to weigh in personally regarding the importance of AMRAAM to the Air Force and to Raytheon, the second-source production contractor located in Massachusetts. The compromise outcome of the conference committee made further authorization of AMRAAM dependent upon certification by 1 March 1986 by the secretary of defense that

- the AMRAAM design was complete;
- system performance had not been degraded from the original development specifications, including a 1985 development concept amendment;
- the flight test program had been revised to incorporate the maximum number of qualified and flight-tested design changes to reduce costs, under a fixed-cost research, development, and testing contract with Hughes Aircraft, set at $556.6 million;
- total production cost of 17,000 AMRAAM missiles for the Air Force would not exceed $5.2 billion (FY 84 dollars); and
- the Navy would receive 7000 copies of AMRAAM at a total cost of $1.8 billion.[22]

Battista's openly expressed intention was to kill the program, whereas that of his Senate counterpart (and former Navy jet pilot), Carl Smith, was to save it intact. The compromise requiring certification at the secretarial level, Battista believed, would make it impossible for the Air Force and the secretary to proceed in good faith, because he thought that the secretary could not "truthfully" meet the certification requirements. Smith, having checked, thought differently.

Secretary Weinberger certified AMRAAM in all of the required respects on the eve of the 1 March deadline.[23] According to numerous Air Force and DOD sources, cost assumptions were altered on what one termed a "lie-until-you-believe" basis. Although there were dissenting voices, the secretary was officially advised by the Air Force to certify the program and did so. The Cost Analysis Improvement Group (CAIG) of the DOD, which had earlier advised that AMRAAM estimates were unrealistic, now begrudgingly went along with assumptions and resulting numbers believed by insiders at the time to be just as unrealistic. As one former CAIG official views it, the cost-certification requirement was like "shutting the barn door after the animals had already escaped. The situation was well out of hand, and certification was required by Congress to posture and to make it appear as if they were performing the role of public guardian."

Cost Cap and Required Reports

Following Secretary Weinberger's certification of AMRAAM design readiness and cost, and repeated challenges to those certifications by Battista,[24] the House Armed Services Committee required Air Force test reports to Congress on AMRAAM missiles that incorporated producibility enhancements and placed an overall *cost cap* on the AMRAAM program of $7 billion in FY 84 dollars.[25] With only minor adjustments, the Senate acceded to the House provisions.[26] This "cap" on overall AMRAAM costs has been followed by a series of House and Senate Appropriations committees' expressions of concern regarding costs, directions, and limits on both current-year fiscal outlays and numbers of missiles allowed into production.[27]

The Air Force and the DOD have complied with clear directives to make tests and transmit reports, but critics point to problems in test assumptions and reliability. Faced with explicit cost caps and statutory appropriations limits, the Air Force and the DOD have complied with the law. Experienced service and DOD personnel point out, however, that although such measures do "work," they are almost certain to yield results that are unanticipated and undesired by those who impose them: long-run unit cost and total cost increases, distorted and unrealistic assumptions, corner-cutting by contractors, reduced weapon capabilities, increased refitting costs, delivery delays, loss of development-production concurrency, and so forth.

A Question of Credibility — The Air Force and the DOD

Implicit in the AMRAAM case from nearly the beginning was the question of Air Force credibility under increasing pressure of the congressional oversight system and the media. Even the most senior Air Force spokesmen, such as Assistant Secretary Thomas Cooper, had to admit that in "the late 1970's ... costs that were projected for AMRAAM were horribly optimistic."[28] Others deeply involved in Air Force estimations for AMRAAM and other programs were more blunt:

> *A former uniformed officer privy to the 1970s estimation process:*
> "I saw the cost numbers they [program office cost estimators] came up with, and they were about like mine. But they weren't allowed to use the realistic numbers. I couldn't believe the technical and cost people could stand behind the numbers they put out. But then success is understood as getting the program approved."
>
> *An Air Force civilian official:*
> "It is the way the Air Force does business. The Air Force lies; Congress knows we lie. If everyone told the truth, the one liar would have the advantage. Studied lying is necessary to sell programs to Congress.... The Navy has some really proficient liars."[29]
>
> *A Defense Department official:*
> "There's been a long history of systematic growth in cost differences between publicly marketed estimates and actual costs. The people in the Air Force and the DOD are not telling the truth."

Congressional perspectives on AMRAAM cost estimation by and large were equally cynical, though perhaps more calloused in understanding a system that, whatever its faults, generally "works":

> *A former House staff specialist:*
> "The whole system is built around, 'Cover it up; don't tell the Hill.' . . . It's just a game; they lie, we know it, and they know we know it."
> *An administrative assistant and former defense specialist in the House:*
> "The Pentagon is afraid to admit problems to Congress for fear of losing funding. . . . Their level of paranoia is high, tending to see constructive criticism as a devastating body blow."
> *A Senate committee staff member:*
> "As is almost always the case, the Air Force came up with an analysis that justified the project, and [Secretary of Defense] Weinberger signed off on just about anything the services wanted. . . . But all told the system works. It doesn't work the way people think it works, but it does work."

It cannot be suggested, however, that there is anything like a uniformity of views on the ethical questions raised immediately and repeatedly in tracing the AMRAAM case. Whether in the Pentagon or on the Hill, both the facts and effects of military service "lying" in weapons acquisitions were contested:

> *A House member:*
> "The Air Force has been very good at briefing—the whole load of hay. . . . Now we're in a horrible mess; civilians realize that the military had been lying to them—hope and wishes triumphed over realism."
> *An experienced DOD civilian analyst:*
> "In the AMRAAM program, people were exaggerating, withholding information, not presenting material in an attempt to provide full clarity. I don't consider it lying exactly, but it is reprehensible behavior."
> *A former military program manager:*
> "The system doesn't permit the truth. I've lied. To get a program through, you have to promise more than you know you can deliver."
> *A senior Air Force officer, now retired:*
> "One man's lie is another man's uncertainty or optimism."

Notwithstanding a diversity of views on this troubling concern, Air Force credibility and likely veracity of its cost and other projections on AMRAAM were at issue from the outset. The following colloquy between Air Force Assistant Secretary Thomas Cooper and the House Armed Services Committee's Anthony Battista in 1986 is illustrative:

> *Dr. Cooper:* In some camps, AMRAAM has been made out a disaster, and has a terrible cost record, and I don't think that is the case. Last year,

we told you there has been some cost growth in it. Mr. Battista was sitting where Mr. Bayer was 6 years ago [in 1980] when the Air Force said in 1978 dollars, they thought they could build an AMRAAM missile for $68,000 a copy.... You laughed at that....

Since 1982, we have been advertising a unit price in 1978 dollars of about $145,000 a copy. That has been briefed to the committee.... As you saw the numbers on the board, we showed you what the unit cost was in 1982, we showed you what we are estimating the unit cost to be in 1986 [$151,000 in 1978 dollars]. They are within a few percentages of each other....

Mr. Battista: Now, Tom, ... I will make you a prediction you will never buy that missile for the numbers you have up on that chart.... Now, you know as well as I do that you won't be here, I won't be here, Secretary Weinberger won't be here, when that program comes in at what it is really going to cost. I still contend you are going to spend $750,000 a copy on that missile.... I have got the internal data from both contractors.... I will take the standard labor hour rate, multiply it by the estimated number of hours, I get higher prices than you have on this chart. I have also got the bill of materials....

Dr. Cooper: We haven't built the first one yet.

Mr. Battista: I am telling you what I have got downstairs. I have got the bill of materials from both contractors. I am telling you, you are not going to build that missile for that kind of money.[30]

In mid-1990, at a point when military acquisitions budgets were clearly on a down slide, a leading aviation industry journal flatly stated the case for a new approach to service credibility in an open letter directed to newly installed members of the Joint Chiefs of Staff: "Mounting instances of misleading statements and withholding information from Congress and the press have undermined the military's credibility at a time when it is needed most.... The attitude of the military toward the public, Congress and the press is ingrained from the top down. The tone you set will be followed by your subordinates.... In this tough fiscal climate, you have little choice. If you are not forthcoming in arguing your case and supporting it with timely and accurate data, you cannot expect a fair hearing from Congress."[31]

Effects of Congressional Intervention
and Executive Response

Results for Policy

Policy directives contained in the initial delegation on AMRAAM from Congress were not followed by vigilant oversight, nor were the results of these directives notably successful. Joint Air Force–Navy program development specified by Congress did result in the establishment of a "joint" program office; however, Navy participation in the program was little more than "window dressing" for what was clearly an Air Force program. The prototyping and dual-sourcing requirements, also specified by the original congressional delegation, oriented the development competition and production plan of the Air Force from the first. Competitive prototyping requirements are widely believed to have been fairly administered, resulting in a development contract award based on merit. Nevertheless, experienced observers from various institutional perspectives regard the current prototyping or "Milestone" process for weapons development to be ineffective in containing the expenditure of large sums of public money on dubious programs. It is widely believed that once a prototype weapons system passes "Milestone Zero" (program initiation/mission-needs decision phase) and then "Milestone One" (concept demonstration/validation decision phase) in a multistage process, it is thereafter almost impossible to stop. In addition, the results of the dual-sourcing policy in cost savings through competition at the production phase of AMRAAM have not achieved earlier predictions. Congressional oversight of AMRAAM, however, has concentrated on matters other than those directed in the initial delegation to support the program.

The concurrency of AMRAAM development and production has been preserved by the Air Force as a result of its initial contract with Hughes Aircraft Company, despite continuing congressional concerns about the risks of concurrency for cost containment and weapons effectiveness. Although Congress could not revoke the Air Force contract with Hughes after the fact, to put AMRAAM on a fly-before-you-buy basis, it required funding for the qualification of a dual-source production contractor (in this case, the Raytheon Company) on the assumption that costs could be controlled through competition. It could also limit annual outlays and purchase numbers for completed missiles. This has been done repeatedly in the appropriations process; however, the almost immediate administrative rejoinder is to lay unit and total production cost increases on the congressional doorstep. In turn congressional analysts point out the limited utility of purchasing cheaper missiles that won't yet fly, requiring expensive refitting later.

Congressional techniques such as certifications, cost caps, and fiscal-year production quotas delayed the government's purchase of unperfected missiles and reduced annual outlays. Statutory cost caps and quotas appeared to be particularly effective because they established legally enforceable limits. Certification requirements, although not without effect, appeared to present a greater challenge to individual and institutional integrity than to decision-making authority. Some view "certifications" as a way for Congress to avoid making the tough decision to kill a program or as a means of finding political compromise. In any case such tactics opened the door to debates over responsibility for the inevitable delays and cost increases to follow.

Results for Management

Increasing congressional attention to and involvement in the AMRAAM program is likely to have encouraged the Air Force to place a higher priority on the program's managerial expertise and continuity. Air Force appointment of Colonel Thomas Ferguson as AMRAAM program director in 1984 coincided with the drawing of congressional attention to the program's difficulties. For the first time since the program's inception, it would have continuity of leadership for a four-year period.

Congressional involvement in AMRAAM raised the program's visibility, which in turn focused greater and higher-level attention on the program in both the Air Force and the DOD. Sustained attention of the Armed Services and Appropriations committees to specific problems and funding of AMRAAM inevitably elevated the priority of the program on the upper-echelon understanding that it might otherwise be lost.

Increased congressional involvement in the AMRAAM program required consequential expenditures of time and effort by program officers and ranking officials in the Office of the Secretary of the Air Force and the Office of the Secretary of Defense. After congressional deauthorization of AMRAAM was threatened in 1985, the Air Force and DOD hierarchies gave substantially more attention to managerial aspects of the program as well as to an increased public relations effort. Various participants conclude that the producibility enhancement process came in direct response to congressional involvement and cost questioning. However, others contend that the Air Force recognized its problems and took independent measures to correct them.

Results for Institutional Relations

Air Force anticipation of negative congressional reactions to realistic estimates of AMRAAM development needs contributed to the service's overoptimism and deceit with regard to technical problem-solving cost projections. The Air Force has its own cynicism with regard to congressional sensitivities, motivations, and intelligence. Congressional reaction is generally anticipated to be negative toward any new program unless it can be presented in such a way as to acknowledge only minimal costs with high payoffs for individual districts. The initial Air Force unit-cost estimation for AMRAAM at about $60,000 per copy (less than a tenth of the current-year purchase price) and the conscious positioning of some 397 AMRAAM subcontractors in twenty-seven states reflect such assumptions.

The Air Force goal to move ahead with AMRAAM at all costs severely compromised the service's honesty and integrity values. Unfortunately, such values run headlong into constant pressures on military officials, particularly during peacetime, to have "their system" succeed as an imperative of career advancement. Both currently serving and retired Air Force and DOD officials interviewed in the course of this study were troubled by a weapons acquisition system that informally, though often not so subtly, demands that they "convince themselves," as one put it, "of a whole new brand of truth." Adjusting to this may involve extreme forms of rationalization, cynicism, or resignation to dishonesty. Whatever the reaction, Air Force morale and sense of high purpose are almost inevitably damaged.

Technically trained and highly experienced congressional members and staff were able to perform more effective and influential roles in AMRAAM's development than those without such backgrounds. Many congressional officials had both the position and opportunity to become active in the AMRAAM case; those who did so most effectively used expertise and experience more than position as aspects of leverage.

The Air Force's overoptimistic reports and misinformation to Congress increased congressional skepticism and reduced Air Force credibility as the AMRAAM case unfolded. Congressional skepticism, particularly that of the House Armed Services Committee and Congressman Smith, was expressed on the record and in press conferences repeatedly. This incredulity was compounded by the Air Force's own seemingly disingenuous presentations of cost data.

Distrust of Air Force information prompted congressional members and staff to contract-out for independent analysis of the AMRAAM program, initiate GAO audits, seek out "moles" within the Air Force, and to develop information resources with Air Force development and production contractors. Failing to receive what appeared to them to be a straight report from the Air Force, interested congressional participants had a rich base of contacts and information resources to which they could turn. Observers repeatedly reported that Battista and Smith in the Congress had better data on AMRAAM development than either the Office of the Secretary of Defense or the Office of the Secretary of the Air Force.

Decreased Air Force credibility in connection with the AMRAAM program provided congressional incentives to apply additional cost and information controls on program reporting and performance. The House Armed Services Committee initiated virtually all of the control techniques directed at AMRAAM, and in case after case congressional distrust of the Air Force was plainly expressed at the time and on the record. Informally, respondents explained that the credibility of the Air Force—and other services as well —had been badly compromised across a wide range of acquisitions programs. As a result, they said, such measures could be expected in the AMRAAM case and elsewhere. Arguably, a more forthcoming information exchange between the Air Force and its congressional overseers might have reduced both the problem and the congressionally understood need for controls. Many participants conclude, however, that a change in organizational cultures must precede any genuine reform of the defense acquisitions process. At the very least, cultural differences—between the uniformed services, the DOD civilian acquisitions hierarchy, and Congress—as they affect the roles of each of these institutions in the process, must be better understood on all sides.

Conclusions

The general purpose of the initial congressional delegation that began the AMRAAM program was unambiguous, and the level of specificity required of policy implementation—excepting the joint-development and prototyping requirements—was relatively low. Member and staff interest in becoming deeply involved in the details of policy and program development at an early stage was quite limited. This level of concern largely coincided with the perception of AMRAAM as, in the Department of Defense context, a relatively modest sized program with initial, informal projections for a total buy of approximately $1.4 to $1.5 billion (in contrast to $14–$15 billion in 1990).

The policy goal of developing an advanced-capability replacement for the radar-guided Sparrow missile was never challenged by congressional direct involvement in policy implementation and program development. The Air Force's needs assessment that a fast, beyond-visual-range, fire-and-forget, air-to-air tactical missile was required to meet air warfare threats of the 1980s and 1990s was never seriously questioned by Congress or its staff even as the intensity of the Cold War diminished. Congressional involvement consistently related to uncontained costs, technical problems, and reliability deficiencies of the AMRAAM system and to potentially more feasible alternatives, such as an advanced redesign of the existing Sparrow missile.

Congressional involvement in the AMRAAM program drew wider attention to cost and technical problems with the system and raised the visibility of the system both in the Air Force and in the DOD generally. Congressional attention, expressed in a variety of intervention tactics, threatened AMRAAM as an Air Force program. In turn this threat stimulated the service and the DOD to rally in support of the program managerially and technically as well as politically. Although AMRAAM was a relatively small program, it was the fundamental "bullet in the gun" of the Air Force's tactical fighter fleet, all the more so as the Sparrow and Sidewinder missiles were being phased out of production. Realization of a threat at this level broadened concern within the Air Force generally and increased the priority of attention to the program at higher levels in both the Air Force and DOD hierarchies.

The policy focus of participants in the AMRAAM case was relatively exclusive to this weapon system and largely did not, in the context of the case, widen to a broader regard for related or overall weapons system priorities, costs, and resources. With only an occasional side glance toward the potential alternative to AMRAAM in a redesigned Sparrow system, the primary context of the AMRAAM case was the AMRAAM system. No decision structures, either in Congress or the executive, appeared to be available for evaluation of AMRAAM with respect to competing priorities even in the field of tactical air warfare. Larger strategic considerations appeared simply to be taken as "givens," and not worthy of related concern. Also held aside were impending and severe budgetary constraints, which would clearly affect a wide variety of weapons systems including AMRAAM.

Epilogue

As of April 1991, the contractors' missile deliveries were behind schedule, and many of the problems that delayed production had not been fully resolved. In response to these delays, the Air Force extended the delivery schedules. A month later the Defense Acquisitions Board concluded that additional testing was needed before the missile could enter full-rate production. In June 1991 the General Accounting Office corroborated the DAB's conclusion, reporting that, although significant improvements in performance and reliability of the weapon had been achieved, still further tests should be successfully completed before beginning full-rate production.[32]

Correspondingly, the initial Air Force–Navy budget for the program for FY 92 requested $997 million for 1191 missiles. In April 1991 that request was reduced by $115 million and 300 missiles, reflecting contractor delays in deliveries. The actual appropriation approved by Congress for FY 92 was $739.9 million for 891 missiles.[33] In addition, subsequent congressional authorization report language required the Operational Test and Evaluation unit to certify that AMRAAM is combat ready before permitting full-rate production. It should be noted that the authorization legislation for FY 90 and FY 91 required the OT&E to certify not only test procedures and results (its initial statutory responsibility) but also the status of production and design issues. The expanded scope of OT&E activities was scaled back by congressional authorizations for FY 92 and FY 93.

Timeline of Major Events in the AMRAAM Case

October 1975 — Air Force–Navy tactical working group defines requirements for 1985 and beyond.

July 1976 — Congress approves missile's development in the Defense Appropriations Act of 1977; requires a joint-service (Air Force–Navy) program.

May 1978 — Senate Armed Services Committee recommends DOD review of missile warhead lethality before prototype program is begun.

November 1978 — Secretary of Defense (Sec Def) approves program's transition to validation stage.

February 1979 — Hughes Aircraft and Raytheon begin thirty-three-month validation phase.

December 1981 — Air Force awards Hughes a fifty-four-month, fixed, price-incentive-fee, full-scale development contract.

April 1984 — House DOD Authorization Act report for 1985 selects AMRAAM for "high value" transitioning review—from development to production readiness. House Armed Services Committee contracts with a private consulting firm for review.

January 1985 — As AMRAAM program approaches "Nunn-McCurdy" limits for program cost overruns, Sec Def appoints "blue-ribbon" panels for program review.

September 1985 — Conference report on Defense Authorization Act for FY 85 recommends funding to qualify second-source production of AMRAAM. $150 million cut from Air Force authorization request for AMRAAM.

December 1985 — Hughes and Raytheon awarded contracts to improve producibility.

National Defense Authorization Act for 1986 requires Sec Def to certify to the House and Senate Armed Services committees completion of AMRAAM design; maintenance of system-performance specifications; procured missile performance in accord with development specifications; and price caps for delivery of completed missiles.

1986 — National Defense Authorization Act for FY 87 establishes "cost cap" (in 1984 dollars) for procurement of 24,000 missiles.

June 1987 — Sec Def approves funding for initial low-rate production.

May 1988 — Defense Acquisitions Board (DAB), after review, approves production of 423 full-capacity missiles; delays Air Force request on long lead-time items.

September 1988 — DAB's Conventional Systems Committee decides that AMRAAM is not ready for full-scale production.

June 1989 — Conventional Systems Committee postpones decision on

	the fabrication of 906 missiles until further reliability data can be obtained.
September 1989	General Accounting Office recommends that the Sec Def defer authorization of AMRAAM full-rate production until tests show missile has met performance and reliability requirements and that contractors can produce quality missiles.
1989	National Defense Authorization Act for FY 90 restricts obligation of funds for full-range AMRAAM production until director of Operational Test and Evaluation unit certifies testing required for full-rate production has been completed and that AMRAAM has met all established performance requirements and has achieved design and configuration stability.
1989	House Appropriations Committee recommends keeping AMRAAM at an initial low rate of production; reduces Air Force requests by 635 missiles and $215 million.
February 1990	In the wake of continued performance failures, the Air Force suspends acceptance of delivery of further AMRAAM missiles.
June 1990	Missile delivery resumed but at a reduced rate.

Notes

1. P.L. 94361 (14 July 1976).

2. Senate Committee on Armed Services, Subcommittee on Tactical Air, *Hearings: Department of Defense Authorization for Fiscal Year 1979*, 95th Cong., 2d sess., 5 April 1978, 5251.

3. General Accounting Office, *Missile Procurement: AMRAAM Cost Growth and Schedule Delays*, GAO/NSIAD-87-78 (Washington, D.C., March 1987).

4. Tony Capaccio, "DAB Says No to Full-Rate AMRAAM Production," *Defense Week*, 25 May 1991.

5. House Committee on Armed Services, *Hearings on Military Posture and H.R 10929*, pt. 3, 95th Cong., 2d sess., 27 February 1978. Initially, there were those in the Navy who would resist the Air Force's lead in AMRAAM in favor of a reconfigured Sparrow missile, but by 1977 the Navy acquiesced to a joint program under Air Force management at Eglin Air Force Base. Throughout the program's development, the Navy provided an officer who would serve as deputy program manager of the project, yet there was no question that the Air Force was "senior partner" in the venture. Also, from the first the Air Force's projected purchase of AMRAAM missiles would be nearly twice that of the Navy.

6. Department of Defense, Directive No. 5000.4, 30 October 1980.

7. House Committee on Armed Services, *Hearings on Military Posture and H.R. 10929.*

8. AMRAAM per-unit cost estimated on the basis of total program costs in 1978 dollars was set at $202,000. Air Force, *Selected Acquisitions Report,* AIM-120A, 31 December 1982.

9. See, for example, House Committee on Armed Services, *Hearings: Department Authorization and Oversight; Research, Development, Test, and Evaluation—Title II,* 99th Cong., 2d sess., February–March 1986.

10. General Accounting Office, *Missile Procurement: AMRAAM's Reliability Is Improving, But Production Challenges Remain,* GAO/NSW-91-209 (Washington, D.C., June 1991), 10.

11. General Accounting Office, *Missile Procurement,* 19.

12. Peter Cary, "The Pentagon's Misguided Missile," *U.S. News and World Report,* 1 May 1989, 33.

13. House Committee on Armed Services, *Report: Department of Defense Authorization Act, 1985,* 98th Cong., 2d sess., 19 April 1984, 124–25.

14. See for example, Senate Committee on Armed Services, *Report: Omnibus Defense Authorization Act, 1985,* 98th Cong., 2d sess., 31 May 1984, no. 98-500.

15. See Mathew D. McCubbins and Thomas Schwartz, "Congressional Oversight Overlooked: Police Patrols versus Fire Alarms," *American Journal of Political Science* 28 (February 1984): 165–79.

16. Nick Kotz, *Wild Blue Yonder: Money, Politics, and the B-1 Bomber* (Princeton: Princeton University Press, 1988), 185.

17. House Committee on Armed Services, *Hearings: Defense Department Authorization and Oversight for Fiscal Year 1987,* 99th Cong., 2d sess., 5, 6, and 7 February 1986, 17.

18. 10 U.S.C.A §2433.

19. House Committee on Government Operations, *Report: Inaccuracy of Department of Defense Weapons Acquisition Cost Estimates,* 99th Cong., 1st sess., 1985, no. 96-656, 2.

20. House Committee on Armed Services, *Report: Department of Defense Authorization Act, 1986,* 99th Cong., 1st sess., 10 May 1985, no. 99-81, 102–3; 126–27.

21. Senate Committee on Armed Services, *Report: National Defense Authorization Act for Fiscal Year 1985,* 99th Cong., 1st sess., 29 April 1985, no. 99-41, 105–6.

22. House Committee of Conference, *Conference Report: Department of Defense Authorization Act, 1986,* 99th Cong., 1st sess., 29 July 1985, no. 99-235, 31.

23. Letter to Les Aspin, chairman, House Committee on Armed Services, 28 February 1986.

24. See House Committee on Armed Services, *Hearings: Defense Department Authorization and Oversight for Fiscal Year 1987; Hearings: Defense De-*

partment Authorization and Oversight; Research, Development, Test, and Evaluation — Title II.

25. House Committee on Armed Services, *Report: National Defense Authorization Act for Fiscal Year 1987,* 99th Cong., 2d sess., 25 July 1986, 91.

26. House Committee of Conference, *Conference Report: National Defense Authorization Act for Fiscal Year 1987,* 99th Cong., 2d sess., 14 October 1986, 384–85.

27. See, for example, House Committee of Conference, *Conference Report: Making Continuing Appropriations for Fiscal Year 1987,* 99th Cong., 2d sess., 15 October 1986, No. 99-1005, 532; *Conference Report: Making Further Continuing Appropriations for the Fiscal Year Ending September 30, 1988,* 100th Cong., 1st sess., 22 December 1987, No. 100-498, 613; *Conference Report: Making Appropriations for the Department of Defense,* 100th Cong., 2d sess., 28 September 1988, No. 100-1002, 60–61.

28. Testimony before the Senate Subcommittee of the Committee on Appropriations, *Hearings: Department of Defense Appropriations for Fiscal Year 1986,* 99th Cong., 1st sess., 1986, 653.

29. Less than a year after this assessment was uttered, the Navy announced the firing of two admirals and a captain who had managed the service's A-12 "stealth" bomber program for allowing top Pentagon officials, including Secretary of Defense Richard B. Cheney, to believe that the program was "on schedule, on cost and on track." Rick Atkinson and Barton Gellman, "Navy Fires 3 Working on Top Jet," *Washington Post,* 15 December 1990; Office of the Secretary, Department of the Navy, "Memorandum for the Secretary of Defense: A-12 Administrative Inquiry—Information Memorandum," 29 November 1990.

30. House Committee on Armed Services, *Hearings: Defense Department Authorization and Oversight for Fiscal Year 1987,* 656–60.

31. "Advisory to New Service Chiefs," *Aviation Week and Space Technology,* 30 July 1990, 7.

32. General Accounting Office, *Missile Procurement: AMRAAM's Reliability Is Improving, But Production Challenges Remain,* 3–4.

33. House Committee of Conference, *Conference Report: Defense Appropriations for Fiscal Year 1992,* 102d Cong., 1st sess., 1991, No. 102-328.

9

Improving Military Coordination: The Goldwater-Nichols Reorganization of the Department of Defense

Thomas L. McNaugher
with Roger L. Sperry

Introduction

In 1986 Congress reorganized the Department of Defense. The Goldwater-Nichols Department of Defense Reorganization Act of 1986 (P.L. 99–433) touched almost every facet of the department's operations, from budgeting to strategy making to planning.[1] At the core of the reorganization, however, lay changes in the nation's military command structure, concern for which had given initial impetus to the overall defense reorganization effort. The act enhanced the power of the chairman of the Joint Chiefs of Staff (JCS) relative to the three service chiefs and the commandant of the Marine Corps. The chairman alone, rather than the JCS as a whole, was made principal military adviser to the president. He was also given greater control over the selection of officers to work on the joint staff, and greater power over the selection of issues they would examine. Meanwhile, commanders of the nation's combatant commands, like the Southern Command (SOUTHCOM) and the Central Command (CENTCOM), most of which deploy components from two or more military services, were given substantially greater authority over service elements within their commands. Against the history of congressional efforts to organize an effective joint military structure out of the nation's separate military services, these were truly significant changes.

Equally significant was the manner in which the 1986 reforms were passed. Historically, Congress had been wary of legislation that consolidated power in an executive branch agency, preferring instead to create divisions in such agencies that could be exploited to retain legislative control.

Nowhere was this more the case than with the military services, where traditional "divide-and-rule" tactics had been buttressed by a strong aversion to anything resembling a "general staff." Thus, the historical pattern of reform in the realm of military command structure generally involved congressional efforts to dilute ambitious executive branch proposals to consolidate power over the military services. In the 1980s, by contrast, Congress pushed for such a consolidation against the wishes of the secretary of defense. Indeed, tension in this period of defense reform was less between the executive and legislative branches than between the Defense Department, on the one hand, and Congress and the White House, on the other—despite the close friendship between Secretary of Defense Caspar Weinberger and President Ronald Reagan.

How did such a pattern emerge? More broadly, how did Congress come to pass major reforms in an area that had little immediate constituency appeal, and about which few legislators knew very much before 1982? Finally, four years and several military operations later, what can be said about the value of the reforms Congress produced? Before turning to a history of how the Goldwater-Nichols bill was born, this case report places that bill in the context of its predecessors, stretching back to World War II, when the joint chiefs of staff system was first created.

Origins of Structural Reform

The arduous process of structural reform began during World War II, when the United States first sought to encourage or impose cooperation on its separate military services.[2] Wartime experience highlighted the need for cooperation; air, sea, and ground forces often had to work together to achieve maximum effectiveness. But wartime experience also highlighted the difficulty of achieving smooth cooperation among military organizations that had emerged from disparate histories, used different technologies, and operated in starkly different milieus. Whole theaters were carved up to give vent to interservice jealousies.[3] And the Army in particular complained of inadequate support from its sister services, even the Air Corps, which until 1947 remained part of the Army itself.[4] It was clear from the start that cooperation would not come easily.

The so-called unification debate about how best to achieve cooperation began before the war ended, with the military services taking positions that have not changed much in the years since. As a rule, the Army favored centralization of the separate services under a "general staff," headed by a powerful "armed services chief of staff," reflecting the Army's greater dependence on the other services for transport and air support, as well as its historical experience in organizing its own disparate activities under a general staff.[5] The Navy preferred decentralization, reflecting its relatively decentralized approach to managing itself, and probably also a desire to protect the operational independence it acquired from possessing its own ground and air forces.[6] The Air Force took an ambiguous middle ground, supporting the Army's centralizing principles, but largely in return for Army support for its independence as a separate service.

These organizational positions found powerful allies in Congress. To some extent this was a matter of constituency politics, with political positions reflecting the presence in states and congressional districts of shipyards, Army bases, aircraft firms, and so forth. Also reflected in congressional debates was the historical legacy stemming from long years in which separate committees in each house had overseen the War and Navy departments.

But members of Congress were moved to action by grander forces as well. Control of the military is a vital political issue in any country, but perhaps especially in the United States, where citizens have traditionally been deeply suspicious of the military. One example of such suspicions was widespread aversion to the Army's use of the phrase *general staff* in presenting its reorganization proposals. The phrase evoked images of the German general staff, hardly a popular image, especially in the years immediately following World War II. As Congressman William S. Cole (R-N.Y.) told Army Chief of Staff Lawton Collins during hearings held in 1949, "If you folks down there would just forget the words 'staff' and 'general' and call it something else, you wouldn't have anywhere near the trouble you are getting about staffing your people."[7]

At the core of congressional suspicions of military unification lay the fragmented nature of the nation's government and the jealousy with which the legislative and executive branches protected their respective powers. Legislating the consolidation of power in an executive branch agency risks ceding power generally to the executive branch. Congressional power to some degree depends on decentralization in the executive branch because decentralization provides legislators with points of entry through which to gain information about, access to, and leverage over action within the executive. Although this general principle holds true whether power is consolidated in a civilian secretary of defense or a uniformed chairman of the JCS, Congress has been more willing on the whole to grant power to the secretary.[8] It has done so, however, partly because legislators have seen the uniformed service chiefs as a source of counterbalancing power to the defense secretary. The political risks inherent in giving the secretary more power thus have encouraged Congress to protect the power of the service chiefs.

Given these considerations, it is hardly surprising that the logical dictates of wartime experience gave rise to heated debate but tentative and incremental action. As it does with most issues, the nation's political system has "muddled through" on the issue of JCS reform, returning to it again and again in the years since World War II. Landmark bills have been passed— notably the National Security Act of 1947, the Department of Defense Reorganization Act of 1958, and, finally, the Goldwater-Nichols Act of 1986. Between those years, innumerable amendments and smaller legislative actions have dealt with the same issue.

None of this legislation has focused exclusively on the military command structure. Much of it has dealt instead with the power of the civilian secretary of defense, an office created by the National Security Act of 1947. Much of it was also driven by a desire to solve problems in the weapons acquisition process. The Defense Reorganization Act of 1958, in particular, increased the size and power of the secretary's staff (the Office of the Secretary of Defense, or OSD), largely in an attempt to eliminate so-called wasteful duplication among weapons projects.[9] Yet each legislative step also dealt with the military command structure, as legislators and political officials sought, slowly but steadily, to curb remaining vestiges of service independence and interservice rivalry.

On the issue of command structure, debate has focused mainly on the composition and leadership of the Joint Chiefs of Staff. President Franklin D. Roosevelt created his own JCS during the war, and there was little doubt that the organization would be formalized by legislation after the war ended. But this left open critical questions about how the body would function. Should it be a loose collegial body of service chiefs capable of presenting political officials with the widest range of alternative courses of action, as the Navy has generally maintained? Or should it reflect the Army's desire for a more centralized organization, run by a reasonably strong chairman, capable of integrating differing service perspectives into a single coherent strategy? In the years after World War II it became increasingly clear that service chiefs found it inordinately difficult to sacrifice the interests of their own service for the general good, making JCS products the "lowest common denominator," that is, mere amalgamations of all service perspectives. Although this encouraged some reformers to create a still more powerful chairman, others sought to reduce each chief's administrative connection to his service; still others argued in favor of the creation of a joint staff composed of retired senior military leaders drawn from each service.[10]

Related to this issue was the question of who should control the joint staff, which supports the JCS. Critics of the decentralized system have argued that to the extent that the JCS as a whole is able to produce only a "lowest common denominator" (i.e., consensus) product, this is what the staff is left to work with. The joint staff's product thus has tended to be an inferior duplication of work done by the separate service staffs. Under the direction of a strong chairman armed with the power to define staff problems on his own, the argument went, the joint staff would work on integrated strategic problems quite distinct from problems confronting the individual services. The power, and presumably also the status, of the joint staff would rise commensurately.

A separate issue has had to do with the nation's operational commands.

Some of these are so-called specified commands, like the Strategic Air Command, that belong to a single service. Given the growing need for interservice cooperation in projecting force, however, it was inevitable that some of these commands, the so-called unified commands, would draw on components from two or more of the services. Given that the individual services still had valid missions to perform and skills to teach, there was an obvious need to balance authority and responsibility between operational commanders and service chiefs. How this balance was struck depended on the relationship of each to the budget process, to the JCS, and to commanders of service components within each unified command.

A variety of histories tell the story of how the nation's political system has handled these issues in the years since World War II. Here it is enough simply to establish the caution inherent in the approach and the practical results it had. The National Security Act of 1947 established a JCS whose members, the chiefs of the three services (the act made the Army Air Corps into an independent third service), were the principal military advisers to the president, secretary of defense, and the National Security Council. Congress gave the JCS a staff of no more than one hundred officers detailed from the services, but it hewed more closely to the Navy's than to the Army's arguments in refusing to create a chairman of the JCS (CJCS). Indeed, Congress left the services with considerable power by placing each unified command under one or another "sponsoring" service, effectively leaving service chiefs in the chain of command, and also in control of resources.

This set of command arrangements was criticized for its lack of coherence almost as soon as it went into effect. Among others, James V. Forrestal, the first secretary of defense and earlier a strong proponent of the Navy position, complained that the system was unable to provide the kind of integrated military advice he needed to generate a reasonable defense budget. In 1949 Congress, at the urging of President Harry S. Truman, amended the 1947 act to give the JCS a chairman. Contrary to Truman's wishes, however, Congress insisted that the chairman remain weak; he was given neither a vote on the JCS nor command of the operational forces. His role was simply to act as liaison between the JCS and higher-level officials.

Critical of these arrangements during his election campaign, President Dwight D. Eisenhower reorganized the Defense Department (DOD), by administrative fiat rather than by requesting legislation, soon after taking office in 1953. The 1953 Defense Reorganization Plan gave the chairman authority to manage the joint staff and to select officers to be part of it. It also removed the service chiefs from the command chain, which instead ran from the president, through the defense secretary and the military departments to the operational commands—an attempt, as William Lynn puts it, to "emphasize that the primary role of the JCS was to act as a planning and advisory group, not as a command organization."[11]

Eisenhower sought to expand on these themes in 1958, as part of a much broader effort to reorganize the Defense Department that culminated in the Defense Reorganization Act of 1958—the last major legislative reorganization of the DOD until 1986. Yet although the DOD Reorganization Act of 1958 substantially strengthened the power of the civilian secretary and his staff, Congress actually reduced some of the powers Eisenhower had earlier given the chairman of the JCS, rejecting in particular the chairman's independent authority over the joint staff. At Eisenhower's request, Congress removed the service chiefs from command of the unified commands, leaving a chain of command that ran from the president through the secretary of defense to each operational commander. Operational commanders were given operational control over component elements, leaving the services with administrative control. But the service chiefs were inserted into the operational chain "to advise the secretary on military operations and to transmit orders to the commands."[12]

This basic set of arrangements remained in place through the 1980s. Clearly, the 1958 reorganization centralized power in the Defense Department, at least in a relative sense. But it did so almost entirely on the civilian side of the department. This allowed defense secretaries anxious to bring interservice rivalry under control to do so through the exercise of their staff (OSD) rather than through the JCS. Yet this applied more to weapons acquisition than to war planning, which remained largely a military function. During Robert McNamara's tenure as defense secretary (1961–67), for example, the civilian director (later assistant secretary) for systems analysis and the director of defense research and engineering (DDR&E) were given substantial control over service acquisition projects in an effort to eliminate wasteful duplication. So great was service resistance to McNamara's civilian "whiz kids," however, that Republican administrations since then have generally sought to get civilians "off the backs" of the military. Indeed, this promise was part of the Republican platform that brought Reagan to office in 1981. Although interservice rivalry has never ceased to be a problem, the Reagan administration's DOD thus suffered from an unusual amount of it.

The lack of centralization in the Reagan administration's Defense Department helped to focus attention on the nation's military command structure in the 1980s. Clearly, however, the issues were long-standing. Indeed, little of the 1980s debate was new; most of the arguments echoed positions developed in the years just after World War II. What was new was the extent to which Congress was willing to grant considerably more power to the chairman of the Joint Chiefs of Staff and to operational commanders as means of solving residual interservice problems in strategy formulation and weapons acquisition. After years of resisting creation of a "general staff," Congress moved some distance in 1986 toward creating one, at the expense of service chiefs whose prerogatives it had traditionally protected.

Moreover, Congress pushed the consensus forward against the wishes of the secretary of defense in a reversal of the historic pattern in which Congress reacted to and generally diluted ambitious executive branch proposals. The substance of the 1980s debate may not have been new, but both its product and the manner of its production certainly were.

Revisiting the Issue: 1982

The specific impetus for returning yet again to the nation's military command structure came, appropriately enough, from the officer who had spent more time than any other serving on the Joint Chiefs of Staff. General David C. Jones had served as Air Force chief of staff from 1974 to 1978 before becoming chairman of the Joint Chiefs of Staff (CJCS) in 1978, giving him nearly eight years of service on that body when he first voiced his concerns for national military organization in 1981. Jones's first lesson in the organizational problems that afflicted the nation's military had come still earlier, during a tour in Vietnam where he witnessed several different U.S. "air forces"—that of his own service plus the Navy's, the Marine Corps's, and even the Army's rotary wing force—fighting largely separate wars. If a single incident piqued his concern, however, it was the abortive Iranian-hostage rescue mission, conducted under his direction in 1980. The need for absolute secrecy in this case made it impossible to rehearse the operation as a whole, thus leaving the lack of normal interservice training painfully obvious. Jones concluded that the services had to train together in truly joint fashion as a routine matter. And that, he felt, would require considerably more "jointness" at the highest levels of the nation's command structure.

Jones sought to move in this direction on his own, but the very problems he wished to solve blocked his path. The service chiefs who constituted the JCS approved of joint studies and actions unanimously or not at all. Jones thus felt forced to seek approval for reform from those whose power and independence his reforms would curb—hardly a likely prospect. The best Jones could do was to commission at his own initiative a special study group on the subject composed of retired four-star generals from each service and headed by civilian William K. Brehm. The Brehm report, as their findings were termed, supported many of Jones's convictions. It called for creation of the position of vice chairman of the JCS, for example, to "assure maximum continuity in the Chairman's position . . ., free the Chairman to participate more actively in field activities . . ., and relieve the Service Chiefs of the need to play the role of Acting Chairman [in the Chairman's absence]."[13] It also called for modestly strengthening the power of the chair over the chiefs and for improving the quality and focus of the joint staff. Many of these recommendations were picked up and advanced by later studies, and in this sense the Brehm report may be said to have launched the intellectual effort that produced the Goldwater-Nichols reform bill four years later. But the report seems to have had no immediate political effects.

Instead, Jones raised the issue both publicly and within the broader political process. Asked by the editors of the journal *Directors and Boards* to ruminate on his role as "chief executive officer" of the world's largest "corporation," Jones submitted an article that described in some detail the failings of the existing JCS system and the serious flaws these imparted to the nation's military operations. The article appeared in December 1981, and was reprinted the next March in *Armed Forces Journal International*, where it was sure to be seen by the appropriate audience.[14] By that time, however, Jones had dropped his bomb on Capitol Hill. In his last annual appearance before the House Armed Services Committee in January 1982, Jones was asked if he had any parting remarks based on his long experience on the JCS. His reply, summarizing his *Directors and Boards* article, took committee members by surprise, "electrifying" many of them, in the words of a staff member present at the hearing.

It did not, however, electrify Defense Secretary Caspar Weinberger, who was present for the testimony and was also aware of the *Directors and Boards* article. Weinberger's antipathy to reorganizing his department would become clear in subsequent years, but evidently it was already well established in 1982. As Weinberger told Jones, he wanted no distractions in his effort to force the largest defense budget possible through the congressional budget process. He took a dim view of Jones's suggestion that it would be in the administration's interest to show some concern for the efficiency with which defense funds were spent as well as with the dollar amount appropriated. That Weinberger saw Jones as tainted by years of service in the Carter administration no doubt only reinforced the defense secretary's antipathy to Jones's ideas.[15] In practical terms, then, Jones lacked support from the secretary of defense as well as the JCS as a body.

Quick Action in the House

Under these circumstances, the issue had to be addressed on Capitol Hill if it was to be addressed at all, and it was. Soon after Jones delivered his testimony, Congressman Richard White (D-Tex.), chairman of the Investigations Subcommittee of the House Armed Services Committee, launched a series of hearings on the subject of JCS reform. Coming from a committee whose members were initially unfamiliar with defense organizational issues, this move owed much to the effect of Jones's presentation. Perhaps members of the committee, like Jones himself, harbored painful memories of the failed Iranian rescue mission. Still, it probably did not hurt Jones's cause that a recently hired subcommittee staff member was also an expert on defense organization. Before retiring from the Air Force and joining the subcommittee in 1981, Colonel Archie Barrett had been involved in a Carter administration study of the nation's military command structure. The Carter administration never produced a final report on the subject, but Barrett used the data from the Carter administration's study to produce a book of his own on the subject.[16] As time went on, Subcommittee Chairman White also became increasingly interested in and informed about defense organizational issues.

Once under way, the subcommittee hearings generated their own momentum. Testifying soon after the hearings began, Army Chief of Staff General E.C. ("Shy") Meyer echoed Jones's concerns and proposed still more radical reforms to solve them, among them replacing the JCS entirely with a panel of retired senior officers no longer institutionally constrained to represent strictly the views of their own services. In contrast, Navy admirals and Marine Corps generals defended the existing command structure, with then Chief of Naval Operations Admiral Thomas B. Hayward the most outspoken defender of the status quo. But retired admirals and Marine Corps generals could be found among the critics as well. The hearings lasted five months and involved thirty-eight witnesses, most of them former senior DOD and military officials. Although a majority of the witnesses favored some kind of JCS reform, they varied substantially on just what reforms they had in mind; most of the critics favored Jones's proposals or mild variations on them, but a substantial minority favored Meyer's more radical position.[17]

The White subcommittee produced a moderate JCS reform bill over the summer of 1982, and this was approved by voice vote in the House in September. The bill's most striking proposal, that of creating a deputy chairman of the JCS, was mild in comparison to reforms proposed during hearings the previous spring, and also, significantly, in comparison to the Goldwater-Nichols reorganization act that would pass both houses of Congress four years later. In part, this was because subcommittee staffers labored under a very short deadline; by the time the bill passed the House there were only seventeen working days left before the congressional session ended, leaving little time for Senate consideration. A considerable debate had swirled around the FY 83 defense budget, and this also restricted the time available to consider JCS reform. Still, it is doubtful that a more radical reform bill would have passed the House at this point.[18] Whatever the case, few on White's staff thought the issue would subside with House passage of the first piece of legislation. All hoped to return to the issue in the next session of Congress.

The Senate Blockade

If White's first JCS reform bill passed easily through the House, it was partly because House members knew theirs was not a serious vote. Senate opposition to the bill was virtually guaranteed, notably by the opposition of Senate Armed Services Committee Chair John Tower (R-Tex.), a conservative Republican and Navy reservist ill-disposed to rapid action on the issue. Tower held desultory hearings on the subject in December 1982, but no one was surprised when these hearings produced no legislation, nor when Tower refused even to consider the House reform bill during the few days that remained in the congressional session. The 97th Congress ended with expressions of interest but no action on JCS reform.

Although Tower's personal antipathy to JCS reform would become clearer subsequently, the Senate's position on JCS reform at this point cannot be attributed entirely to him. The House bill was not taken seriously. The Senate was not interested in it, one staffer asserted, because it was not an interesting bill, nor even one whose simple provisions required legislative approval.[19] Senators were accustomed to receiving the most outrageous bills from the House, this staffer continued, passed in part because representatives tended to move more quickly than senators, but also in part because the House leadership knew such bills would be dumped in conference. Thus the general feeling in the Senate Armed Services Committee was that JCS reform would come, if at all, only after long and careful consideration—and not in response to a quickly written House bill.

White House Interest

Significantly, at this point the White House may have been more interested in the issue than the Senate. In June 1982 the president's assistant for national security, William Clark, passed a memo to Weinberger suggesting that the president himself was interested in JCS reform, or at least that Weinberger should not be seen to be stonewalling on the issue. In response, Weinberger informed Congressman White on 23 July that he had asked currently serving members of the JCS for their views on the need for reform and would provide their responses by 1 October.[20]

Behind the White House position stood Clark's deputy, Robert C. McFarlane. A retired Marine Corps officer with joint staff experience, McFarlane held views similar to those of General Jones when it came to the failings of the military command structure.[21] He was also no friend of Weinberger's. Having served as counselor to the Department of State during the Reagan administration's first year, McFarlane was aware of tensions already emerging between Weinberger and Congress, and he feared that these might undermine support for the president's ambitious defense program.[22] (Evidently Tower himself shared these sentiments; although he had blocked the early White reform bill, he reportedly advised the White House that it was not in the Defense Department's interest to be perceived as stonewalling on this particular issue.) For both strategic and domestic political reasons, then, McFarlane favored some action on JCS reform and was able to move the White House gently in this direction.

Gestation: 1983–84

Action on JCS reform picked up again soon after the 98th Congress convened in January 1983 and continued episodically over the next two years.

No practical legislation emerged during this period, however, because the constellation of forces highlighted in 1982—House support, Senate opposition —remained intact so long as Tower remained at the head of the Senate Armed Services Committee. Still, these were important years of gestation on both sides of the Hill. The JCS issue had arisen only the year before, after years of dormancy; members of Congress remained relatively uninformed on questions of military organization and slightly uncomfortable legislating on issues of such consequence. What they learned in these years of legislative inaction helped prepare them for the more eventful legislative sessions to follow.

Two seriously flawed military operations that occurred during this period encouraged interest in military organization. One involved the bombing by a Shiite muslim terrorist of a U.S. Marine Corps battalion stationed at the Beirut International Airport. Investigation of both the bombing and bungled U.S. retaliatory air strikes against targets in Lebanon's Bekaa Valley exposed a confused U.S. command structure and a weak JCS, which together helped to produce tragic results. More than this, however, the bombing itself took much of the gloss off the first two years of the Reagan administration's defense-spending surge. As Archie Barrett of the House Armed Services Committee put it, "Here we had the largest defense buildup in history and it looked like we were powerless, disarmed. It was chaos. When Weinberger, [Marine Corps Commandant P.X.] Kelley and [General Bernard] Rogers came up to the Hill to testify [on the Beirut bombing], you could tell they knew they were in trouble. Weinberger especially."[23]

Within a week of the Beirut bombing, U.S. forces invaded the tiny island of Grenada. Their sheer size left little doubt as to the outcome. At the same time, however, the fact that each service had a role in the operation seemed to confirm arguments that a weak JCS was incapable of decisive organizational and strategic action. Again, investigation produced a strong impression of malaise and indecisiveness in the military command structure. It also exposed continuing incompatibilities among the equipment used by different services; incompatible radios prevented Army troops from calling in air strikes by Marine aircraft, for example. Thus, the Grenada operation, like operations in Lebanon, proved to be a strong goad to JCS reform.

Significantly, domestic politics also encouraged congressional interest in JCS reform. If the problem was JCS weakness in the face of service power, after all, there was no better example of it than the Reagan Defense Department. Republicans had for years campaigned against civilian meddling in service affairs, but Weinberger took this philosophy to practical extremes, largely removing himself and his staff from service decision making. Legislators could see the results in the duplicative service procurement projects that marked Weinberger's defense budgets, clear evidence of the "wasteful duplication" that had encouraged their predecessors to pass the Defense Reorganization Act of 1958. Even those supportive of the Reagan defense program tended to see this as squandering the very buildup they favored.[24]

House Action

House action on JCS reform in this period started with a useful distraction. In April 1983 Congressman Ike Skelton (D-Mo.) introduced a truly radical JCS reform bill calling for wholesale elimination of the JCS. In its place Skelton proposed creating a "chief of staff of the National Command Authority," with one deputy for operations, another for logistics. The ideas came largely from the previous year's testimony of General Maxwell Taylor. They were too radical to have a serious prospect of passage, even in the House. Yet for that very reason the Skelton bill drew attention to the issue and may have expanded the realm of politically practical reform legislation.

Defense Secretary Weinberger was also working on legislative proposals for management reform, and under some pressure from House Armed Services Committee Chairman Melvin Price (D-Ill.), he presented these to the committee on 19 April 1983. Not surprisingly, these were considerably more conservative than Skelton's, or even those contained in the White reform bill. Weinberger wanted to place the chairman of the JCS in the chain of command, to extend duty on the joint staff to four years, and to expand the joint staff.[25] However, Weinberger's proposals were silent about the chairman's power over the staff and the power of unified commanders over component forces of their commands.

Weinberger's input in hand, the Investigations Subcommittee then moved along lines established the year before. Although Richard White had retired from the House at the end of the previous session, William Nichols (D-Ala.), his successor at the subcommittee's helm, was also an advocate of JCS reform; he became more enthusiastic still after his subcommittee's investigations into the Lebanon and Grenada operations exposed their organizational and strategic flaws. After brief hearings involving only eight witnesses, the subcommittee pieced together a new JCS reform bill from the previous year's bill and Weinberger's proposals. Called the "Joint Chiefs of Staff Reorganization Act of 1983," this one gave the chairman of the JCS more control over military field commanders and also made him a member of the National Security Council. But it refrained from giving him a deputy largely out of deference to General John Vessey, the chairman at that time, who opposed the idea.

Introduced in August 1983, the Nichols reorganization bill passed the full House by voice vote in October, just like its predecessor. And, just like its predecessor, it met with Senate inaction. Frustrated, members of the House Armed Services Committee the next year attached the Nichols bill to their FY 85 Defense Authorization Act, hoping to force Tower to discuss it in conference. Yet even this ploy failed. Although the Armed Services Committee conference session lasted more than four months, Tower accepted only the most meager of the House committee's proposals.[26] The best the conferees could do was to produce a list of questions on defense management issues that was delivered to Weinberger for review by the serving JCS,

CINCs, and service secretaries. Answers were required by 1 March 1985, ensuring that these issues would be raised again early in the next Congress.

Senate Action and Inaction

Despite his refusal to consider House reform bills in 1982 and 1983, Senator Tower was not completely idle when it came to JCS reform. And if the activities he set in motion before his retirement moved in directions contrary to his wishes, they still helped to generate serious Senate interest in JCS reform.

Tower was not so much opposed to JCS reform as he was opposed to the kind of reform sent his way by the House. Not surprisingly, perhaps, given his long career in the U.S. Navy Reserve, Tower's own views, like those of most naval officers, leaned away from further centralization and the creation of a strong chairman of the JCS. Like Weinberger, Tower opposed civilian meddling in service affairs. So long as JCS reform fell into line with these precepts, Tower was happy to sponsor it. Indeed, according to one aide, Tower saw championing the right kind of JCS reform as a vehicle for furthering his own ambition to become secretary of defense.

In June 1983 Tower and the late Senator Henry "Scoop" Jackson (D-Wash.), the committee's ranking minority member, directed staffer James Locher to prepare a comprehensive study of the Defense Department's organization and decision-making procedures. A month later the Senate committee began a series of hearings on defense management, broadly defined to include the budget process and the organization of the secretary's staff—the OSD as well as the joint staff. The hearings lasted through November, involved testimony from thirty-two witnesses, and delved into virtually every aspect of defense management.[27] The Senate, it seemed, was finally starting to move on the issue.

Indeed, both the hearings and Locher's study played crucial roles in what would become a major and successful Senate effort to reform the nation's military command structure. Senator Sam Nunn (D-Ga.), for example, later called the Tower hearings "more important than any we [on the Armed Services Committee] have had."[28] And in June 1984 Senator Barry Goldwater (R-Ariz.) himself stated that JCS reform "is going to receive very deep study and, it is hoped, some resolution," suggesting that, among other things, the hearings had spurred his interest in the subject.[29] Meanwhile Locher's study, expanded under Goldwater's and Nunn's tutelage, would figure importantly in educating members of the Armed Services Committee and in expanding the range of practical political action on JCS reform and other defense management issues.

Yet none of this would happen so long as Tower reigned over the committee. Having set the hearings and Locher's study in motion, Tower soon realized that the emerging consensus on defense reform did not resonate with his own views. With interest growing among members of his committee, he was in no position simply to kill the hearings or the study outright. Yet he was in no mood to sponsor legislation that would contradict his own precepts. Hence, he soft-pedaled the issue in 1984, allowing hearings to continue and Locher to work on his study but refusing to produce legislation. The stage was slowly being set for Senate action, but only after Tower retired at the end of 1984.

The Outside Studies

It was not just in the halls of Congress that legislators were learning the intricacies of defense management and JCS reform. Beginning in 1983 two think tanks and one academic group took up these subjects in ways that, to varying degrees, influenced the political process.

A book project launched by professors—Samuel Huntington (Harvard), Robert Art (Brandeis), and Vincent Davis (University of Kentucky)—early in 1983 produced a collection of papers by noted experts, including chapters on defense organization in Great Britain, West Germany, France, and the Scandinavian countries, as well as a series of chapters on specific organizational problems haunting the U.S. defense establishment.[30] It is not clear that the book, although academically the most respectable of the outside studies, had much influence on the political debate then emerging, but it helped to place that debate in its international and historical context.

In its 1984 edition of *Mandate for Leadership II,* the conservative Heritage Foundation published a chapter-length critique of the defense-management problem. Written by former Army officer Theodore J. Crackel, the chapter covered all aspects of defense management.[31] Its treatment of strategy formulation and the military command structure echoed many of the complaints General Jones had raised some years previously. At the same time, Crackel criticized Weinberger's marginal changes as insufficient.

The most influential study in terms of the political debate then unfolding was conducted under the auspices of Georgetown University's Center for Strategic and International Studies (CSIS) and resulted in the publication of *Toward a More Effective Defense* in February 1985.[32] The study's influence stemmed as much from the method of its production as from its substance. Defense experts and members of Congress were brought together in study panels that focused on selected defense management issues: the budget process, weapons procurement, the command structure, and so forth.[33] Although it is impossible to separate the influence of this project from that of hearings, the Locher study, and the various botched military operations that helped sustain interest in defense management during the early 1980s, congressional staffers agree that the CSIS study was a crucial part of the education process that raised awareness of and familiarity with the issue of JCS reform, among a variety of defense-management issues. Moreover, the study and its originator, Barry Blechman, seem to have had direct influence over House legislation on the subject of JCS reform during 1985–86.

Expanding the Boundaries: 1985

On the issue of JCS reform, 1985 began much as the previous three years had begun, with the House Armed Services Committee preparing to write and pass yet another JCS reform bill. As in the past, the Investigations Subcommittee, still chaired by William Nichols, held hearings early in the year. Much later the subcommittee wrote another bill, which passed the committee 38–2 on 29 October. The bill passed the full House shortly thereafter, this time by formal rather than voice vote, a signal of growing House frustration and seriousness.

On the surface, at least, the year had much in common with each year since 1982, the first in which the House passed a JCS reform bill. Yet a simple rendition of the facts obscures the extent to which momentum was gathering behind the Hill's defense-management reform effort. Having spent two years involved with the CSIS defense-management study, House Armed Services Committee Chairman Les Aspin (D-Wisc.) entered 1985 committed to JCS reform of a kind simply not possible in preceding years. In 1982 Investigations Subcommittee Chairman Richard White had said that a bill making the chairman of the JCS the "principal military advisor" to the president "wouldn't get through Congress."[34] In February 1985, by contrast, the CSIS study made that suggestion among many others, all of them endorsed by the several key members of Congress who had taken part in the study. The bill the Investigations Subcommittee produced in 1985 read very much like those portions of the CSIS study that dealt with JCS reform. It advocated making the chairman of the JCS the principal adviser to the president, creating a vice chairman of the JCS, and placing the joint staff directly under the chairman.[35] The boundaries around what was politically feasible in the realm of JCS reform had expanded substantially since 1982.

Those boundaries continued to expand over the course of the year, and not just in the House of Representatives. Indeed, key action in 1985 lay in the Senate and the White House rather than in the House. John Tower's retirement from the Senate broke the logjam there. Tower's successor at the helm of the Senate Armed Services Committee, Barry Goldwater, was already on record as favoring JCS reform, as was the committee's ranking minority member, Georgia Democrat Sam Nunn. Over 1985 these two senators pushed their colleagues on the Armed Services Committee to consider a range of defense-management reforms extending far beyond JCS reform alone. There was little doubt that some action on these issues would be taken.

Meanwhile, in 1985 the small crack that had opened between the Defense Department and the White House on these issues as early as 1982 widened substantially, as both Congress and the president cooperated in chartering a new commission to examine all aspects of Pentagon management. The commission soon became known as the "Packard Commission," after its chairman, David Packard, a defense industrialist and former deputy secretary of defense. Although the commission's interim report was not published until early in 1986, well before then it was clear that Packard, too, envisioned major defense-management reform.

As in previous years, background events continued to favor such reforms. But in the mid-1980s the impulse for reform had shifted from bungled military operations to waste in the weapons-procurement process. The budget deficit, the result of borrowing to finance the Reagan-era defense spending surge, increased incentives on Capitol Hill to chip away at each year's defense budget proposal. Because it was politically difficult to be "for" higher taxes or "against" higher defense spending, the obvious compromise was to be "for" more efficiency in defense spending. And with stories about defense contractors charging $435 for hammers and $1,000 for tiny plastic stool caps filling the nation's newspapers, it was easy enough to generate support for reforming the way the Pentagon managed itself and its contractors. To be sure, contracting inefficiencies—so-called fraud, waste, and abuse in the acquisition process—bore no direct relation to questions of military organization. Yet one way to spend defense dollars more efficiently was to eliminate duplicative projects among the services, and that meant curbing service power— precisely the problem General Jones had alluded to in 1982. Pentagon reform, in short, tended to be an all-or-nothing affair.

In missing this point, Caspar Weinberger continued to fuel the reform effort he bitterly opposed. It would be wrong to say that Weinberger did nothing to meet critics of defense inefficiency, but his actions were aimed almost exclusively at disciplining the defense industry. The DOD inspector general mounted an aggressive campaign against defense contractors, for example, while at Weinberger's direction the military services developed new and seemingly more efficient ways to buy equipment and spare parts. Weinberger also reorganized his own OSD logistics and procurement staff repeatedly, albeit adding more assistant secretaries rather than "streamlining" the staff, which most critics called for. Such actions implied that all was well with Pentagon management, especially with the military command structure, as Weinberger himself said repeatedly over the course of the year. Although members of Congress may have lauded Weinberger's attack on the industry, most saw it as inadequate.

The Senate Takes Off

In June of 1984, recognizing that Tower would retire at the end of the 98th Congress, Goldwater said of JCS reform that "whether Senator Nunn is Chairman [of the Senate Armed Services Committee] or I am Chairman, this is a subject that is going to receive very deep study and, it is hoped, some resolution."[36] With the Republicans retaining control of the Senate, it was he who won the chance to make good on that prediction. From the start Goldwater made the effort bipartisan by working closely with Nunn. Debate in the Senate, as in the House, broke down less along party than along service lines, with the Navy's supporters, especially Senator John Warner (R-Va.), working hard to block or dilute reform legislation.

Goldwater and Nunn launched their effort to reform defense management in January 1985 by setting themselves up as the only two members of a task force on Defense Department reorganization. They gave staff member James Locher authority to work full-time on the study Tower had originally commissioned him to write. Locher was given two staff members—one majority and one minority— to help. Significantly, Locher's was to be a staff study rather than one that would carry either senator's imprimatur. This gave Locher latitude to explore more radical positions than the senators might wish to endorse.

In May, Goldwater and Nunn added seven other senators to their task force in an effort to expand the base of support on the Armed Services Committee for defense reorganization. By this time the CSIS study was available, as was the Heritage Foundation's chapter on defense organization. In March Weinberger shipped to the Hill the answers to questions Armed Services conferees had posed as part of their FY 85 Department of Defense Authorization Bill, adding still more voices to the debate on reorganization.[37] By summer, individual chapters of the Locher study became available and were circulated to task force members, sparking a lively debate covering a growing range of defense-management issues. Task force members also had the chance to discuss defense reform issues over breakfasts that summer with former defense secretaries Melvin Laird and James Schlesinger. Even in the absence of hearings, there was more than enough activity going on in the first half of 1985 to impart increasing momentum to the Senate debate concerning defense reorganization.

When published in October 1985, the Locher report, as it was called, created quite a stir.[38] This was and would remain the most radical of the reform studies. In the realm of JCS reform, for example, it called for eliminating the JCS entirely in order to allow the service chiefs to concentrate on service administration. In place of the JCS, the report called for creation of a "joint military advisory council" consisting of a chairman and a four-star military officer from each service on his last tour of duty. The chairman of the advisory council would have the authority "to provide military advice in his own right," rather than summing views of other council members, and would have independent control over the joint staff.[39] To strengthen operational commanders, the report called for making unified commanders senior in rank to service chiefs, and for giving them substantially greater authority over component commanders.[40] These recommendations made the Locher report the lightning rod for criticism of JCS reform and subjected Locher himself to a good deal of verbal abuse; interviewees referred to a "lynch-Locher" mentality among many in the Pentagon after the report appeared. On the other hand, Locher's recommendations made those of other studies appear more moderate and appealing, suggesting that Locher helped pull the ongoing legislative effort toward more far-reaching reforms.

The Locher report did not end with needed reforms in the Defense Department; it turned a critical eye on Congress as well. Locher and his colleagues noted, for example, that congressional action had historically "served to frustrate mission integration efforts in DoD," a reference to the traditional congressional preference for diluting executive branch recommendations for consolidating power in the Pentagon. Indeed, the report asserted that the congressional tendency to dwell on policy or program conflict within the Defense Department often reinforced interservice conflicts. Beyond this, the report noted that "the current practice of congressional review and oversight has resulted in substantial instability in defense policies and programs." A variety of committees and subcommittees handled portions of the DOD's operations in stylized and often inconsistent ways, producing confusion and inefficiency in the Pentagon's operational routines. And in focusing largely on artificial accounting inputs rather than mission outputs, Congress rarely confronted the crucial trade-offs that crossed service boundaries.

Finally, of course, there was the problem of mushrooming congressional oversight of the defense budget. In the 1950s the Pentagon's budget had been overseen annually by the Defense subcommittees of the House and Senate Appropriations committees. Annual authorization of portions of the defense budget had begun in 1959, and in the ensuing decade Congress had gradually but consistently expanded the portions of the defense budget requiring prior authorization through the Armed Services committees.[41] Adoption of the congressional budget process in 1974 added yet another layer of congressional review. Locher noted that in 1970 the defense authorization act had totaled 9 pages with an accompanying conference report of 33 pages. In 1985 the bill totaled 169 pages and the conference report 354 pages. Congressional intervention in Pentagon programs had climbed commensurately; whereas in 1970 Congress made 830 detailed program adjustments to service budgets, in 1985 it made 3163.[42]

The Locher report offered a number of options for addressing these problems, such as adopting a biennial budget process, consolidating congressional committees, and clarifying committee jurisdictions. Like the report's suggestions for executive branch reform, some of these went well beyond what was politically practical. In contrast to the report's effects on political debate as regarded command structure, however, these suggestions did not expand the realm of what was politically feasible in reforming Congress. The wave of organizational reform centered on the Goldwater-Nichols reorganization did little to change relations between Congress and the Pentagon.

With the Locher report in hand, the pace of events in the Senate began to pick up considerably. Early in October—the Locher report was finished but not yet published—Goldwater organized a dinner for committee members and a number of experts on defense management, held in the lodge at Fort A.P. Hill, Virginia. Although most of the experts present were reluctant to endorse Locher's more radical proposals, they nonetheless agreed that there was a serious need for reform. The dinner, which acquired a certain notoriety in the months that followed, tended both to increase support on the committee for defense reorganization and to isolate opponents of reform.

The day after Locher's report appeared in print, the Armed Services Committee launched a series of hearings on reorganizing the Defense Department. When the series ended on 12 December, the committee had heard from twenty-eight witnesses, among them several present and former service chiefs, defense secretaries, service secretaries, and a few operational commanders. The hearings exposed an enormous range of opinions; the first two witnesses, for example, were James Locher and Caspar Weinberger, whose views on defense reform were diametrically opposed. Significantly, after Weinberger had testified, Goldwater stated that the defense secretary's remarks implied "that you haven't really studied the matter. . . . You better go back and read this report of ours. . . . We're going to get you back again. We want some answers."[43] The hearings thus gave Weinberger a strong sense of what was to come so far as defense-management reform was concerned.

As he chided Weinberger, Goldwater also complained of "premature lobbying efforts which seek to polarize the debate" on defense reorganization.[44] There had been minor signs of opposition in the past—Congressman Nichols had complained of anonymous letter-writing campaigns and so forth—but opposition had been marginal so long as the Senate seemed unlikely to pass reform legislation. With the Senate Armed Services Committee increasingly committed to reform, critics became more committed in their opposition. The Department of the Navy, in particular, became increasingly strident in its criticism of the reform effort and increasingly active in seeking ways to dilute or kill reform legislation. As one journalist put it, behind passage of the final reorganization bill lay "acrimonious debate, behind-the-scenes political maneuvering and vicious bureaucratic battles."[45] Given the Senate's key role, it was toward the Senate that much of the acrimony was directed.

Acrimony and bureaucratic maneuvering aside, thoughtful arguments *against* reorganizing the military command structure were at this point being made energetically in scholarly and service journals. Opponents asserted, first, that centralizing military advice in a single, more powerful chairman of the JCS was incompatible with the nation's political culture. "There is a strong anti-militarist strain in the American experience," MacKubin Thomas Owens argued, "and incorrectly or not, a central military staff is perceived as an instrument of militarism."[46] By design the

Founding Fathers created a political system so decentralized that efforts to centralize often backfired, producing more bureaucracy. As Deputy Under-secretary of the Navy Seth Cropsey put it in 1985, "Any experience in federal government should dispel [the tendency to] equate centralization with simplification." Cropsey cited no less a military figure than General Douglas A. MacArthur, who had observed, while serving as Army chief of staff in 1931, that "the history of Government demonstrates that the parasitical development of bureaucracy springs from the setting up of superfluous echelons of control." MacArthur thus had flatly opposed early efforts to centralize the nation's defense establishment.[47]

Second, and more to the point, opponents of reform worried that strengthening the chairman would provide the nation's political leadership with worse, rather than better, military advice. As Owens put it,

> Under the geopolitical conditions faced by the U.S., the variety of strategic opinions produced by the corporate JCS is a strength, not a weakness. On the other hand, to strengthen the Chairman in the interest of curbing inter-service rivalry is merely to ensure that a *single* strategic view will be imposed upon policymakers at the expense of the corporate JCS's diverse and broad perspective on strategic and operational matters and on service conditions and capabilities.[48]

Worse still, an empowered chairman might be pressured to offer political leaders what they wanted to hear rather than the "disagreeable truths" and the "full, balanced information" already available from the existing JCS.[49]

These arguments were summarized and extended by Navy Secretary John Lehman, who remained the most outspoken critic of JCS reorganization within the Defense Department itself. JCS reorganization, Lehman noted in an article that appeared in December 1985, as both Senate and House prepared reorganization bills, "would increase bureaucracy and layers of organization. It would decrease policy control by elected leadership. It would strip our national decision-making process of needed information and expertise. And it would make no contribution whatsoever to the crucial question of efficient defense spending."[50] On the basis of these arguments, Lehman marshaled his political forces to battle those seeking to reorganize the military command structure.

If these arguments, and the arguments of reform advocates, seemed new, it was only because the nation's politicians had not seriously faced the issue of JCS reform since 1958. In fact, the debate that raged around the Locher report was as old as the effort to create a unified defense establishment. Even service positions in the debate were the same as always, with advocates coming mostly from the Army and the Air Force, opponents still associated with the Navy. Arguments for and against reform were deeply rooted in the U.S. political process and key military institutions. All that would change this time around would be the outcome, as the nation "muddled" toward a still stronger chairman of the JCS.

The Packard Commission

Although acquisition had been a source of concern on Capitol Hill almost from the start of the Reagan-era defense-spending surge, press reporting about exorbitantly priced toilet seats and spare parts made 1985 an especially troublesome year. Even the president's most ardent supporters realized that such reports could endanger his program in the absence of some effort to reform the weapons acquisition process.[51] Thus, in May 1985 the Senate attached to its version of the FY 86 defense authorization bill an amendment calling for establishment of a bipartisan, twenty-one-member "Commission on Defense Procurement"—an amendment that ultimately helped give birth to the Packard commission. Sponsored by Senators William D. Roth, Jr. (R-Del.) and Dennis DeConcini (D-Ariz.), the proposal met with little resistance in the full Senate.

Significantly, when the commission was finally established by the president in July, it was dubbed the President's Blue Ribbon Commission on Defense Management, reflecting a broadening of its charter beyond a strict focus on procurement. Despite obvious concern for "fraud, waste, and abuse" in procurement, there was general agreement in the Senate that "the commission would look into the overall management of DOD and not just at ways to improve Pentagon procurement practices."[52] Roth made this explicit in a letter to Weinberger dated 27 March, in which he suggested that the commission look into the JCS as well as procurement reform.[53]

Key members of the White House staff, notably Robert McFarlane, agreed on both the need for a commission and an expansive interpretation of its charter. From McFarlane's perspective, creating commissions had become a useful way of bypassing tension between the secretaries of state and defense that had made it increasingly difficult to develop coherent national strategies through the normal processes of government. The Scowcroft commission, for example, had sought consensus on strategic forces issues, while the Kissinger commission was created to generate consensus on U.S. policy toward Latin America. These had worked reasonably well, so it seemed logical to use the same device to tackle growing concern for defense management. Given McFarlane's views on JCS reform, he not surprisingly worked in coordination with members of the Senate Armed Services Committee to ensure that the commission's charter extended well beyond weapons acquisition.[54] Thus the executive order that established the President's Blue Ribbon Commission on Defense Management referred specifically to the commission's obligation to examine the nation's military command structure as well as the adequacy of its defense acquisition process.[55]

Weinberger resisted creation of the commission but was overruled by the president. Weinberger's resistance apparently fell somewhat when the president assured him that the commission would examine problems in the defense industry, the area in which Weinberger had focused his own reform drive. Weinberger was also given veto power, along with McFarlane and Packard, over appointments to the commission's membership. In the weeks following creation of the commission in July, Weinberger stated repeatedly that the commission's role was simply to "validate" reforms already undertaken in his department. No one on the commission, nor in the public, agreed with this interpretation.[56]

Indeed, several of the newly selected members of the commission, including Brent Scowcroft, R. James Woolsey, and James L. Holloway, all of whom had testified on defense reorganization issues in previous years, were anxious to tackle defense management broadly, to include the command structure, strategy making, and the budget process. Packard had testified during the House Investigations Subcommittee's first JCS reform hearings in 1982, and had come down then in favor of General Meyer's reform proposals, which were more radical than those proposed by General Jones.[57] Hence, commission members agreed soon after they first met that they would examine procurement first, but then turn to broader management issues.

Interest among commission members in JCS reform grew as time went on. In part, it grew as they discovered that problems in procurement could not be solved in isolation from deeper organizational problems in the Defense Department. One source of procurement inefficiency, for example, stemmed from lack of interservice coordination in the acquisition process—the "wasteful duplication" that had motivated the Defense Reorganization Act of 1958. Insofar as the problem stemmed from continuing service power, it raised questions about the functioning of the JCS and its chairman. Meanwhile, staff studies for the commission piqued interest in the military command structure. One in particular, outlining the hopelessly complicated command structure connecting the U.S. Army's commander in Korea with the Pacific Command, generated strong interest in reform.

Although the commission's first report was not due out until early in 1986, Packard kept in touch fairly regularly with members of Congress concerned with DOD organization, and by December 1985 it was reasonably clear that the commission was entertaining organizational reforms closely akin to those then under serious discussion on Capitol Hill. By the time the commission began work that month on its interim report, a consensus already existed on reforms in the four areas around which the commission organized its final report: (1) national security planning and budgeting, (2) military organization and command, (3) acquisition organization and procedures, and (4) government-industry accountability.[58] As for the military command structure, the interim report called for many of the reforms then under consideration in both houses of Congress. It sought to make the chairman of the JCS the principal uniformed military adviser to the president, the National Security Council, and the secretary of defense, for example, and to give the chairman exclusive control of a larger joint staff. The commission recommended creation of a vice chairman of the JCS, with duties focused particularly, although not exclusively, on weapons acquisition. Finally, the interim report asked the president to give the unified commanders broader authority over subordinate commanders, and to give unified commanders a direct line to the chairman of the JCS, so that the latter "may better incorporate the views of senior combatant commanders in his advice to the Secretary [of Defense]."[59]

Weinberger Shifts Position

On 2 December 1985 Weinberger sent a letter to both Goldwater and the Packard commission that reflected a fundamental change in position. Although Weinberger rejected the Locher report's call for creation of a joint military adviser council, he now supported the idea of making the chairman of the JCS principal military adviser to the president, provided that "his duty to present the alternative views of the JCS is clearly established in law." The letter favored establishing a vice chairman of the JCS, although Weinberger insisted that this individual should fall sixth in rank behind the service chiefs rather than second. Finally, Weinberger supported placing the chairman of the JCS in the chain of command.[60] Few in the White House or on Capitol Hill took the letter to mean that Weinberger had seen the value of defense reform; rather, it was seen as evidence that he had finally realized that reform was inevitable.

In fact, reform legislation was then being written in both houses of Congress. In the Senate, Locher and other Armed Services Committee staff members began writing a major defense-management reform bill soon after the committee's hearings ended on 12 December. At about the same time the House Armed Services Committee set aside the JCS reform bill that had passed the full House less than two months before and began work on a "concept paper" outlining reforms covering the full panoply of defense-management issues. Much debate had yet to occur; the Goldwater-Nichols Department of Defense Reorganization Act would not be passed for some nine months, but by the end of 1985 the language that would find its way into that act was being written.

Action: 1986

Senate Armed Services Committee staffers finished writing their Defense Department reorganization bill late in January 1986. Markup, which began on 4 February, involved a running battle between the Navy department and advocates of reform. Working out of offices in the Pentagon as well as one on the Hill supplied by Senator John Warner, opponents of reform produced some eighty-seven amendments to the basic bill, most funneled by the Navy through Warner.[61] Goldwater retaliated by refusing to allow the committee to consider any other action—promotions, reprogramming, and so forth —until the Defense Department reorganization bill had been passed. After fourteen sessions in which the committee considered each amendment but allowed none to dilute the bill seriously, the full Armed Services Committee passed its version of the DOD reorganization bill unanimously (19–0) on 6 March.[62]

Although debate in preceding months had focused largely on the Locher report's recommendations, the Senate bill fell far short of that report's radical proposals. Rather than abolishing the JCS, the Senate merely designated the JCS chairman as the principal military adviser to the president, although it required him to submit to civilian policymakers the views of dissenting chiefs of staff. The bill created a vice chairman of the JCS and, after much debate, made him second rather than sixth in rank among the JCS. It increased the power of the various unified commanders over component commanders.[63]

Dubbed the "Barry Goldwater Department of Defense Reorganization Act of 1986," the bill was approved 95–3 by the Senate on 7 May. The lopsided nature of the full Senate vote testified in large part to Goldwater's prestige, and to the care both he and Nunn had exercised in developing a consensus on defense reform. As one senator stated on the floor of the Senate, "Only Goldwater could produce this.... If anybody else had been the one who had been advocating this reorganization, every military man and woman in the Pentagon would have been down on our backs as 'Communist Sympathizers.'"[64] Significantly, by this time even Warner had become an advocate of the bill, asserting to the press that he wished the military had been "less strong in their criticism" of the reorganization effort and urging them to "give the bill a chance to work."[65]

By the time the Senate voted, events in the executive branch may also have helped convince Senate fence sitters of the popularity of DOD reform. The Packard commission's interim report was published on 28 February 1986. Although its substance surprised no one who had been following the issue, its publication gave Reagan an executive branch document recommending defense reforms similar to those under consideration in both houses of Congress. In National Security Decision Directive (NSDD) 219, dated 2 April 1986, Reagan formally ordered the Defense Department to implement virtually all of the Packard commission's recommendations—a move that apparently surprised many in the department as well as on Capitol Hill.[66] Later that month Reagan sent members of Congress a letter praising both the Senate's and the Packard commission's reforms, and on 24 April he sent Congress a special message calling for early enactment of reform legislation. Overall, the White House conveyed its support of the Senate's reform bill, provided marginal changes were made in the mandated term of office for the chairman of the JCS. The full Senate vote on the Goldwater reform bill came less than two weeks later, in the full glow of this White House endorsement.[67]

Ironically, the House Armed Services Committee, which had been pushing for JCS reform since 1982, was now running behind the Senate. In March 1986 the committee held extensive hearings (twenty sessions in thirty days) on the broad-concept paper Aspin and his staff had begun writing the previous December. Over April and May committee staffers wrote the House bill, which was approved by the Investigations Subcommittee (10–2) on 12 June. JCS reform never having been as controversial in the House as it had been in the Senate, markup was less arduous for Nichols and Aspin than it had been for Goldwater and Nunn. Thus, the "William Nichols Department of Defense Reorganization Act of 1986" passed out of the committee, 39–4, on 26 June, and passed by the House, 382–17, on 5 August.

Although conceptually akin to the Senate bill, the House bill called for more radical departures in several reform areas, especially those concerning the power of commanders of the unified and specified commands. The Senate bill gave these "CINCs" "operational command" of component forces; the House bill gave them "full command." The House bill also gave them power to select and if necessary relieve commanders of component forces in their commands, and to organize their commands as they saw fit. It also and for the first time gave the CINCs limited authority over support functions like fuel and munitions, and an operations budget for joint training and selected operations—measures likely to bring the CINCs into conflict with the services, whose mission remained that of training and equipping component forces.[68]

The Senate-House conference began on 13 August, with the House conferees trying to pull the Senate bill toward more far-reaching positions. As a rule, they succeeded, though less with regard to the powers of the JCS chairman than those of the CINCs. As expected, the chairman of the JCS was made principal military adviser to the president; subject to the wishes of the secretary of defense, the chairman became the spokesman for the combatant commands in the DOD, especially on operational issues. Still, catering to fears that the nation's civilian leadership should hear varying opinions, the bill required the chairman to present contrary advice from dissenting service chiefs, were there any, alongside his own recommendations. The president and defense secretary could also, not surprisingly, request the views of the service chiefs as they wished.[69] The conference bill created the office of the vice chairman of the JCS, making it second in rank, rather than sixth, behind the chairman.[70]

As for the CINCs, rather than haggle over the differences between "operational" and "full" authority for unified and specified commanders, the conferees listed the CINCs' authorities, which included authority to direct subordinate commands and forces in all aspects of military operations, training, and logistics. CINCs were also given the power to establish ways in which component commanders would communicate with their respective services—this in response to the complaint in testimony of Army General Bernard Rogers, former CINC of the European Command, that component commanders often bypassed their CINCs to go directly to component chiefs of staff.[71] Although the services would continue to choose commanders for component commands within each unified and specified command, the conference bill gave the CINCs veto authority over these nominations. Finally, the CINCs were given authority to submit budget proposals for joint training and exercises as well as "selected operations," which were then to be included in the annual DOD budget request.[72]

The conferees approved what was at that point called the Goldwater-Nichols bill on 11 September, and the full Senate and House followed suit on 16 and 17 September, respectively. Reagan signed the bill into law on 1 October 1986.

Effects: Goldwater-Nichols in Practice

Thus far, it would be difficult indeed to argue that the Goldwater-Nichols reorganization bill has not done what it set out to do, with positive results. In the Iraq crisis of 1990–91, leading to Operation Desert Storm in January and February 1991, Commander in Chief of U.S. Central Command General H. Norman Schwarzkopf was able to exercise powerful centralizing and integrating control over component service elements. Marine Corps aircraft, for example, were in some cases pulled away from the corps and given over to Air Force component commander Lieutenant General Charles Horner for operational control. A U.S. Army brigade was controlled by Marine Corps commander Lieutenant General Walter Boomer. Logistics priorities were established by Central Command rather than by individual services. After the war Lieutenant General "Gus" Pagonis, the Army logistician who more than any other single officer handled Desert Storm's staggering logistics challenge, told Senator Nunn that "he could not have done his job—moving a city the size of Charleston, S.C., halfway around the globe in five months—before Goldwater-Nichols."[73]

Meanwhile, Chairman of the Joint Chiefs General Colin Powell served conspicuously as the principal military adviser to the nation's civilian leadership during the Panama and Iraq crises, while the service chiefs were probably less visible during Operation Desert Storm, in particular, than ever before. The chairman of the JCS has clearly assumed greater authority over the joint staff, which in turn seems to be functioning in a serious way for the first time in its history, absorbing functions like budget and quantitative military analysis that have been performed largely by analysts in OSD. With the CINCs now more firmly in command and the chairman of the JCS and the joint staff expanding their purview, the budget process too seems to be shifting slightly away from the services and service secretariats and toward the unified and specified commands.[74]

All of these were central goals of the Goldwater-Nichols Act and flow at least in part from it. To be sure, Powell's central role in recent military operations and the expansiveness of joint staff operations are partly a reflection of Powell's previous acquaintance with the president, his congenial relationship with Defense Secretary Richard Cheney, and his astute grasp of how power flows in the nation's capital. Meanwhile, the CINCs' role in the budget process may stem in part from the fact that Cheney is, in the words of a former CINC, "very considerate of what the CINCs have to say."[75] Personality inevitably plays a role in determining power relationships in the nation's highly fragmented political system. But so does law, and Powell's position and influence, not to mention Schwarzkopf's command authority during Desert Storm, derived ultimately from the legal basis established by the Goldwater-Nichols Act.

A few weeks after the fighting in the Gulf war was stopped, a hearing was held before the House Armed Services Committee on the operation of the Goldwater-Nichols Act in the wake of Operation Desert Storm.[76] The general reactions of the individuals testifying were quite positive. Former Secretary of Defense Harold Brown stated that no significant changes were needed in the 1986 reorganization act; the minor changes he thought necessary could be implemented without legislation. General David Jones testified that before Goldwater-Nichols, Defense Department organization rated about a 3 on a scale of 10. He now believed it rated a 7, especially insofar as it allowed General Schwarzkopf much greater control over logistics during Operation Desert Storm. Admiral Harry Train, former commander in chief of the Atlantic Command, argued that the CINCs ought to have still more power over their own budgets, but agreed that they had substantially greater power to carry out their military missions.

These witnesses had been in favor of greater centralization of the command structure all along, and thus were merely expressing satisfaction that the Goldwater-Nichols Act had actually done what it was meant to do. Not surprisingly, those suspicious of the need for greater centralization remain so. Noting the extent to which General Powell has made himself the sole source of military advice to the nation's civilian leaders, for example, strategist Eliot Cohen echoed the Navy's long-standing concern for the lack of options likely to be made available to the president in future wars: "[W]hen the use of force was contemplated in Panama and the Persian Gulf, the civilian leaders were briefed not on several military options, with their associated risks and benefits, but on one plan and one plan only."[77] In fact, during the Iraq crisis the president met with the chiefs at least twice, although Cohen considered these meetings to have been largely pro forma. Arguably, however, the absence of serious debate at these meetings may have signaled reasonably strong consensus on military strategy.

Still, Cohen's remarks and others like it suggest that the debate about the nation's command structure goes on, as well it should; there is no "perfect" solution to this vital political and military issue. Advocates of reform have, with some justification, invoked the conspicuous success of postreform military operations to justify their effort. For this very reason, however, future military failures—and there will surely be some—will no doubt reinvigorate the critics. Personalities will change as well, leading to friction where at the moment harmony reigns.

It is at least arguable that Congress itself may become less enamored of its own work over time, not because it fails to produce the desired military operational outcome but because it reduces congressional access to and power over Pentagon decision making. In passing the Goldwater-Nichols Act, after all, Congress stepped out of its usual role of diluting executive branch proposals to consolidate power in an executive branch agency. Congress may yet return to past behavior and dilute its own reorganization. Given the momentousness of the issues involved, however, it is unlikely that Congress is anxious to return soon to the question of military organization save to make marginal changes in the existing law.

Conclusions

For those impressed by the incoherence and fragmentation of Congress, the degree of consensus generated on Capitol Hill in passing the Goldwater-Nichols Department of Defense Reorganization Act was a pleasant and encouraging surprise. Congress took up an issue with which it was not deeply familiar (the last legislative reform having been passed in 1958), one on which it has historically divided sharply, and one for which there were no strong constituency pressures for action. Over a period of four years, the Armed Services committees in both houses became familiar with the issue and ultimately passed what most would call thoughtful, coherent reform legislation. Most would also agree that those reforms have produced the intended effect, at least in the area of JCS reform.

What motivated the Congress to do such a thing? Clearly it was not party politics. Perhaps the key advocate of reform was Barry Goldwater, as staunchly conservative a Republican as one could find on Capitol Hill. The second key advocate was Sam Nunn, a Democrat. Votes in the House from 1982 on did not break down along party lines.

Nor was Congress as a whole driven by constituency interests, narrowly defined. To the contrary, the absence of multiple and narrowly defined constituencies in this issue area helps account for the coherence of both the debate and the final Goldwater-Nichols bill. As in the past, debate was generated more by service than by more narrowly defined economic or political constituencies. To be sure, service advocates were motivated at least partly by constituency considerations; Senator Warner's opposition to reform no doubt derived partly from the presence of a major naval base and shipyards in and around Norfolk, Virginia.[78] But constituency connections like these defined a broad position—in Warner's case, support for the Navy's opposition to greater centralization—with historical and empirical validity. To the extent that constituency concerns defined positions, in short, they contributed to an important and coherent debate.

But why engage in the debate in the first place? A central driving force behind JCS reform in this case apparently was a genuine concern for the nation's ability to equip and use its military forces. The Reagan-era defense-spending surge, and the deficit that financed it, created powerful incentives to improve efficiency in the Defense Department. President Reagan made it politically difficult to be against defense or for more taxes, so the only option was to be for greater efficiency. It is at least arguable that had Reagan-era defense budgets been financed from tax revenues rather than by borrowing, there would have been substantially less pressure on Capitol Hill for defense-management reform.

But interest derived from military as well as fiscal issues. In talking frequently of reviving the military strength of the United States, and in occasionally using military forces, Reagan highlighted the organizational problems that haunted U.S. military operations. It is doubtful that JCS or other defense reform issues would have acquired much momentum without Reagan's emphasis on defense spending and military operations. Nor should the role of Beirut and Grenada in generating concern for reform be forgotten.

Personalities also played a role. Senator Goldwater's singular importance, noted earlier, was matched by that of Defense Secretary Caspar Weinberger, whose tendency to stonewall on virtually every issue raised management and efficiency issues to much higher levels of salience. To be sure, stonewalling is a tried and true tactic in U.S. politics, based on the verifiable premise that to give up anything before interbranch negotiations begin is merely to launch the negotiations from a lower baseline or weaker position. What Weinberger lacked, however, was a politician's subtle sense of when to give, or at least to appear to give.

By giving so little and so reluctantly, Weinberger's stonewalling tactic proved ultimately to be counterproductive. Because Weinberger gave on so little, for example, members of Congress resorted to touting "horror stories" from the weapons acquisition process, less because the stories made sense (some did, but often they were exaggerated) but, rather, to keep Weinberger off balance, to weaken him before his next appearance on the Hill. By giving so little, Weinberger also reinforced the growing impression that his stonewalling was merely a cover for his own lack of competence at defense management, encouraging members of Congress to organize defense management out from under him. Finally, Weinberger's strong preference for letting the services have their way starkly highlighted the problem JCS reformers wanted to solve, and no doubt increased support for their cause. A more politically savvy and competent defense secretary willing to negotiate with Congress probably could have reduced the reform urge on Capitol Hill, ending up with a much less radical reorganization.

In the absence of any willingness in the Defense Department to cooperate with members of Congress, Congress was forced to produce its own reforms. Lack of flexibility in the DOD left Congress, and think tanks as well, the time to investigate an issue of enormous complexity. Thus, among other things, what began as concern for JCS reform ultimately expanded into concern for defense management in the broadest sense. In this sense, at least, those who favored defense reform should probably give their loudest applause to the man who most vehemently opposed it.

Timeline of Major Events in the Goldwater-Nichols Department of Defense Reorganization Act of 1986 Case

January 1982   In his last appearance before the House Armed Services Committee, departing chairman of the Joint Chiefs of Staff General David C. Jones criticizes then-current JCS structure and calls for reorganization. Written copies of Jones's arguments appear in the journals *Directors and Boards* and *Armed Forces Journal International.*

Spring 1982   The Investigations Subcommittee of the House Armed Services Committee launches five months of hearings, involving thirty-eight witnesses, on the subject of JCS reform.

August 1982   Modest JCS reform bill originating in the Investigations Subcommittee passes the full House by voice vote. Although it holds desultory hearings on the subject of JCS reform, the Senate Armed Services Committee refuses to consider the House bill, which dies at the end of the session.

June 1983   Senator John Tower (R-Tex.), chairman of the Senate Armed Services Committee, launches major series of hearings on defense management, including but not confined to JCS reform.

Summer 1983   Georgetown Center for Strategic and International Studies begins major study of defense reorganization that yields the influential *Toward a More Effective Defense* in 1985.

August 1983   The House Armed Services Committee's Investigations Subcommittee, chaired by William Nichols (D-Ala.),

	approves a "Joint Chiefs of Staff Reorganization Act of 1983." This carries the full House, by voice vote, in October 1983. As in 1982, the Senate Armed Services Committee refuses to consider the bill in conference.
Fall 1983	Senator Tower sets staffer James Locher to work on a reorganization study. Ultimately, this will become the influential *Defense Organization: The Need for Change,* published by the Senate Armed Services Committee in October 1985.
Summer 1984	In an effort to force Senate consideration in conference, the House attaches its "Joint Chiefs of Staff Reorganization Act" (the Nichols bill of the previous year) to its FY 85 Defense Authorization Bill. The Senate Armed Services Committee nonetheless avoids prolonged discussion, and few parts of the bill find their way into the conference report. Conferees do, however, agree to forward a long list of questions on defense management to Secretary of Defense Caspar Weinberger, requesting answers by 1 March 1985.
January 1985	Senator Barry Goldwater (R-Ariz.) takes over as chairman of the Senate Armed Services Committee in the wake of John Tower's retirement. Goldwater immediate sets James Locher to work full-time on his study of defense organization.
February 1985	*Toward a More Effective Defense* is published by the Center for Strategic and International Studies. According to one congressional staff member, this and a few related studies "radically expand the boundaries" of what is possible in defense reorganization.
March 1985	Weinberger, service chiefs of staff, and unified and specified commanders in chief respond to questions delivered the previous fall by the House-Senate Armed Services committees. All oppose reform, but unified and specified commanders criticize the current command structure.
May 1985	Senate approves an amendment to its FY 86 Defense Authorizations Bill calling for the establishment of a twenty-one-member "Commission on Defense Procurement," with industrialist and former Deputy Defense Secretary David Packard as the suggested chair. White House creates the commission and names Packard to head it in June.
August 1985	Weinberger makes modest changes in defense department's management structure, but leaves the military command structure untouched.

October 1985	The "Locher Study" (*Defense Organization: The Need for Change*) is published. It takes a far more radical position on reform than all previous studies. It thus serves as a lightning rod for criticism, and by so doing expands the boundaries of what is possible in actual reform.
	House Investigations Subcommittee, with strong backing from Congressman Les Aspin (D-Wisc.), chairman of the House Armed Services Committee, writes a JCS reform bill more far-reaching than previous House reform bills. This passes the House late in 1985.
November–December 1985	Senate Armed Services Committee holds elaborate hearings on the subject of JCS reform.
December 1985	In letters to Senator Goldwater and members of the Packard commission, Weinberger accepts the idea of making the chairman of the JCS the principal military adviser to the president. Weinberger also now favors creating the position of a vice chairman of the JCS. The letters express a fundamental change in Weinberger's position.
December 1985–January 1986	Senate Armed Services Committee staff members write their version of a JCS reform bill.
February 1986	Packard commission's interim report appears. Its conclusions reinforce many of the reform arguments then being heard by the Senate Armed Services Committee.
February–March 1986	Senate Armed Services Committee markup of the JCS reform bill—thirty days of extremely heated debate in which some eighty-seven amendments to the bill are considered, most proposed by Senator John Warner (R-Va.) at the Navy's behest. Bill is approved, 19–0, on 6 March.
March 1986	House Armed Services Committee launches series of twenty hearings in thirty days on general issue of defense management.
April 1986	In a surprise move seen by many observers as a rebuff to Weinberger, on 2 April Reagan orders the Defense Department to implement virtually all Packard commission recommendations.
April–May 1986	House Armed Services Committee staffers write what is now called the "William Nichols Department of Defense Reorganization Act," calling for somewhat more radical reforms that those in the Senate bill. Bill passes out of the committee late in June.
May 1986	Senate unanimously (95–0) approves what is now called the "Barry Goldwater Department of Defense Reorganization Act of 1986."

July 1986	Final report of the Packard commission, *A Quest for Excellence,* is published.
August 1986	House passes the Nichols bill, 382–17.
August–September 1986	House-Senate conference on the reorganization bills. Senate and House approve the Goldwater-Nichols Department of Defense Reorganization Act of 1986 on 16, 17 September, respectively.

Notes

1. The act sidestepped only weapons acquisition, reform of which tended to be handled by a special set of subcommittees operating separately from those focused on overall reform. The largest single set of acquisition reforms was packaged in the Acquisition Improvement Act of 1986 (P.L. 99-661, §§ 901–963).

2. The history of this process has been outlined in several books, among them Paul Y. Hammond, *Organizing for Defense: The American Military Establishment in the Twentieth Century* (Princeton: Princeton University Press, 1961); Demetrios Caraley, *The Politics of Military Unification: A Study of Conflict and the Policy Process* (New York: Columbia University Press, 1966); and Lawrence Korb, *The Joint Chiefs of Staff: The First Twenty-Five Years* (Bloomington: Indiana University Press, 1976). An excellent short history is William J. Lynn, "The Wars Within: The Joint Military Structure and Its Critics," in *Reorganizing America's Defense: Leadership in War and Peace,* ed. Robert J. Art, Vincent Davis, and Samuel P. Huntington (New York: Pergamon-Brassey's, 1985).

3. The creation of separate Army and Navy theaters in the Pacific, for example, resulted from "stormy interservice negotiations" designed, among other things, to salve the ego of General Douglas MacArthur while giving substantial independence to the Navy, traditionally paramount in the Pacific. See John Keegan, *The Second World War* (New York: Viking, 1989), 291.

4. A sore point then that lingers to the present is the Air Force's unwillingness to provide close air support to Army ground troops. The complaint has some legitimacy; long before it became a separate service in 1947 the Army Air Corps showed a marked preference for strategic bombing over close air support precisely because the former offered maximum independence from ground force control. See Perry M. Smith, *The Air Force Plans for Peace, 1943–45* (Baltimore: Johns Hopkins University Press, 1970), especially 27–38.

5. On the differing Army and Navy approaches to internal management, see Hammond, *Organizing for Defense,* chaps. 2, 3.

6. During the unification debate the status of the Marine Corps and naval air assets came into serious question; with some justification, Navy officials feared that the Army and its Air Corps were seeking to relieve their service of these assets. See ibid., 186–226, especially 221ff. So real was this fear, and so anxious were the Marine Corps's supporters on Capitol Hill to dispel it, that in 1953 Congress legislated a minimum size for the Marine Corps of three divi-

sions, making it the only service to enjoy legislative protection. The same fears resurfaced in the 1980s reorganization debate; in 1985, Congressman William Nichols, chairman of the House Armed Services Committee's Investigations Subcommittee and a leader in pushing for reorganization, complained publicly of being the target of an anonymous letter-writing campaign accusing him of seeking to "do away with the Marine Corps and the Navy air arm."

Although such fears may have motivated some Navy and Marine Corps opponents of reorganization, they do not seem to have played a prominent role in the overall debate. See Michael Ganley, "Hill Again Promises JCS DoD Reform, But Timing for Legislation Is Unclear," *Armed Forces Journal International* (May 1985): 12.

7. As quoted in Hammond, *Organizing for Defense*, 267. Derisive use of the phrase resurfaced in the debates leading up to the 1986 reorganization, especially in criticism leveled by Navy Secretary John Lehman. But the mythology surrounding the general staff may have been laid to rest in the 1980s as historians debunked the idea that the German general staff had enjoyed the power many Americans accorded to it. See, for example, John M. Nolen, "JCS Reform and the Lessons of German History," *Parameters* 14, no. 3 (1984): 12–24.

8. As Robert J. Art puts it, organizational changes in the Defense Department since World War II have been "modest on the military side but radical on the civilian side."

See his introduction to Art, Davis, and Huntington, *Reorganizing America's Defense*, xiii. Radical in this case is a relative term; in fact, Congress has consistently given the defense secretary less power than administrations have sought. Moreover, even when legislators have granted greater legal power to the secretary, they have subsequently found ways of curbing the secretary's ability actually to exercise that power. See Thomas L. McNaugher, *New Weapons, Old Politics: America's Military Procurement Muddle* (Washington, D.C.: Brookings, 1989), 56–58.

9. See McNaugher, *New Weapons, Old Politics*, 38–41.

10. Many of these arguments surfaced during the Korean War. See Hammond, *Organizing for Defense*, 256–66.

11. Lynn, "The Wars Within," 176.

12. Ibid., 179.

13. Joint Chiefs of Staff, Chairman's Special Study Group, *The Organization and Functions of the JCS*, Report for the Chairman (Arlington, Va.: Systems Research and Applications Corporation, April 1982), 66.

14. General David C. Jones, "Why the Joint Chiefs of Staff Must Change," *Armed Forces Journal International* (March 1982): 62–72.

15. Jones had been singled out by several of the retired military officers advising the Reagan campaign as being antimilitary and representative of the "Carter approach" to defense. According to some interviewees, William Van Cleve, head of Reagan's Pentagon transition team, even suggested replacing Jones as the administration took office. Although Jones remained in office for his full

four-year term, reportedly his relationship with Weinberger was chilly from the start.

16. Archie D. Barrett, *Reappraising Defense Organization: An Analysis Based on the Defense Organization Study of 1977–1980* (Washington, D.C.: National Defense University Press, 1983).

17. See Deborah M. Kyle and Benjamin F. Schemmer, "Navy, Marines Adamantly Oppose JCS Reforms Most Others Tell Congress Are Long Overdue," *Armed Forces Journal International* (June 1982): 61–67.

18. Asked why he had not pushed for more far-reaching reforms, White stated simply that these would have encountered "tremendous opposition . . . such a bill wouldn't get through the Congress." "AFJI Talks to Congress: Richard C. White," *Armed Forces Journal International* (September 1982): 18.

19. On this point at least one interviewee raised questions about General Jones's assertion that most of his reforms could not be accomplished by the defense department alone.

20. Deborah M. Kyle, "DoD Deadline on JCS Reform Recommendations May Delay Reorganization Bill," *Armed Forces Journal International* (September 1982): 17–19.

21. Jones pointed to the Iranian hostage rescue mission as perhaps the key event in validating the need for JCS reform; McFarlane pointed to the *Mayaguez* incident, in which President Gerald Ford used force to free U.S. citizens captured by Cambodian Khmer Rouge forces in 1975. The need for speed and secrecy in this operation forced Marines to use U.S. Air Force helicopters stationed in Thailand, producing the same lack of coordination evident in the Iran rescue mission. McFarlane served on the joint staff from 1968 to 1971, where he witnessed the general problem of service logrolling against a relatively weak JCS.

22. According to McFarlane, Weinberger's credibility began to fall early in the Reagan administration, during hearings on Capitol Hill to determine a proper basing mode for the MX missile. Having worked on the Senate Armed Services Committee staff from 1979 to 1981, McFarlane remained in close touch with many senators as well as Senate staffers. From them he received the strong impression that Weinberger had made a poor showing in delivering testimony on the MX issue, and that even senators who supported the administration's choice of an MX basing mode were reluctant to back Weinberger for fear that he would reverse himself as time went on.

23. Quoted in Mark Perry, "How Cap Weinberger Lost the Fight over Defense Reform," *American Politics* (February 1988): 7.

24. William Kaufmann, *The 1986 Defense Budget* (Washington, D.C.: Brookings, 1985), 35–40. Kaufmann saw a need to develop highly accurate delivery vehicles for nuclear weapons, for example, but believed that "the administration has not adequately explained why it needs the MX, the D-5 (Trident II), which will be much less vulnerable, and the slower but still very accurate cruise missile." Similarly, he accepted the wisdom of developing ways to penetrate Soviet airspace, but criticized as "lack of discipline rather than a demonstration of

prudence" the Reagan administration's development of the air-launched cruise missile, the B-1B bomber, an advanced cruise missile, and the stealth bomber (B-2).

25. For a discussion of both the Skelton bill and Weinberger's proposals, see Deborah M. Kyle, "JCS Reform *Still* a Hill Issue," *Armed Forces Journal International* (May 1983): 14.

26. The conferees agreed to make the chairman of the Joint Chiefs of Staff the spokesman to the secretary of defense for the commanders of the nation's combatant commands on operational requirements. Recognizing that "the House has performed an important service in bringing JCS reform to the fore," they agreed to make the issue of JCS reform "high priority during the next session of Congress." Senate Committee on Armed Services, *Department of Defense Authorization for Appropriations for Fiscal Year 1985,* Conference Rept. (Washington, D.C.: Government Printing Office, 1984), 330.

27. See Senate Committee on Armed Services, *Organization, Structure, and Decisionmaking Processes of the Department of Defense, Hearings,* 98th Cong., 1st sess., 1983, pts. 1–12.

28. Quoted in Deborah Kyle, "Weinberger Challenges Senate Committee at Defense Reform Hearing: Ease Up," *Armed Forces Journal International* (September 1983): 16.

29. Quoted in Clinton H. Schemmer, "House JCS Reform Stalled: Tower Promises Separate Senate Bill," *Armed Forces Journal International* (September 1984): 9.

30. Art, Davis, and Huntington, *Reorganizing America's Defense.*

31. Theodore J. Crackel, "Defense Assessment," in *Mandate for Leadership II: Continuing the Conservative Revolution,* ed. Stuart M. Butler, Michael Sanera, and W. Bruce Weinrod (Washington, D.C.: Heritage Foundation, 1984), 331–48. Much later the Heritage Foundation published Backgrounder #508, which was similarly favorable to Pentagon reorganization: Kim R. Holmes, "A Solid Case for Pentagon Reorganization" (5 May 1986). Although it appeared while House and Senate Armed Services Committees were working out the details of the final reorganization bill, it was nonetheless significant in demonstrating broad support for defense reform across the political spectrum.

32. *Toward a More Effective Defense: The Final Report of the CSIS Defense Organization Project* (Washington, D.C.: Center for Strategic and International Studies, Georgetown University, 1985). Although it is often referred to as the "CSIS Study," this project was launched at the Roosevelt Center under the direction of Barry Blechman, then one of the center's vice presidents. Blechman's mandate at the center was to generate work on issues of strategic merit, yet issues on which political action was a practical possibility. Scanning the political horizon late in 1982, Blechman encountered the interest already generated by Jones's speech earlier that year and the subsequent House Armed Services Committee hearings on JCS reform. He launched the project, bringing notables like General Andrew Goodpaster and Philip Odeen in to raise its visibility and ex-

pand its focus. In 1983, however, the Roosevelt Center changed hands and also direction, at which point Blechman took the project to CSIS.

33. The CSIS project's steering group included Senators Sam Nunn (D-Ga.), Nancy Kassebaum (R-Kan.), and William S. Cohen (R-Me.) and Congressmen Les Aspin (D-Wisc.), Samuel S. Stratton (D-N.Y.), and Newt Gingrich (R-Ga.). Still other members of Congress were involved on one or another of the study's working groups. Although former defense secretaries were notably absent from steering or working groups, six former defense secretaries—all who had served in that office since 1961 save Donald Rumsfeld—stated in a covering letter included with the published report that they were "united in support for the general thrust of its proposals."

34. "AFJI Talks to Congress: Richard C. White," *Armed Forces Journal International* (September 1982): 18.

35. For a brief summary, see "Subcommittee Clears New JCS Bill," *Armed Forces Journal International* (October 1985): 22.

36. Quoted in Charles H. Schemmer, "House JCS Reform Stalled; Tower Promises Separate Senate Bill," *Armed Forces Journal International* (September 1984): 9.

37. See Michael Ganley, "DoD Leaders Defend Command Structure, But Joint Commanders Ask for More Say," *Armed Forces Journal International* (June 1985): 26. As a rule, Weinberger and the serving chiefs opposed significant reform, while operational commanders asserted that although the DOD was giving them more attention than it had in the past, they still felt the need for more control over resources. Significantly, Admiral William J. Crowe, commander-in-chief Pacific Command (PACOM) but soon to become chairman of the JCS, complained that on occasion "the results of major service decisions, not previously coordinated with me, have affected my ability to execute USPACOM strategy." Crowe went on to argue that "giving the unified commanders an earlier and stronger voice in the resource allocation process would strike a better balance between responsibility and accountability." Rather than calling for a stronger chairman, however, Crowe suggested opening a direct line between operational commanders and service chiefs, who at that point communicated only through component commanders working in each unified command. See ibid., 32. Although Crowe remained noticeably silent on JCS reform issues after he became chairman, interviews suggest that behind the scenes he supported the reform effort.

38. Senate Committee on the Armed Services, *Defense Organization: The Need for Change*, Staff Report, 16 October 1985 (Washington, D.C.: Government Printing Office, 1985).

39. Ibid., 240–42.

40. Ibid., 351–53.

41. For a more detailed survey of the evolution of congressional oversight, see McNaugher, *New Weapons, Old Politics*, 56–58, 68–70.

42. Senate Committee on the Armed Services, *Defense Organization,*

591–93. See also John G. Kester, "Under Siege," *Military Logistics Forum* 1 (September-October 1984): 27, 30.

43. Quoted in Michael Ganley, "Weinberger Opts for 'Evolutionary,' Not 'Radical,' Fixes in DoD Reform," *Armed Forces Journal International* (December 1985): 20. In fairness to Weinberger, his testimony was directed at the Locher report, the conclusions of which were too radical for many who otherwise supported JCS and defense-management reform. By this time Weinberger was not arguing against reform so much as he was urging the Armed Services Committee to delay reform legislation until the Packard commission report was available.

44. Ibid.

45. Perry, "How Cap Weinberger Lost the Fight over Defense Reform," 4.

46. MacKubin Thomas Owens, "The Hollow Promise of JCS Reform," *International Security* 10 (Winter 1985/86): 102.

47. See Seth Cropsey, "One Officer at the Top?" *United States Naval Institute Proceedings* (December 1985): 81, 82. For an empirical argument that efforts to centralize weapons procurement have backfired in precisely this way, see McNaugher, *New Weapons, Old Politics,* 64–66.

48. Owens, "The Hollow Promise of JCS Reform," 105.

49. Cropsey, "One Officer at the Top?" 83, 84.

50. As quoted in Department of Defense News Summary, "Joint Chiefs of Staff," 3 March 1986, 5. For more of Lehman's views, see his "Let's Stop Trying to Be Prussians," *Washington Post,* 10 June 1984, C7 (op-ed).

51. See in particular Michael R. Gordon, "Data on Production Inefficiencies May Spur New Debate on Defense Contracting," *National Journal,* 1 June 1985, 1283–86.

52. Michael Ganley, "Reagan to Name Blue-Ribbon Panel on DoD Buying as Reform Calls Mount," *Armed Forces Journal International* (July 1985): 12.

53. Ibid. The letter also suggested Packard and former Defense Secretary Melvin Laird (both good Republicans) as possible chairmen.

54. McFarlane was not alone in this effort. The president's new assistant for national security, Admiral John Poindexter, was apparently anxious to make changes in the military command structure. And Chief of Staff Donald Regan, a former marine but otherwise inexperienced in defense management, nonetheless showed great interest in the Packard commission's deliberations. Finally, interviewees suggest that the president himself realized that growing criticism of his Defense Department endangered his military buildup.

55. For a copy of Executive Order 12526, dated 15 July 1985, see *A Quest for Excellence: Final Report by the President's Blue Ribbon Commission on Defense Management, Appendix* (Washington, D.C.: Government Printing Office, June 1986), Appendix B, 27–28. Cited hereafter as *Quest for Excellence, Appendix.*

56. On 7 June at a conference at the Aspen Institute in Colorado, Weinberger told a group of former high-level officials that the commission was formed to "validate" DOD procurement and management reforms already under

way. According to *Armed Forces Journal International,* the former officials "gasped at Weinberger's perception of its purpose." Michael Ganley, "Packard Panel on DoD Management May Derail DoD Reforms in Congress," *Armed Forces Journal International* (August 1985): 16.

57. For excerpts from Packard's testimony, see Kyle and Schemmer, "Navy, Marines Adamantly Oppose JCS Reforms Most Others Tell Congress Are Long Overdue," 65.

58. President's Blue Ribbon Commission on Defense Management, *Quest for Excellence.* The final report appeared in July 1986, while the interim report was available by 31 January of that year.

59. Ibid., xx.

60. Michael Ganley, "Rogers Says Eliminate Service Chiefs to Strengthen CinCs, JCS Chairman," *Armed Forces Journal International* (January 1986): 20.

61. The most difficult issue had to do with whether the newly created position of vice chair of the JCS would fall sixth in rank behind the service chiefs or second behind the chair. See Michael Ganley, "Senate Armed Services Resolves Most Issues in DoD Reorganization Bill," *Armed Forces Journal International* (March 1986): 18. Section 154 of the Goldwater-Nichols bill makes the vice chair second to the chair. Still, the vice chair may not vote on matters before the JCS, nor is he allowed to command either the chiefs or the combatant commands. Interviews suggest strongly that reformers saw the vice chair as responsible for weapons acquisition, not strategy or command, and that he was meant to be the military counterpart to the undersecretary of defense for acquisition, a position created by the Acquisition Improvement Act of 1986.

62. Senate markup produced interesting, sometimes comical, drama. Although the Navy secretary denied that his department had organized a "crisis center" to kill the reorganization bill, as the committee's markup session began Goldwater was given the center's telephone number. He promptly called the center, located in the Navy department's Pentagon offices, to offer his services —proving that the center existed, and acquiring a list of those in charge of it. See Michael Ganley, "How's That Again? You're Opposed to What?" *Armed Forces Journal International* (March 1986): 18.

63. Michael Ganley, "Reorganization Bill Almost Certain to Reach President's Desk This Year," *Armed Forces Journal International* (April 1986): 16.

64. Quoted in Perry, "How Cap Weinberger Lost the Fight over Defense Reform," 4.

65. Quoted in Ganley, "Reorganization Bill Almost Certain to Reach President's Desk This Year," 16.

66. According to Michael Ganley, reorganization advocates on the Hill feared that Weinberger might persuade the president to veto a reorganization bill. Ibid., 16. On the Pentagon's response, see Michael Ganley, "Reagan's Order to Implement Packard Reforms Catches DoD by Surprise," *Armed Forces Journal International* (May 1986): 15. Unclassified portions of NSDD #219 can be found in *Quest for Excellence, Appendix,* Appendix B, 33–37.

67. See *Quest for Excellence,* 4, and Michael Ganley, "DoD Reorganization Bill Sweeps Through Senate on Unanimous Vote," *Armed Forces Journal International* (June 1986): 14, 16.

68. The description of the House bill in this and the following paragraphs is taken from Michael Ganley, "Reform Bill Called 'Sea Change' for Navy, 'Revolutionary' for Pentagon," *Armed Forces Journal International* (July 1986): 23.

69. Department of Defense Reorganization Act of 1986, P.L. 99–433, 1 October 1986, Title II, pt. A, sec. 151(d).

70. Ibid., Title II, pt. A, sec. 151(d), and pt. B, sec. 163(b)(2).

71. Michael Ganley, "DoD Reorganization Awaits Reagan's Pen After Compromise Bill Clears," *Armed Forces Journal International* (October 1986): 21.

72. Department of Defense Reorganization Act of 1986, Title II, pt. B, sec. 166.

73. See Larry Grossman, "Beyond Rivalry," *Government Executive* (June 1991): 10–15.

74. See, for example, Neil Munro, "Role of CINCs Increases as Budget Forces Shift," *Defense News* (2 September 1991): 26.

75. The words of General Maxwell Thurman, commander of Southern Command during the invasion of Panama, quoted, ibid. It is worth noting as a possible example of Cheney's "considerateness" that the budget role Munro describes goes beyond that required by the Goldwater-Nichols bill.

76. Hearing before the House Committee on Armed Services, 12 April 1991.

77. See Cohen's thoughtful review of Robert Woodward's book *The Commanders;* "In DoD We Trust," *New Republic,* 17 June 1991, 35.

75. Warner had also been secretary of the Navy during the Nixon administration and had served as a Marine Corps officer during the Korean War.

Part Three

Foreign Affairs Issues

Resolving Policy Differences: Foreign Aid and Human Rights

G. Calvin Mackenzie

Introduction

Picture two giant sumo wrestlers, each powerful, experienced, and unrelenting. They battle round after round. One applies a hold to gain the advantage until the other develops a counterhold to reclaim control. These two giants know each other well, and they know their own strengths. Their power derives from self-respect and skill and the desire to represent their regions ably. When the end comes, the art of combat has been refined, but neither has vanquished the other. It is a draw. Nobody wins. They will have to fight again another day.

For almost two decades, Congress and the executive branch have fought in much the same way to determine the role that human rights concerns should play in foreign aid decisions. The advantage has shifted from branch to branch, as power energized counterpower, technique invited countertechnique. But neither branch has won, and the struggle continues.

Twenty years ago, one rarely heard human rights and foreign aid mentioned in the same hearing. Now they are often mentioned in the same breath. Human rights has moved to a place of prominence in foreign assistance policy, but it did not get there without much argument and distrust. Nor is the dust yet settled. The principle that foreign assistance decisions should address the human rights policies of recipient countries is embedded in statute, in bureaucratic organization, and in widely shared understandings and expectations. It is the law of the land. But the application and interpretation of the principle continue to generate debate and political struggle.

This case explores the transition in foreign assistance policy over the past two decades, focusing especially on the central contest between Congress and the executive branch over the role that human rights should play in the policy. The question here is not which branch won, for neither did, but how they fought and why. What role did Congress play in the transition? What strategies and techniques did it employ? Did it overreach the proper bounds of legislative authority and trespass too far into the details of administration?

This is not a case about a single decision. It is about many decisions, most of them encompassed by the annual debate over foreign assistance appropriations. The players changed throughout. The constant was the institutional struggle between a determined set of executive agencies and officials and an equally determined set of congressional committees and individual members. Institutional prerogatives are at the center of this case. Institutional incentives are the source of its energy. Institutional limitations are the principal determinants of its outcomes.

The Issue

The Struggle Begins

In the spring of 1973 Don Fraser (D-Minn.) initiated a series of discussions with members of his staff about the problem of human rights. Fraser was chairman of the House Foreign Affairs Committee Subcommittee on International Organizations. His work on the subcommittee had raised troubling questions in his mind about the state of U.S. relations with countries such as Pakistan, Greece, and South Vietnam, regimes supported by the United States in spite of routine violations of the human rights of their own citizens. At what point and in what way, Fraser wondered, must the United States hold the recipients of its assistance responsible for their domestic human rights policies?

Fraser hired a staff member that spring named John Salzberg. At Fraser's direction, Salzberg arranged a series of about fifteen hearings in the latter half of 1973 on the subject of human rights. From these followed a report that the Subcommittee on International Organizations adopted in the spring of 1974, *Human Rights in the World Community: A Call for U.S. Leadership.* Principal among the report's recommendations were a number of organizational changes in the State Department aimed at giving greater emphasis and priority to human rights.[1]

Although Fraser played an important leadership role in all this, other members of both houses shared his concern about human rights. That became evident in 1975 when human rights restrictions were added to the foreign aid authorization bill during floor debate in each house.[2] Those provisions prohibited development aid to any country "engaging in a consistent pattern of gross violations of internationally recognized human rights" unless Congress determined that the aid benefited "needy people." In making decisions under the provisions, the Foreign Affairs committee of the House or the Foreign Relations Committee of the Senate could require a report from the Agency for International Development (AID). If either committee disagreed with the report, it could initiate action to terminate development aid to the country in question.

The provisions embodied several of the elements that became routine in Congress's effort to enhance human rights concerns in foreign assistance policy: (1) mandatory reports from executive agencies on human rights policies in individual countries; (2) congressional authority to cut foreign aid to countries that were consistent and gross violators of human rights; (3) "escape hatches" that permitted the provision of foreign aid, under certain executive determinations, even to countries that violated human rights.

The Foreign Assistance Program

The focus of this early congressional activity, and most of the efforts that followed, was foreign aid. The foreign aid program had come into existence during the 1940s, first to win the war then to sustain the peace. Initially, it took the form of predominantly humanitarian aid for the war-ravaged countries of Europe. Then, as the postwar communist threat materialized, military assistance became the primary focus of the aid program. Later, developmental aid to less developed countries emerged as a priority. Figure 10.1 indicates changes in the composition of the foreign aid program over time.

From the start, the foreign aid program became a stage upon which a wide range of political objectives were played out. Strings and conditions of broad diversity were attached to the aid. At one time or another, for example, Congress required one-half of aid shipments to be transported on American-flag vessels, prohibited aid to countries selling certain goods to the Soviet Union or Cuba, and ordered the cessation of aid to Indonesia and countries in Eastern Europe.

For the first twenty-five years of the foreign aid program, there was little interest or effort in either Congress or the executive branch to hold recipients of aid to any standard of human rights. The reason was not diffidence or blindness on the part of U.S. policymakers, nor commitment to human rights on the part of many aid recipients. It was instead the powerful, dominating force of the Cold War and the perceived need for allies and friends in a bipolar world. Better a repressive friend than an enlightened enemy. If a country's government was committed to the struggle against communism, aid was likely to flow in its direction regardless of its internal human rights policies.

Even when objections were raised to the policies of some friendly regimes, they were quickly rebutted with arguments about the strategic importance of alliance with those governments and the significant role that aid played in maintaining their friendship and support. Congress rarely raised the flag of human rights to challenge any aid proposal from the executive branch.

That began to change in the 1970s in the context of some broader changes in relations between the two branches. In few periods in this cen-

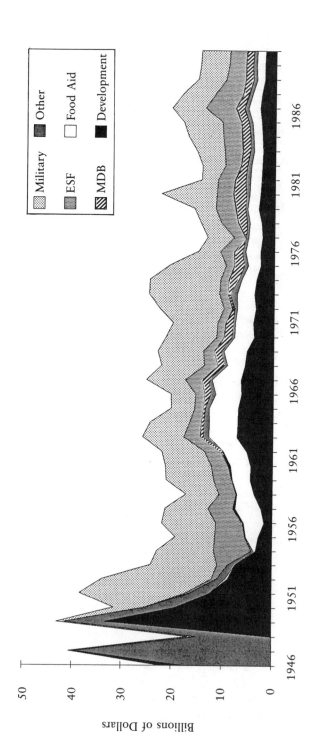

FIGURE 10.1
FOREIGN AID BY CATEGORY (IN CONSTANT 1989 DOLLARS)

NOTE: ESF = Economic Support Fund; MDB = Multilateral Development Banks.
SOURCE: Unpublished data supplied to the author by the Congressional Research Service.

tury has so emboldened a Congress faced so enfeebled an executive as in the few years that began in 1973. The cruelly painful conclusion of the war in Vietnam, the elongated bloodletting over Watergate, the resignation of one president and the succession of another without benefit of election yielded public and congressional distrust of a badly weakened presidency. This coincided with an uncommonly large turnover in Congress, in the House especially, which brought a host of young and aggressive new legislators to Washington. Their impatience with the old ways of Congress soon produced wide-reaching reforms in legislative procedure and organization. It was one of these reforms, in fact, that permitted a relatively junior member like Don Fraser to chair a subcommittee.

The events of the mid-1970s turned the customary relationship between the president and Congress on its head. Traditionally, the president's role is to draft and initiate, Congress's to deliberate and amend or defeat. But in this period, on the issue of human rights, the initiatives were all coming from Congress while the executive stalled, dodged, fudged, and caterwauled.

Challenging the executive branch became an increasingly common form of congressional behavior in the 1970s. Some commentators of the time attributed this to the tensions of divided government, of a Republican administration juxtaposed for eight years with large Democratic majorities in Congress. But the election of Democrat Jimmy Carter in 1976 modified congressional assertiveness only slightly. Congress continued to feel its oats and to seek a larger and larger role in matters of public policy.

That significant change in congressional-executive relations found constant expression in the annual foreign assistance debate. And, increasingly, human rights concerns became a principal center of attention and confrontation. Congress sought new ways to enlarge concern for human rights; the executive branch resisted those efforts that threatened to superimpose human rights on more traditional diplomatic concerns with stability, consistency, and self-interest. By 1975 the battle lines were drawn and the issue was joined.

Congressional Actions in Detailing Foreign Aid Implementation

Congressional efforts to enhance human rights considerations in foreign aid decisions have evolved over time. They have followed no clear blueprint, adhered to no rules of consistency, nor produced any grand consensus or smashing breakthroughs. Because this case covers two decades of activity, involves five administrations, dozens of members of Congress and several subcommittees, and encompasses the expenditure of almost $250 billion (in constant 1989 dollars), it is not easily reduced to a few simple generalizations. But it is fair to say that members of Congress have searched widely for techniques and strategies to impose their concerns about human rights on executive decision making. Over time, the efforts have brought the full legislative arsenal into play. The most common patterns of interaction are identified below.

Broad Legislative Statements of Guiding Principle

Congress has often felt the need to state or restate its collective views on human rights. Part of this was intended to frame the terms and contours of the issue, part to provide a constant reminder to executive, public, and foreign constituencies of continuing congressional interest in the issue. In foreign aid bills, in other foreign policy legislation, and in sense-of-the-Congress resolutions, the legislature has frequently restated its commitment to human rights and its intention to seek to improve human rights in other countries.

In the Foreign Assistance Act of 1973, for example, Congress inserted language stating that "it is the sense of Congress that the President should deny any economic or military assistance to the government of any foreign country which practices the internment or imprisonment of that country's citizens for political purposes."[3] Congressional intentions were amplified and given greater force by the 1974 Harkin amendment (so called after its sponsor, then Democratic Congressman Tom Harkin of Iowa) to section 116 of the Foreign Assistance Act of 1961:

> No assistance may be provided under this part to the government of any country which engages in a consistent pattern of gross violations of internationally recognized human rights, including torture or cruel, inhuman, or degrading treatment or punishment, prolonged detention without charges, causing the disappearance of persons by the abduction and clandestine detention of those persons, or other flagrant denial of the rights of life, liberty, and the security of persons unless such assistance will directly benefit the needy people in such country.[4]

The 1978 amendments to section 502B of the Foreign Assistance Act of 1961 prohibited security assistance to "any country the government of which engages in a consistent pattern of gross violations of internationally recognized human rights."[5] And the Foreign Assistance and Related Programs Appropriations Act of 1982 included language indicating that "funds appropriated by this act may not be obligated or expended to provide assistance to any country for the purpose of aiding efforts of the government of such country to repress legitimate rights of the population of such country contrary to the Universal Declaration of Human Rights."[6]

These examples are but a few of the many occasions on which Congress has included statements of this sort in foreign aid legislation. Their principal effect is to provide "touchstones" or "baselines" for ongoing legislative executive deliberations. They are frequently cited in hearings, committee reports, and State Department communications. Congress employs them often as criteria for assessing State Department proposals and sensitivity on human rights matters.

Some of these legislative statements of principle are quite general, others are more specific in describing disapproved practices, but all are essentially hortatory in nature. They are not self-enforcing. They impose expectations, but no decisive constraints, on the executive branch. By themselves, they do little to change specific decisions or behavior. A member of the House Appropriations Committee staff who has participated in the drafting of many of these statements and provisos noted their limited effect: "The trouble with them is that the interpretation is with the administration. And they're not going to interpret any country they want to give foreign aid to as a gross violator."[7]

In addition, Congress has nearly always included "escape hatches" in these statements. Escape hatches allow the executive branch to avoid congressional restrictions on awarding aid to countries guilty of human rights abuses, for example, "in extraordinary circumstances"; when "such assistance will directly benefit the needy people in such country"; or "if the national security so requires." Determinations of the appropriate time to open these escape hatches are left to the administration, and no definitions are provided in law. Thus, they provide some flexibility to the president, but in so doing they weaken the impact of legislative restrictions.

Reporting and Certification Requirements

On many occasions, Congress has required executive branch agencies to provide reports on matters relating to human rights. These have been the most common form of congressional intervention in the implementation of the foreign aid program. Fourteen statutes requiring human rights reports currently exist.[8] In addition, Congress often uses hearings or committee reports to impose other reporting requirements. The most important of these reports is the State Department's annual "Country Report on Human Rights Practice." This was first mandated by Congress in 1976 and required to cover human rights conditions in all countries that received U.S. security assistance.[9] Because that seemed to focus attention on the human rights failures of U.S. allies only, the coverage was broadened by Congress in 1979 to include all members of the United Nations. The State Department now routinely goes beyond the requirements of the law by including reports on human rights conditions in countries that are not UN members.

At the outset State Department Secretary Henry Kissinger was reluctant to issue this annual report as a public document, arguing that its report-card nature could only harm our relations with countries that received low grades for their human rights policies. Congress was not deterred and began to require that the State Department's annual country report be issued as a public document. The relevant committees of Congress then initiated the practice of holding hearings to review the annual report.

The earliest versions of the annual report in the 1970s drew criticism from members of Congress and human rights groups for pulling punches and failing to detect or to report widely known human rights violations. Over time, the candor and quality of the reports have improved and they are now widely regarded, on Capitol Hill and elsewhere, as reliable and straightforward assessments of human rights conditions around the world.

Other reporting requirements are more specific in nature. As a Congressional Research Service (CRS) study observed, "In some areas, Congress has given the President broad discretionary authority and significant flexibility, but has attached detailed reporting requirements to these provisions so that it can oversee the Administration's use of these discretionary authorities."[10] Typically, Congress does this by imposing certification requirements. These mandate a report from the executive branch to Congress certifying that a particular precondition to the provision of foreign aid has been met. In the foreign aid authorization for FY 82, for example, Congress required that certain kinds of aid could be delivered to Chile only upon presidential certification that Chile had made "significant progress" in complying with internationally recognized principles of human rights.

In that same year, Congress imposed even stiffer restrictions on aid to El Salvador, requiring the administration to submit a certification within 30 days of the passage of the legislation and every 180 days thereafter that El Salvador was "making a concerted and significant effort to comply with internationally recognized human rights" and was "achieving substantial control over all elements of its own armed forces." If the president did not make these certifications, shipments of aid and arms to El Salvador would be suspended.[11]

The value of the reporting and certification requirements has been hotly debated. Some critics see them as a cop-out, a way for Congress to maintain face while submitting to executive branch pressure to continue aid to countries with bad human rights records. One congressional staff member with long experience in human rights matters said, "We're learning more and more about all of these certifications.... Once you put in presidential certification, you might as well assume the money is going. In the five years I've been here, I don't know of one case where the administration has cut off aid to a country."[12]

Others simply doubt whether an institution like Congress could ever fit these reports in a consistent and meaningful way into its decision-making routines. A CRS specialist who has monitored foreign aid reporting requirements for years remarked: "Most of the reports are never used. Some are never called for. It's hard to get a sense of how they're used. It's especially hard to determine what role they play in foreign aid determinations. The problem is not their quality, which most people think is pretty high, but the system—or lack of system—for receiving them, reviewing them, and integrating them into future decisions."[13]

Still other criticisms focus on the burden that reporting requirements impose on both branches. A congressional task force that studied the foreign assistance program concluded in 1989 that "in spite of 1,300 pages of congressional presentation, over 700 congressional certifications annually, and innumerable reports, Congress does not know what actual progress is being made towards the solution of serious global problems."[14]

Those who defend the use of reporting and certification requirements do so on both practical and political grounds. They serve, first, as a method for Congress to obtain information. Prior to congressional enforcement of the requirement for an annual, comprehensive country report on human rights, there was no systematic reporting on that topic, nor was there so reliable a source of country-by-country information or so systematic a basis for assessing progress. As Congressman Wayne Owens (D-Utah), a member of the Subcommittee on Human Rights, stated, "The reports have generated a great degree of interest and reflect an official U.S. policy position. The reports are an extremely important resource for policymakers when considering human rights criteria, both generic and country-specific, contained in U.S. foreign assistance laws."[15]

Reports also encourage the communication between members of Congress and their counterparts in the executive branch that is essential to consensus building in foreign policy. "The underlying presumption of reporting requirements," concluded a CRS study, "is that if Congress has the necessary information on actions being undertaken by the executive branch, members can let the executive branch know of any actions of which they disapprove. Thus, such reports can be a starting point for consultation."[16]

Although individual members of Congress often take the lead in these consultations with the executive branch, personal and committee staffers are frequently the day-to-day conduits for interbranch communications. It is now quite common, for example, for both House and Senate staff members to travel to countries that are suspected of human rights violations, to undertake their own investigations while there, and to meet with government officials and government critics in those countries.

Professional courtesy and prudence generally require that staffers remain anonymous while credit for their work goes to the member who employs them. But the practical reality is that much of the initiative and most of the follow-up on the human rights dialogue between the branches is provided by congressional staff members. As reporting and certification requirements and other elements of congressional involvement in human rights have expanded, the burdens on Congress have grown and the bulk of the added load has been shouldered by staffers. The clear consequence is that they have become increasingly important players in this domain of congressional-executive relations.

Reporting requirements produce a peculiar form of consultation. Indeed, one Senate staff member referred to them as an "illusion of consultation."[17] They may contribute to better informed communication between the branches, and they may lead to genuine discussions of policy, but the human rights reports are rarely specifically integrated into foreign aid or other foreign policy decisions. So, they constitute only an oblique form of congressional-executive consultation.

Reports do often generate hearings. The annual country report on human rights, for example, is now routinely followed by extensive congressional hearings. The hearings provide significant opportunities for executive branch officials to inform Congress about the human rights situation in individual countries and to explain U.S. efforts to improve human rights conditions. A senior State Department official commented that "we do a lot of reporting in the context of giving testimony rather than just submitting a formal report."[18] The hearings also afford members of Congress opportunities to communicate their concerns about policy and progress in countries of special interest.

Reporting and certification requirements are also valuable political tactics because they provide an avenue of compromise when Congress is at loggerheads with the administration over human rights policy. Instituting a reporting or certification requirement is a moderate stroke by Congress, a way to command attention to its views without taking the more draconian step of cutting off foreign aid. When a significant portion of the membership of Congress took issue with the Reagan administration's proposal for continued aid to El Salvador in the early 1980s, the threat of an aid cutoff hung heavy in the air. A showdown was averted when Congress mandated the certification requirements described above. Showdowns of this sort, when the denial of aid is at stake, come infrequently. Congress rarely wins when they do. Hence, reporting and certification requirements offer Congress a middle ground, one the administration usually accepts if the alternative is a full-tilt battle over a foreign aid cutoff.

Finally, it is important to note the cumulative effect of the reporting requirements Congress has imposed in recent years. Although there are critics who question the impact of any specific such requirement in changing the policy of the administration or the human rights activities of the targeted country, there is almost universal agreement that the accumulation of reporting requirements has had a significant and constructive effect. They have forced every embassy, every country desk, and every regional bureau in the State Department to spend part of each year examining, reflecting upon, and reporting about the human rights practices of the countries in their jurisdiction. They have made human rights a routine part of the State Department's agenda in a much more comprehensive way than was the case before the reporting requirements began to be enforced in the 1970s.

Felice D. Gaer, director of the International League for Human Rights and a frequent critic of U.S. human rights policy, noted the importance of the "mainstreaming" of the annual country reports within the State Department. "The pattern established whereby every embassy must now think about and report back on human rights concerns is a powerful bureaucratic tool to institutionalize human rights concerns," she said.[19] Mark Tavlarides, staff director of the House Foreign Affairs Subcommittee on Human Rights and International Organizations and longtime aide to its chair, Congressman Gus Yatron (D-Pa.), stated that "Congress institutionalized human rights. It was Congress that created the human rights report."[20] And Terry R. Peel, director of the staff of the House Appropriations Subcommittee on Foreign Operations, pointed out that the reports have some influence on foreign countries because "they worry about getting in there.... Sometimes they argue with what's been said. Sometimes they make changes."[21]

For all of these reasons, the establishment of reporting and certification requirements has played an important role in congressional efforts to focus executive branch attention on human rights and to guide administration policy. The reports have often failed to meet the standards of their stiffest critics, and there is little evidence that they have had a consistent or broad effect on human rights conditions abroad. But they have become a central and convenient arena for negotiation between the legislative and executive branches on human rights policy.

Administrative Controls

In its efforts to impose human rights considerations on foreign aid decisions, Congress has also relied on some tried-and-true administrative controls or oversight techniques. The purpose and, to some degree, the effect of these has been to extend the reach of Congress beyond the legislative process into the arena of policy implementation.

In 1977 Congress enacted legislation, in the face of concerted State Department opposition, to create a Bureau of Human Rights and Humanitarian Affairs in the department. The prevailing view in Congress was that human rights could be brought to a higher level of priority in State Department deliberations only by the creation of an advocate for that position in the department.

The creation of the Human Rights Bureau was the outcome of a process that began in 1974 with the report on human rights issued by Congressman Fraser's Subcommittee on International Organizations. That report called for the establishment of just such a bureau. Anxious to avoid congressionally imposed alterations of its internal organization, the department responded to the issues raised in hearings before Fraser's subcommittee with initiatives of its own. George Aldrich, then the department's deputy legal adviser, indicated in testimony that he had established the position of assistant legal adviser on human rights and had appointed Charles Runyon, a man well-regarded by the human rights community on Capitol Hill, to it.

After Fraser pressed department witnesses vigorously on human rights matters at hearings in 1974, he was visited by Robert Ingersoll, a senior department official, who told Fraser that he had set up a small human rights office in the department and introduced James Wilson, the man he had selected to serve as human rights coordinator. One congressional staff observer of these events has remarked, "The administration did this without any direct prodding from Congress. But sometimes I wonder if we don't give enough credit to the effects of hearings as opposed to legislation."[22]

These fledgling efforts by the department briefly mitigated but did not stanch congressional interest in having a forceful, institutional advocate for human rights within the department. In 1976 Congress formally mandated the appointment of a coordinator for human rights and humanitarian affairs by the president with the advice and consent of the Senate.[23] In 1977 further congressional action elevated the coordinator to assistant-secretary status.[24] The Bureau of Human Rights and Humanitarian Affairs was taking shape at a high level of organizational visibility. "The intent," declared John Salzberg, a staff assistant to Fraser at the time, "was that the Human Rights Bureau would be the watchdog for human rights. Just like there's a Bureau of Economic Affairs and a Bureau of Politico-Military Affairs, why not a Bureau of Human Rights?"[25]

As often occurs when Congress imposes organizational changes on an executive department, the integration of the new bureau into State Department routines was anything but seamless. Part of the difficulty was the natural suspicion that attached to any uninvited or unsought interloper. The bureau bore the stigma of an "alien creature."[26] This perception was strengthened when President Carter staffed it with human rights activists whose backgrounds were largely in domestic politics. More significant, however, was the natural resistance in the State Department to the bureau's mission.

One official of the bureau described the sources of that tension:

> This bureau has never been particularly welcomed as part of the State Department.... You can't do human rights without stepping on toes. Most of our human rights work as a government is, by its very nature, going to be negative. The nature of the State Department is to pursue a goal of frictionless relations, to avoid bilateral friction. We, on the other hand, are creating friction.... The culture [at State] is negotiate and compromise. No ripples, please.... For a lot of people throughout the State Department, there's a motivation of let's just not have anything blow up on my watch. This is not conducive to an activist approach.... You can't do human rights without being active.[27]

In many ways the Bureau of Human Rights has had better relations with Congress than with its counterparts in the department. The bureau's philosophy more closely aligns with the views of its congressional creators than with prevailing routines, incentives, and policies in the diplomatic corps. Hence, its strength and its weakness come from the same source: its dominant commitment to serve as an advocate for human rights. It is trusted and well regarded in Congress for its persistence and independence; it is avoided and resisted in the department for the same reasons. Accordingly, the impact of the bureau on U.S. policy and the behavior of foreign governments has been limited. Its impact on foreign aid decisions has been particularly scant, for it intersects only peripherally with the annual foreign aid determination process.

Congressional efforts to impose a human rights emphasis on State Department routines have not been limited to the creation of the Bureau of Human Rights and Humanitarian Affairs. It has paid close attention to the staffing of that bureau as well. Evidence of that occurred most dramatically in 1981 when the Senate forced the withdrawal of the nomination of Ernest W. Lefever, Ronald Reagan's first nominee for the position of assistant secretary of state for human rights and humanitarian affairs. Lefever had been a vigorous critic of the human rights policies of the Carter administration and his appointment was opposed by a coalition of thirty-five groups called the Ad Hoc Committee of the Human Rights Community. The coalition charged that Lefever was indifferent to human rights and therefore unqualified for the position.[28] The Senate Foreign Relations Committee, though controlled by the Republicans, voted 13–4 to reject the nomination, and Lefever withdrew from consideration thereafter.

Cutting Off Foreign Aid

The power of the purse remains Congress's most effective lien on administrative discretion. When it cuts off foreign aid to a country with an unacceptable human rights record, or when it threatens to do so, it takes control of foreign aid decision making more effectively than in any other way. "The leverage of the funding," noted a House staff member with long experience in foreign aid appropriations, "has as much to do with putting pressure on human rights as anything.... Probably the best leverage is the leverage of giving and taking money, threatening to give and take money, to countries that aren't performing on human rights."[29]

A direct cutoff of foreign aid, the heaviest weapon in the congressional arsenal, is rarely used. From time to time in the past two decades, Congress has reduced assistance levels proposed by the administration as a way to indicate its disapproval of the recipient country's human rights policies. On even rarer occasions, it has cut off all aid to a country. In 1983, for example, in exasperation over the persistent human rights abuses of the Guatemalan regime, Congress denied the Reagan administration's request for aid to that country.

But an aid cutoff is a very blunt instrument of congressional-executive relations and of foreign policy. It is both difficult to employ and potentially counterproductive in its effects. The political burden of cutting off foreign aid is enormous. It requires a fabric of consensus in Congress strong enough to resist the full force of presidential pressure. Experienced congressional hands know how difficult it is to forge and sustain such a consensus when the president is willing to commit White House resources and personal time to win a showdown. When there was strong opposition in Congress in 1980, for example, to President Carter's request for $75 million in aid for the Sandinista government in Nicaragua, the administration pressed hard for its position and won. Although Congress attached strings, it voted the aid nevertheless.

Given this political difficulty, Congress tends to avoid showdowns of this sort. The incentive is strengthened by the realization that an aid cutoff may well reduce U.S. influence on the country in question. Robert W. Ferrand, former deputy assistant secretary of state for human rights, spoke of the problem with labeling a country a gross violator of human rights and cutting off its aid: "Once you have so labeled a government, you have in fact, in a way, hit them so hard that the effect may very well be that they say, fine, take your aid, we don't need it, we don't want it. In that case, the lever that you had chosen to use to change behavior, to improve behavior ... breaks off in your hand."[30]

Even among members of Congress most concerned over human rights, there is a deep reluctance to cut off aid. Fraser, an early leader in Congress's efforts to force human rights concerns to a higher level of priority, generally opposed congressional efforts to cut off aid to particular violators. Aid cutoffs, he felt, were a meat-axe approach when more delicate strategies were needed, and such cutoffs permitted little flexibility for Congress to react when the targeted country began to make progress in human rights.[31] The current staff director of the House Subcommittee on Human Rights echoed this view: "Some people think that the hammer is the only tool, that we should just cut off aid and that's it. There's nothing else in between. But there are a lot of people up here, principled advocates of human rights, who don't support cutting off aid in many countries with human rights violations because they see larger problems.... Our policies are far more effective abroad when both Congress and the executive branch speak with one voice and agree on policy."[32]

Efforts to cut off aid continue to occur in Congress. In 1990 some Democratic members of the House Appropriations Subcommittee on Foreign Operations moved to cut off all aid to the government of Zaire. The subcommittee's staff director declared at the outset that it would be a "major undertaking." "The administration is opposed to it, and members, mostly Republicans but some others too, are opposed to a complete cutoff. But with some of these countries, you just get to the point where you've tried everything."[33]

For the most part, the congressional power to deny foreign aid to a country that violates human rights remains a kind of club behind the door. It is used as a threat, and it is a threat that hangs in the air whenever there is a significant dispute between the legislative and executive branches over the acceptability of the human rights policies of a recipient country. Knowing that Congress has the ultimate power to cut off aid, the executive branch will often work more aggressively to bring about changes in the country in question or accept conditions that Congress seeks to impose on the provision of aid. One senior State Department official stated:

> I wouldn't underestimate [the impact of] the prospect of [Congress's] cutting off aid. One of the reasons that they seldom cut it off is that they make their concerns known to the administration long enough and loud enough ahead of time that the administration says, "Look, we don't need a big fight over that. We don't need to jeopardize all our programs in the region with other countries for the sake of that country. So let's see if we can quietly work out with the committee staff what would be an acceptable level to them or what conditions would be acceptable to them. Then we'll come back and say we don't want any conditions, and they'll come back and say we don't want any aid, and we'll work out this wonderful compromise." The threat of cutting off aid brings the State Department to the table when it otherwise would not go.[34]

Knowing how difficult and potentially unproductive an aid cutoff can be, Congress will look for places to compromise, usually by the attachment of conditions or by symbolic, but not total, reductions in the administration's aid requests. Serious efforts to cut off foreign aid to human rights violators are rare, but their potential shapes the broad contours of debate and adjustment between the two branches.

Effects of Congressional Intervention in Foreign Assistance

These events of the past decade and a half have altered U.S. foreign policy, and they have altered relations between Congress and the executive branch in the area of foreign assistance. But the natural constraints in the U.S. Constitution, in the byplay of domestic politics, and in U.S. international obligations have channelized and moderated those alterations. Rip Van Winkle, awakening today from a twenty-year nap, would not find the relative power positions of Congress and the president significantly changed, nor would he notice a major outbreak of human rights in the countries that receive U.S. foreign aid. He would notice much more talk about human rights, yielding only marginally increased activity in their pursuit.

Results for Policy

In debates over foreign assistance—indeed, over all of U.S. foreign policy—human rights is significantly more prominent than it was at the beginning of the 1970s. There is now legislation that makes acceptable human rights policies a precondition of receipt of U.S. aid. There is a House Subcommittee on Human Rights. Appropriations subcommittees in both houses give ample attention to human rights in their annual deliberations. There is a congressional Human Rights Caucus. Within the State Department, there is a Bureau of Human Rights and Humanitarian Affairs. And an array of human rights interest groups have spawned and become a visible presence in Washington. If only human rights had multiplied as rapidly as the groups and institutions that have emerged to protect them, the problem would have long since been solved.

Observers of the foreign policy struggles of the past two decades are unanimous in one conclusion: sensitivity to human rights has been heightened throughout the diplomatic corps and the making of foreign policy. The *principle* that U.S. influence should seek to improve human rights in other countries is now widely supported in both the executive and legislative branches.

That is no small change, for political debate in the early 1970s often questioned whether the United States had any right to examine and question the internal policies of its allies. Leading U.S. policymakers—of whom Richard Nixon was the most prominent—argued for a foreign policy based on power and self-interest. "We deal with individual nations on the basis of their foreign and not their domestic policy," Nixon had stated in 1972.[35] A growing determination by some members of Congress and by President Carter to give a larger role to human rights in shaping our foreign relations has altered what had been a long-standing predisposition in U.S. policy.

But the principle has changed more fully than the policy. If there has been growing consensus that human rights concerns ought to be a central element of U.S. foreign policy, there has been little precision in the definition of acceptable human rights standards and no standing consensus on how best to deal with human rights violators. The political debate over human rights rolls on, with crescendos of intensity almost every year. But systematic human rights abuses also roll on, even in countries that are major recipients of U.S. aid. Why is that?

The principal explanation is that despite the growing consensus on the importance of human rights, there are few participants in the making of foreign policy who believe that human rights should be the primary element in foreign policy. In a complex and often dangerous world, most argue, we cannot afford the luxury of basing our relations with other countries solely on our comfort with their human rights policies. Our need for friends and allies is too great; our ability to influence internal policies abroad is too limited. Hence, the incentives for the State Department and the administration to picture human rights violations in the broader frame of the international balance of power are strong. Jeri Laber, executive director of the human rights group Helsinki Watch, observed, "The administration often falls down because it wants to continue giving aid, it tends to judge conditions in a country more favorably than they should be judged instead of saying straight out this country violates human rights. . . ."[36]

Congress's ability to force human rights to a higher level of priority has also suffered from internal dissensus. Human rights are important to different members in different ways. Liberal members tend to be more troubled by the human rights violations of rightist governments; conservative members worry more about the abuses of leftist governments. This yields widespread support for improved human rights abroad, but that support begins to disintegrate when the focus narrows to individual countries. The frequent debates in Congress during the 1980s on foreign aid to El Salvador, Guatemala, and other Central and South American countries often split Congress along ideological as well as partisan lines. Without a solid and determined congressional consensus, efforts to redirect the attention or policies of the executive branch are rarely very successful.

Even if consensus were more common in Congress, a shortage of resources limits congressional ability to monitor and respond to human rights conditions in more than 150 foreign countries. "It's pretty hard to do it," lamented the staff director of the House Appropriations Subcommittee with responsibility for the foreign aid budget. "We've got three staff people here for the whole world. We pay attention to the country that's squeaking the most, the one that the human rights organizations are raising or Americans who are in the country are bringing out information. We can't do that much."[37]

The impacts of congressional assertiveness on human rights policies have been felt in two principal ways. First, at the margins. The reports that Congress has mandated are read in the countries that are their subject. They are reported in the world press. Governments do not like publicity for their human rights violations. Sometimes, therefore, in response to or in anticipation of an unfavorable mention in a human rights report, governments will cease certain gross human rights violations. The cessation may be temporary; it may have limited effect; other human rights abuses may continue. But there has at least been a marginal impact.

Congress has also been able to alter human rights violations abroad when it focuses on specific cases. Said Mark Tavlarides, staff director of the House Subcommittee on Human Rights, "Does it help? If you're asking me if I've deluded myself into thinking that we've democratized the rest of the world, no. Have we made a little bit of a difference? Yes. I know, for example, on specific human rights cases, a member of Congress has written the ambassador based let's say on an alert from Amnesty International, and asked for a stay of execution or for someone to be released, and they'll do it."[38]

The common view, however, is that the efforts of the past two decades have added up to little real change in human rights practices abroad. The voice of the United States is too muted or too cacophonous. Beyond the water's edge, our reach exceeds our grasp. A moral concern like human rights will often, inevitably, take a back seat to the other practical concerns that dominate international relations. We have huffed and we have puffed, but we have blown down very few torture chambers and political prisons.

Results for Institutional Relations and Processes

In foreign policy, Congress has always suffered a shortage of handles. In a famous scholarly treatise, Professor Edward S. Corwin made the oft-quoted remark that the Constitution "is an invitation to struggle for the privilege of directing American foreign policy."[39] Maybe so. But the fact has always been that the Constitution, court interpretations thereof, and historical precedent have defined broad areas of activity in which the president is relatively free of congressional restraint. The president has the sole power to receive ambassadors and, through that, to recognize foreign governments as legitimate. In 1948, for example, President Truman recognized the government of Israel before many in Congress—and even his own secretary of state—were prepared to do so. Presidential authority to negotiate executive agreements with foreign nations is only rarely subject to congressional intervention. And even with the War Powers Act in place, recent presidents have suffered few constraints on their freedom to dispatch U.S. armed forces to hot spots around the world.

So, if the Constitution has invited Congress and the president to struggle over foreign policy, it has also required Congress to be inventive in creating arenas for that struggle, in devising new handles by which to restrain presidential discretion. We have seen that effort unfold in this case. When some members of Congress became unhappy in the early 1970s with the direction of foreign policy, and especially with its indifference to human rights violations by our allies and aid recipients, they initiated an effort first to build a set of procedural and structural restraints on foreign aid decisions and then to employ them to enlarge congressional participation and influence.

Informal, then mandatory proscriptions were placed on aid to gross human rights violators. Human rights reporting requirements were created, multiplied, and refined. An outpost for human rights advocacy was established in the State Department. An unsatisfactory nominee to head that bureau was rejected. Human rights hearings became commonplace and sense-of-the-Congress resolutions on specific human rights violations poured forth. A multitude of conditions and certification requirements were placed on foreign aid appropriations. In egregious cases, aid cutoffs were threatened and occasionally carried out. All of this generated much conflict between Congress and the president. But did it alter, in any meaningful and permanent way, the relative roles of the two branches in determining U.S. foreign assistance policy?

Opinions differ. Some believe that Congress has asserted itself beyond its constitutional role and beyond its capabilities. They suggest that Congress is now often guilty of "micromanagement." Ronald Reagan noted in 1986 the tendency of recent Congresses "to try to curb and take away from the presidency some of the prerogatives that belong there—the handling of foreign policy and so forth—and placed restrictions on the office that in effect would have foreign policy determined by a committee of 535."[40] The frequent result of this kind of micromanagement, the critics allege, is inconsistency in policy and embarrassment to loyal friends abroad.

Others take a very different view. Congress, they note, did only what it had to do to ensure a responsible foreign policy based on traditional and widely supported U.S. values. A Senate Appropriations Committee report argued that Congress has had to act because "there are major flaws within the U.S. Government bureaucracy in the manner in which U.S. human rights policies are formulated and implemented."[41] Jerome J. Shestack, the chairman of the International League for Human Rights, has suggested that "the Administration regularly complained about congressional interference in the specifics of foreign policy. But it was the Administration's blatant bypass of human rights legislation properly within the congressional prerogative that compelled these congressional directives."[42]

A senior congressional staff member argued that "when the administration takes care of it, then we won't micromanage. They're not doing it. Every time there's a void up here, people are going to step in, and there's a void there. I don't think Congress micromanages this issue enough."[43] And Congressman Lee Hamilton (D-Ind.), the cochair of a panel created to study foreign aid policy, suggested, "We could strike a deal: that the executive branch will pay attention to the initiatives of Congress and not ignore them, and Congress will not try to micromanage the foreign aid program."[44]

Has Congress trespassed the line of propriety into micromanagement? It is a difficult and probably not very profitable inquiry. There is no consensus in either branch, in the law, or in the scholarly literature on where congressional authority properly ends and executive authority begins. In fact, they overlap constantly almost everywhere and the only meaningful restraints are those that are self-imposed and politically driven.

Significant elements of Congress have disagreed with recent administrations about the proper level of U.S. concern for human rights abroad. In the absence of intrabranch or interbranch consensus, fighting has ensued. The fighting has resembled trench warfare more than grand strategy. Minor gains and losses have occurred for each branch. Fragile truces are made and then violated. Presidential efforts and objectives have rarely been significantly deterred, but they have often been hard-won, with compromise and modification and conditions the implements of conflict.

Conclusions

What does this case tell us about the current status of relations between the president and Congress? Several instructive generalizations can be drawn from the events and experiences we have examined here.

1. *Where public opinion provides little clear policy guidance, conflict within and between the two branches is inevitable.*

Over time, public opinion on foreign aid has provided only one consistent cue to public officials: the American people do not like it. In the past two decades, opinion poll after opinion poll has confirmed the unpopularity of foreign aid as a U.S. policy.[45] Congress has responded to that not by killing the foreign aid program or curtailing it significantly but by violating normal legislative procedure to reduce the number of recorded votes necessary to enact the annual foreign aid program. Throughout the 1980s, for example, Congress rarely passed a foreign aid authorization bill. In most years, the requirement for an authorization was waived and Congress enacted foreign aid entirely through the appropriations process.

Public opinion on the role of human rights in foreign policy was ambiguous at best. There were no broad national movements for or against human rights in foreign policy, nor has this been a subject of widespread public debate. The efforts of President Carter to make human rights a centerpiece of foreign policy during his administration were met largely with indifference in the United States. The information gathering and lobbying efforts of a handful of human rights groups were important in helping to identify problems abroad and helped to keep the human rights issue on the agenda of the executive and legislative branches, but those groups represented no large or active constituency and were no substitute for the policy guidance and constraints that come from mobilized public opinion.

In the absence of that kind of public opinion, policymakers in both branches were free to act on their own concerns. When those concerns differed, as they often did, they fought it out. The fights occurred in public view but with little public interference. The frequent dissensus between Congress and the executive branch was encouraged by a lack of consensus—and interest—among the American people.

2. *In important ways, the State Department and the foreign affairs community in Congress represent two different cultures. Congressional-executive conflict is often rooted in a clash of those cultures.*

The State Department operates in a world of many sovereign actors and is governed by a commitment to deliberate, often painstaking, negotiation and bargaining. It respects the principle of deference to foreign traditions and domestic policies that is one of the bases of international diplomatic practice. The department prefers predictability, stability, and consistency. It often views its constituency as the world diplomatic community and its clients abroad, rather than the American people or their representatives in

Congress (or sometimes even their representative in the White House). It abhors and resists externally imposed changes that force it to violate normal diplomatic procedure.

Congress is quite a different kind of organization. Change is its business; substantive consistency is a stranger in its midst. It rides on ebbs and flows in the public mood and the rise and fall of political tides. One senior State Department official said of the department's view of Congress: "Elected officials are more prone to look at what is right and what is politically doable than to look at 'is someone going to be offended because we are doing it,' particularly someone who is not a U.S. citizen constituent. The Capitol Hill culture is more advocacy oriented." The official contrasted that perception of Congress with the typical State Department view: "Here, the best of all possible quos is the status quo. Anything that you do, other than the status quo, is bound to either offend the country that you're dealing with or possibly backfire. There are lots of incentives for bureaucracy to just ride with it."[46]

It is inevitable that these two different cultures will clash constantly; Congress pushing new initiatives, the State Department holding out for stability and consistency. The president, with one foot in the political world and the other in the bureaucracy, often ends up as a mediator in these conflicts of institutional culture.

3. Divided government exacerbates all the inherent tensions in a system of separation of powers.

One of the dominant characteristics of this case is that it has occurred in a period when the presidency and at least one house of Congress were controlled by different parties most of the time. That, in fact, has been the case in eighteen of the twenty-two years from 1969 to 1990. Divided government, inevitably, undermines congressional-executive cooperation and comity.

For much of the period under review here, human rights have been an issue with potent partisan connotations. The Republican administrations under Nixon and Ford gave little priority to human rights as a factor in the foreign aid calculus. The realpolitik to which they were committed emphasized power and self-interest as the principal ingredients in U.S. policy making. Indeed, it was this perceived indifference to human rights that first energized congressional activism in the 1970s.

The election of Carter, the only Democrat to fill the presidency in this period, brought a new emphasis—in rhetoric and sometimes in practice—on human rights in foreign aid determinations. The Reagan campaign in 1980 criticized that emphasis, and Reagan's election brought an avowed effort to reduce the weight of human rights considerations in aid decisions. During the Reagan administration and the first two years under President George Bush, the Bureau of Human Rights and Humanitarian Affairs sought to emphasize low-volume rhetoric and "quiet diplomacy" as the primary approach to improving human rights abroad. David Burgess, policy director of the bureau, noted that "quiet diplomacy can get important results, and . . . it should generally precede (but not exclude) the kind of public denunciations that get high levels of media attention, but achieve little real progress in human rights."[47]

There have been human rights advocates in both parties in Congress, but the leadership on human rights initiatives has usually come from Democrats and from the committees they controlled. Some of the incentives for that, no doubt, were ideological and institutional. Democratic members asserted their own policy views when those differed from the administration's. They sought to enlarge the congressional role in foreign aid determinations when they grew uncomfortable with directions proposed by the executive branch. Those are natural inclinations whatever the partisan composition of the federal government, but the rift between the two branches and the intensity of debate over human rights during this period was aggravated by partisan conflict.

The post-Watergate, post-Vietnam Congress is a more independent and feisty institution than Congresses of previous decades. It is not clear, because we have had so little opportunity to discern, whether one-party control of both branches could tame the conflict that now often occurs between them. It is clear, however, that divided government only encourages interbranch differences and compounds the difficulty in resolving them.

4. *Congressional initiatives often strengthen the hand of U.S. diplomats in dealing with their foreign counterparts.*

For all of their objections to congressional "interference," those who implement policy in the executive branch often find congressional mandates a useful stick in dealing with their own counterparts and clients. Career diplomats are almost always uncomfortable when duty requires them to criticize, or seek domestic policy changes from, their foreign counterparts. It is easier for them to do that when they can place the blame on Congress. "This is awkward for us, but Congress has required us to raise some concerns about your human rights violations," goes this approach.

One experienced congressional staff member said of congressional initiatives in human rights, "I think the administration has viewed those conditions and resolutions as useful tools. They can say to that government: 'We didn't do it to you, Congress did.' Good cop, bad cop."[48] Another staff member made the same point: "I think the administration uses our leverage, too, to their advantage. They say that Congress is going to cut off funds unless you make changes."[49]

5. *In Congress, and often in the executive branch, policy is more important than process.*

The architectural imperative that form should follow function is a legislative imperative as well. Over its two centuries of existence, Congress has developed fat books full of legislative rules, procedures, and precedents. Its members pay them great lip service, but they also try to circumnavigate or violate them whenever they stand in the way of important policy objectives.

The one overarching lesson of the congressional budget debate in the past two decades is that no procedural innovations can force members of Congress to vote for spending cuts or tax increases against their will. The Budget Reform Act of 1974 failed fully to accomplish that and the Gramm-Rudman-Hollings deficit reduction act of 1985 has also fallen far short of its objectives. Legislative ingenuity reaches its zenith when a procedural requirement stands in the way of a policy objective.

We have seen that pattern repeatedly in foreign aid determinations as well. One of the bedrocks of congressional rules is that no funds will be appropriated until a program has been duly authorized. Yet, in the 1980s Congress frequently passed a foreign aid appropriation bill without any prior authorization. Conditions and requirements on foreign aid distribution were routinely written into committee reports rather than legislation. Waivers of those were just as routinely granted by committees or their chairs. State Department officials certified human rights progress to ensure a continuation of aid to countries where human rights abuses were commonplace.

All of this points up the important distinction between law and will. The imperatives of law are highly subject to fluctuations of will. If Congress and the president had the will to balance the budget, they have the legal tools to do so. To the extent they have the will to use foreign aid to enforce a higher commitment to human rights in recipient countries, they have tools to do that as well. But without that will—at least, without a collective will—laws and procedures are mere words.

In the foreign assistance program, law and policy have often differed. We have given foreign aid, billions of dollars in foreign aid, to countries that systematically violate the human rights of their citizens. We have done that, even though U.S. law enjoins it, because Congress and the executive branch have frequently lacked the collective will—often because of deference to other considerations—to observe the stiff requirements of the law.

6. Prescriptions about proper legislative and executive roles are rarely binding, unless they come from the federal courts.

The dominant lesson of this case, as indeed of all cases of congressional-executive relations, is that the separation of powers is more often a political than a legal matter. On this subject, the Constitution is an ambiguous document. That may be its genius, and the source of its durability. With but few exceptions, the framers of that document were unable to achieve the consensus necessary to define precise boundaries between the legislative and executive branches. Subsequent generations have found that consensus just as elusive.

So, the two branches have been locked in continuing conflict on a moving front. Assertions of executive authority have brought counterassertions of legislative authority. Victories have been won not through compelling legal arguments but through the construction of majority coalitions. Few of those were permanent and few of the victories they wrought have lasted beyond Congress or the generation in which they occurred.

The closest we have come to clear demarcations of legislative and executive authority have resulted from those infrequent Supreme Court interventions in these disputes. The prevailing wisdom of the Court over the years has been that these are "political questions," best left to Congress and the executive to settle on their own terms. Sometimes the two branches could not settle their conflicts, and the Court was asked or forced to intervene. The number of such cases is small. Each has defined, usually in the narrowest way possible, a division of legislative and executive authority. But those are exceptions. In most areas of congressional-executive conflict—foreign affairs especially—the boundaries remain unsettled. All the scholarly analyses and all the weighty statements from presidents and members of Congress pale in the face of contemporary political disputes. Uncertainty is opportunity. And those who seek policy change will explore every crevice of possibility to achieve their goals. Few institutional boundaries constrain or impede them.

Timeline of Major Events in the Foreign Aid and Human Rights Case

1941	Lend-Lease program begins, providing the first instance of U.S. foreign aid. By V-J Day, lend-lease assistance to the Allies exceeds $40 billion, mostly in war materiel.
1943	Government and Relief in Occupied Areas (GAROIA) program begins with invasion of Italy.
1944	Bretton Woods Agreements create World Bank and International Monetary Fund (IMF).
1945	United Nations created. U.S. participation in Bretton Woods and in creation of UN indicates a commitment to the recovery of war-ravaged countries and a willingness to spend to maintain conditions for peace abroad.
1947	President Truman recommends $400 million in bilateral U.S. aid to Greece and Turkey, which are perceived to be under Soviet threat. Some in Congress object that bilateral aid will undermine the UN, but Congress appropriates the funds Truman requested.
1948	Truman administration initiates the European Recovery Program (Marshall Plan) following comprehensive review of U.S. foreign policy. Program will provide $17 billion in grants and loans over four years to sixteen participating countries. There is broad bipartisan support in Congress.
1949	North Atlantic Treaty Organization (NATO) formed. Mutual Defense Assistance Act shifts emphasis of foreign aid from

humanitarian relief to military aid. Of $26.3 billion in net aid distributed between 1945 and mid-1950, only $1.4 billion is for military purposes. From mid-1950 to mid-1955, military aid constitutes $14 billion of $26 billion in total aid.

1951   Foreign aid comes to be viewed increasingly as a relatively cheap way to extend national security and implement the policy of containing communism.

1954   P.L. 83-480, sec. 112(d) is the first legislation to require the executive branch to report on human rights policies in countries receiving U.S. aid.

1957   Eisenhower Doctrine seeks to emphasize foreign aid to nations of the Middle East following Suez Crisis of 1956.

1961   President Kennedy announces the Alliance for Progress, a program of financial aid and cooperative development for the countries of Latin America.

By executive order, Kennedy creates the Agency for International Development (AID) to replace the International Cooperation Administration and Development Loan Fund.

1973   House Foreign Affairs Subcommittee on International Organizations holds extensive hearings on human rights abroad.

1974   Congress adds sec. 502B to the Foreign Assistance Act of 1974 (P.L. 93-559), stating "the sense of the Congress that, except in extraordinary circumstances, the President shall substantially reduce or terminate security assistance to any government which engages in a consistent pattern of gross violations of internationally recognized human rights." The section also requires an annual report to Congress on human rights conditions in all countries receiving U.S. security assistance.

1975   For the first time, both houses of Congress divide military and economic assistance into separate bills.

The Harkin amendment to the foreign economic aid authorization bill (P.L. 94-161) establishes a procedure (sec. 116) specifically prohibiting economic assistance to any country that engages in gross violations of human rights, "unless such assistance will directly benefit the needy people in such country."

1976   Sec. 28 of the Inter-American Development Bank Act (P.L. 94-302) directs the U.S. executive director of the bank to vote against any loan to any government that grossly violates the human rights of its citizens.

The International Security Assistance and Arms Export Control Act (P.L. 94-239) establishes the Office of Coordinator for Human Rights and Humanitarian Affairs in the State Department. The act also requires the department to submit an annual report on human rights practices in each country proposed by the administration as a military aid recipient.

1977   Inauguration of President Carter initiates new emphasis on indigenous human rights policies of foreign countries as a factor in bilateral relations with the United States.

P.L. 95-118 seeks to insert human rights considerations into indirect U.S. aid provided through all international lending institutions by requiring U.S. officials working at those institutions to try to direct loans away from countries violating human rights.

1978   Military aid authorization (P.L. 95-384) bars security aid to any country violating human rights of its citizens, unless secretary of state finds that extraordinary circumstances necessitate continuation of aid.

1979   Congress approves Carter's plan to reorganize the administration of foreign aid programs. A new independent agency, the International Development Cooperation Agency (ICDA) takes over responsibility for most direct and indirect economic aid programs.

1981   In the foreign aid authorization for FY 82 (P.L. 97-113), Congress establishes human rights conditions for aid to El Salvador, beginning an ongoing struggle with the Reagan administration over aid to that country. In the same legislation, Congress conditions aid to Chile on presidential certification of progress in human rights.

1983   Congress denies Reagan request for aid to Guatemala, citing the repressive policies of the military government.

1989   Foreign Operations Appropriations Act of 1989 (P.L. 100-461) denies aid to any country whose duly elected head of state has been deposed by military coup d'état.

Notes

1. This narrative is based on newspaper reports of the period and the author's interview with John Salzberg, 20 July 1990, Washington, D.C.

2. The bill is H.R. 9005; it became P.L. 94-161.

3. P.L. 93-189.

4. P.L. 94-161.

5. P.L. 95-384.

6. P.L. 97-377.

7. Interview with Terry R. Peel, staff assistant, House Committee on Appropriations, Subcommittee on Foreign Operations, Export Financing, and Related Programs, Washington, D.C., 26 July 1990.

8. See Congressional Research Service, Foreign Affairs Division, *Required Reports to Congress on Foreign Policy,* prepared for the House Committee on Foreign Affairs, 100th Cong., 2d sess., 1 August 1988). Committee Print.

9. P.L. 94-329.

10. Congressional Research Service, Foreign Affairs Division, *Foreign Assistance Reporting Requirements,* prepared for the House Committee on Foreign Affairs, 100th Cong., 2d sess., December 1988, Committee Print, 6.

11. The Chile and El Salvador certification requirements are included in P.L. 97-113.

12. Peel interview.

13. Interview with Vita Bite, analyst in international relations, Congressional Research Service, 16 July 1990.

14. House Committee on Foreign Affairs, Task Force on Foreign Assistance, *Report of the Task Force on Foreign Assistance,* 101st Cong., 1st sess., February 1989, H. Doc. 101-32, 32.

15. House Committee on Foreign Affairs, Subcommittee on Human Rights and International Organizations, *Review of the State Department's Country Reports on Human Rights, 1988, Hearings,* 101st Cong., 1st sess., 1989, 1.

16. Congressional Research Service, Foreign Affairs Division, *Executive-Legislative Consultation on Foreign Policy: Strengthening the Legislative Side,* prepared for the House Committee on Foreign Affairs, 97th Cong., 2d sess., April 1982, Committee Print, 46.

17. Ibid., 48.

18. Interview with David Burgess, policy director, Bureau of Human Rights and Humanitarian Affairs, Department of State, Washington, D.C., 18 July 1990.

19. House Committee on Foreign Affairs, Subcommittee on Human Rights and International Organizations, *Review of the State Department's Country Reports on Human Rights, 1988,* 95.

20. Interview with Mark J. Tavlarides, staff director, House Committee on Foreign Affairs, Subcommittee on Human Rights and International Organizations, Washington, D.C., 17 July 1990.

21. Peel interview.

22. Salzberg interview.

23. P.L. 94-329.

24. P.L. 95-105.

25. Salzberg interview.

26. Burgess interview.

27. Ibid.

28. *Congress and the Nation,* vol. 6, 1981–1984 (Washington, D.C.: Congressional Quarterly, 1985), 141.

29. Peel interview.

30. House Committee on Appropriations, Subcommittee on Foreign Operations, Export Financing, and Related Programs, *Foreign Operations, Export Financing, and Related Program Appropriations for 1990, Hearings,* 101st Cong., 1st sess., 1989, 81.

31. Salzberg interview.

32. Tavlarides interview.

33. Peel interview.

34. Burgess interview.

35. Quoted in Charles W. Kegley, Jr., and Eugene R. Wittkopf, *American*

Foreign Policy: Pattern and Process, 3d ed. (New York: St. Martins Press, 1987), 77.

36. House Committee on Appropriations, Subcommittee on Foreign Operations, *Foreign Operations, Export Financing, and Related Programs Appropriations for 1990,* 52.

37. Peel interview.

38. Tavlarides interview.

39. Edward S. Corwin, *The President: Office and Powers,* 4th ed. (New York: New York University Press, 1957), 171.

40. Quoted in Kegley and Wittkopf, *American Foreign Policy,* 415.

41. *Senate Report 101-131,* 29.

42. Jerome J. Shestack, "An Unsteady Focus: The Vulnerabilities of the Reagan Administration's Human Rights Policies," reprinted in House Committee on Foreign Affairs, Subcommittee on Human Rights and International Organizations, *Hearings: Review of the State Department's Country Reports on Human Rights,* 101st Cong., 2d sess., 1990, 200.

43. Peel interview.

44. "Foreign Aid System Criticized as Cumbersome, Ineffective," *Congressional Quarterly Weekly Report,* 11 February 1989, 272.

45. National Opinion Research Center poll in 1988 found that 68 percent of the American public believed that the United States was spending "too much" on foreign aid. A national poll published in the *New York Times* on 27 May 1990 indicated that 83 percent of the respondents were willing to reduce the amount of U.S. foreign aid.

46. Burgess interview.

47. Letter to the author, 2 October 1990.

48. Tavlarides interview.

49. Peel interview. A CRS study found this to be a common tactic of U.S. diplomats. See Congressional Research Service, *Human Rights and U.S. Foreign Assistance: Experiences and Issues in Policy Implementation (1977–1978),* November 1979, 7.

II

Interjecting Constituency Concerns: Foreign Military Arms Sales

G. Calvin Mackenzie

Introduction

Virtually all countries, save the very smallest, have armed forces. But most countries have no arms industry or, at best, have one that is primitive and inadequate even to domestic needs. Hence, most countries have to import arms to equip their military forces. As weapons technology grows more sophisticated, developing countries rely more heavily on the industrial countries as arms suppliers, a circumstance that has created an enormous worldwide commerce.

This commerce is hardly a free market, where willing buyers seek out willing sellers. It is, instead, a market dominated by the security interests and international relations of the arms-exporting countries. Their sales are closely governed by their own definitions of national self-interest and by their efforts to shape alliances and relationships. Even in the democracies with free-market economies, arms exports are highly regulated by governments. In no other country, however, are they so tightly controlled nor is control so widely shared as in the United States. It was not always so.

Foreign military sales (FMS) emerged as a regular component of U.S. foreign policy in the 1960s. Then and in the years that immediately followed, overseas weapons sales were a business conducted by the executive branch of government with minimal congressional involvement. This was especially true of direct cash sales, which required no congressional appropriations. Employees of the Defense Department negotiated directly with their foreign counterparts. As long as the State Department raised no objections on policy grounds, the sales took place. Congress was informed—when it was informed at all—haphazardly and after the deals were done.

Congressional indifference was dissipating by the late 1960s, and by the middle of the next decade Congress was carving out a significant role for itself in foreign military sales decisions. From the early 1970s to the present, Congress and the executive branch have been engaged in skirmishes over the substance of arms sales policy and the procedures for making arms sales decisions.

The conflict has unfolded on many fronts, engaging the interests of many actors, domestic and foreign. Some of the most prominent foreign policy clashes between the two branches have emerged from the disputes over arms sales. So, too, have some significant tests of the parameters of executive authority and legislative power. Disagreements over policy have frequently turned into fundamental debates about institutional prerogatives.

This case study explores congressional-executive conflict in arms sales over the past two decades. It focuses especially on the efforts of Congress to enlarge its role in this policy area. The central questions here are these: By what tactics and methods did Congress seek a larger institutional role in shaping FMS policy? Where did Congress succeed and where did it fail? What are the principal effects of its efforts on FMS policy, on policy-making procedures, and on institutional relations? What lessons can we draw from this case to help us understand more clearly the capabilities and constraints on Congress as a participant in making and implementing contemporary public policy?

Contemporary Arms Sales Program

The first significant transfer of U.S. arms to a foreign nation occurred in 1940, when President Franklin Roosevelt negotiated with British Prime Minister Winston Churchill the exchange of fifty aging destroyers for basing rights on British soil for U.S. troops and ships. Under the Lend-Lease program that subsequently emerged, large amounts of weapons and materiel were provided to U.S. allies during World War II.

Postwar relief, especially under the Marshall Plan, continued to provide military assistance to the allies. It included both arms and defense services, virtually all in the form of grants rather than sales. The pattern continued after passage of the Mutual Security Act of 1954. The Foreign Assistance Act of 1961 marked a turning point in arms-transfer policy. Grant aid began a steady decline through the 1960s; this was matched, in almost direct proportion, by an increase in arms sales. As the dollar value of arms sales grew, so too did congressional interest. That was signified in 1968, when Congress passed the first Foreign Military Sales Act, separating, for purposes of legislative review, sales from grants-in-aid.

Components and Magnitudes

As the United States became a more active participant in the world arms trade, the character of the U.S. arms-transfer program grew more elaborate. The current program has three principal components. The *Military Assistance Program* (MAP) covers grants of military equipment and services to friendly nations, financed through the Foreign Assistance Act (FAA). Since 1982 the grants have been merged with foreign military sales credits extended under the Arms Export Control Act (AECA). The *Foreign Military Sales program* (FMS) includes sales of major military equipment and services by the U.S. government to friendly foreign governments for cash or credit. The Department of Defense (DOD) may order and buy the equipment from private companies, manufacture it in government facilities, or draw it from existing stocks. FMS also includes sales of military construction services under the Foreign Military Construction Sales (FMCS) program. The largest portion of the dollar value of arms transfers occurs under FMS government-to-government sales. The *Commercial Sales program* (CS) involves sales of military and police hardware by U.S. corporations to foreign governments or companies. The U.S. government is not the seller in these transactions, but they must be licensed by the Office of Munitions Control (OMC) of the State Department.

The value of U.S. arms sales can be demonstrated in several ways: trends in dollar value over time (table 11.1), principal recipients (table 11.2), and exports as a percentage of worldwide exports (table 11.3).

Rationales

Why do Americans sell and give arms to foreign countries? The answer is a complex mixture of domestic politics, economics, foreign policy, and military policy. A common rationale is that providing arms to foreign countries enhances the self-defense capabilities of those countries and raises the sophistication of their armed forces. This helps to bring stability to geographical regions and simplifies the task of conducting joint military operations with the United States should the need ever arise. Francis J. West, Jr., then assistant secretary of defense for international security affairs, noted in 1982 that by selling arms, "we help to secure access to port and air facilities, overflight rights and base privileges abroad; we help to modernize regional armed forces; and we foster greater complementarity between regional and U.S. force structures, which really improves our mutual ability to engage hostile forces should regional deterrence fail and U.S. involvement become necessary.[1] The joining of U.S. and Saudi Arabian military forces in response to the Iraqi invasion of Kuwait was simplified, for example, by the fact that the most sophisticated Saudi weapons were made in the United States.

Another common rationale for foreign military sales is that they are good for business in the United States, especially for the weapons industry. Increased sales lead to increased employment and profits. They allow manufacturers to produce more units of a particular weapon, thus lowering unit cost. A weapon, such as a sophisticated fighter plane, that is very expensive to develop and test can cost less to the U.S. government if units are also produced for sale abroad. That way, research and development costs can be amortized over a larger number of sales.

Table 11.1.
U.S. Foreign Military Sales, FY 50–87
(Billions of Current Dollars)

Fiscal Year	Foreign Military Sales[a] Agreements	Commercial Exports[b]
1950–77	54.5	5.2
1978	6.7	1.7
1979	11.2	1.5
1980	12.6	2.0
1981	6.6	2.2
1982	17.7	1.8
1983	15.0	4.0
1984	13.7	3.8
1985	11.4	5.6
1986	7.0	3.7
1987	6.9	2.2
1950–87	163.4	33.7

SOURCE: U.S. Defense Security Assistance Agency, *Foreign Military Sales, Foreign Military Construction Sales and Military Assistance Facts* (Washington, D.C: Government Printing Office, 1987).

a. Total dollar value of defense articles and services purchased with cash, credit, and Military Assistance Program merger funds by a foreign government or international organization.

b. Total dollar value of deliveries made against purchases of munitions-controlled items by foreign governments directly from U.S. manufacturers.

Harry J. Gray, retired chairman of the board of United Technologies and spokesperson for the American League for Exports and Security Assistance, a trade association of arms manufacturers, told a congressional hearing that

> international sales are an essential revenue source for funding defense related R&D, and international sales represent well understood cost savings for DOD in its domestic procurements spending. In addition, overseas sales allow the defense industry to maintain a larger production base—a larger production base with lower unit costs, than would be possible providing for just the domestic market alone. Additionally, this enlarged production base provides the U.S. with a comfortable surge capacity. We are aware of cases in which an entire production line would have been shut down had it not been for the foreign sales.[2]

Arms sales abroad are also valued by some because they contribute positively to the U.S. balance of trade. The United States exports a much larger

TABLE 11.2
U.S. ARMS TRANSFERS TO SELECTED COUNTRIES
AND REGIONS, 1984–88
(BILLIONS OF CURRENT DOLLARS)

Region	Amount	Country	Amount
Middle East	16.3	Saudi Arabia	7.5
Europe	19.0	Israel	6.1
East Asia	13.2	Japan	4.9
Oceania	4.2	Australia	4.0
Latin America	2.2	United Kingdom	3.3
Africa	1.3	Taiwan	3.0
South Asia	1.4	Egypt	2.8
North America	0.9	South Korea	2.5
		West Germany	2.5
		Netherlands	2.1
		Spain	2.1
		Turkey	2.0
		Belgium	1.5
		Pakistan	1.2

SOURCE: U.S. Arms Control and Disarmament Agency, *World Military Expenditures and Arms Transfers, 1989* (Washington, D.C.: Government Printing Office, 1990), 115–18.

dollar volume of arms than it imports. Indeed, there are few other industries in which the ratio of exports to imports is so favorable to the trade balance. The common view among foreign policy analysts is that countries with the desire to purchase weapons will find a supplier somewhere, even if they need to do so covertly. If the United States declines to sell weapons, or to sell a certain kind of weapon, to a particular country for reasons of policy, that country is likely to take its business elsewhere; it is not likely to remain un-armed. Hence, the argument is often made by arms sales advocates that the United States should be aggressive in its arms sales policies because it is in the nation's economic interest and because turning aside sales very probably is not in its foreign policy or military interests.

Finally, the argument is frequently heard that arms sales can contribute to the development and domestic tranquility of the purchasing countries. Lieutenant General Charles W. Brown, a recent director of the Defense Security Assistance Agency, testified,

We also believe that we can have a positive influence on the countries we assist. Promoting democracy, human rights and nation-building is desirable for its own sake. If the United States cuts relations with Third World mili-

TABLE 11.3.
U.S. Arms Exports, 1978–88
(Billions of Dollars)

Year	U.S. (Current Dollars)	U.S. (Constant 1988 Dollars)	World (Current Dollars)	World (Constant 1988 Dollars)	U.S. as Percentage of World Arms Exports
1978	6.4	10.7	26.5	44.5	24.2
1979	5.9	9.1	31.9	49.3	18.5
1980	6.4	9.1	35.6	50.4	18.0
1981	8.5	11.0	44.0	56.8	19.3
1982	9.3	11.3	47.8	58.0	19.5
1983	11.6	13.5	49.3	57.6	23.5
1984	10.7	12.0	52.4	59.0	20.4
1985	11.1	12.1	46.2	50.5	24.0
1986	9.2	9.8	46.1	49.1	20.0
1987	14.3	14.7	54.3	56.1	26.3
1988	14.3	14.3	48.6	48.6	29.4

SOURCE: U.S. Arms Control and Disarmament Agency, *World Military Expenditures and Arms Transfers, 1989* (Washington, D.C.: Government Printing Office, 1990), 73, 111.

taries, we lose all influence with those militaries, which remain strong, if not the strongest, institution in many countries. In many of these countries the military is the only effectively functioning modern institution, often with a disproportionate concentration of technical and engineering skills. They are a critical part of nation building. Security assistance is essential to maintain the ties and influence needed.[3]

Over the two decades since arms sales abroad began to grow with gusto, these arguments have been woven into a fabric of rationale and explanation that has proved surprisingly strong. But there has been plenty of criticism as well, particularly of the notions that arms sales lead to regional stability abroad and to internal development in countries with strong militaries. Much of that criticism has found voice and force in Congress and, as we shall see, has been a primary motive for increasing congressional activism on FMS policy.

Participants in the Foreign Military Sales Process
The U.S. government usually engages in four to five thousand military sales a year to foreign governments. These can range from small sales of helmets or canteens to very significant sales of missiles, fighter aircraft, or Airborne

Warning and Control System (AWACS) battlefield command systems. The small, routine sales are handled largely within the Defense Department, with reviews and approvals by the State Department. The largest country-to-country sales are treated quite differently. Those that pass the thresholds established in the Arms Export Control Act (described below) must journey around all three points of a triangle before they can be consummated.

Most arms sales begin abroad in the form of discussions between foreign military leaders and members of the U.S. Military Assistance Groups (MAGs) or other embassy personnel in each country. Many foreign military officers, especially those of developing countries, also come to the United States for training and are thereby exposed to advanced weapons. This encourages their interest in having their countries purchase some of the weapons they have seen.

The Foreign Military Sales program (FMS) system is highly complex and technical. The government's own flow chart of the process spreads across many pages. Its basic elements include the following:

- A request by a foreign government for price and availability (P&A) data on the desired weapon.
- The provision of that P&A data, usually by the military departments.
- The negotiation of a Letter of Offer and Approval (LOA) between the military department responsible for the sale and the representatives of the purchasing country. This specifies the arms to be purchased, the costs, the means and timing of payment, and a host of statutory and other restrictions on the use of those arms. The request for an LOA does not commit either side to the sale, but it initiates the review process. The Defense Security Assistance Agency (DSAA) in the Defense Department reviews the sale and countersigns the LOA.
- The proposed sale is reviewed, usually simultaneously, by the DSAA and the Bureau of Politico-Military Affairs (PM) in the State Department.
- If both approve the sale and it is of a character or magnitude that requires congressional review, the DSAA submits informal notification to Congress that a proposed sale will be coming forward for review and begins preparation of a formal congressional notification. (If congressional review is not required, this step may be skipped. Sometimes, however, when it anticipates congressional concern, the DSAA may informally notify Congress of a proposed sale that falls below the thresholds for formal congressional review.)
- Once the DSAA, State's PM, and Congress (if required) have all agreed to the sale, the relevant military department submits a signed LOA to the DSAA. The LOA is reviewed once more by the DSAA and State's PM and then countersigned by the DSAA comptroller. The purchaser is then normally allowed sixty days or less to accept the offer.[4]

Two characteristics of this process are especially noteworthy, and highly relevant to the discussion that follows. One is that the executive branch is the clear and inevitable initiator in FMS. There is simply no way nor any precedent for Congress to take the lead in making arms sales agreements with other nations. The nature of the function determines the initiative and reactive roles of the executive and the legislature.

Second, there is little way for Congress to get involved in the process until it is well along. By the time a potential sale has come to Congress for review, there may have been months, perhaps even years, of discussion among Defense Department officials, U.S. embassy personnel, and representatives of the foreign government. Although some members of Congress may know of the discussions, and may even have expressed reactions to them, there has been no formal congressional participation. When Congress does get officially involved, if it does at all, foreign governments have already conducted a good deal of internal discussion and have made a commitment to purchase arms from the United States rather than some other country. Should Congress choose to oppose the sale, its opposition comes relatively late in the process and at the cost of embarrassment to U.S. officials who negotiated the sale and the officials of foreign countries who advocated it within their own governments. The normal schedule of the FMS process imposes an inevitable constraint on congressional action and influence.

Developing Patterns of Congressional-Executive Relations

Major changes in the congressional role in foreign military sales began to occur in the mid-1970s. They can be understood only in the context of the events that surrounded and motivated their occurrence.

By 1974 relations between the presidency and Congress had been rocked by a protracted war in Vietnam and the deterioration of presidential influence and credibility that resulted from the attempted cover-up of the Watergate break-in. Richard Nixon's congressional support approached zero on the eve of his resignation from office. His appointed successor, though a former leader in Congress, was unable to effect a significant reversal of legislative distrust of the presidency. It was a period in which, on many fronts, Congress sought to fortify its own ability to shape public policy and to narrow the scope of executive discretion. The War Powers Act, the Impoundment Control Act, and the creation of intelligence oversight committees were just a few of the landmarks of that period of uncommon and intense congressional-executive hostility.

Beyond Washington other events were casting a shadow on the politics of arms sales. In 1969, Nixon had announced a major new thrust in foreign policy, what came to be known as the Nixon Doctrine. Among its principal elements was the proposition that when U.S. allies were faced with non-nuclear aggression, "we shall furnish military and economic assistance when requested in accordance with our treaty commitments. But we shall look to the nation directly threatened to assume the primary responsibility of providing the manpower for its defense."[5]

To put the Nixon Doctrine in place, it became necessary to increase substantially the provision of arms to U.S. allies. Richard F. Grimmett, a Congressional Research Service (CRS) foreign policy specialist who has followed arms sales policy for years, noted the effect of this on Capitol Hill:

> And how are you going to help [the Nixon Doctrine] come to pass? You're going to take someone like the shah of Iran and you're going to make him the policeman of the Persian Gulf. You have a massive infusion of weapons sales to the Persian Gulf countries in the late sixties and early 1970s. Nearly every mainline system in the United States inventory outside of nuclear weapons was going to the shah.
>
> The only way Congress found out about what was going on was through the newspapers. There was no institutionalized mechanism for reporting to Congress, except the possibility that you might get some kind of a briefing much after the fact. That's not consultation. The actions that were being taken had a potentially significant effect on U.S. foreign policy. Consequently, the folks down here started asking questions about the process.[6]

The October War between Israel and Egypt and Syria had occurred in 1973. This had two deeply felt effects on FMS policy. First, it emphasized the threat to Israel's security and encouraged Israel's friends in the United States to seek even larger transfers of advanced U.S. weaponry to enhance Israel's military security. Arms transfers to Israel increased from $310 million in 1973 to more than $2 billion in 1974 and averaged $1.43 billion a year in the following decade.[7]

The October War also led to the OPEC oil embargo. This was a retaliation by the Arab-dominated OPEC cartel for U.S. support of Israel. The embargo was the first step in an escalation of oil prices that (1) had a profound negative effect on the U.S. balance of trade, and (2) had a profound positive effect on the national treasuries of the oil-producing countries. The first effect encouraged increased arms sales as a way to improve the U.S. balance of trade. The second provided several of the Arab countries in the Middle East with cash resources to purchase sophisticated weapons to enhance their own national security. The U.S. desire to increase arms sales was a perfect match for the Arab desire to increase arms purchases.

Supply and demand came together in a way that threw U.S. foreign policy toward the Middle East into something of a tizzy. That this occurred precisely at a time of executive weakness and growing congressional assertiveness virtually guaranteed that FMS policy would become a significant arena in the unfolding struggle between the legislative and executive branches.

The Nelson-Bingham Amendment

The first two major salvos in this struggle were fired in 1974. They both occurred as part of the Foreign Assistance Act for Fiscal 1974 (P.L. 93-559). One demonstrated the ability of an aroused Congress to shape arms sales policy; the other sought to institutionalize that ability.

In July of 1974 Turkey invaded the island of Cyprus, using U.S. weapons that had been supplied through the military assistance program. Cyprus had long been a source of conflict between Greece and Turkey, and the Turkish invasion angered many Americans of Greek descent. They lobbied Congress intensely to cut off aid to Turkey until it withdrew from Cyprus or agreed to negotiate a settlement of the crisis there. Greek-American members of Congress repeatedly made the point that Turkey's use of U.S. weapons in offensive action of this sort was a violation of the Foreign Assistance Act.

By the time this debate occurred in Congress, Nixon had resigned and Gerald Ford had succeeded him. The Ford administration opposed an arms embargo on Turkey, arguing that it would eliminate the flexibility needed to encourage negotiations and that it would irritate the Turks and thus weaken the NATO alliance in southern Europe. But Congress persisted and forced the administration to accept a suspension of arms shipments to Turkey until there was progress toward a military solution on Cyprus. "The Turkish arms embargo," concluded a CRS study of this decision, "was essentially a unilateral congressional initiative to set American policy toward an important ally.... For many members of Congress, the embargo was a way of responding to the administration's apparent reluctance to implement provisions of arms sales law."[8]

The broader question of the congressional role in arms sales had been troubling some people on Capitol Hill for years. One of those was Paula Stern, an aide to Senator Gaylord Nelson (D-Wisc.). She and Norvill Jones, a staff member on the Senate Foreign Relations Committee, had often discussed ways to give Congress a formal role in arms sales decisions. By 1974 they had fixed on the notion of mandating congressional review and approval of the most important military sales through the device of the legislative veto. "It evolved," said Stern of these discussions, "that the best way would be reports and a crack at vetoing arms transactions."[9]

Legislation embodying that approach was introduced by Nelson in the Senate and by Jonathan B. Bingham (D-N.Y.) in the House. After some congressional debate, the procedure took shape and was included in P.L. 93-559. As approved, Congress would have twenty calendar days to review a pending sale after formal notification from the executive branch. Review would be required only for military sales valued at $25 million or more.

Such a sale could be killed by passage (in both houses) of a concurrent resolution of disapproval. The president could waive congressional review by declaring that "an emergency exists which requires the proposed sale in the national security interest of the United States."

This was a significant departure from existing practice. Previous foreign military sales acts had been passed in 1968 and 1971, but neither established any formal role for Congress. In fact, prior to the Nelson-Bingham amendment, there was not even a systematic procedure for informing Congress of foreign sales before they were consummated. Most were handled entirely by the Defense Department with little other participation in either branch.[10] In arguing for passage of this amendment, Nelson underscored the inability of Congress to get a handle on foreign military sales:

> Despite the serious policy issues raised by this tremendous increase in Government arms sales, these transactions are made with little regard for congressional or public opinion. The Department of Defense is consulted. The manufacturers of weapons and providers of military services are consulted. The foreign purchasers are involved. But Congress is hardly informed of these transactions, much less consulted as to their propriety. As it stands now, the executive branch simply presents Congress and the public with accomplished facts.[11]

The first test of the new process came about in 1975 when the Ford administration proposed to sell fourteen batteries of Hawk missiles to Jordan. The Hawk is a mobile air defense missile, and it worried many in Congress that its possession by Jordan would diminish the strategic superiority of the Israeli air force in the region. The House Foreign Affairs Committee reacted to the proposed sale by voting a resolution of disapproval. At that point, the administration withdrew the proposal and initiated negotiations with leaders of the congressional opposition to the sale. They agreed to a modification of the terms of the arms transfer. Jordan would get the Hawk missiles, but it would be required to install them at fixed sites from which they could not be moved. Once that agreement had been negotiated, the sale was resubmitted and allowed to proceed.

The Arms Export Control Act

The tinkering with procedures continued through the mid-1970s. Once the Nelson-Bingham process was in effect, staff and members in Congress found that the twenty days provided for review of proposed sales was inadequate. So, in February of 1976 they forged a "gentleman's agreement" with officials in the Defense Department providing for an informal twenty-day preliminary notification. This would precede the twenty-day formal notification required under the law, effectively doubling the length of time available for Congress to review and respond to a proposed arms sale.

Later in 1976 Congress further enlarged its role in FMS policy by passing a landmark bill, the International Security Assistance and Arms Export Control Act (P.L. 94-329), usually referred to simply as the Arms Export Control Act, or AECA. The first version of this bill reduced the arms sale threshold for congressional review from $25 million to $7 million and placed an annual limit on all arms sales of $9 billion. President Ford vetoed the bill, arguing that it was an inappropriate congressional trespass into the jurisdiction of the executive branch, making Congress a "virtual co-administrator" of foreign policy. Lacking the votes, Congress never attempted to override the veto.

Congressional interest in arms sales remained strong, and a new version of the AECA soon came forward. It eliminated the annual ceiling on total arms sales, but kept the threshold for congressional review at $7 million. It provided Congress thirty days in which to review such sales and maintained the concurrent resolution legislative veto procedure. It also established the first congressional limits on commercial arms sales, prohibiting private companies from selling any major equipment costing $25 million or more directly to other governments. Under the AECA the president was also required to submit an annual estimate to Congress of the amount of sales, credits, and loan guarantees expected to be extended to foreign governments in the following year. Ford signed this version of the AECA into law on 30 June 1976.

Tinkering with the AECA has continued, with most of the changes imposing a higher level of reporting obligations or constraints on the executive branch. The principal features of the current law are outlined in table 11.4.

Table 11.4.
Selected Provisions of the Arms Export Control Act Relative to Congressional-Executive Relations

---

- President must *notify* Congress of any proposed sale of
  - Major defense equipment amounting to $14 million or more;
  - Defense articles or services amounting to $50 million or more; and
  - Design and construction services worth $200 million or more.

- Additionally, though not required by statute, DSAA (Defense Security Assistance Agency) informally provides Congress with at least *twenty days advance notice* prior to the statutory certification to permit sufficient time for congressional review of the proposal.

- Once notification is made,
  - Congress has *thirty days in which to act,* or fifteen days in the case of NATO countries, Australia, New Zealand, and Japan.

- The International Security and Development Cooperation Act of 1981 shortened the time for NATO countries, Australia, New Zealand, and Japan reviews from thirty to fifteen days and eliminated the twenty-day, informal prior notification for these countries. This shortening applies only to FMS sales; commercial sales still require thirty days notification for NATO countries, Australia, New Zealand, and Japan.
- Congress may prevent a sale from proceeding by passing a joint resolution to that effect.

- President may *waive* Congress's right to block a sale by stating in the notice to Congress that "an emergency exists which requires such sale in the national security interests of the United States."
  - In 1979 Congress tightened up the emergency waiver provision in the AECA. It added a new provision requiring the president to submit to Congress a "detailed justification" of any decision under the president's emergency powers to waive the requirement that Congress be given thirty days to disapprove major sales abroad (P.L. 96-92). This did not eliminate the waiver provision, but it enlarged the burden on the president to justify its employment.

- In 1978 Congress amended the AECA to require an annual report to Congress by 15 November of each year, providing information on all arms sales requiring congressional review that were likely to be proposed in the following year. The requirement was sponsored by Senator Jacob Javits (D-N.Y.) and has come to be known as the "Javits report."

- A 1979 amendment (inspired by the Iranian revolution) requires that arms sales certifications include a "sensitivity of technology statement" regarding the extent to which the major defense items proposed to be sold contained sensitive technology. This applies only to FMS, not to direct commercial sales. The reporting requirement applies only to sales that fall under the $14-, $50-, $200-million arms sales criteria.

- A 1985 amendment requires the administration to expand the "statement of sensitivity" accompanying the certification of a proposed sale to include *a detailed justification for selling major defense items containing sensitive technology.* This amendment also requires advising Congress at least forty-five days before delivery of a major defense item in which the sensitivity of technology or the capability is enhanced from that described in the original certification. The administration is also required to submit a new certification if the value of the enhancement or upgrade exceeds the $14-, $50-, or $200-million thresholds identified above. The statement of sensitivity and the report on upgrades apply to any nation.

Congress was not long in flexing the new muscle that it possessed under the AECA. In September 1976, Ford submitted $6 billion worth of proposed sales to eleven countries for congressional review. Many in Congress reacted angrily to what they viewed as an overload of the review process and the absence of an overall arms sales policy on the part of the administration. Members also felt that most of the sales included in the package were well along in negotiations before Congress received notification of them. Said Senator Frank Church (D-Idaho) of the Foreign Relations Committee, "By the time [the sales] come to this panel, it's practically a *fait accompli*. The contracts are already negotiated, the pressures are there."[12]

Congressional opponents, though reluctant to single out just one country, finally decided to focus their opposition on the proposed sale of 1000 Sidewinder and 1500 Maverick missiles to Saudi Arabia. The Foreign Relations Committee voted 8–6 in favor of a resolution of disapproval of that sale. Before the resolution reached the Senate floor, the administration negotiated a compromise with opposition leaders, reducing the sale to 850 Sidewinders and 650 Mavericks. The resolution of disapproval was then tabled and the sale went ahead.

A New President Seeks a New Policy

The election of Jimmy Carter brought a promise of significant change in FMS policy. In May 1977 Carter ordered a government-wide review of arms sales and stated, "The United States will henceforth view arms transfers as an exceptional foreign policy implement, to be used only in instances where it can be clearly demonstrated that the transfer contributes to our national security interests."[13] Administration officials trumpeted this as a new approach, aimed at reducing the growing levels of worldwide trafficking in arms.

Less than two months later, however, Carter notified Congress that he intended to sell seven AWACS planes to Iran at a cost of $1.2 billion. Congressional opposition was strong. AWACS was the cutting edge in U.S. technological capability and, although the shah of Iran had long been a reliable ally, the fear that his government could be overthrown, allowing AWACS to fall into less friendly hands, sent a collective shudder through Congress. The House International Relations Committee voted out a resolution of disapproval and the Senate Foreign Relations Committee was about to do so when Carter withdrew the proposal. A few weeks later, after modifying the terms of the sale to satisfy the major congressional objections, Carter resubmitted it and Congress did not disapprove.

Early in 1978, Carter intended to propose a sale of F-15 long-range fighter jets to Saudi Arabia. Recognizing that there would be substantial opposition to the proposal in Congress, the administration packaged the F-15 sale to Saudi Arabia with sales of F-15s to Israel and F-5E fighter/bombers to Egypt. Secretary of State Cyrus Vance hinted that if Congress disapproved any one of the sales, the president would withdraw the others. There was, nevertheless, very considerable congressional opposition to the sale of F-15s to Saudi Arabia, which many in Congress saw as a grave threat to the security of Israel. A resolution to disapprove the Saudi Arabia portion of the sale was narrowly defeated in the Senate, 44–54, only after Defense Secretary Harold Brown promised that the F-15s would be based outside striking distance of Israel and that the planes would not be equipped with bomb racks or air-to-air missiles.

Reagan and AWACS

The most ferocious congressional-executive battle to date over arms sales occurred in 1981. President Ronald Reagan had promised upon coming to office that he would not follow the Carter policy of using arms sales only as a last resort in foreign affairs—a policy that the Carter administration had honored more in rhetoric than practice, in any case. Reagan said that arms transfers would instead be treated by his administration as "an essential element of [the U.S.] global defense posture and an indispensable component of foreign policy."[14]

Evidence of that approach developed dramatically on 1 October, when the Reagan administration proposed to sell five AWACS planes to Saudi Arabia for $8.5 billion. To the friends of Israel this was the gravest threat ever posed by a U.S. arms sale. The American-Israel Public Affairs Committee (AIPAC) led an intensive lobbying and organizing effort to defeat the sale. On 14 October the House disapproved the sale, 301–111. Two weeks later, after a concerted "full-court press" by the administration, the Senate failed, 48–52, to pass the resolution of disapproval. So blistering was this battle that a subsequent proposal to sell forty F-16 planes to Pakistan, which would have been similarly controversial at most times, succeeded with minimal opposition because neither house was anxious to gear up for another major contest with the president.

The Effects of *Chadha*

In the period of nearly a decade that followed enactment of the original Nelson-Bingham amendment, Congress had never formally disapproved a proposed arms sale, but the legislative veto procedure had nonetheless proved to be a valuable handle on FMS policy. Its existence forced administrations to contemplate likely congressional responses in negotiating arms sales, and it provided members of Congress who opposed a sale with a mechanism for engaging the administration in a pointed dialogue.

All the congressional effort of the previous decade was thrown into considerable jeopardy, therefore, by the Supreme Court's 1983 decision in *INS v. Chadha*. The *Chadha* decision invalidated a legislative veto provision in which the veto could be exercised by only one house of Congress. A few weeks after the decision, however, the Court affirmed a lower court decision that found the concurrent resolution, or two-house veto, approach unconstitutional as well. None of these cases dealt directly with section 36(b) of the Arms Export Control Act, but the consensus among legal experts and in Congress was that their effect was to annul the existing procedures under which Congress could disapprove proposed arm sales.

Congress responded early in 1986, when it enacted legislation to revise the AECA in light of the *Chadha* decision.[15] Under the new procedures, disapproval of a proposed sale would require passage of a joint, rather than a concurrent, resolution. This was a significant change. A joint resolution takes effect only when it is signed by the president; a concurrent resolution requires no presidential signature.

In practice, this meant that a joint resolution of disapproval of a sale could be vetoed by the president (the likely outcome because the president would have initially proposed the sale that Congress would be seeking to disapprove). To have its way, Congress would then have to override the president's veto, a process that requires a two-thirds majority in each house. Simple arithmetic suggests that an arms sale proposed by the president can take effect even if it is able to garner the support of only one-third plus one of the members of one house of Congress. This made the task of killing a proposed sale all the harder for congressional opponents.

Dire predictions of loss of congressional influence following *Chadha* seemed to be borne out a few months after the new procedure was enacted. Reagan proposed the sale of $265 million worth of arms to Saudi Arabia. Congressional opposition was broad, and Congress passed Senate Joint Resolution 316 to disapprove the sale. As expected, the president vetoed the joint resolution. The Senate upheld the veto—and thereby permitted the sale to proceed—by the narrowest of margins, 66–34. Still, the closeness of the vote indicated that the president could not disregard Congress, even though *Chadha* might have yielded procedural advantages in FMS decisions.

Congressional opposition leading to negotiated compromises reemerged in 1987 when Reagan proposed a $1 billion arms sale to Saudi Arabia. The sale went through, but only after Reagan agreed, at the insistence of several senators, to remove 1600 Maverick missiles from the package. The same pattern was repeated the following year when the administration proposed to sell forty F-18 planes and associated missiles to Kuwait. Some House members sought to strip the Maverick missiles from the sale proposal, withdrawing their opposition only after intense negotiation produced a letter from Secretary of State George Shultz that identified restrictions to be placed on the use of the weapons. Afterward, opponents of the sale noted the administration's willingness to negotiate. Congressman Lawrence Smith (D-Fla.) said the administration had engaged in "unprecedented consultation" on the sale, and Congressman Mel Levine (D-Calif.) called the Shultz letter of assurances "something new" in arms sales discussions between the two branches.[16]

Explanation: Creating a Congressional Role

Over nearly two decades Congress has struggled to make a place for itself in FMS policy making. It has done that by changing the rules of congressional-executive relations to permit itself a broader role, then by developing strategies to gain advantages under those new rules. When the strategies failed, the usual response was to change the rules again, enlarging the area of legislative influence while narrowing the area of executive discretion.

For Congress, the experience has been simultaneously rewarding and frustrating. Congress clearly participates more fully and effectively in FMS decisions than it did before this spate of change began in the mid-1970s, but it is not yet a full partner in the decisions in the way that many of its members would like it to be. It continues to struggle to shape its role and to fill that role successfully.

Defining the Rules and Playing the New Game

One of the ways in which Congress has sought to participate in arms transfer decisions is through the diligent exercise of the power of the purse. It has scrutinized presidential budget requests carefully and often altered them in significant ways. That has been particularly true of foreign aid, a program that requires annual appropriations from Congress. In the past several decades military assistance has become an increasingly important portion of all foreign assistance. Perhaps the most notable measure of congressional influence on the military assistance program is the extent to which military aid funds are now "earmarked" by congressional action.

In recent years, for example, more than 90 percent of the Foreign Military Sales Credit (FMSCR) program budget, which provides loans to selected foreign governments to enable them to acquire U.S. defense articles and services, has been earmarked to four countries (Egypt, Greece, Israel, and Pakistan). Since FY 80, as a lingering echo of the Turkish arms embargo of the 1970s, Congress has also employed what is called the "7:10 ratio," guaranteeing that military assistance to Greece will never fall below 70 percent of that provided to Turkey.[17]

The appropriations handle fails to provide Congress with much leverage over cash sales of weapons to foreign countries; these require no appropriation of funds by Congress. Here Congress has had to be constantly creative in defining new methods of participating in these decisions, designing and employing several devices to achieve its ends.

One of Congress's most important needs is for information on pending, future, and potential military sales and their impacts. To obtain that information, Congress has enacted a lengthening list of reporting requirements. There are currently more than forty statutory provisions that mandate reports on arms sales from the executive branch to Congress. As a consequence, Congress now receives approximately 350 reports a year on arms sales issues. Although not the sole source of information, the reports and the hearings they sometimes generate are surely the most important source.[18]

Congress has also enacted a host of statutory restrictions on who can purchase U.S. arms and under what conditions. The number is too large to identify them all here, but table 11.5 gives a sense of the diversity of these restrictions. Their intent has always been to narrow executive discretion in selling arms.

TABLE 11.5.
STATUTORY RESTRICTIONS ON PRESIDENTIAL DISCRETION
IN ARMS SALES, EXAMPLES

1. *Terrorism.* Prohibits military sales for one year "to any government which aids or abets, by granting sanctuary from prosecution to, any individual or group which has committed an act of international terrorism." (Sec. 3(c), Arms Export Control Act [AECA])

2. *Foreign intimidation.* Prohibits military sales, sales credits, guarantees, or the issuing of export licenses for "any country determined by the president to be engaged in a consistent pattern of acts of intimidation or harassment directed against individuals in the United States." (Sec. 6, AECA)

3. *Human rights.* "No security assistance may be provided to any country, the government of which engages in a consistent pattern of gross violations of internationally recognized human rights." (Sec. 502B, Foreign Assistance Act [FAA])

4. *Communist countries.* No assistance under the FAA may be provided to any communist country. (Sec. 6209(f), FAA)

5. *Military coups.* No foreign assistance funds may be appropriated or expended for "any country whose duly elected head of Government is deposed by military coup or decree." (Sec. 513, P.L. 99-591)

6. *Restrictions on marketing.* U.S. diplomatic and military personnel serving in overseas missions are required to be instructed by the president "that they should not encourage, promote or influence the purchase by any foreign country of United States military equipment, unless they are specifically instructed to do so by an appropriate official of the executive branch." (Sec. 515(f), FAA)

Country-specific:

7. *Greece and Turkey.* Security assistance will be provided only for defensive purposes, including its use in fulfilling NATO obligations. (Sec 101(f), P.L. 99-83)

8. *Chile.* No military assistance was permitted in FY 87. (Sec. 557, P.L. 99-591)

9. *Pakistan.* All sales of military equipment and technology are conditioned on presidential certification to Congress that "Pakistan does not possess a nuclear explosive device and that the proposed U.S. assistance program will

reduce significantly the risk that Pakistan will possess a nuclear explosive device." (Sec. 902, P.L. 99-83)

10. *Jordan.* Notification to Congress of any proposed sale of "United States advanced aircraft, new air defense systems, or other new advanced military weapons shall be accompanied by a Presidential certification of Jordan's public commitment to the recognition of Israel and to negotiate promptly and directly with Israel under the basic tenets of United Nations Security Council Resolutions 242 and 338." (Sec. 130, P.L. 99-83)

NOTE: For a more complete compilation of restrictions, see Larry A. Mortsolf and Louis J. Samelson, "The Congress and U.S. Military Assistance, Part II," *DISAM Journal* 10 (Fall 1987): 44ff. Also see House Committee on Foreign Affairs, Subcommittee on Arms Control, International Security and Science, *U.S. Military Sales and Assistance Programs: Laws, Regulations, and Procedures,* 99th Cong., 1st sess., 1985, Committee Print, 65ff.

Most important, as noted in the historical narrative above, Congress has sought to establish formal procedural restraints on arms decisions initiated by the executive branch. It did that at first with the legislative veto procedure devised by the Nelson-Bingham amendment and then refined in section 36(b) of the Arms Export Control Act. On several subsequent occasions it broadened the definition of arms transfers subject to this review procedure. When the *Chadha* decision invalidated that approach, Congress responded with a new joint resolution procedure.

In each case Congress has tried to construct and then fortify its own position as a partner in significant FMS decisions. In few areas of congressional-executive relations has so much new law been created in the past two decades. But Congress was not satisfied merely to make its point legislatively, then turn its attention elsewhere— an argument some have made about the passage of the War Powers Act and the Impoundment Control Act. Instead, it has stayed in the fray, adjusting and refining its legislative handles to improve the congressional grip on arms sales policies. Failure to achieve a satisfactory role—sensed usually when Congress has failed to disapprove an arms sale to which there was significant opposition—has often resulted in new recommendations for procedural changes. In the late 1980s yet another proposal for such change—one that would require specific congressional approval in law of all arms sales—was proposed by Senator Joseph Biden (D-Del.) and Congressman Levine.[19]

Some observers have referred to these legislative efforts to build a larger institutional role in arms sales as the "3 R's" approach, relying on reports, restrictions, and restraints. Congress has sought leverage wherever it could be found, and over a period of nearly two decades has steadily broadened the foundation of its own participation in arms sales. Defining the rules has been only part of the congressional effort to take a fuller role in the shaping of arms sales policy. Members of Congress have also been remarkably aggressive in using the new rules for their own policy objectives.

Congress has never successfully disapproved an arms sale by formal action,[20] but it has often used the implied or explicit threat of such action to force the withdrawal of proposed sales or to encourage negotiations with executive branch officials. Such negotiations usually result in changes in the terms or components of the sale that mollify congressional opposition. So, the power to review and disapprove has become a wedge, forcing the executive branch to open up the sales process to congressional view and, when members desire, to congressional participation.

Arms sales have also become an area of persistent conflict within Congress, within the executive branch, and between the two branches. The conflict was rarely apparent before 1974; now it is in constant evidence. The vast majority of arms sales each year generate little interest or opposition in Congress, but a small number attract very substantial interest and intense opposition. The causes of that are political and institutional.

Political Pressures and Influences

Foreign military sales have a domestic and economic, as well as an international security, component. Arms are manufactured in individual states and congressional districts. Decisions on what to sell, in what amounts, and to which countries have direct effects on the prosperity of certain companies and the work forces they employ in those states and districts. Arms sales also affect the balance of military power in the geographical regions of the countries making the purchases. Some U.S. ethnic groups are especially sensitive to the effects of the sales on the security of the countries of their ancestry or kinship. When an arms sale seems to pose a threat to a country to which they are sympathetic, these groups are often stirred to action. All of this provides an important political dimension to arms sales decisions and often inspires special congressional attention to those decisions for reasons other than national security. If arms sales are often motivated by international concerns, opposition to them often results from domestic concerns. It is a potentially combustible mix.

Since passage of the Nelson-Bingham amendment, most of the controversial arms sales have involved executive branch efforts to sell sophisticated weapons to Arab countries: to Jordan, Saudi Arabia, and Kuwait, in particular. Such sales invoke the concerns of the politically potent American Jewish community about the security of Israel. The primary representative of that concern is the American-Israel Public Affairs Committee (AIPAC).

AIPAC has long been regarded as one of the most skillful and effective private organizations in Washington. It has a grass-roots network in communities and congressional districts all over the country and a talented, diligent Washington office. It has also seemed to Washington observers to have a remarkable information-gathering capability, often informing its contacts on Capitol Hill about potential arms sales before they receive notification from the executive branch. AIPAC is usually heavily involved in efforts to build coalitions in opposition to sales of advanced weapons to Israel's adversaries.

AIPAC is not alone in this kind of involvement. Greek-Americans have also been active in trying to curb arms sales to countries that threaten the security of Greece, especially sales to Turkey. Other ethnic groups have also made occasional appearances in arms sales debates. As Congressman Henry Hyde (R-Ill.) once noted, when "you get into having to approve arms sales to some of these countries ... every ethnic group, and there are limitless ethnic groups in this country, and they have causes, and they go back generations. They are going to be here and they are going to have something to say."[21]

Domestic economic interests also provide an angle of vision on arms sales. As table 11.6 indicates, foreign military sales are a multibillion-dollar source of commerce, with especially important impacts on the companies that manufacture weapons and the local economies where their facilities are located. The arms manufacturers are not very visible in congressional debates on arms sales. They rarely lobby openly because of their sensitivity to the negative reaction that would come from appearing to support an arms trade driven by profit motives, but they work closely with the Defense Department in the development of potential sales, and they often seek to use indirect leverage on sales that are controversial in Congress. Glenn Rudd, who has served at the DSAA for almost two decades and is now its highest-ranking civilian, commented:

TABLE 11.6.
NATIONWIDE INCOME IMPACT OF FMS DISTRIBUTIONS,
1980–86 (BILLIONS OF CURRENT DOLLARS)

Year	Foreign Military Sales Disbursement	Income Generated
1980	$ 8.8	$17.4
1981	9.9	19.6
1982	12.0	23.6
1983	12.4	24.2
1984	9.6	18.9
1985	9.8	18.6
1986	10.5	20.8
Average	10.5	20.4

SOURCE: U.S. Defense Security Assistance Agency.

We deal with [the arms manufacturers] fairly closely. They give advice on markets. Do countries have financing? That sort of thing. What are their needs? We dialogue with the defense industry all the time. It's to our advantage to sell, as long as it's to a friend, and keep our industrial base strong. . . .

The [arms manufacturers] will also try to get support on the Hill, but of course they've got a fairly low profile. They can't be up there looking like greedy corporate so-and-so's.[22]

The profile may be low, but the efforts by arms manufacturers to win congressional support for proposed sales are well-noticed by members of Congress. Congressman Dante Fascell (D-Fla.), chairman of the House Foreign Affairs Committee, once told a representative of the arms manufacturers: "I will give you credit for this. . . . Your lobbying has been—well, let me put it this way. I have not seen your lobbying effort where I have seen you. [Laughter] We all know the lobbying on the other side has been effective. It has been open and direct. You gentlemen have done it some other way, I don't know how, but it too has been very effective."[23]

One of the tactics used most successfully by the arms industry and the Defense Department has been to keep members of Congress constantly aware of the economic benefits that will come to their districts when companies there receive the contracts that new arms sales will stimulate. Levine, a frequent critic of arms sales, declared that "the Administration is not shy about reminding Members of Congress just who will have what built where."[24] The Defense Department, in fact, now routinely prepares and circulates information on the likely economic benefits to individual districts that particular sales will produce.

Even some of the nations that wish to purchase of U.S. weapons have begun to take part in these efforts to build domestic, grass-roots support for arms sales. Prince Bandar bin Sultan, the Saudi Arabian ambassador to the United States, has traveled to seek support in individual districts where weapons for Saudi Arabia would be built. "Prince Bandar," remarked Glenn Rudd, "has recognized who really votes in this country. He's made lots of trips around to talk to the workers at lots of plants. He gets a very good reception."[25]

Public opinion, in the way that term is normally conceived, is largely mute on arms sales policy. In the absence of such broad or visible expressions of public sentiment, members of Congress take other cues in deciding to support or oppose individual arms sales. The cues may come from a member's personal worldview or political philosophy; they may come as well from aggressive administration lobbying, which often weighs heavily on the decisions of members of the president's party. But reactions may also be affected by the prism of domestic politics—electoral politics—through which active interests try to present their views.

Institutional Perspectives
There is more at work here than electoral politics. Much of the legislative creativity and the controversy of the past two decades is directly attributable to divergent legislative and executive perspectives on arms sales and to the desire of members of Congress to construct a larger role for their own institution in this increasingly important area of foreign policy.

It is no accident that congressional assertiveness on arms sales coincided with the growth in dollar value—and policy impact—of those sales. Biden observed, "Congress became interested in arms sales as a component of foreign policy when they increased from $1.7 billion to about $16 billion in four years. It looked as though arms sales were becoming almost the sole criterion for determining our role abroad."[26]

Initial congressional endeavors in this area and subsequent congressional activism grew out of a collective sense that (1) arms sales were becoming an increasingly significant element of U.S. foreign policy, and (2) the national interest could not be served merely by congressional participation in defining the broad parameters of that policy. In the view of many in Congress, no real line could be drawn between policy formulation and policy implementation. Congress could not exercise meaningful control over FMS policy through broad pronouncements. Requiring that arms sales "serve U.S. national security interests" or other such ambiguous objectives offered too little guidance to the executive branch and provided too little leverage for the legislature. Congress had to have a say at least in the most significant individual sales.

It was inevitable that conflict would occur between the two branches over both the propriety and the nature of congressional review of individual arms sales. President Ford vetoed the original proposal to establish such review. Once Congress had overcome those objections and legislated a role for itself through the Arms Export Control Act (AECA) in 1976, then conflict occurred over the character of congressional participation.

A common executive branch perspective is that Congress too easily loses sight of the national interest and national security needs, that its members are blinded by domestic politics, especially by ethnic politics. Analyzing executive branch reactions to the Turkish arms embargo, a Congressional Research Service study concluded, "For executive branch actors, the role of Greek Americans was the unpalatable interconnection between domestic and foreign policies. . . . Many in the foreign policy bureaucracy were highly critical of what they saw as parochial, unenlightened views from Capitol Hill."[27] Said Glenn Rudd of the DSAA:

> The effect of AECA has gotten Congress more in the act and it's got what I'd call the special interests or ethnic politics playing a much larger role than they did before the Act. The Israeli-Arab situation is the primary place where it occurs. It has also played larger and larger in the Greek-Turkish af-

fair.... A minority of people there feel very strongly about it and a majority go along with it. You may only be goring a few oxes, but those people feel very strongly about it and the rest of them go along because they may need some help when their ox is gored.[28]

Another common perspective in the executive branch is that foreign policy is an area that traditionally and principally falls within the jurisdiction of the executive branch. The assertiveness of Congress on matters of arms sales seems, to many in the executive branch, a violation of that tradition. Congress, in this view, has intervened too deeply into the details of arms sales, which denies needed flexibility to the administration and slows the arms sale process to a snail's pace. Lieutenant General Charles W. Brown, a former director of the DSAA, told Congress:

> There have been problems over the last several years in managing security assistance programs because of the differences in priorities between the Administration and Congress and the narrowing flexibility available to the Administration. Over the years, as funding for security assistance has declined, the levels of congressional earmarking have increased. But the world has changed. It does not serve the best interests of U.S. foreign policy to lock up all but tiny percentages of security assistance funds in earmarks. In an uncertain world we need more flexibility, not less.[29]

Rudd described the difficulty in adjusting arms sales to congressional decision-making patterns:

> The 30-day notice period has been aborted over the years so that now it seems like it takes 6 months.... Then comes the question of "Hey, you guys are sending over too many Saudi sales all at once." So you start looking for the right time for controversial sales, and you find the right time never happens. So you start glomming them together. You send them over, maybe two or three at once, and they say, "Not right now, this is a bad time." You find that you run into problems of consolidating your sales, lumping them all together, and then they say that you're giving them too much on a plate at once.[30]

Executive branch concern with congressional encroachment into the president's foreign policy turf was highlighted in 1989 during the debate over the licensing of so-called FSX technology to Japan. The executive branch had proposed, after much internal debate, joint U.S.-Japanese codevelopment of a new jet fighter, Fighter Support Experimental, or FSX, for the Japanese defense forces. The proposal was criticized primarily for granting Japanese companies access to U.S. technology that they might later exploit for their own profit, with a consequent loss of business for U.S. manufacturers.

Congress passed a joint resolution setting conditions on the codevelopment venture.[31] President Bush vetoed it, and sent a veto message to Congress admonishing it for its infringement on presidential authority. The language is most revealing:

> [T]he resolution contains binding provisions that unconstitutionally infringe on the powers of the Executive.
>   ... In the conduct of negotiations with foreign governments, it is imperative that the United States speak with one voice. The Constitution provides that that one voice is the President's. While of course Congress has authority under the Constitution to regulate commerce with foreign nations, it may not use that authority to intrude into areas entrusted by the Constitution exclusively to the Executive.
>   ... [A]cceptance of this resolution would constitute a setback in our objective of achieving a close working relationship and mutual respect between our two branches through the minimization of legislative micromanagement of both foreign affairs and Executive branch internal deliberations.[32]

Many members of Congress possess a different set of perspectives about arms sales. A widespread view is that the executive branch has been neglectful of Congress, failing to consult even on the most controversial arms sales. It was the absence of any pattern of consultation that led to passage of the Nelson-Bingham amendment in the first place. Dissatisfaction with the subsequent character of executive consultation led to refinements of the procedures that Nelson-Bingham initiated.

Even after these procedures went into effect, the feeling prevailed in Congress that executive branch personnel had little understanding of the purpose of legislative consultation, that their primary interest was "damage limitation."[33] In this view, it was necessary constantly to hold executive feet to the fire, to grant no benefit of the doubt to the executive branch on arms sales matters.

Legislative skepticism and mistrust have been encouraged as well by the perception that executive branch interest in arms sales is not always driven by national security or foreign policy concerns. There lingers in Congress a good deal of suspicion about the relationship between the Defense Department and the arms manufacturers—the old military-industrial complex. There is suspicion as well that arms sales abroad are part of the strategy for developing expensive new weapons technologies for U.S. armed forces. A former State Department official expressed a criticism of arms sales policy that is often echoed on Capitol Hill:

> There have been some weapons systems where the Defense Department was desperate to get foreign sales. They do it all the time. One of the biggest ex-

amples was the AWACS. The only way the Air Force could justify it was if it was sold to Europe. Then they wanted to sell it to Iran. That was just a very blatant attempt to get the unit cost of the AWACS down by selling it overseas.[34]

The security of Israel is also a persistent bone of contention between the two branches, especially from the perspective of members of Congress for whom Israel is a high priority. An assistant secretary of state underscored what is perceived in Congress as the standard executive branch view when he told members of Congress that "our interests in that region go beyond the Arab-Israeli conflict. . . . We have other interests in the region, and we have other interests in a solid Saudi-American relationship.[35]

To some members of Congress, however, that pursuit of "balance" in the Middle East often leads executive branch officials to overlook or undervalue what they perceive as Israel's security needs. Congressman Levine put it this way: "It is interesting that in [my] eight years in Congress the Administration has testified that not a single missile, not a single plane, not a single tank, not a single bullet will have any impact on Israel's security in the region. At some point in time that simply does not remain credible. That is one of the great frustrations that we have."[36]

For members of Congress, there is also a common suspicion that executive branch officials are often more interested in maintaining good relations with their friends—by selling them whatever weapons they want—than they are in protecting peace and security abroad. Some in Congress worry that executive personnel become too cozy with their foreign clients and domestic arms manufacturers. Deals take shape, in this view, without adequate concern for the deals' geopolitical or national security impacts. Defense and State Department officials worry too much about upsetting the leaders of foreign countries by denying them weapons they seek to buy. Hence, members of Congress often feel bound to impose a dose of perspective and responsibility on this process, to participate actively in it to prevent bad foreign military sales decisions.

Many in Congress, for example, have been distressed by recent executive branch proposals to sell Stinger missiles to Arab countries. The Stinger is a shoulder-fired antiaircraft missile, one of the wonders of modern weapons technology. On several occasions in the 1980s Congress forced the administration to remove Stingers from proposed sales. The principal objection was that they could easily fall into the hands of terrorists and be used against the United States or the aircraft of friendly countries. Executive branch officials minimized the danger of that happening; congressional opponents maximized it. It became an important source of interbranch conflict.

Another foundation of congressional activism in this area is the argument that foreign military sales are not foreign policy in the strict and conventional sense. Instead, they fall into a canyon of uncertainty between foreign policy and commerce. In the former, Congress has traditionally deferred to presidential leadership, but the latter—foreign commerce—is clearly and constitutionally an area of congressional jurisdiction. That was the argument made by members of Congress in response to Bush's veto of the Japanese FSX disapproval cited above. The president chastised Congress for usurping executive authority in this matter, but Capitol Hill opponents took stern issue with the president's constitutional interpretation. Senator John Danforth (Mo.), a Republican like the president, cited section 8 of Article I of the Constitution, which grants Congress the power "to regulate commerce with foreign nations," and he pointed out that acceptance of Bush's interpretation would result in "a very substantial rollback in the authority of Congress.... It would be a violation of our own oath of office if we were to agree that the role of Congress in international trade is something less than the Constitution of the United States says it is."[37]

The two branches disagree persistently about who is the more responsible. Executive branch officials often criticize Congress for acting irresponsibly, for forcing changes in arms sales that are harmful to relations with client countries. Members of Congress deny the charge, arguing that the dangers to relations with individual countries are usually overstated by executive branch officials anxious to complete a sale, that there are often higher priorities than individual relationships in any case, and that Congress always includes "escape hatches" in its legislative restrictions that permit the president to waive the restrictions if legitimate national security needs so require.

Filling the gulf that separates Congress and the executive branch on arms sales matters is one basic and fundamental difference. On foreign policy matters, the two branches represent two quite different cultures. The executive branch foreign policy establishment is dominantly other-directed; the legislative branch is dominantly inner-directed. The former has a primary concern with the effect of foreign policy decisions on international constituencies; the latter has a primary concern with the effect of foreign policy decisions on domestic constituencies. Virtually all of the arguments between the branches over individual sales have their roots in this fundamental difference of perspective. When the cultures clash, as they often do, Congress grasps for leverage wherever it can be found.

Effects of Congressional Intervention and Executive Response

Congress and the executive branch have now completed almost two decades of conflict and negotiation over foreign military sales (FMS). What has come of all that? Has it affected FMS policy in any significant way? How has it altered relations between the two branches?

Results for Policy

The primary thrust of all congressional efforts in this period has been to provide the legislature with larger opportunities to participate in shaping decisions. In the eyes of virtually all observers, larger opportunities have been achieved. But their effects on FMS policy are not easy to measure simply because there is no sure way of knowing in what directions FMS policy might have gone had Congress not sought to participate so actively in it.

The long-term trends (see table 11.1) suggest an increase in arms sales from the 1970s into the early 1980s, leading to a more recent decline. Most people close to the process expect that decline to continue into the foreseeable future.[38] But it is not clear that increased congressional activism contributed either to the initial increase or the subsequent decline.

In general, Congress has been a voice of moderation in arms sales policy. Nowhere in this period is there a case of Congress's opposing a sale proposed by the executive branch because it was too small. There is simply no record of Congress pushing for more sales, even to friendly countries. The closest Congress has come to that has been its effort to ensure that sales to Greece kept pace with sales to Turkey through the 7:10 ratio. By and large, Congress has had a distaste for arms sales and has used its avenues of participation to limit them. It sought during the Ford administration to place a dollar ceiling on total arms sales. That was vetoed. In subsequent years it has intervened in individual sales to limit the size or the weapons components of the sale.

Given this historical pattern, it is reasonable to argue that congressional participation has probably forced an overall reduction in U.S. arms sales abroad. Congress has played the role of skeptic and critic, not of cheerleader. It has directly acted in some cases to reduce individual sales. The executive branch, no doubt, has declined to propose others in anticipation of congressional opposition.

There have been other policy impacts as well. One of the broader problems with the provisions that permit Congress to intervene in specific military sales is that they seem to encourage congressional involvement that is spasmodic, uncoordinated, and potentially incoherent. Rather than participate in the continuing development of a sensible arms export policy, Congress tends to respond to the political pressures that surround particular arms sales decisions (e.g., Turkey, Jordan, Saudi Arabia). Hence, congressional activism is less a kind of appropriate responsiveness to broad public opinion—of which there is little on arms sales—than a divisive and often inconsistent set of responses to highly vocal interests opposed to particular arms sales because of their perceived effects on the adversaries of the purchasing countries.

The rare congressional efforts to define a national arms sale policy, principally through the Arms Export Control Act (AECA) and the Foreign Assistance Acts, have combined broad statements of objectives, detailed descriptions of decision-making procedures, and lists of restrictions on possible sales. They seem to have aimed more at ensuring a continuing role for Congress in implementation than in establishing the kind of clear guidance that bureaucratic agencies need to perform responsibly. The legislative histories of statutes affecting arms sales and military assistance read more like recipes for ongoing congressional-executive relations than the kind of marching orders that one branch might leave to the other's discretion in carrying out.

The obvious consequence of this is that much of arms sales policy is made through implementation rather than legislation. We create the policy as we go along, paying lip service to certain broad and consensual objectives like creating a world "free from the scourge of war and the dangers and burdens of armaments,"[39] but actually sculpting the contours of policy through the accumulation of individual decisions on sales to particular countries and regions.

For example, the language of the AECA reaffirms U.S. policy to "encourage regional arms control and disarmament agreements and to discourage arms races."[40] But what does that mean in application? If Turkey comes to the Pentagon seeking to buy arms, should we sell? If Egypt wants the most advanced U.S. planes, should we sell? As a practical matter, the legislation does not answer such questions. It is unlikely that legislation could ever be written with sufficient insight, foresight, and precision to do so. Defining regional balance is a political question. Answers depend on political perspectives. They can be determined only through a political process. And, not surprisingly, an intensely political institution like Congress can never be comfortable leaving those political questions to someone else. It wants to bring its own perspectives to bear.

When substantive policy is made by accumulation rather than by legislation, inconsistencies are inevitable. In jurisprudence—which is the art of policy by accumulation—consistency is created by *stare decisis,* by devotion to precedent. But that does not work, at least not very effectively, in congressional-executive relations. There is no devotion to precedent; the politics of the moment is always the guiding light. Hence, inconsistency is inevitable. And the broader the range of political actors participating in any set of decisions, the greater the likelihood of inconsistency in their outcomes. If arms sales policy has seemed inconsistent over the past decade—and to most observers it has—that should be no surprise, given the participation of two branches of government riven by internal conflicts and separated by fundamental differences of perception and purpose.

Results for Institutional Relations and Processes

It is useful to view the events of the past two decades through a long lens. What one sees is a process of constant, mutual adjustment as Congress and the executive branch seek to cope with conflict. Conflict is inherent in democratic government; democracies can survive only by developing procedures and practices that permit its expression and resolution.

In this case, over time, the two branches have sought to do that by developing a set of conflict-channelization procedures. Recognizing that there was no way to eliminate conflict from arms sales decisions, and little likelihood that conflict from such disparate perspectives and sources could actually be "resolved," the procedural coping strategies employed by the two branches have been aimed at controlling the impact of their inherent disagreements. They have forced their conflict over arms sales into narrow channels where each could garner information, express its views, and use its instruments of authority and political influence to try to forge an outcome to its liking.

Fundamental to this approach was conflict containment. Each victory or defeat is self-contained, neither advancing nor diminishing the broader interests or opportunities of either branch. A failure to win approval for one arms sale was no deterrent to the executive branch to propose another of similar nature later on. Nor was a failure to disapprove an arms sale a deterrent to the legislative branch to oppose another of similar nature. You win some, you lose some.

A good deal of institutional learning has also taken place over time, on both sides. Nowhere is that more clearly demonstrated than in the notification procedures that the two branches have devised and refined. H. Allen Holmes, director of the Bureau of Politico-Military Affairs in the State Department, said in 1987, "Current notification procedures ensure effective coordination between the executive and Congress. . . . The present arms transfer process operates in a prudent and controlled manner, is carefully managed and it contains numerous opportunities for congressional comment and input."[41] Michael Van Dusen, staff director of the House Subcommittee on Europe and the Middle East, takes a similar view: "The legislation has been useful in terms of getting justifications, making people go through the loops in terms of why they're doing what they're doing. As an exercise, I think it has been therapeutic and, to a degree, useful."[42]

This paper has focused on conflicts over arms sales because those have been the cutting edge in shaping congressional-executive relations, but it is important to note that the United States makes thousands of arms sales each year that generate no significant conflict. Attribute some of that to indifference and limited resources for review in Congress. Attribute some of it as well to the development of a process of information and consultation that permits Congress to focus its attention and concerns on the handful of arms sales that seem, in the view of some members, to represent genuine and significant differences in legislative and executive objectives or viewpoints.

All political systems are imperfect, but a system works like a system when it resolves conflict where it is resolvable and channelizes it into narrow confines where it is not. Though never explicitly stated, that has been the primary impact of the congressional-executive minuet over arms sales policy in the past two decades.

The resulting partnership has some notable characteristics. Congress has little or no role in initiating arms sales proposals. Its posture is reactive. Its formal authority to impose its views, in contradiction to the president's, is difficult to exercise, especially after the invalidation of the legislative veto by *Chadha*. In practical terms, in an ultimate show of strength, the president can make an arms sale even with the opposition of more than two-thirds of the members of one house and all but one-third plus one of the members of the other.

Formal authority defines only the very outer limits of this partnership. In reality, both branches have much to gain from the good faith of the other. They brandish their sharpest implements of authority very rarely, preferring to share information, to express their concerns openly and straightforwardly in forums designed for that purpose, and to seek compromise whenever possible.

It is a widespread understanding in both branches that U.S. foreign policy is strengthened when it has the support of both branches. A decision that carries the full voltage of Congress as well as the president conveys a clearer and stronger message abroad than one that has been won by one branch over the intense opposition of the other. Accordingly, there are incentives on both sides to join forces—and thus to participate in procedures that facilitate a tandem relationship.

Government is a hard business. Executive branch officials would find life much easier were it not for the burden of satisfying congressional scrutiny. Members of Congress would happily prefer an even stronger hand in controlling executive branch discretion. Neither change is going to occur, so conflict will persist. And the need to devise procedures to manage the conflict has been a prominent feature of congressional-executive relations on this issue and the dominant motivation in the actions of the branches toward each other over the past two decades.

Conclusions

The recent history of arms sales policy provides a rich case study of congressional-executive interaction. It is full of procedural and political efforts at institutional assertion, of conflict and compromise, of shifting advantage. And it yields some revealing lessons—lessons about the peculiar nature of arms sales policy and the broader character of the relationship between the legislative and executive branches.

1. *Though Congress has created the tools to do so, it has rarely intervened in the implementation of arms sales policy.*

It is striking in reviewing the U.S. arms sales program of the past two decades, a program in which arms worth more than $100 billion have been exported, to see how infrequently Congress has objected in any significant way to arms sales proposed by the executive branch. By focusing only on controversial cases, one could easily form the impression that Congress is a compulsive meddler, seeking a handle on every arms sale. That is simply not the case.

Even in the years of its greatest activism, Congress has rarely given more than passing attention to as much as 10 percent of the dollar value of sales proposed in those years. Most sales require no congressional review because they fall below the statutory thresholds that trigger review. Among the sales that exceed those thresholds are many to reliable allies, sales that almost never trouble members of Congress. The bulk of congressional attention has focused on a few large sales of highly sophisticated weapons to adversaries of Israel or to a few other countries like Turkey or Pakistan that were part of a delicate regional military balance.

Criticisms that Congress too often micromanages arms sales are difficult to support, given the limited evidence of congressional participation in arms sales decisions. Even where Congress has intervened, it has had a limited impact on the sales that some of its members sought to oppose. On only a few occasions in the past two decades have arms sales proposals been completely withdrawn in the face of congressional opposition. Most have gone ahead as proposed or been modified slightly to win minimum necessary congressional support.

For all the congressional effort devoted in this period to legislating new restrictions and exercising oversight, presidents have been little deterred in their arms sales objectives. Arms sales policy has been very much what presidents wanted it to be.

2. *Congressional activism has improved the quality of arms sales decisions.*

The larger role played by Congress in FMS policy has "raised the cost of doing business" for the executive branch. Knowing that they are being more closely watched and are subject to more effective control mechanisms, executive branch officials who negotiate arms sales have had to be more careful and more thoughtful in their work. They now have to meet a higher standard of explanation and rationale. They not only have to convince themselves that a particular arms sale is wise, they have to convince a couple of often skeptical congressional committees as well. Hans Binnendijk, a Senate Foreign Relations Committee staff member, declared:

> We use the threat of an ultimate sanction, an ultimate veto, to try to make adjustments in the sales so that we get assurances, understandings, adjustments in numbers, modifications. What we have done was to take a fairly blunt instrument ... and we have tried to sharpen it in practice so that you are not really in the business of killing arms sales, but rather in the business of fine-tuning them.[43]

Congress has become an institutionalized second opinion in arms sales decisions. That second opinion usually concurs with the first, or at least acquiesces in it, but it does not always do so. And executive branch officials now have to be more alert and sensitive to the national security and domestic political impacts of the arms sales they negotiate than was the case before Congress began to carve out a more active role for itself in the early 1970s.

3. More active congressional participation has added little consistency to arms sales policy.

Consistency is the hobgoblin of journalists and scholars, not legislators. One of the arguments that members of Congress have made to justify their participation in arms sales decisions is that they could discern no consistent pattern of sales that seemed to add up to a policy. In the view of many in Congress, the executive branch was simply too willing to sell arms to almost anyone, and it became incumbent upon Congress to apply the brakes, to set broad restrictions and review individual decisions.

Congress has done that, but it is still difficult to discern a coherent arms sales policy. If anything, the larger congressional role has made the pattern of sales less coherent rather than more so. Recent administrations, for example, have sought to be more evenhanded in distributing arms to Middle Eastern countries, seeing that as a way to expand the number of friends of the United States among those countries. A powerful and intense group of opponents in Congress, seeking to protect the security of Israel, has often opposed those sales—with varying degrees of effectiveness.

The outcome has been mixed but hardly consistent. Hawk missiles were sold to Jordan in 1975 to strengthen the U.S. relationship with King Hussein. But Congress intervened in the sale and required that the Hawks, designed to be mobile missiles, be installed in fixed sites. This was insulting to King Hussein and significantly undercut the benefits that the sale was intended to achieve. Even the staff director of the subcommittee from which much of the opposition to the sale arose said, "We've never recovered with King Hussein. We've never had the relationship we had pre-1975."[44]

Congressional intervention has been sporadic and politically driven. Little of it has been inspired by a consistent or coherent vision of the national interest. Virtually none of it has followed from any congressional effort to deliberate upon a proper arms sales policy. Thus, though congressional intervention in arms sales has often been motivated by concerns about lack of coherence, it has tended to exacerbate rather than cure the problem.

4. Both branches have powerful incentives to resolve their differences through compromise rather than direct exercise of power or authority.

There have been some bruising showdowns between the two branches over arms sales policy, but the number has been small and they have tended to be aberrant cases in which normal conflict resolution procedures simply failed. No one on either side relishes the showdowns. Presidents dislike them intensely because they suggest to both domestic and foreign constituencies how real are the limits on presidential authority. Reagan worried aloud during the 1981 battle with Congress over selling AWACS planes to the Saudis, "How can I meet with a foreign leader and have him believe I'm in charge of the government if I can't sell five airplanes?"[45] Presidents dislike showdowns also because they often result, even if the president wins, in congressional enactment of tighter restrictions on executive discretion. It is, in fact, a common pattern in this relationship for Congress to try to recapture by procedural restraint what it has lost in substantive conflicts with the president.

Congress has a similar distaste for showdowns with the executive branch because it knows that it is unlikely to win. In a one-on-one confrontation with Congress, the president is a formidable adversary. That is especially true under current procedures, where extraordinary majorities are necessary in Congress to disapprove a sale if the president is determined to go ahead with it.

The president can muster the resources of the executive branch, of his supporters across the country, of foreign governments, and of defense manufacturers, and he can draw heavily on the loyalty of members of his own party in Congress. That usually adds up to enough support to carry a close vote. In fact, as we have seen, there have been several such close votes on controversial arms sales—some decided by a single vote—and the president has won them all.

So, for Congress the message is clear: half a loaf is better than none. Negotiate and compromise. Seek changes in the components or size of a sale. Go to the mat with the president only as a last resort.

5. In shaping effective relations between the two branches, no policy pronouncement or procedural innovation is as valuable as good faith.

Though structured by laws and regulations, congressional-executive relations always boil down to interactions among people. Because people often bear different institutional perspectives and political views, their interactions are potentially conflict-laden. The only effective way to orchestrate harmony from the discord is through diligent exercise of openness, consideration, honesty, and respect: the interpersonal traits that add up to mutual trust.

Richard Grimmett, the CRS specialist who has been the principal chronicler of the history of congressional involvement in arms sales, has underscored the importance of all this:

> The reason things worked with those examples that never elevated themselves to the level of controversy was because there was a willingness to explore ways to deal with the concerns. Good faith, I think, was the underlying factor. That's how you deal with distrust. The whole Nixon, Watergate period created a poisonous atmosphere of distrust. And good faith is the best antidote for any kind of distrust.[46]

Good faith cannot be crystallized from thin air, nor can it be legislated into existence. It can emerge and survive only when the participants in arms sales decisions recognize how essential it is to successful, long-term patterns of interaction. They must be willing to place the value of their working relationships on a par with the value of their policy objectives so that they are able to manage effectively the conflicts that are endemic to the issues they confront and the institutional and political perspectives they represent.

6. *Procedural change is a logical extension of policy conflict.*

With a nod to Clausewitz, one might well argue that changes in the structure of congressional-executive relations are substantive policy struggles carried on by other means. Congress commonly alters procedures in order to gain objectives it has been unable to achieve in policy confrontations with the executive branch. When it fails to win a policy battle, a normal reaction is to seek a change in the rules of engagement.

This case tells a story of constant tinkering with the legislative underpinnings of congressional-executive relations. From the late 1960s, when a foreign military sales act was passed, up to the present, Congress has repeatedly defined and redefined its own role in arms sales decisions, required more and more reports from executive agencies, and steadily increased the number of restrictions on executive discretion. Time after time, the addition of new procedures or restraints has followed a policy dispute in which a substantial number of members of Congress were dissatisfied with the outcome.

Little of this congressional tinkering was inspired by some clear or carefully deliberated philosophy of congressional-executive relations. No blueprint was ever in evidence. It was inspired instead by the search for political advantage, for ways to improve Congress's strategic position vis-à-vis the executive branch so that the legislature could play a larger role in shaping policy outcomes. Sometimes that resulted in trespassing into what even many in Congress regarded as areas of proper executive jurisdiction. "When you put conditions on a sale to go ahead," said one knowledgeable congressional staff member, "that is micromanaging. There have been a good many of those."[47] Congress always found justification for that in the perceived failure of the executive branch to abide by the law or in the sharp differences of philosophy between the two branches—differences compounded during this period by divided partisan control of the government.

In the face of these policy differences, calls for respect of traditional institutional boundaries are of little avail. There is no consensus on the proper alignment of those boundaries in any case. And even if there were, that would probably not stand in the way of the policy pursuits of legislators in a system where political pressure will always seek out the weak points in procedural restraints.

7. *Participation in the details of administration is sometimes the only effective way for Congress to shape public policy.*

Purists would like to believe that the roles of the legislature and the administration can be neatly separated. The legislature passes laws that make policy, the administration implements it. That is a simplification of reality that assumes impossible things. It assumes, first of all, that policy can be fully "made" in legislation, that by enacting a statute, Congress can resolve all the political conflicts, address all the technical issues, and provide all the guidance necessary to help the implementers navigate through the future. No such luck. Even in the best of circumstances, no legislature is wise enough to foresee and comprehend the multiple futures in which policy will be implemented. Congress—setting aside the nagging problem of politics for the moment—might have been able in 1976 to write language in the Arms Export Control Act that directed the administration to sell only certain kinds of weapons to certain kinds of countries in certain amounts. It did not, of course, because it was unable to answer those questions for itself. Even if it had, that guidance would have been quickly out of date. Three years later, one of the most powerful allies of the United States in the Middle East, Iran, had become its arch adversary. Egypt had signed peace accords with Israel. The Soviet Union had invaded Afghanistan. And so on. Legislation is black print on white pages. Policy needs to be a living organism.

There is an even more compelling reason that Congress is always tempted to meddle in the details of administration. Implementation is— broadly across all of the U.S. government—the primary point of conflict resolution, and thus the place where many important decisions actually get made. Congress seeks a role in implementation because that, so often, is where the action is.

Congress is a collectivity, not a person. It is a shifting frenzy of coalitions and fissures. Discipline is insufficient and leadership inadequate. Consensus comes rarely and flees quickly. When Congress is riven by internal conflict and doubt—its normal condition—it will hedge its bets and retain maximum control over program implementation. That is simply a way of doing what Congress does best: avoiding conflict by postponing difficult decisions. It leaves to the implementation process what cannot be resolved in the legislative process.

Timeline of Major Events in Foreign Military Arms Sales Case

1940	Decision by President Roosevelt to give the British fifty aging U.S. destroyers in exchange for certain base rights marks the first significant transfer of U.S. arms to a foreign government.
22 October 1968	P.L. 90-629, Foreign Military Sales Act of 1968, restricts arms sales and credit sales to underdeveloped nations solely to annual appropriations. This legislation is requested by the administration after Congress has eliminated existing methods of financing arms sales.
31 December 1971	P.L. 91-672, Foreign Military Sales Act, authorizes government-to-government arms sales.
18 December 1974	P.L. 93-559. This foreign aid authorization act includes a provision, originating in the House, that requires the president to give advance notice to Congress of any offer to sell defense items worth $25 million or more. Congress then has twenty days in which to disapprove such sales by concurrent resolutions. The president can waive the review requirement if he determines a sale would be in the national interest and reports it to Congress. This is called the Nelson-Bingham amendment, after its Senate and House sponsors.
1975	Congress mandates the suspension of military assistance and sales to Turkey after the intervention of Turkish forces in Cyprus. The administration objects that congressional action is harmful to U.S. interests and represents an unsound congressional intrusion into the conduct of foreign relations.
	President Ford notifies Congress of a proposed sale to Jordan of Hawk and Vulcan missile air defense systems. The administration temporarily withdraws the proposal after the House Foreign Affairs Committee votes a resolution of disapproval. After some negotiation, in which the administration agrees to require that the Hawk missile batteries be permanently installed at fixed sites, the sale is resubmitted and allowed to occur.
18 February 1976	Defense Department agrees to an informal procedure whereby Congress would be provided a twenty-day, preliminary notification of possible government-to-government sales that might be formally submitted for congressional review.
25 June 1976	P.L. 94-329. International Security Assistance and Arms Export Control Act, S. 2662 reduces the arms sales threshold for congressional review from $25 million to

$7 million for both public- and private-sector contracts and places a $9 billion annual limit on total arms sales. President Ford vetoes the bill, saying it makes Congress a "virtual co-administrator" of foreign policy. Lacking the votes, Congress never attempts to override.

Congress revises the bill, eliminating the $9 billion ceiling. Congress also prohibits private companies from selling any major equipment costing $25 million or more directly to other governments; such sales would have to be made through government rather than commercial channels. Congress also receives the authority to review (but not veto) all commercial arms sales exceeding $7 million. This is the first time Congress has required a review of commercial arms sales. P.L. 94-329 lowers the threshold for congressional veto on government arms sales to $7 million. Congress would have thirty days' advance notice of such sales, during which time it could prevent them by concurrent resolution of disapproval.

This legislation also requires the president to submit to Congress an annual estimate of the amount of sales, credits, and loan guarantees expected to be extended to foreign governments in the following year and an arms control impact statement for each country estimate.

The administration proposes to sell 1000 Sidewinder and 1500 Maverick missiles to Saudi Arabia. Opposition arises in Congress, and negotiations between the two branches leads to a reduction in the number of missiles to 850 Sidewinders and 650 Mavericks. The Senate Foreign Relations Committee still reports a resolution of disapproval, but the resolution is subsequently returned to the committee and the sale is made in its revised form.

19 May 1977   President Carter orders a review of U.S. military sales practices, concluding, "the United States will henceforth view arms transfers as an exceptional foreign policy implement, to be used only in instances where it can be clearly demonstrated that the transfer contributes to our national security interests."

7 July 1977   Carter notifies Congress that he will sell seven AWACS to Iran at a cost of $1.2 billion. He is forced to withdraw the sale after the House International Relations Committee votes 19–17 on a resolution to veto the sale. Had Carter not withdrawn the sale, the Senate

Foreign Relations Committee was expected to support the veto resolution later the same day. Many members say they needed more than the allotted thirty days to examine all the questions raised by the sale and thus support the veto.

On 7 September Carter resubmits the proposal with assurances that the deal has been modified to resolve most of the problems. A veto resolution is introduced in the Senate Foreign Relations Committee, but there is no action on it, nor in the House, before the deadline passes.

28 April 1978   Carter proposes a package sale of F-15 long-range fighters to Israel, F-5E short-range fighter bombers to Egypt, and F-15s to Saudi Arabia (total value of $4.8 billion). Congress objects principally to the sale to Saudi Arabia. Carter wins a significant victory when the Senate votes 44–54 to reject a resolution of disapproval. The House never votes after the Senate fails to endorse the resolution, though objections to the sale are reported to be high there.

12 September 1978   P.L. 95-384, military aid bill. Includes a provision expressing the sense of Congress that the president adhere to a policy of restraint in conventional arms transfers and that not later than 31 December 1979 the president transmit to Congress a detailed report assessing the results and commenting on the implications of multilateral arms sales discussions with other arms suppliers.

Congress amends sec. 25 of the Arms Export Control Act to require the president to transmit to Congress, no later than 15 November of each year, a report to be termed the "Arms Sales Proposal," which would include data on all arms sales requiring congressional review that were likely to be proposed in the coming year. This is usually called the "Javits report," after Senator Jacob Javits, who introduced the amendment suggesting it.

16 October 1979   P.L. 96-92, foreign military aid authorization. Includes a provision requiring the president to submit to Congress "a detailed justification" of any decision, under the president's emergency powers, to waive the requirement that Congress be given thirty days to disapprove major arms sales abroad.

1 October 1981   President Reagan proposes to sell five AWACS to Saudi Arabia for $8.5 billion. A ferocious fight ensues. On 14 October the House votes 301–111 to disapprove

the sale. On 28 October, after intensive lobbying, the Senate votes 48–52 to defeat the resolution of disapproval. President narrowly wins and the sale goes through.

23 October 1981   Reagan proposes to sell forty F-16 planes to Pakistan for $1.1 billion. Congressional objections are muted after the bruising battle over AWACS to Saudi Arabia. A resolution of disapproval is defeated 7–10 in the Senate Foreign Relations Committee, and 13–13 in the House Foreign Affairs Committee.

1983   In its decision in *INS v. Chadha,* the Supreme Court invalidates the legislative veto, in most instances, as a technique of legislative oversight. The decision does not apply directly to the Arms Export Control Act, but most legal experts believe the *Chadha* precedent undermines the validity of the concurrent resolution procedure included in sec. 36(b) of that law.

8 August 1985   Reagan signs P.L. 99-83, the foreign aid authorization law for 1986–87, despite objections to a provision banning sales of warplanes and other advanced weapons to Jordan unless that country agrees to begin peace negotiations with Israel. The law also includes a provision requiring the president to seek congressional approval for any upgrade in the level of technology to be included in a foreign arms sale after the sale has been approved by Congress.

1986   Congress investigates the Iran-*contra* affair, which involves alleged violations of arms sales restrictions imposed by Congress.

3 February 1986   Secretary of State Shultz notifies Congress that the Reagan administration is postponing indefinitely a planned arms sale to Jordan. The arms sale proposal first came to Congress in 1985. Congress negotiates a delay with the administration. Pro-Israel members of Congress use the delay to maneuver to block the sale completely. When it appears they are nearing success, the administration withdraws the proposal to avert a rejection.

Congress passes a bill (P.L. 99-247) designed to revise the Arms Export Control Act in light of *Chadha.* Under the original law, Congress could disapprove a proposed arms sale by passing a concurrent resolution of disapproval. Under the new procedures, disapproval would require a joint resolution. A joint resolution requires a presidential signature to take effect; a concurrent resolution requires only passage by both houses.

Reagan submits a proposal to sell weapons worth $265 million to Saudi Arabia for congressional approval. Both houses support S.J. Res. 316, a resolution of disapproval. Reagan vetoes the joint resolution, and his veto is sustained 66–34 in the Senate. To secure Senate support for the veto, Reagan writes a letter to Majority Leader Robert Dole in which he promises to remove Stinger missiles from the arms package if his veto is upheld, allowing the sale to go through. This is the first time that both houses have voted to disapprove a proposed weapons sale.

August 1986

P.L. 99-399 takes effect, barring arms sales to countries that the secretary of state has found to support international terrorism. The president can waive the ban on a case-by-case basis by declaring that it is in the "national security interests" of the United States to do so. He is required to consult with Congress at least fifteen days in advance and submit a report detailing any proposed sales under such a waiver.

October 1987

Reagan wins support for a $1 billion arms sale to Saudi Arabia after working out a compromise agreement with Congress. The package includes twelve F-15s and a variety of other weapons and parts. At the insistence of some members of the Senate, Reagan withdraws 1600 Maverick air-to-ground missiles from the proposal.

August 1988

A proposed sale to Kuwait of forty F-18 planes and associated missiles survives congressional opposition after the Reagan administration agrees to alter the types of Maverick air-to-surface missiles that would be sold. Intense lobbying by the administration overcomes an effort by some House members to kill the sale by stripping all Maverick missiles from the package.

September 1988

The Reagan administration, as part of its foreign aid proposals (P.L. 100-461), recommends the elimination of all FMS loans and replacing them with outright grants. The objective is to reduce the debt burden carried by many poor countries that have purchased arms from the United States on credit. House Foreign Operations Subcommittee Chair David Obey opposes the conversion of the FMS program to all-grant aid. In final congressional action, the mix of loans and grants is changed in the direction the administration sought, but the loan component of the program is retained. Conferees also agree to a watered-down version of an amendment sponsored by Tom Harkin in the Senate bill, requiring the administration to inform Congress in advance of any potential overseas sale of missiles, rockets, or artillery projectiles, regardless of the price. The conferees limit the new requirement only to ground-to-air missiles such as Stingers and air-to-ground missiles like Mavericks.

Notes

1. Quoted, *Congressional Quarterly Weekly Report*, 3 April 1982, 722.

2. House Committee on Foreign Affairs, Subcommittee on Arms Control, International Security and Science, *Hearings: Proposal to Reform the Arms Export Control Act*, 100th Cong., 1st sess., 1987, 34.

3. Statement prepared for delivery before the Senate Appropriations Foreign Operations Subcommittee, 22 June 1990 (Mimeographed), 6.

4. This process is described in much fuller detail in House Committee on Foreign Affairs, Subcommittee on Arms Control, International Security and Science, *U.S. Military Sales and Assistance Programs: Laws, Regulations, and Procedures*, 99th Cong., 1st sess., 1985, Committee Print, 17–39. The brief description offered here applies only to government-to-government sales; a different procedure applies for direct commercial sales between U.S. arms manufacturers and foreign governments.

5. Richard M. Nixon, "Address on Vietnam," 3 November 1969. Quoted, Congressional Quarterly, *Congress and the Nation*, vol. 3, 1969–72 (Washington, D.C.: CQ Press, 1973), 869.

6. Interview with Richard F. Grimmett, specialist in national defense, Congressional Research Service, Washington, D.C., 18 July 1990.

7. Nitza Nachmias, *Transfer of Arms, Leverage, and Peace in the Middle East* (Westport, Conn.: Greenwood Press, 1988), 13.

8. House Committee on Foreign Affairs, *Congressional-Executive Relations and the Turkish Arms Embargo*, 97th Cong., 1st sess., 1981, Committee Print, 3.

9. Quoted, *Congressional Quarterly Weekly Report*, 10 April 1982, 798.

10. Interview with Glenn Rudd, deputy director, Defense Security Assistance Agency, Washington, D.C., 19 July 1990.

11. *Congressional Record*, 93rd Cong., 2d sess., 38074.

12. Quoted, *Congress and the Nation*, vol. 4, 1973–1976 (Washington, D.C.: CQ Press, 1977), 877.

13. Quoted, *Congressional Quarterly Weekly Report*, 10 April 1982, 797.

14. Quoted, ibid.

15. P.L. 99-247.

16. Both quoted, *Congressional Quarterly Almanac, 1988* (Washington, D.C.: CQ Press, 1989), 507.

17. For more detail on earmarking practices, see Larry A. Mortsolf and

Louis J. Samelson, "The Congress and U.S. Military Assistance, Part I," *DISAM Journal* 9 (Summer 1987): 75.

18. House Committee on Foreign Affairs, *Foreign Assistance Reporting Requirements*, 100th Cong., 2d sess., 1988, Committee Print.

19. See House Committee on Foreign Affairs, Subcommittee on Arms Control, International Security and Science, *Hearings: Proposal to Reform the Arms Export Control Act.*

20. One could argue that the Turkish arms embargo, voted by Congress in 1974, had much the same effect as disapproval of an arms sale.

21. House Committee on Foreign Affairs, Subcommittee on Arms Control, International Security and Science, *Hearings: Proposal to Reform the Arms Export Control Act*, 61.

22. Rudd interview.

23. House Committee on Foreign Affairs, Subcommittee on Arms Control, International Security and Science, *Hearings: Proposal to Reform the Arms Export Control Act*, 66.

24. House Committee on Foreign Affairs, Subcommittee on Arms Control, International Security and Science, *Hearings: Proposed Tank Sale to Saudi Arabia*, 101st Cong., 1st sess., 1989, 3.

25. Rudd interview.

26. Quoted, *Congressional Quarterly Weekly Report*, 3 April 1982, 722.

27. House Committee on Foreign Affairs, *Congressional-Executive Relations and the Turkish Arms Embargo*, Committee Print prepared by CRS, 1981, 4–5.

28. Rudd interview.

29. Prepared statement of Lieutenant General Charles W. Brown, director, DSAA, before the Senate Foreign Operations Subcommittee, 22 June 1990 (Mimeographed), 7.

30. Rudd interview.

31. S.J. Res. 113, 101st Cong., 1st sess., 1989.

32. *Congressional Record*, 101st Cong., 1st sess., 31 July 1989, S9132.

33. House Committee on Foreign Affairs, *Executive-Legislative Consultation on U.S. Arms Sales*, 97th Cong., 2d sess., 1982, Committee Print, 3.

34. Quoted, *Congressional Quarterly Weekly Report*, 3 April 1982, 724.

35. Statement by Richard W. Murphy, assistant secretary of state for Near Eastern and South Asian Affairs, to the House Foreign Affairs Subcommittee on Europe and the Middle East, in *Hearings: Presidential Certification on the Delivery of AWACS to Saudi Arabia*, 99th Cong., 2d sess., 1986, 53.

36. House Committee on Foreign Affairs, Subcommittee on Arms Control, International Security and Science, *Hearings: Proposed Tank Sale to Saudi Arabia*, 55.

37. *Congressional Record*, 101st Cong., 1st sess., 13 September 1989, S10933, S10994.

38. Rudd interview; Grimmett interview.

39. Sec. 1, Arms Export Control Act.

40. Ibid.

41. House Committee on Foreign Affairs, Subcommittee on Arms Control, International Security and Science, *Hearings: Proposal to Reform the Arms Export Control Act,* 67.

42. Interview with Michael Van Dusen, staff director, House Foreign Affairs Subcommittee on Europe and the Middle East, Washington, D.C., 26 July 1990.

43. Quoted, *Congressional Quarterly Weekly Report,* 10 April 1982, 799.

44. Van Dusen interview.

45. Reported by Senator Ed Zorinsky (D-Neb.) from a personal conversation with the president; quoted, *Congressional Quarterly Weekly Report,* 31 October 1981, 2097.

46. Grimmett interview.

47. Van Dusen interview.

Conclusion

12

Co-Managing Policy and Program Development

ROBERT S. GILMOUR AND ALEXIS A. HALLEY

The case studies of this volume are used as tools to understand the motivations, means, and effects of detailed congressional intervention in an area traditionally regarded as the prerogative of the executive branch: policy and program development and implementation. Familiar terms used to describe the congressional role in the policy process—*overseer, policymaker, legislator, micromanager*—are inadequate to characterize the congressional behavior and results witnessed in these ten case studies.

As the discussion in this chapter will show, the cases reveal significant institutional change in the relationship between Congress and the executive branch, leading to the overall conclusion that the Congress observed in these cases was not only an active and authoritative overseer but also a thoroughly involved participant—a co-manager—with (or sometimes in spite of) the executive in directing the details of policy implementation and program execution.[1] The cases collectively suggest that the term *congressional co-management* of policy implementation and program execution characterizes the transition from a congressional reliance on postaudit oversight of executive branch performance to preaudit congressional program controls and direct congressional participation with the executive in the full scope of policy and program development and implementation. The cases show a "congressional co-manager" intervening directly in the details of policy development and management rather than enacting vague, wide-ranging, sweeping statutes to change fundamental policy directions. The cases also suggest that congressional co-management is as much a result of actions in the executive branch as it is a result of actions in the legislative branch.

Congressional Co-Management with the Executive Branch

The basic questions that guided the research for each case study were when, why, how, and with what results does Congress enter the executive domain to direct the details of policy development and implementation? The same elements can be used to describe the institutional behavior across the cases that we characterize as congressional co-management of policy and program development and implementation (see figure 12.1): (1) catalysts that trigger congressional co-management; (2) procedures, techniques, or tools that enable Congress to sustain its intervention as a co-manager; and (3) mixed effects—some unexpected—for policy-making and program management and for the function and performance of the institutions involved.

The discussion thus far assumes that congressional co-management is a metaphor describing a relatively uniform pattern of behavior—or that all ten cases show identical forms of congressional co-management. That, of course, is not so. The cases are examples or prototypes to suggest more discrete or finer-grained arrangements of congressional co-management. We distinguish five styles of congressional co-management illustrated by the cases: (1) strategic leadership, (2) consultative partner, (3) superintendent, (4) combative opponent, and (5) passive observer. Each style characterizes a different pattern of catalysts, procedures and techniques, and effects that shows a particular form of congressional co-management (see figure 12.2). All these styles have enough in common to be considered congressional co-management, yet they differ enough also to indicate something unique.

Each of these elements will be considered in turn to clarify what congressional co-management of policy development and program implementation with the executive branch implies for overall (that is, co-management in general terms) and discrete (that is, styles or subtypes of co-management) forms of interinstitutional behavior. Whether overall or discrete, congressional co-management is here described using a framework that includes motivations or catalysts; congressional-executive actions and counteractions through procedures, techniques, and tools; and the ensuing effects.

Catalysts for Congressional Co-Management

The historical timelines developed in the case studies sometimes extend as far back as forty years. This perspective yields the insight that Congress typically began its involvement in each of the cases with a broad delegation of authority to the executive branch. Collectively, the cases show a common evolution in congressional delegations. The path of change began, in all cases, with Congress's assuming, first, that broadly stated laws or initiatives would be implemented in good faith and in ways generally congruent with

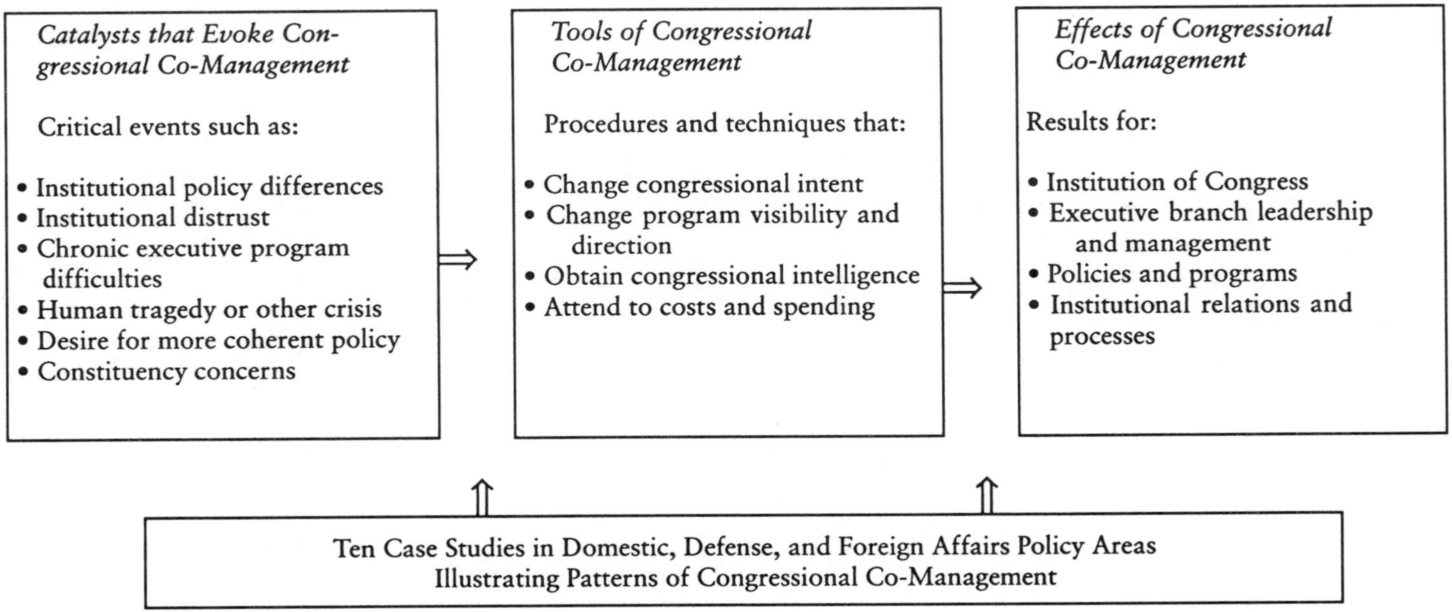

Catalysts that Evoke Congressional Co-Management

Critical events such as:

- Institutional policy differences
- Institutional distrust
- Chronic executive program difficulties
- Human tragedy or other crisis
- Desire for more coherent policy
- Constituency concerns

Tools of Congressional Co-Management

Procedures and techniques that:

- Change congressional intent
- Change program visibility and direction
- Obtain congressional intelligence
- Attend to costs and spending

Effects of Congressional Co-Management

Results for:

- Institution of Congress
- Executive branch leadership and management
- Policies and programs
- Institutional relations and processes

Ten Case Studies in Domestic, Defense, and Foreign Affairs Policy Areas Illustrating Patterns of Congressional Co-Management

FIGURE 12.1.
FRAMEWORK FOR DESCRIBING (GENERAL CASE OF) CONGRESSIONAL CO-MANAGEMENT OF POLICY DEVELOPMENT WITH THE EXECUTIVE BRANCH

Framework for General
Case of Co-Management

Styles (Subtypes) of Congres-
sional Co-Management

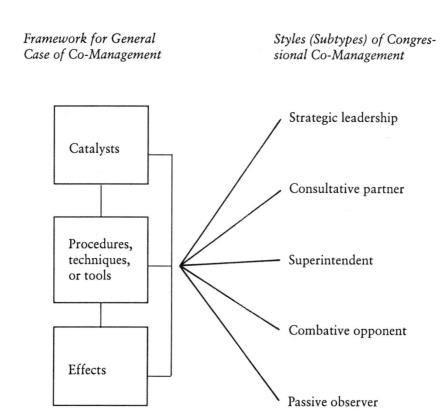

FIGURE 12.2.
STYLES OF CONGRESSIONAL CO-MANAGEMENT WITH THE
EXECUTIVE BRANCH, TEN ILLUSTRATIVE CASE STUDIES

congressional mandates, and second, that the ambiguity inherent in such broad prescriptions would still provide adequate parameters for executive branch implementation and postaudit congressional oversight.

But the broad congressional delegations were typically followed by critical events that cumulatively triggered the onset of a period of change—in substantive policy or the administrative role of Congress, or both. During and following significant social, political, economic, and policy events, Congress (particular members and staffs interested in or jurisdictionally relevant to specific issues) actively intervened in the executive branch domain in both the substance and execution of policy and programs. Congress, as co-manager, intervened directly in the details of program management rather than with sweeping statutes to change fundamental policy directions. Gone almost entirely are the vague, wide-ranging delegations of new authority from Congress to executive. Delegations made two and three decades past have been retrieved to a large extent with the imposition of nearly countless requirements, limits, directions, prohibitions, reporting requirements, personnel restrictions, deadlines, hammers, "no-expenditure" clauses, and other controls or means of direct congressional access to policy redirection and implementation. As a result, congressional committees, members, and staffers have become vital participants, along with their executive branch counterparts, in the execution and management of public policies and programs, as well as in their planning and development.

What was the nature of the "catalytic events" that set off such assertedly overwhelming institutional change? The domestic, defense, and foreign affairs cases examined included five common catalytic events, woven into different patterns in each individual case. The change to congressional co-management was triggered by one or more of the following types of events: (1) profound institutional policy differences between Congress and the executive, or congressional distrust of executive intentions, competence, or veracity; (2) chronic executive program difficulties—delays, cost inefficiency, program failures or escalation of costs, executive refusal to adhere to congressional directives, or even outright management failures and deceit; (3) human tragedy or other crisis; (4) a desire for more coherent policy; and (5) constituency concerns. Rarely could congressional intervention be attributed to only one of these events. Instead, several events were typically observed as necessary and sufficient conditions for Congress to change its role.

Institutional Policy Differences and Distrust

Intense interbranch policy differences that could not be resolved informally were in some cases resolved by congressionally imposed statutory provisions, which structured process and procedures, organization, priorities, sites, timetables, and expected results. At least half of the cases explored here (*Goldwater-Nichols Defense Reorganization; Hazardous Waste Disposal; Human Rights and Foreign Aid; High-Level Nuclear Waste Policy;* and *For-*

eign Military Arms Sales) illustrate deep-seated interbranch policy disagreement as a source of the imposition of congressionally dictated directions and controls.

Policy disagreement can also be a place where congressional distrust of executive intentions, competence, or veracity is acted out. In the *Hazardous Waste Disposal* case, the 1984 congressional amendments were preceded by a period of thoroughgoing policy disagreement between Congress and the Reagan administration. It became difficult to disentangle the policy disagreement from the intense and reciprocal distrust. Similarly for the *Medicare Prospective Payment System* case, where policy differences between a presidential administration and a democratic Congress over time expanded the distrust as well as the disagreement. The two foreign affairs cases, *Foreign Military Arms Sales* and *Foreign Aid and Human Rights,* were characterized in the 1970s by a profound distrust of the presidency brought on by the Vietnam war and Watergate scandal. When the policy disagreement went beyond the normal bounds of difference toward institutional distrust, congressional co-management—taking the forms of preaudit program controls and direct congressional intervention in implementation—often followed.

Executive Program Difficulties

In an environment where interbranch distrust is a strong undercurrent, any number of conditions or events could trigger a change in the congressional role from delegator of authority and passive overseer of administration to active program co-manager. Some of the most powerful initiators of congressional co-management of the policy process involved chronic program failures and cost overruns. Throughout these cases there is a pattern of congressional response to administrative inadequacy in the executive branch (that is, program mismanagement, neglect, or breakdown; excessive costs; prolonged delays in policy implementation; misinformation and outright deceit). The significance of program failures was often accentuated by a crisis atmosphere, and further heightened by extensive media coverage. For example, in the *Goldwater-Nichols Defense Reorganization* case, the reorganization act was prompted in major part by cumulative military failures of coordination among the armed services—in Vietnam, in the Iran rescue mission, and in Grenada. Similarly, once made visible by repeated press accounts, chronic Energy Department inattention to safety and health concerns in the *Defense Nuclear Weapons Complex Cleanup* case prompted the imposition of a wide range of congressional directives and controls on the program. The Goldwater-Nichols defense reform was also fueled by escalating military acquisitions costs in program after program.

Irrespective of actual cause, a number of the case studies illustrate a belated congressional recognition of troubled or languishing programs: *AMRAAM; High-Level Nuclear Waste Policy; Defense Nuclear Weapons Complex Cleanup; Medicare Prospective Payment System; Hazardous Waste*

Disposal; Foreign Military Arms Sales; and the *Traffic Alert and Collision Avoidance System* (TCAS). The particulars of congressional problem recognition and response are somewhat different in each, but the same pattern is evident.

General policy guidelines developed in an initial delegation (or in a series of delegations) from Congress to an executive agency were not followed by vigilant oversight or effective intelligence gathering until after a serious program breakdown had occurred. The Defense Appropriations Act of 1977, for example, initiated development of a new advanced medium-range air-to-air missile (AMRAAM) as a joint Air Force–Navy project. Afterward little was done by Congress to track the progress of AMRAAM's development until 1983, nearly seven years later. At that time, reports of mounting costs and intractable—possibly insurmountable—technical obstacles began to filter back to senior staffers of the House Armed Services Committee. Only then did Congress become actively involved. In the *Traffic Alert and Collision Avoidance System* case, after three committees held hearings on midair collision avoidance in 1979, the House Appropriations Committee expressed its intent that the Federal Aviation Administration develop a national standard (regulations) for a collision avoidance system. Thereafter, a modest effort to develop a system was begun by the FAA. But it was not until the furor over the Cerritos, California, collision in 1986—seven years later—that Congress again asserted itself directly to elevate the collision avoidance system's priority in the FAA by setting a definite deadline.

In some situations, congressional and executive neglect of program deficiencies may be long-term in the extreme. In the *Defense Nuclear Weapons Complex Cleanup* case, health and environmental risks from more than a hundred nuclear defense production facilities, including fourteen primary facilities in twelve states, had been hidden from public view for more than thirty years. Congressional staff members had complained about the high levels of secrecy extending to the pollution and radiation threats of these facilities for some time, yet it was not until a series of hard-hitting reports in the *New York Times,* following extensive GAO studies, cited both the dangers and the likely $100-billion-plus cleanup costs that congressional committee leadership began to take a serious interest. Then, with the added impetus of the Soviet Union's Chernobyl disaster and reports of leakage and contamination at two primary U.S. weapons facilities, the pace of congressional involvement escalated. More than a score of committees and subcommittees held some fifty hearings during the 1980s, as Congress required new plans, deadlines, and reports, and imposed other controls.

Human Tragedy or Other Crisis

In some instances program failure or ineffectiveness is more dramatic when punctuated with a human disaster such as the Cerritos midair collision, the waste contamination crises of Love Canal, or the OPEC oil crisis. There seems little question that the torpid pace of the FAA's traffic alert and collision avoidance regulatory process would have continued but for the Cerritos incident. Surely, as well, congressional interest in safety and environmental problems in the Department of Energy's nuclear weapons complex was accentuated by the Chernobyl disaster.

In the *Medicare Prospective Payment System* case, the hospital insurance trust fund crisis, coupled with the beginning of a significant expansion of the federal budget deficit, prompted Congress to pass the Tax Equity and Fiscal Responsibility Act and prompted the Health Care Finance Administration to continue, and even accelerate, its efforts to design a prospective payment system.

Desire for More Coherent Policy

A significant dimension of Congress's role as co-manager with the executive branch is its interest in substantive policy. In the *Goldwater-Nichols Defense Reorganization* case, an element of congressional behavior was rooted in a desire to address the broad issues of defense organization and strategy. Similarly, the *Hazardous Waste Disposal* case showed a Congress with a deep desire fundamentally and forcefully to redirect policy in a legislative design that would guarantee an end to the status quo. In the *Foreign Aid and Human Rights* case, Congress was interested in assuring humane treatment of citizens in other countries—or playing a role in shaping that policy. The *Medicare Prospective Payment System* case showed a Congress with a strong desire, shared by the executive branch, to revolutionize national policies for reimbursing hospital costs for Medicare.

The *Goldwater-Nichols Defense Reorganization* case offers what is surely, among the cases studied here, the most profound example of a Congress increasingly frustrated by uncoordinated and sometimes incoherent executive branch policies. It was this frustration that resulted in a comprehensive legislative effort to reorganize and impose procedural reforms to improve the quality and management of defense policies and programs.

Constituency Concerns

The classic congressional role of protecting and enhancing district and constituency concerns is also demonstrated in a number of the cases. "Not-in-my-backyard" motives triggered much of the action in the *High-Level Nuclear Waste Policy* case. Conversely, pork-barrel incentives played a prominent part in the *Highway Demonstration Projects* case (along with coalition-building needs of Public Works committees). Locations of governmental projects and institutions also illustrated the role of constituency concerns in triggering congressional co-management. Examples included securing federal funds for parochial purposes (siting a highway demonstration project in the home district) or avoiding selecting the location for necessary but unpleasant projects, such as a nuclear waste disposal site. Constituency concerns were also an element in the *Medicare Prospective Payment System* case with respect to members' moving hospital boundaries (typically changing the official location of the hospital from rural to urban) in order to alter the basis on which payment rates would be set.

Tools of Congressional Co-Management

No single event thus appears to be sufficient to trigger a profound change in congressional behavior. For Congress to intervene as a co-manager, a combination of circumstances seems essential. But given the appropriate catalysts, how—with what procedures, techniques, and tools—does Congress intervene?

Congressional directives to the agencies are numerous and varied. They may specify conditions, methods, quantities and dollar amounts, deadlines, organizational and staffing designs, and contingency arrangements. Congressional directives are also issued in a variety of forums. They may be embedded in an agency's organic (initial enabling) act, in amendments to such statutes, or tucked into omnibus budget reconciliation bills or continuing (appropriations) resolutions. They may appear in committee reports, in hearings of all sorts, in "sense-of-the-Congress" resolutions, in colloquies in the *Congressional Record,* and in informal "letters of understanding" between agencies and senior members and staffers who hold critical jurisdictional authority.

For the most part, the mechanisms that enable Congress to play a role in administration have long histories of use in a wide variety of situations. Each of the cases investigated in this volume demonstrates the use of at least a few of the familiar control techniques, to the point that a complete catalog of devices actually used across the ten cases would list several dozen varieties. When familiar controls were inadequate, Congress searched for and invented new and different ways to sustain its involvement. Table 12.1 provides examples of familiar and more recent congressional co-management tools of intervention.

The intended congressional purposes in employing these co-management controls can be classified in three broad categories: (1) changing congressional intent and program direction; (2) obtaining intelligence in the form of congressionally relevant information; and (3) controlling or at least appearing to control the escalation of program costs and budgetary outlays. It is the context, sequence, combination, and frequency of use of these controls that indicates a significant change in legislative role.

Changing Program Direction and Legislative Intent
Congress frequently communicates its directives formally in statutory language. The *Medicare Prospective Payment System* case offers an extraordinary example of the voluminous detail and complexity of such statutory

TABLE 12.1.
EXAMPLES OF TOOLS OF CONGRESSIONAL CO-MANAGEMENT

Case Study	Program Direction Tools	Intelligence Tools	Cost and Spending Tools
Traffic Alert and Collision Avoidance System	Legislation to force FAA to proceed to full implementation		
Highway Demonstration Projects	Authorization and reauthorization bills with congressional priorities		Highway trust fund Earmarking highway funds for specific localities
High-Level Nuclear Waste Policy	Selecting a site in legislation Procedures, schedule, and organizational arrangements for site characterization in legislation	100 hearings between 1980 and 1990 Numerous "go-do-a-study" funds Creation of intelligence offices in legislation	Authorized nuclear waste trust fund to enable DOE to recover costs of developing disposal system
Hazardous Waste Disposal	Reauthorization legislation contains policy framework, schedule, regulations in form of hammers	Statutory requirement to notify Congress within a reasonable time before publishing regulations Few oversight hearings	Hammers invented by authorizing committee, some say to get attention and ensure actions from appropriations committee and OMB
Medicare Prospective Payment System	Policy and restrictions through budget reconciliation process	Reporting requirements Creation of ProPAC in legislation Increased number of congressional staffers	Hospital insurance trust fund Specification of payment formulas in legislation, often reconciliation legislation Moving hospital boundaries in legislation

| Department of Energy's Cleanup of the Defense Nuclear Weapons Complex | Informal agreements, telephone calls, staff-to-staff discussions
Directions to spend in particular manner in appropriations bill
65 hearings between 1980 and 1990 to give specific management and policy direction
Ordering reorganization in legislation
Setting cleanup priorities in legislation
Requiring independent oversight bodies to report cleanup issues | GAO reports identifying management problems
Request by committees for data on types of waste at complexes
Monitoring by OTA, GAO, EPA, NRC, and CRS
Informal network of informants that tells Congress realistic costs
Use of *Five-Year Plans* and OTA and CRS reports to gather and publicize information | Increasing environmental funding in appropriations bills
Consolidation of agency responsibility in legislation |
| Advanced Medium-Range Air-to-Air Missile | Specification of multiple testing requirements, cost ceilings, annual production quotas in legislation | GAO reports
Private consultants and moles
Member inquiries
Committee-financed studies | Competition in contracting requirements
Secretary of defense certification requirements in law
Cost caps in legislation
Appropriations act cutbacks in executive budget requirements |

Continued ...

TABLE 12.1. — *Continued*

EXAMPLES OF TOOLS OF CONGRESSIONAL CO-MANAGEMENT

Case Study	Program Direction Tools	Intelligence Tools	Cost and Spending Tools
Goldwater-Nichols Reorganization of the Department of Defense	Goals of reorganization set in law Riders to authorization bills Informal attention by congressional leadership	Intelligence from internal and external studies; Congress builds coherent data base Packard commission Numerous hearings Statute including reporting requirements	
Foreign Aid and Human Rights	Sense-of-the-Congress provisions in foreign assistance acts Creating a new bureau in legislation Human rights restrictions in foreign aid authorization bills	Hearings Reporting requirements Certification requirements Bureau of Human Rights	Conditions and requirements on foreign aid distribution routinely written into committee reports
Foreign Military Arms Sales	Adding general and country-specific restrictions on both sales and assistance 30-day formal congressional review period for proposed sales; can stop a sale by concurrent-resolution legislative veto procedure	Mandating scores of reports and certifications Congress is briefed by the executive branch in preparation for legislative review of proposed sales	Arms sales dollar thresholds for congressional review Annual dollar limits on total arms sales Congressional dollar limits on commercial arms sales

instructions and requirements, written by Congress annually as a part of the budget reconciliation process.

In the *Foreign Military Arms Sales* case, in addition to requiring a thirty-day congressional review period prior to the consummation of a major weapons sale, Congress legislatively added numerous general and country-specific restrictions on both sales and assistance. In the *High-Level Nuclear Waste Policy* case, Congress enacted *the* location for "site characterization" as well as specific organizational arrangements for the testing and selection processes to follow. In other situations, congressional direction and indications of concern have been less formalized: foreign aid conditions and requirements written into report language, not law; requested GAO audits and OTA monitoring in the Energy Department's nuclear production facilities; and the informal initiation of member inquiries and committee-financed studies by private consultants in the *AMRAAM* case.

In several of the cases, incremental legislative directives amounted, over time, to a fundamental change in prior-expressed congressional intent or program direction. The *Defense Nuclear Weapons Complex Cleanup* case demonstrated Congress's ability to set specific priorities among particular weapons plants for the cleanup effort. So too did the *Highway Demonstration Projects* case, where congressional parochial priorities were substituted for systemic ones. The *Hazardous Waste Disposal* case describes legislation containing congressionally determined environmental priorities and regulations that would take effect if the agency did not meet the statutory deadlines. In the *Foreign Aid and Human Rights* case, Congress clearly meant to introduce human rights considerations into foreign assistance decisions, and did.

Obtaining Intelligence

Information is the lifeblood of the legislative enterprise. Absent relevant intelligence, the consequences of legislative action are not only misinformed but potentially ruinous. Congress is well aware of this, to the point that the primacy placed on information access on Capitol Hill is unmistakable to even the most casual observer.

Traditional sources of information and intelligence available to Congress from the executive branch have been politicized or otherwise compromised in recent years; agency communications and data are widely distrusted in Congress.[2] At the same time there is considerable executive misapprehension and distrust of actual and potential congressional roles in the policy implementation process. For example, executive secrecy and congressional distrust of Department of Energy information were evident in both the *High-Level Nuclear Waste Policy* and the *Defense Nuclear Weapons Complex Cleanup* cases. In this area, the *AMRAAM* case offers but one illustration of congressional skepticism of weapons-acquisition data, analysis, and projections offered by the armed services and the Department of

Defense. A subcommittee of the House Government Operations Committee found, for example, that initial planning estimates for weapons systems acquisitions and more refined full-scale development estimates both turned out to be far below actual costs. Not once, the subcommittee concluded, did the Department of Defense accurately estimate or underestimate the cost of any major weapons system.[3] Distrust of motivations on the part of both sides, as well as of information, is highly evident in the *Medicare Prospective Payments System* case. The Health Care Finance Administration and the Office of Management and Budget looked askance at congressional intent to protect certain hospitals without regard for the public fisc, and congressional participants doubted HCFA support data for its PPS proposal as well as the HCFA's future capacity to generate accurate, trustworthy hospital-cost data during implementation of the new payment system.

With the decline of "neutral competence" in the executive branch as a source of trusted information and institutional memory, Congress has increasingly turned to alternative sources for intelligence. In years past it was not at all uncommon for Congress to have executive branch experts—even those from the president's Bureau of the Budget (now the Office of Management and Budget)—detailed to Capitol Hill so that their talents and experience could be brought to bear on legislative problems. Such contacts between the branches are increasingly rare now. Instead of relying upon the executive bureaucracy for expertise, Congress of the late-twentieth century has created administrative intelligence resources of its own. Congressional committees tripled their staffs between the early 1960s and the mid-1970s, and have subsequently maintained House and Senate committee staff levels at over 3000 employees. During the 1980s House and Senate personal staffers have consistently numbered over 10,000. Also during this period Congress developed large, highly professional staffs in its institutional support agencies: General Accounting Office, about 5000 employees; Congressional Research Service, about 850; Congressional Budget Office, about 220; and Office of Technology Assessment, about 140, figures that have remained relatively stable for over a decade.[4]

Increased congressional staff size and expertise have meant greater reliance upon staffs by members and the congressional leadership for intelligence and advice. Congressional staff participation and expertise were important, even pivotal, to every case examined in this study. The action in the *AMRAAM* case was initiated and largely sustained by senior staffers of the House and Senate Armed Services committees. Staff analysis and recommendations in the *Goldwater-Nichols Defense Reorganization* case were crucial to the development of the legislation and subsequent restructuring that followed. In the *Foreign Aid and Human Rights* case, the staff-developed series of hearings and a staff-written report initiated a process of change in policy implementation. Congressional staffers converted the barebones executive branch proposal for a *Medicare Prospective Payment Sys-*

tem into an highly detailed statutory procedure for implementation. By 1990 three congressional staff members were said to be concerned with PPS for every one executive staff person in the HCFA. Congressional staffers were largely responsible for conceiving the land-ban hammers in the *Hazardous Waste Disposal* case.

In at least four of the cases (*Defense Nuclear Weapons Complex Cleanup, High-Level Nuclear Waste Policy, Medicare PPS,* and *AMRAAM*), General Accounting Office policy audits—in continuing series—were instrumental in the elevation of critical issues and in bringing attention to continuing programmatic problems and costs. In two other cases, *Hazardous Waste Disposal* and *Traffic Alert Collision Avoidance System,* Congress's Office of Technology Assessment performed a critical role in providing a trusted source of technical data analysis.

Congress is also likely to be prompted and assisted in its participation not only by its own staff institutions, such as the General Accounting Office (GAO), Congressional Budget Office (CBO), and Office of Technology Assessment (OTA), but also by new, highly specialized institutions—the Prospective Payment Assessment Commission (ProPAC), for example—that Congress itself has created specifically to perform particular tasks and to keep legislators informed.

In some of the same cases, and in numerous others explored elsewhere, Congress has turned to independent consultants, educational institutions, and single-purpose commissions to evaluate programmatic and administrative problems. The House Armed Services Committee engaged the services of an independent consulting firm to investigate progress and prospects of the troubled AMRAAM program. As a preface to the Department of Defense Reorganization Act of 1986, both congressional and executive officials cooperated in the evaluation by Georgetown University's Center for Strategic and International Studies (CSIS) of the defense management structure. CSIS was later chosen for extensive evaluation of the effects of the defense reorganization effort. Congress and the White House (over Defense Department objections) cooperated in creating the Blue Ribbon Commission on Defense Management (Packard commission).

Where Congress has found existing intelligence resources to be inadequate, and where sources of independent and sustained input and reporting were believed to be needed, Congress has not hesitated to create new institutions. Some have been established as "independent" executive branch agencies, but with reporting responsibilities to Congress. For example, the Operational Test and Evaluation (OT&E) office was established by Congress in the Department of Defense as an antidote to numerous and often scandalous reports of inadequate preproduction testing of newly developed weapons systems in the early 1980s. The director of OT&E was to prescribe, monitor, coordinate, and analyze all DOD policies and procedures for operational tests and evaluations of new weapons systems, and to report findings on all major defense acquisition programs not only to the secretary of defense but also to the House and Senate Armed Services committees.

Attending to Costs and Spending

The congressional agenda of the 1980s was largely dominated by the politics of the budget and deficit reduction. Virtually all other legislative contests were played out in a constant tension between pressures for cost containment and legislators' desires to spend on behalf of national and constituency needs. Like many other policy and program developments of the decade, both defense and domestic cases of this study reflect this tension and demonstrate a variety of the techniques of budgetary politics. Three main routes for coping with budget constraints were observed in the case studies: (1) policy making through the budget reconciliation process; (2) the special use of trust funds; and (3) general congressional controls appearing within authorization and appropriations legislation directed toward the special case of spiraling costs in military acquisitions programs.

POLICY MAKING THROUGH THE BUDGET RECONCILIATION PROCESS. Begun in 1974 as a means of reconciling decisions on individual authorizations and appropriations with overall congressional budget targets, the budget reconciliation process was transformed by 1981 into an annual catharsis of deficit reduction. During the 1980s, annual omnibus budget reconciliation laws also became major, "must-pass" legislative vehicles. Chronic and growing budget deficits were addressed frontally within the scope of this process, making some programs perennial targets for budget reductions. In this context, budget scores (savings in federal dollar outlays projected by the Congressional Budget Office for the succeeding fiscal year) became powerful motivators for both congressional and executive involvement in cost-driven policy issues. Of the cases of this study, the *Medicare Prospective Payment System (PPS)* offers a clear—if complex—example of budget reconciliation incentives for detailed congressional intervention in annual program redefinition.

When PPS was enacted in 1983, the reconciliation process had just emerged as a vehicle for making policy changes. The system itself was put in place to help control rapidly escalating federal costs for Medicare-financed hospital care. Moreover, the PPS statute had been designed so that any procedural change in the relationship between the branches would make a difference in how the system was administered. The Gramm-Rudman-Hollings legislation enacted in 1985 proved to be a major turning point in the congressional-executive relationship. Mandated budget ceilings escalated the search for budget savings. This set the stage for the scenario observed in the *PPS* case. In essence, if the administration proposed a change to the system through regulation, it would get credit for savings. If Congress took the initiative and proposed a change through reconciliation, it would get the credit. That there is credit to be appropriately assigned by someone external to the process is evidently taken as an article of faith among those involved. Virtually every reconciliation law since the Omnibus Budget Reconciliation Act of 1986 contains PPS provisions.

SPECIAL USE OF TRUST FUNDS. Budgetary stringency has also encouraged Congress to use what were otherwise exempt funds to satisfy constituent demands without breaching deficit control limits. Again, this became particularly evident after passage of the Gramm-Rudman-Hollings law. The *High-Level Nuclear Waste Policy* and *Highway Demonstration Projects* cases both illustrate the ways in which special trust funds were used to mask the size of the federal deficit and to support parochial projects. For example, the Nuclear Waste Policy Amendments of 1987 authorized the Nuclear Waste Fund (NWF) to make it possible for the Department of Energy to recoup the costs of disposing of spent nuclear fuel and high-level waste from those who generated it, most notably the electric utility companies. The NWF requires a one-mill-per-kilowatt-hour levy on nuclear-generated power as well as one-time fees from the utilities for spent fuel created before the fund was established. Although some of the fund has been expended in Nevada to facilitate development of the Yucca Mountain disposal site, provisions of the Gramm-Rudman-Hollings legislation have made possible—even encouraged—use of the NWF to offset marginally related energy and water projects, protecting them from budgetary cutbacks and the funding of new projects that are at best tangential to nuclear waste disposal.

Similarly, "new money" has also been found by members of Congress in the National Highway Trust Fund (maintained by revenues from federal gasoline excise taxes) to support highway demonstration projects. Such projects were made more attractive to the states by exempting them from state obligation ceilings of the trust fund, making it possible for members to take credit for new highway expenditures in their districts while avoiding the strictures of deficit reduction. From the perspective of career highway administrators, however, such projects are likely seen as failing to "demonstrate" anything "except how to get an extra dip in the public till."

AUTHORIZATION AND APPROPRIATIONS CONTROLS. Several case studies showed Congress inserting detailed language in authorizing and appropriations legislation. In at least two cases—*Hazardous Waste Disposal* and *Highway Demonstration Projects*—the detailed language amounted to a significant change in congressional method and role for that policy area. By contrast, another case, *Foreign Aid and Human Rights,* showed Congress writing conditions and requirements into committee reports rather than legislation.

Pressures exerted as the general result of budget and deficit growth appear likely to have encouraged some congressional attention to program effectiveness and cost control across most policy areas; however, this effect is most obvious in defense. Faced with unforecast, runaway costs in virtually every military acquisitions program as well as a steady stream of reports cataloging system failures and unreliable performance in many programs, the House and Senate Armed Services committees initiated a series of reforms to mandate weapons testing prior to production and to assure contract competition and cost controls. Specific programs such as AMRAAM became targets of congressional inquiry and concern regarding both cost and performance issues. Initial directions in appropriations law from Congress to the Air Force and the Navy at the beginning of the AMRAAM program specified (1) a joint missile acquisitions program with the Air Force taking the lead, (2) competition in awarding the development contract, and (3) dual sourcing (more than one contractor) in construction of the final product. Later as problems developed, Congress specified multiple testing requirements, cost ceilings, and annual production quotas by statute.

Effects of Congressional Co-Management

The few recent studies of direct congressional intervention in the details of public policy development and implementation, as well as assorted executive laments, may convey the impression that these devices or "levers" of direct congressional involvement in policy development and implementation are more a meddlesome, "micromanaging" nuisance than effective mechanisms of policy orientation and program control.[5] Such an impression underestimates their purpose, power, and effects. As understood in the cases investigated for this volume, the techniques of direct congressional involvement in policy administration can be—often are—forceful levers for change. Once set in motion, they can have profound impacts on overall policy and programs, on Congress itself, and on executive branch management. Examples from the cases illustrate these effects.

Effects on Policy and Programs
First, congressional intervention in administration changed the content, scope, and future of policy and programs:

1. Congressional intervention has prompted or forced changes in program priorities, directions, the speed of program implementation, and the visibility of programs on the executive policy agenda.

In the case of the *Traffic Alert and Collision Avoidance System* administered by the Federal Aviation Administration and in the case of the Environmental Protection Agency's *hazardous waste disposal regulatory program,* not only did legislative deadlines and hammers increase the speed of program implementation but congressional mandates also changed executive priorities. For example, congressional mandates made TCAS a prominent

FAA program, not just a languishing project in FAA's research and development unit. In the case of the *Advanced Medium-Range Air-to-Air Missile*, legislative investigation and certification requirements focused much greater executive attention on the program, not just in the Air Force but also in the Department of Defense, ultimately involving the secretary of defense himself. Similarly, in the *Defense Nuclear Weapons Complex Cleanup* case, congressional intent was to shake the Department of Energy out of its lethargy and to speed administrative attention to environmental and health concerns. The effort was successful. Congressional challenges to proposed *Foreign Military Arms Sales*, under threat of a legislative veto, forced executive attention to underlying legislative policy concerns up to the level of the president.

In some cases, the intent of congressional co-managers was to change critically the content of established policy at the administrative level. The *Foreign Aid and Human Rights* case demonstrated the ability of Congress to advance human rights considerations in State Department decision making through reporting and certification requirements and through other administrative controls as well. In the case of *High-Level Nuclear Waste Policy* Congress made the nuclear waste site selection for the Department of Energy, thus forcing a single solution on the department.

2. Congressional intervention has had both intended effects on substantive policy outcomes and other effects that were neither intended nor anticipated.

In the case of *Foreign Military Arms Sales*, had Congress not carved out a larger formal role for itself in foreign military sales decisions, the United States would have sold more arms abroad than it had during the 1970s and through the mid-1980s. Moreover, larger numbers and more sophisticated weapons would have been sold to Middle Eastern countries that have historically been enemies of Israel. With congressional direction, the Department of Energy's *Defense Nuclear Weapons Complex Cleanup* funding increased from \$1.7 billion in FY 89 to \$4.3 billion in FY 91, to a requested nearly \$6 billion for FY 92, and the department shifted its focus from production to environmental restoration. In the case of *AMRAAM*, Congress was able to slow the flow of budgeting outlays and delay full-rate production of a still unreliable weapon. In each of these cases, the effects of congressional involvement were both intended and expected.

Yet not all of the effects of congressional intervention—in details of the *AMRAAM* case, for example—were those that congressional participants had in mind. Specifically, the Air Force's response to congressional intervention yielded higher levels of distrust, unreliable information, and damage to Air Force morale. Certifications demanded of the Defense Department by Congress regarding missile cost, performance, and reliability were intended to induce the Air Force to admit that its projections and assurances for the weapon system had been unrealistic. They were also intended to promote a searching review of more promising and effective alternatives. Nevertheless, civilian and military insiders reported that the required certifications merely forced official disinformation (some called it "lying") about the program to higher levels of military and civilian authority and to Congress. In significant measure, career advancement initiatives attached to the success of weapons development programs appear to have triumphed over the traditional ethical restraints of military honesty and integrity.

In the case of *Highway Demonstration Projects,* initial sums of dollars for demonstration projects have been relatively small. Congressional participants argued the legitimacy of elected legislators' judgments as set against the determinations of unelected state highway officers, emphasizing that demonstration projects represented less than 2 percent of the Omnibus Transportation Act of 1987. Yet, many demonstration projects are related to the interstate highway system, and they entail a huge potential commitment to future spending for a system that for all practical purposes is complete. The trend continued in the 1992 authorization bill—489 demonstrations were included in the House bill, at a cost of roughly $5.4 billion.

3. Congressional intervention has operated to keep both branches focused on narrowly defined, short-run programs and inclined to continue existing programs while submerging hard questions about alternatives or large policy issues.

Discrete and relatively narrow programs have the characteristic of defining policy in the absence of self-consciously determined courses of action. Program definitions often begin as reflections of relatively narrow subcommittee jurisdictions. Subsequently, direct congressional intervention can further shift scarce human and financial resources to sustain an ever-narrowing focus on these programs, thereby precluding attention to other critical areas or larger policy concerns. For example, as the complexity and political intensity of the *High-Level Nuclear Waste Policy* problem increased, a comprehensive approach to finding alternative solutions was submerged and a single solution was forced on the Department of Energy by Congress.

In the case of the *Medicare Prospective Payment System,* although the declared overall goal was to contain federal costs across the entire health system without affecting access or quality of care or depriving providers of adequate compensation, these issues cannot be adequately addressed without confronting a wide array of policy concerns beyond the hospital payment system. Congressional and executive actors focused their efforts on the details of the technology of PPS in the budget reconciliation process; however, the policy product of this process, by all accounts, does not mesh well with comprehensive, long-term national health needs.

In the *Hazardous Waste Disposal* case, Congress invented priorities, deadlines, and regulations, in part as a proxy for broad policy, in part as the only way known to address the issues, given existing knowledge. Congressional intervention, as well as actions by the executive branch, resulted in programs and policies that focused resources on implementing the land-ban provisions, thereby downgrading the priorities of other environmental initiatives.

Overall, congressional co-management also appears to be related to an increased tendency to persist with existing programs, even though they may be performing poorly, rather than considering the merits of alternative approaches. The cases studies suggest that there are powerful incentives at work that transcend bureaucratic inertia: staff career needs; procedural mechanisms that can be adopted in place of hard decisions; and the absence of structural devices to force a broader view.

In contrast to other examples, however, the *Goldwater-Nichols Defense Reorganization* case illustrates the realization of comprehensive policy development as a result, in part, of congressional co-management where both structure (broad jurisdictions of the House and Senate Armed Services committees) and determined leadership are present. In addition, Congress has used the 1986 Defense Reorganization Act as a platform for further reforms of defense organization, management, and process. For example, in the FY 91 authorization act, Congress attempted to strengthen long-range defense planning. The House Armed Services Committee report on the bill stated, "Congress must be a partner in the development of strategy ... it must participate in the final solution."[6]

Effects on Congressional Oversight
Second, congressional intervention in administration changed the character of congressional oversight.

1. The Congress observed in these ten case studies was not a gadfly. Once particular committees, members, and staffs were involved in the details of implementation, they tended to stay involved until the situation changed or until safeguards were in place to assure that desired progress would continue.

In two cases—the *Defense Nuclear Weapons Complex Cleanup* and *AMRAAM*—Congress seemed to be taken by surprise, coming late and with little warning to an already well-developed problem or serious program crisis. In other cases Congress had passively monitored developing issues for some time but rallied to action only after a crisis (for example, the *Traffic Alert and Collision Avoidance System, High-Level Nuclear Waste Policy, Goldwater-Nichols Defense Reorganization,* and *Foreign Military Arms Sales*). Once involved in each of these cases, however, instead of displaying a short attention span during a burst of investigatory publicity then departing for showier problems, congressional committees and staffs remained engaged.

Characteristically, the routines of the budget, appropriations, and periodic reauthorization processes, as well as other structures of institutional review, such as the General Accounting Office, helped to sustain congressional intervention with a constancy that would have been relatively unusual in prior decades (for example, in the *Medicare Prospective Payment System,* the *Highway Demonstration Projects,* the *Foreign Aid and Human Rights,* the *AMRAAM,* and the *Defense Nuclear Weapons Complex Cleanup* cases).

2.*Congress has created a new network of agencies, commissions, staffs, and other entities to conduct oversight functions, thereby supplementing some committees and subcommittees in their oversight roles. Congress also places great reliance on the investigatory and oversight roles of its own support agencies.*

In the *High-Level Nuclear Waste Policy* case, the major congressional redirection embodied in the Nuclear Waste Policy Act of 1982 and the Nuclear Waste Policy Act Amendments of 1987 increased oversight of the program by organizations independent of DOE and reporting to Congress. These organizations include the Monitored Retrievable Storage Commission, the Nuclear Waste Technical Review Board, and the Office of the Nuclear Waste Negotiator. Similarly, in the *Medicare Prospective Payment System* case, Congress created the Prospective Payment Assessment Commission as a quasi-independent body to oversee implementation by providing advice to both Congress and the HHS secretary. Subsequently, the Omnibus Budget Reconciliation Act of 1990 effectively made ProPAC a congressional agency.

Congress has also placed great reliance on the investigatory and oversight roles of its own support agencies (General Accounting Office, Office of Technology Assessment, Congressional Budget Office, and Congressional Research Service). In the *Defense Nuclear Weapons Complex Cleanup* case, for example, the General Accounting Office produced some sixty reports of environmental, health, and managerial problems at the production reactor facilities. In the *High-Level Nuclear Waste Policy* case, the GAO again performed critical and continuing oversight roles, as it did in virtually every significant weapons acquisition program, including *AMRAAM.* The Office of Technology Assessment played significant oversight and analysis roles in the *Traffic Alert and Collision Avoidance System* and the *Defense Nuclear Weapons Complex Cleanup* cases. The director of the OTA was also given authority to appoint members of the Prospective Payment Assessment Commission in the *Medicare Prospective Payment System* case. The Congressional Budget Office's annual involvement in cost assessment is pivotal in the *Medicare Prospective Payment System* case and in virtually every program change undertaken through the budget reconciliation process. Finally, the Congressional Research Service (CRS) provides the background documentation, analysis, and current tracking for an untold range of issues and program debates, including almost all those studied in this book.

3. *The influence, expertise, and commitment of members of Congress and their staffs were critical to sustaining detailed congressional involvement.*

In the *Goldwater-Nichols Defense Reorganization* case, Barry Goldwater (R-Ariz.) and Sam Nunn (D.-Ga.), respectively as chair and ranking minority member of the Senate Armed Services Committee, committed themselves to passage of the Defense Reorganization Act of 1986. On the basis of their personal reputations for experience and knowledgeability in defense issues, as well as the extensive foundation of research reflected in the Packard commission study and the committee's own staff work, Goldwater and Nunn were able, in two sessions of Congress, to bring to closure a far-reaching managerial reform effort that had been stalled for years and stoutly resisted by the Department of Defense. In the *High-Level Nuclear Waste Policy* case, J. Bennett Johnston (D-La.), as chair of both the Senate appropriations subcommittee and the authorization committee with prime jurisdiction over the nuclear waste program, provided pivotal and determined leadership to redefine the Energy Department's mandate and authority for nuclear waste management.

Well-situated and determined staff members can also perform such roles. A highly skilled senior staff veteran on the House Armed Services committee, Anthony Battista, tracked *AMRAAM* until he left the staff in 1985. He was the major force behind pressuring the Air Force to submit more accurate cost information and was largely responsible for the certification requirements and cost caps that were written into the reauthorization legislation. Determined individual members can also insinuate themselves importantly into the process. Congressman Denny Smith (R-Ore.), although not a member of any relevant committee and not necessarily an opponent of the AMRAAM missile, through his personal staff team also kept a watchful eye on AMRAAM and requested several GAO reports on the missile's capacities and reliability. The result, because of Smith's particular background as a decorated jet fighter pilot, was to generate considerable press attention to the program and its problems.

In the main, across the cases reported in this volume, Congress has exchanged its role as an after-the-fact reviewer of executive fidelity to legislative intent for that of preaudit director of the specifics, even the minutiae, of policy and program management. In one case, the *Hazardous Waste Disposal* case, such legislative specificity at the outset of a policy redirection even resulted in reduced (and ineffective) oversight of any kind for a considerable period thereafter. In this case, the guiding statute, the 1984 Hazardous and Solid Waste Amendments, established a policy framework, an implementation schedule, and a set of congressional regulations that would take effect if the Environmental Protection Agency (EPA) failed to meet the deadlines. One subtle result of this kind of statutory framework for co-management of policy was that Congress and EPA had little communication during the first two years of implementation. When they did, it was initially explosive and highly controversial for both branches.

Effects on Executive Management

Third, detailed congressional intervention forced powerful changes in program implementation by the executive branch.

1. Congressional initiatives both strengthened and burdened the hands of agency administrators, sometimes one more than the other. The burden came in the form of the added workload of new requirements and the erosion of the long-term capacity to manage. The strength came in the form of "an added stick" in dealing with the OMB and the regulated community and in forceful incentives to comply with statutory mandates and to avoid public censure.

Yearly congressional changes to the *Medicare Prospective Payment System* and the increasing planning and analytic capacity of the Prospective Payment Assessment Commission contributed to asserted weakening of the organizational capability of the Health Care Finance Administration, evidenced by turnover and widely perceived morale problems. Yearly congressional changes also created an excessive workload for the agency, caused it to miss unrealistic deadlines, and eroded organizational learning systems that surfaced broader issues and provided the research and development for future policy initiatives.

Similar congressionally imposed burdens in the *Hazardous Waste Disposal* case were offset to some extent by the creation of subtle new agency resources. There, congressional hammers on the land-ban provisions gave the EPA the assurance of an unusually timely response from the OMB on its proposed promulgation of regulations. These same congressional hammers also gave EPA managers the assurance of resources and prompt internal responses to their requests from other EPA officials during implementation of the land ban provisions.

In the Department of Energy's *High-Level Nuclear Waste Policy* and *Defense Nuclear Weapons Complex Cleanup* cases, congressional intervention was also both a burden and a strength to DOE administrators. Virtually all of the controls were a management burden. Some operated to limit the agency from taking a broader view of the program (for example, of the cleanup in the DOE weapons-complex-site prioritization and of the locations at which site characterization studies would be conducted). However, these burdens were at the same time offset to some degree by more or reallocated funding and a programmatic focus for the cleanup effort as well as increased media and public attention.

2. Congressional initiatives changed the structure of governmental activities and functions. This shift is characterized by the creation of an array of commissions, boards, and specially designated offices within and between both branches.

In the *Foreign Aid and Human Rights* case, Congress created the Bureau of Human Rights and Humanitarian Affairs in the Department of State, responsible to the secretary of state for matters pertaining to human rights and humanitarian affairs. The bureau is also required to prepare statements for, and reports to, Congress. Congressional intent was for the new bureau to be the watchdog for human rights; however, there was suspicion and a natural resistance to the bureau's mission in the State Department. As one official noted, "The nature of the State Department is to pursue a goal of frictionless relations ... to negotiate and compromise. But you can't do human rights without stepping on toes and creating friction." The bureau enjoyed good relations with Congress because its philosophy was closely aligned to the views of many members of Congress. Over time, the executive branch came to embrace and applaud human rights objectives as well.

In the *Medicare Prospective Payment System* case, Congress, in reconciliation legislation, created the Geographical Review Board (GRB) in the Department of Health and Human Services (HHS) to make decisions about moving hospital urban-rural boundaries for cost purposes. The HHS secretary appoints the members of the board but has no further decision-making authority unless an applicant appeals a final GRB decision. Observers suggested that the way Congress structured the GRB reflected continuing distrust of the executive branch. The Prospective Payment Assessment Commission was not part of the executive branch or Congress until 1990, when legislation effectively made it a congressional agency. ProPAC is regarded by many observers as confusing responsibility for policy analysis to guide implementation; others argue that it plays a valuable role that only a quasi-independent group outside the executive branch can fulfill.

In the *High-Level Nuclear Waste Policy* case, Congress created the Technical Review Board to oversee the nuclear waste site characterization. The board oversees the DOE program, but because it is part of neither the DOE nor Congress, an institution between the executive and legislative branches of government has been established.

Styles of Congressional Co-Management

In a political system premised on the separation of governmental powers, styles of institutional relations and action can become the critical elements of governance. Such styles are consistent patterns or habits of behavior that develop between institutions as they define their roles and relationships in the same fashion under similar conditions.

Fundamental relations between Congress and the executive branch are traditionally described in relatively simplistic terms: "The President (impliedly, the executive) proposes and Congress disposes"; "Congress makes the laws; the Executive Branch administers them"; and "Congress exercises administrative oversight." Deviations from these simple divisions of function—congressional "micromanagement," for example—are likely to be described in pejorative terms or rebuked as "encroachments." However, close observation of real-world policy and programmatic interplay between the branches discloses patterns that are more subtle and complex.

Each case investigated for this volume was chosen *because* it would be likely to feature intense, characteristic, or particularly revealing *congressional involvement* in the details of policy development and implementation. Consequently, these cases are unlikely to represent those issues, policy areas, and programs in which co-involvement of Congress and the executive is minimal or uninteresting. Still, the variety of policies and programs that were studied for this volume make it clear that the styles of congressional co-management with the executive are also quite varied. In the ten cases examined, Congress (typically key members, congressional committees, and staffs) can be observed in at least five relatively distinct roles in its co-management relationship with the executive branch: (1) strategic leader; (2) consultative partner; (3) superintendent; (4) combative opponent; and (5) passive observer.

Strategic Leader

When Congress adopts a strategic-leader style of co-management, its leadership—or at least committee leadership—seeks to address broad national issues through policies that will enhance executive capacity. To craft the policy, Congress is likely to consider the issue in both depth and breadth: to conduct extensive, businesslike hearings; to produce well-researched, comprehensive studies; and likely, during an elaborate process, to establish one or more blue ribbon commissions to review and recommend alternatives. Members of Congress and congressional staffs operating in this mode are also likely to participate in roundtable discussions conducted by leading think tanks and policy research institutes to deepen their understanding and to sensitize themselves to the views of multiple actors. Such thoughtful investigatory activities have the combined effects of developing a data base for action, educating members and staffs, and mobilizing broad support for reform.

A Congress performing the role of strategic leader is probably correlated with the interest, institutional position, stature, and commitment of one or more members who marshal a significant policy reform through to its adoption, likely winning respect on all sides. Several aspects of this style are characteristic. First, critical elements of Congress are organized and motivated to take a strategic and comprehensive focus on a broad policy issue while at the same time handling the routine details of legislation in specific subordinate programs. Second, Congress may be encouraged to act this way when the executive branch (or affected executive agency) is weakened or divided on the issue. Third, Congress, in seeking to enhance managerial capacity in the executive branch, may run the risk of reducing its access to and power over executive decision making. Thus, in its strategic leadership style, Congress engages in a systematic process of analyzing the key dimensions of an issue, developing a range of options, and ultimately producing at least the appearance of coherent and comprehensive reform.

The case suggesting a broader prototype for Congress as a "strategic leader" is that of the *Goldwater-Nichols Defense Reorganization,* which sought to change the way the Defense Department does business in almost every facet of its activities, from procurement to budgeting to the direction of military field operations. The personal determination of senior members of Congress and their staffs to effect change was pivotal to reforming the command structure. And the degree of consensus generated on Capitol Hill in this case was extraordinary. Overall, Congress took up an issue with which it was not deeply familiar (the last legislative reform having been passed in 1958), one on which it has historically been sharply divided, and one for which there were no strong constituency pressures for action. Over a period of four years, Armed Services committees in both houses became familiar with the issue and ultimately passed what most would call thoughtful, coherent reform legislation. In July 1985 Congress created the Blue Ribbon Commission on Defense Management (the Packard commission), which was given the charter to study all areas of defense reform. Four months later, the Senate committee published the staff study originally commissioned by Senators John G. Tower (R-Tex.) and Henry "Scoop" Jackson (D-Wash.). It covered the full range of defense organization issues, including Congress's review and oversight roles, and it helped set the stage for the legislation to follow.

Years of hearings and analysis were required in Congress, complemented by outside discussions, debate, and study. Congress demonstrated it could successfully deal with a complex institutional reform issue on which executive leadership was lacking and opinions divided. The Goldwater-Nichols act itself made Congress a stronger, more active player in defense organization and process issues while strengthening the DOD in managerial effectiveness (the latter possibly at Congress's expense, however).

Consulting Partner

When Congress adopts a consulting-partner style of co-management, it is likely that its formal legislative authority unilaterally to impose congressional views on the executive will be difficult to exercise. This style became particularly evident in the foreign affairs cases. Over a period of time, Congress changed the rules of congressional-executive relations to create a system of policy co-determination or a process of early, thorough consultation and sharing of the decision making process and tactics to enlarge its participation and influence.[7]

In the consulting-partner style, traditional congressional devices (for example, reporting requirements, hearings, statutory restrictions, earmarked funds, and the creation of congressionally oriented institutions and agents in the executive branch) are used with the intent of encouraging communication and consensus building and seeking compromise whenever possible. Showdowns between the branches are avoided. The congressional power of the purse is used as a kind of club behind the door to induce desired executive branch action.

Although some players characterize reporting requirements as creating the illusion of consultation in that they are rarely integrated into actual policy decisions, the overall pattern is one in which both branches have much to gain from the good faith of the other. Congress behaves as a consulting partner with the executive when formal authority defines the outer limits of the relationship, when both branches prefer to share information in forums designed for that purpose, and when Congress is more reactive than proactive in its posture.

Foreign aid decisions offer a fair case in point. Members of Congress searched for some time for effective techniques to impose their concerns about human rights on executive decision making. Congress was deeply reluctant to use its ultimate weapon: a congressionally imposed cutoff of foreign aid to offending countries. However, aid cutoff has been used as a threat whenever there is a significant dispute between the branches over the acceptability of human rights policies of a recipient country—this in combination with mandated reports on human rights abuses and State Department certifications.

Knowing that Congress has the ultimate power to cut off aid, the executive branch has often worked aggressively to bring about changes in a country in question or to accept conditions that Congress seeks to impose on the provision of aid. Knowing how difficult and potentially unproductive an aid cutoff can be, Congress has typically looked for places to compromise, usually by attachment of conditions or by symbolic, not total, reductions in the administration's aid requests. Serious efforts to cut off foreign aid to human rights violators are rare, but their potential shapes the broad contours of debate and adjustment between the two branches.

Similarly, the executive branch must be assessed to be the clear and inevitable initiator in the *Foreign Military Arms Sales* case. There are simply no effective means, nor any precedents, for Congress to take the lead in making arms sales arrangements with other nations. Indeed, it is difficult for Congress to become involved in such sales in any respect until the process of negotiations is well under way, for months or even years. Consequently, Congress struggled for decades to make a place for itself in foreign-arms-sales decision making. At least partial success toward such a goal has come through a change in the rules permitting a broader congressional role. Congress has defined new methods, including a lengthening list of reporting requirements, statutory restrictions on which countries can purchase U.S. arms and upon what conditions, and formal procedural restraints on arms decisions initiated by the executive branch. Congress tried to construct and then fortify its own position as a partner in significant foreign military sales decisions. Yet, although it has created the tools to do so, direct congressional intervention in the implementation of arms sales policy has been infrequent, directed primarily in response to particular constituency interests.

Congressional Superintendent

When Congress adopts a superintending style to co-manage a policy or program, its role is forceful and its communications are precise. It uses as many control mechanisms and levers—formal and informal—as thought necessary by key legislative players. This may include the invention of new ones to achieve results from the executive branch as quickly as possible.

Congress superintending a policy or program issues legislative mandates characterized by detailed policy frameworks, program implementation schedules and procedures, and explicit statements of expected outcomes. It may even write regulations in its legislation as a forcing or enabling device for executive action. If the issue or crisis is a critical one, numerous committees may conduct extensive and sustained oversight hearings and commission special studies to understand the situation and identify alternatives. Where a situation lacks a plan, Congress may require the executive agency to prepare a long-range plan and to update it regularly. In short, when engaged in the superintending style of co-management, Congress both tells the executive branch what to do and creates an infrastructure of informal and formal devices that will enable it to shift to some other style of co-management once the critical problem or issue is capped, defused, or resolved. The superintendent style of co-management is evident in a number of the cases explored in this volume.

In the *Defense Nuclear Weapons Complex Cleanup* case, following a period (1940s through 1980) in which Congress generally "sat back and waited for information to come in," Congress used a variety of approaches to help improve the management of the nuclear weapons complex safety and environmental policy. For example, Congress asked the Department of Energy to provide plans and budgets to address defense waste and environmental contamination problems. With the urging of congressional committees, DOE cleanup funding has escalated from $1.7 billion in FY 89 to $4.3 billion in FY 91, and a request for nearly $6 billion in FY 92. At the urging of Congress, DOE Secretary James D. Watkins ordered the preparation of a new five-year plan to outline how the DOE should begin tackling its environmental problems. Implementation and annual updating of the five-year plan is required by Congress and carried out by the DOE's new Office of Environmental Restoration and Waste Management. In the environmental restoration program, Congress mandated consolidation of environmental compliance and waste responsibility under a single office. Congress also directed that the targeting of a DOE facility for review will trigger a series of deadlines for the completion of a remedial investigation and feasibility study at the facility and, as necessary, the selection and implementation of remedial action.

In the *Traffic Alert and Collision Avoidance System* case, Congress made clear its determination since at least 1957 that the executive branch solve the problem of midair collisions. Within a month of an August 1986 crash near Cerritos, California, the House Appropriations Committee reported a continuing appropriations resolution that required the Federal Aviation Administration (FAA) to initiate rule making to require altitude encoding and reporting (Mode C) transponders in aircraft flying in all terminal airspace where the FAA provides radar coverage, and in all airspace above an altitude to be determined by FAA, and to implement the rule as soon as possible and report quarterly to the Appropriations Committee on its adherence to the recommended schedule. In late 1987, also in response to the Cerritos incident, the House Public Works and Transportation Committee and the House Science, Space, and Technology Committee reported, and the House passed nearly unanimously, a bill requiring FAA to move forward on TCAS II and Mode C transponders on precise timetables specified in the legislation. In short, Congress "stepped in and mandated dates for the implementation of a requirement for highly technical and complex aviation equipment." Ultimately, Congress loosened the schedule.

Other cases that provide the elements for building a broader prototype of a superintending style of co-management include *Highway Demonstration Projects, High-Level Nuclear Waste Policy,* the Air Force's *AMRAAM* program, and the *Hazardous Waste Disposal* case at EPA.

Combative Opponent

With emergence of the immense, escalating budget deficits of the 1980s, Congress has frequently taken on a style of co-management that with respect to the executive might best be characterized as a combative opponent. In the war over credit taking for "savings" in deficit reduction and control of federal outlays, the opponents are the congressional committees versus the executive Office of Management and Budget and the relevant executive agency. The winner is the side that scores the "savings" points.

When Congress performs as an adversary, it acts forcibly to win by taking back, postponing, or otherwise limiting the discretion it may have granted to an executive agency. Congress in protracted conflict with the executive branch becomes involved in the details of administering the policy to the extent necessary to ensure it gets the "credit" for significant savings. To enable it to sustain and even expand its advantage, Congress in this style of co-management uses analytic information provided by its own staff and by institutions it created to be sources of neutral competence. It is in the interest of neither branch to be open and forthcoming with information when the incentives reward activities that score the most savings points. Thus, the atmosphere surrounding the performance of this role is characterized by high distrust and controversy over details affecting costs. This style of co-management is practically the mirror opposite of both strategic leadership and consultative partnership.

The *Prospective Payment System* (PPS) for hospitals under Medicare well illustrates Congress as a combative opponent of the executive branch in a case of protracted fiscal conflict. The catalytic events that triggered a marked change in Congress's legislative style during PPS implementation were passage of the Balanced Budget and Emergency Deficit Reduction (Gramm-Rudman-Hollings) Act in 1985 and the prominently featured agendas of presidential administrations since 1983 to reduce the federal deficit. The budget reconciliation process has become not only a primary site for formal interbranch communications on the substance of PPS policy but effectively the only place where Congress can make changes in the system. This has resulted in a number of "gaming techniques" that are used to achieve required budget savings, to add new spending, and to communicate with the OMB. The budget reconciliation process has also played a major role in fiscalizing congressional-executive debate on PPS, and in maintaining the PPS point-scoring game between the branches.

Passive Observer

Congress adopts a passive-observer style of co-management at two points: first, *before* it becomes involved in detailed policy implementation and program management; and second, *after* or at the conclusion of a period of detailed congressional intervention in policy development and implementation.

Before a period of implementation, the passive-observer style shows a Congress less than vigilant in its oversight of what were typically broad policy and program delegations to the executive. Whatever congressional attention exists in this style is likely to be initiated and almost wholly sustained by staff and congressional support agencies. As both the *Defense Nuclear Weapons Complex Cleanup* and *High-Level Nuclear Waste Policy* cases illustrate, Congress may maintain a relatively passive stance even as its own audit and research agencies report alarming developments that suggest major management problems and likely crisis ahead.

The passive-observer style of co-management may also be adopted by Congress at the conclusion of a period of detailed congressional intervention in a policy or program. In this mode, Congress relies on mechanisms it has created to oversee policy and program implementation during the prior period of detailed intervention (for example, establishment of the Nuclear Waste Technical Review Board, Nuclear Waste Negotiator, and Monitored Retrievable Storage Review Commission in the *Nuclear Waste Policy* case).

Having put additional institutional mechanisms or legislative specifications in place, and especially when reinforced by a surrounding atmosphere of cooperative relations, Congress—its jurisdictionally relevant members and committees—may readopt the passive-observer style for an area of policy that was once the intense focus of attention and shift its concern to another area. For example, for two years after passage of the 1984 Hazardous and Solid Waste Amendments, there was little or no congressional oversight of the approach EPA was taking to implement the land-ban provisions. As the deadline for promulgating the first rule approached, the EPA formally notified Congress (the day before the document was published in the *Federal Register*). Relevant congressional committees had assumed that the detail stated in the 1984 statute was so specific that it left little discretion to the EPA as to how it would proceed. But the lack of dialog between the branches, the conflicting interpretations of the statute, and the EPA's assumption that the Senate-based version of the provisions (health-based approach to defining treatment standards) could guide implementation all led to a highly conflictual confrontation. Subsequently, however, congressional attention shifted to other policy issues in the area—active formal oversight of further land-ban implementation was limited, and informal staff-to-staff contacts and interest group notifications were relied upon instead.

Conclusion

Congress's revised role in policy and program management occurs across the board with regard to dozens, perhaps hundreds, of specific programs and policy-making delegations. Gone almost without trace is the post-New Deal Congress that optimistically delegated broad-scale public problems and policy questions for solution and resolution by the executive branch. Much diminished as well is an executive branch relied upon by Congress for neutral competence and specialized expertise. Instead, the story of the ten cases studied here is one of the retrieval of executive discretion and the highly specific redefinition—by Congress—of prior delegations of authority. Yet, the pattern is idiosyncratic.

When Congress does actively intervene, its involvement in policy and program implementation is both detailed and sustained—regularized by the authorization, budget, and appropriations processes, and usually continued over many years' time. Once motivated in these and similar cases, Congress has often exhibited both the will and the resources to remain involved and to do so with powerful results. But managing national policy involves more than Congress and the executive branch. The cases reflect a growing host of new "private" or quasi-governmental institutions and unofficial actors—beyond the traditional branches of government—that have also been engaged as managers of public policies and programs.

In some cases Congress has involved itself in the details of program implementation to promote narrow parochial or institutional concerns. In other cases Congress has been unable or unwilling to decide upon or even to consider the alternatives of broader policy questions. But overall, once a basic policy has been established—by most accounts and according to a variety of perspectives—Congress more often than not has demonstrated a remarkable capacity to contribute positively to coherent policy implementation and program performance. This has been especially true where programs were failing, falling behind the pace desired by influential members (or staffs) of the popularly elected branch, or where there was a fundamental disagreement with the policy judgment or ideological posture of the executive.

As it stands, both the congressional and executive focus on narrowly defined programs is almost certainly detrimental to broad and comprehensive direction and evaluation of policy choices and performance. Program overlap and duplication may be useful in some instances, but the proliferation of related but uncoordinated policies, programs, and administrative structures—developed and managed by a multiplicity of overlapping committee jurisdictions and legislative managers—is wasteful of administrative time and resources. Such competitive duplication also cannot help but undermine any comprehensive attempt to integrate policy and program development. Ironically, the organization of both Congress and the executive branch—and, in addition, the growing numbers of institutionalized third-party administrators and analysts of federal programs—reinforces both the rigidity and narrow gauge of current program management structures.

Congress's role as a co-manager can erode its role as an oversight body. Its function as co-manager inherently conflicts with (or redefines) its performance of an effective, albeit traditional, postaudit oversight role. Congressional committees have become so deeply involved in the supervision of (and functional responsibility for) program administration that it may now be difficult, if not impossible, for many of them to act in good faith in an effective "oversight" capacity. Nonetheless, it is still possible for congressional agencies (GAO, OTA, CBO, CRS) to perform admirably as investigators and evaluators. It is also possible for effective oversight to be performed by nonlegislative congressional committees with exclusive jurisdictions for that purpose.

Congressional co-management raises significant questions about executive capacity. The conflict observed in several cases between the president's Office of Management and Budget (OMB) and agencies was noted to be a factor in increasing the depth of congressional intervention in a policy. In domestic cases especially, the observations of morale problems, declining analytic capacities, declining leadership on policy initiatives, and extraordinary difficulty in designing and overseeing complex policy implementation all point to issues of responsibility and relationship. Some might argue that in domestic cases, the executive acted on occasion to "shoot itself in the foot," in particular when a long view is taken of a policy issue. Few structures and processes in the executive branch have kept pace with the complexity of policy implementation and few facilitate the kinds of exchanges necessary to address or even identify the problems arising during implementation. When Congress and the president conflict over policies and programs, executive agencies can be caught in the cross fire, making it difficult for them to propose solutions or comply with congressional guidelines. But whether caught in a policy dispute, a program breakdown, or a network of conflicting interests, when the executive branch cannot meet its responsibilities in accordance with congressional expectations, the vacuum will somehow be filled. In the cases under study, it was filled by Congress.

Congressional co-management has both improved and blurred the clarity of executive accountability for results. Increased accountability was documented in the form of new independent entities to check on the performance of the executive and more frequent or more extensive reporting requirements. Complicated lines of authority, responsibility, and accountability were more frequently observed, especially in domestic policy where an emerging congressional "parabureaucracy" significantly affects interbranch relations and executive capacity.

As a matter of general complaint among some executive branch officials and other observers, Congress's members and their staffs have insinuated themselves inappropriately and unaccountably into administrative management. Although the anecdotal evidence to support such assertions is enormous, they are not given much weight by the ten cases investigated for this study. For the most part, particular members and staffs were well-known players in the implementation process reviewed in these cases. Accordingly they could be—and were—held accountable for their actions by the press and by publics attentive to these policy areas. Similarly, appointed executive officials and senior career civil servants in these cases were easily identified by position and performance for purposes of holding them accountable politically and bound by the constraints of law.

The cases certainly support what many have already observed, namely, that the nation has entered a new era of governance for which familiar labels are no longer descriptive and conventional wisdom provides limited guidance. The Constitution permits a matrix of possibilities for arranging the power to govern. The form wherein the division between Congress and the presidency is a division between Democrats and Republicans pushes the limits of institutional procedures designed for earlier eras and other governing arrangements. Congressional co-management with the executive branch, while not a universal phenomenon at the present, may be, in part, an artifact of the partisan distrust that develops in a government in which the executive and legislative sides are in the hands of opposing political parties. Yet, congressional co-management appears also to be an institutional phenomenon, independent of divided-party government. The central question is not whether Congress will co-manage policy and programs with the executive branch but how effectively both branches can use this form of governance to ensure vigorous partisan debate about and resolution of public policy choices affecting the long-term vitality of the nation, while at the same time respecting and preserving the boundaries that have been the mark of the durability of our constitutional democracy.

Notes

1. Louis Fisher points out that in 1974 President Gerald R. Ford warned Congress that its attempt to become a virtual coadministrator in operational decisions would seriously detract from its proper legislative role (*The Politics of Shared Power,* 2d ed. [Washington, D.C.: CQ Press, 1987], 73). Thomas Franck and Edward Wiesband coined the phrase "policy co-determination" to characterize the system of shared power between the branches in foreign policy (*Foreign Policy by Congress* [New York: Oxford University Press, 1979]).

2. See, for example, Chester A. Newland, "Executive Office Policy Apparatus: Enforcing the Reagan Agenda," in *The Reagan Presidency and the Governing of America,* ed. Lester M. Salamon and Michael S. Lund (Washington, D.C.: Urban Institute Press, 1985), 135–68.

3. House Committee on Government Operations, *Inaccuracy of Department of Defense Weapons Acquisition Cost Estimates,* 99th Cong., 1st sess., 1985, H. Rept. 96-656, 2. Other studies, however, have concluded that Congress is much implicated in activities that escalate such costs. See, for example, J. Ronald Fox, with James L. Field, *The Defense Management Challenge: Weapons Acquisition* (Boston: Harvard Business School Press, 1988); Nick Kotz, *Wild Blue Yonder: Money, Politics, and the B-1 Bomber* (New York: Pantheon, 1988).

4. Norman J. Ornstein, Thomas E. Mann, and Michael Malbin, *Vital Statistics on Congress: 1989–1990* (Washington, D.C.: CQ Press, 1990), 130.

5. Gordon S. Jones and John A. Marini, *The Imperial Congress: Crisis in the Separation of Powers* (New York: Pharos Books [Heritage Foundation and Claremont Institute], 1988); L. Gordon Crovitz and Jeremy A. Rabkin, eds., *The Fettered Presidency: Legal Constraints on the Executive Branch* (Washington, D.C.: American Enterprise Institute, 1989); Joel D. Aberbach, *Keeping a Watchful Eye: The Politics of Congressional Oversight* (Washington, D.C.: Brookings, 1990).

6. House Armed Services Committee, *Report on Fiscal Year 1991 Authorization Act,* 101st Cong., 2d sess., 1990, H. Rept. 101-665, 329.

7. Also see Thomas M. Franck and Edward Weisband, *Foreign Policy by Congress* (New York: Oxford University Press, 1979).

Selected Bibliography

Congress, the Executive, and Public Policy

Aberbach, Joel D. (1990). *Keeping a Watchful Eye: The Politics of Congressional Oversight.* Washington, D.C., Brookings.

Arnold, R. Douglas (1987). "Political Control of Administrative Officials." *Journal of Law, Economics, and Organization* 3 (2): 279–86.

Best, Judith A. (1987). "Legislative Tyranny and the Liberation of the Executive: A View from the Founding." *Presidential Studies Quarterly* 17 (Fall): 697–709.

Blumenthal, Barbara (1979). "Uncle Sam's Army of Invisible Employees." *National Journal* 5 May, 730–33.

Bradley, John P. (1980). "Shaping Administrative Policy with the Aid of Congressional Oversight." *Western Political Quarterly,* December, 492–501.

Bruff, Harold H., and Ernest Gelhorn (1976). "Congressional Control of Administrative Regulations: A Study of Legislative Vetoes." *Harvard Law Review* 90: 1369.

Calvert, Randall L., Mathew D. McCubbins, and Barry R. Weingast (1989). "A Theory of Political Control and Agency Discretion." *American Journal of Political Science* 33 (August): 588–611.

Chubb, John E., and Paul E. Peterson (1989). *Can the Government Govern?* Washington, D.C., Brookings.

Claybrook, Joan (1983). "Congress: A View from the Agencies." In *The United States Congress,* edited by Dennis Hale. New Brunswick, N.J., Transaction Books.

Cohen, Richard E. (1990). "Crumbling Committees." *National Journal,* 4 August, 1876–81.

Congressional Budget Office (1991). *Controlling the Risks of Government-Sponsored Enterprises.* Washington, D.C., Government Printing Office.

Cooper, Phillip J. (1985). "Conflict or Constructive Tension: The Changing Relationship of Judges and Administrators." *Public Administration Review,* November, 643–52.

Corwin, E.S., H.W. Chase, and C.R. Ducat (1978). *The Constitution and What It Means Today.* Princeton, Princeton University Press.

Craig, Barbara Hinkson (1983). *The Legislative Veto: Congressional Control of Regulation.* Boulder, Colo., Westview Press.

———. (1988). *Chadha: The Story of an Epic Constitutional Struggle.* New York, Oxford University Press.

Craig, Barbara Hinkson, and Robert S. Gilmour (1992). "The Constitution and Accountability for *Public* Functions." *Governance: An International Journal of Policy and Administration* 5 (1): 47–67.

Crovitz, L. Gordon, and Jeremy A. Rabkin (1989). *The Fettered Presidency: Legal Constraints on the Executive Branch.* Washington, D.C., American Enterprise Institute.

Davidson, Roger H. (1988). "Invitation to Struggle: An Overview of Legislative-Executive Relations." *Annals of the American Academy of Political and Social Science* 499 (September): 9–21.

———. (1992). *The Postreform Congress.* New York, St. Martin's Press.

Davidson, Roger H., and Walter Oleszek (1990). *Congress and Its Members.* 3d ed. Washington, D.C., CQ Press.

Davies, Susan M. (1990). "Congressional Encroachment on Executive Branch Communications." *University of Chicago Law Review* 57 (Fall): 1297–1321.

Douglas, Arnold R. (1979). *Congress and the Bureaucracy: A Theory of Influence.* New Haven, Yale University Press.

Ethridge, Marcus E. (1985). *Legislative Participation in Implementation: Policy Through Politics.* New York, Praeger.

Fenno, Richard F. (1978). *Home Style: House Members in Their Districts.* Boston, Little, Brown.

Fiorina, Morris P. (1981). "Congressional Control of the Bureaucracy: A Mismatch of Incentives and Capabilities." In *Congress Reconsidered,* 2d ed., edited by Lawrence C. Dodd and Bruce I. Oppenheimer. Washington, D.C., CQ Press.

———. (1989). *Congress: Keystone of the Washington Establishment.* 2d ed. New Haven, Yale University Press.

Fisher, Louis (1987). *The Politics of Shared Power: Congress and the Executive.* 2d ed. Washington, D.C., CQ Press.

———. (1989). "Micromanagement by Congress: Reality and Mythology." In *The Fettered Presidency: Legal Constraints on the Executive Branch,* edited by L. Gordon Crovitz and Jeremy A. Rabkin. Washington, D.C., American Enterprise Institute.

———. (1990). "Congressional-Executive Struggles over Information: Secrecy Pledges." *Administrative Law Review* 42 (Winter): 89–107.

———. (1991). "Congress as Micromanager of the Executive Branch." In *The Managerial Presidency,* edited by James P. Pfiffner. Pacific Grove, Calif., Brooks/Cole.

Fitzgerald, John L. (1986). *Congress and the Separation of Powers.* New York, Praeger.

Fluckiger, Stephen L. (1985). "The Changing Relationship of the Judiciary to the Policy and Administrative Processes of Governments: An Overview of Recent Commentary on the Nature, Causes, Consequences, and Proposals for Reform of Contemporary Judicial Encroachment," *Brigham Young University Law Review,* 671–743.

Foreman, Christopher H., Jr. (1988). *Signals from the Hill: Congressional Oversight and the Challenge of Social Regulation.* New Haven, Yale University Press.

Franck, Thomas M., and Edward Wiesband (1979). *Foreign Policy by Congress.* New York, Oxford University Press.

Frye, Alton (1979). "Congress and President: The Balance Wheels of American Foreign Policy." *Yale Review* 69 (1): 1–16.

Gilmour, Robert S., and Barbara Hinkson Craig (1984). "After the Congressional Veto: Assessing the Alternatives." *Journal of Policy Analysis and Management* 3 (3): 373–92.

Goldstein, Mark L. (1990). "The Shadow Government." *Government Executive,* May, 30–57.

———. (1992). *America's Hollow Government: How Washington Has Failed the People.* Homewood, Ill., Business One Irwin.

Gormley, William T. (1991). "The Bureaucracy and Its Masters: The New Madisonian System in the U.S." *Governance: An International Journal of Policy and Administration* 4 (1): 1–18.

Halpert, Leon (1981). "Legislative Oversight and the Partisan Composition of Government." *Presidential Studies Quarterly,* Fall, 479–91.

Harris, Joseph P. (1946). "The Reorganization of Congress." *Public Administration Review* 6 (3): 267–82.

———. (1964). *Congressional Control of Administration.* Washington, D.C., Brookings.

Havens, Harry S. (1990). "The Erosion of Federal Program Evaluation." *American Review of Public Administration* 20 (March): 1–6.

Hummel, Ralph P. (1989). "Toward a New Administrative Doctrine: Governance and Management for the 1990's." *American Review of Public Administration* 19(3): 175–96.

Jones, Charles O. (1991). "The Diffusion of Responsibility: An Alternative Perspective for National Policy Politics in the U.S." *Governance: An International Journal of Policy and Administration* 4 (April): 150–67.

Jones, Gordon S., and John A. Marini (1988). *The Imperial Congress: Crisis in the Separation of Powers.* New York, Pharos Books (Heritage Foundation).

Kaiser, Frederick M. (1988). "Congressional Oversight of the Presidency." *Annals of the American Academy of Political and Social Science* 499: 75–89.

Katzman, Robert A., ed. (1988). *Judges and Legislators: Toward Institutional Comity.* Washington, D.C., Brookings.

———. (1991). "Building Bridges: Courts, Congress, and Guidelines for Communications." *Brookings Review,* Spring, 42–49.

Kettl, Donald F. (1988). *Government by Proxy: (Mis/)Managing Federal Programs.* Washington, D.C., CQ Press.

Kirst, Michael W. (1969). *Government Without Passing Laws: Congress' Non-Statutory Techniques for Appropriations Control.* Chapel Hill, University of North Carolina Press.

Krent, Harold J. (1990). "Fragmenting the Unitary Executive: Congressional Delegations of Administrative Authority Outside the Federal Government." *Northwestern University Law Review* 85 (Fall): 62–112.

Larson, James S. (1980). *Why Government Programs Fail: Improving Policy Implementation.* New York, Praeger.

Leazes, Francis J., Jr. (1987). *Accountability and the Business State: The Structure of Federal Corporations.* New York, Praeger.

Lowi, Theodore (1979). *The End of Liberalism: The Second Republic of the United States.* 2d ed. New York, Norton.

McCubbins, Mathew D., and Thomas Schwartz (1984). "Congressional Oversight Overlooked: Police Patrols versus Fire Alarms." *American Journal of Political Science* 28: 165–79.

McCubbins, Mathew D., Roger G. Noll, and Barry R. Weingast (1987). "Administrative Procedures as Instruments of Political Control." *Journal of Law, Economics, and Organization* 3 (2): 243–77.

Macmahon, Arthur (1943). "Congressional Oversight of Administration: The Power of the Purse." Parts I, II. *Political Science Quarterly* 58: 161–90.

Mansfield, Harvey C. (1982). "Accountability and Congressional Oversight." In *Improving the Accountability and Performance of Government,* edited by Bruce L.R. Smith and James D. Carroll. Washington, D.C., Brookings.

Mayhew, David R. (1991). *Divided We Govern.* New Haven, Yale University Press.

Melnick, R. Shep (1985). "The Politics of Partnership." *Public Administration Review,* November, 653–60.

——. (1991). "Introduction to Symposium on the New Politics of Public Policy." *Journal of Policy Analysis and Management* 10 (3): 363–68.

Moe, Ronald C. (1990). "Traditional Organizational Principles and the Managerial Presidency: From Phoenix to Ashes." *Public Administration Review* 50: 135–45.

Moe, Terry M. (1985). "The Politicized Presidency." In *The New Direction in American Politics,* edited by John E. Chubb and Paul E. Peterson. Washington, D.C., Brookings.

Mosher, Frederick C. (1980). "The Changing Responsibilities and Tactics of the Federal Government." *Public Administration Review,* November/December, 541–48.

National Academy of Public Administration (1974). *Watergate: Its Implications for Responsible Government.* Washington, D.C.

——. (1983). *Revitalizing Federal Management.* Washington, D.C.

——. (1988). *Congressional Oversight of Regulatory Agencies: The Need to*

Strike a Balance and Focus on Performance. Washington, D.C. (September).
———. (1988). *The Executive Presidency: Federal Management for the 1990s.* Washington, D.C.
———. (1989). *Senior Policy Makers on Congress and Public Management: Proceedings of a Meeting at the U.S. Capitol, February 7, 1989.* Washington, D.C.
———. (1991). *Organizing the Administration of Surface Transportation Policies and Programs to Meet National Needs.* Washington, D.C.
———. (1992). *Beyond Distrust: Building Bridges Between Congress and the Executive.* Washington, D.C.
O'Leary, Rosemary, and Charles R. Wise (1991). "Public Managers, Judges, and Legislators: Redefining the New Partnership." *Public Administration Review* 51 (4): 316–27.
Ogul, Morris S. (1976). *Congress Oversees the Bureaucracy: Studies in Legislative Supervision.* Pittsburgh, University of Pittsburgh Press.
Ogul, Morris S., and Bert A. Rockman (1990). "Overseeing Oversight: New Departures and Old Problems." *Legislative Studies Quarterly* 15 (1): 5–24.
Ornstein, Norman J., Thomas E. Mann, and Michael J. Malbin (1990). *Vital Statistics on Congress: 1989–1990.* Washington, D.C., CQ Press.
Rieselbach, Leroy N. (1986). *Congressional Reform.* Washington, D.C., CQ Press.
Ripley, Randall B. (1988). *Congress: Process and Policy.* New York, Norton.
Rockman, Bert A. (1984). "Legislative-Executive Relations and Legislative Oversight," *Legislative Studies Quarterly* 9: 387–440.
Rohr, John A. (1986). *To Run a Constitution: The Legitimacy of the Administrative State.* Lawrence, University Press of Kansas.
Rosen, Bernard (1989). *Holding Government Bureaucracies Accountable.* 2d ed. New York, Praeger.
Rosenbloom, David (1983). "Public Administrative Theory and the Separation of Powers." *Public Administration Review,* May/June, 219–27.
———. (1987). "Public Administrators and the Judiciary: The New Partnership." *Public Administration Review,* January/February, 75–83.
Salamon, Lester, ed. (1989). *Beyond Privatization: The Tools of Government Action.* Washington, D.C., Urban Institute Press.
Schick, Allen (1976). "Congress and the 'Details' of Administration." *Public Administration Review,* September/October, 516–27.
———. (1983). "Politics through Law: Congressional Limitations on Executive Discretion." In *Both Ends of the Avenue: The Presidency, the Executive Branch and Congress in the 1980s,* edited by Anthony King. Washington, D.C., American Enterprise Institute.
Seidman, Harold, and Robert Gilmour (1986). *Politics, Position, and Power: From the Positive to the Regulatory State.* 4th ed. New York, Oxford University Press.
Smith, Steven S., and Christopher J. Deering (1990). *Committees in Congress.* 2d ed. Washington, D.C., CQ Press.

Sundquist, James L. (1981). *The Decline and Resurgence of Congress.* Washington, D.C., Brookings.

————. (1987). "Congress as Public Administrator." In *A Centennial History of the American Administrative State,* edited by Ralph Clark Chandler. New York, Free Press.

————. (1988). "Needed: A Political Theory for the New Era of Coalition Government in the United States." *Political Science Quarterly* 103 (4): 613–35.

Thurber, James A. (1991). *Divided Democracy: Cooperation and Conflict between the President and Congress.* Washington, D.C., CQ Press.

————. (1991). "The Dynamics of Policy Subsystems in American Politics." In *Interest Group Politics,* 3d ed., edited by Allan J. Cigler and Burdett A. Loomis. Washington, D.C., CQ Press.

————. (1992). "New Rules for an Old Game: Zero-Sum Budgeting in the Post-Reform Congress." In *The Postreform Congress,* edited by Roger H. Davidson. New York, St. Martin's Press.

U.S. Senate. Committee on Governmental Affairs (1986). *Office of Management and Budget: Evolving Roles and Future Issues.* 99th Cong., 2d sess. Committee print.

Vogler, David J., and Sidney R. Waldman (1985). *Congress and Democracy.* Washington, D.C., CQ Press.

West, Darrell M. (1988). "Gramm-Rudman-Hollings and the Politics of Deficit Reduction." *Annals of the American Academy of Political and Social Science* 499 (September): 90–100.

West, William F., and Joseph Cooper (1989–90). "Legislative Influence v. Presidential Dominance: Competing Models of Bureaucratic Control." *Political Science Quarterly* 104 (4): 581–606.

Wildavsky, Aaron (1992). *The New Politics of the Budgetary Process,* 2d ed. New York: HarperCollins.

Wilson, James Q. (1989). *Bureaucracy: What Government Agencies Do and Why They Do It.* New York, Basic Books.

Wilson, Woodrow (1885). *Congressional Government.* Boston, Houghton, Mifflin; Baltimore, Johns Hopkins University Press.

Domestic Policy Case References

General Domestic Policy References

Bryner, Gary (1988). *The Constitution and the Regulation of Society.* Albany, SUNY Press.

Conlan, Timothy J. (1991). "And the Beat Goes On: Intergovernmental Mandates and Preemption in an Era of Deregulation." *Publius,* Summer, 43–57.

Cooper, Phillip J. (1989). *Hard Judicial Choices.* New York, Oxford University Press.

Derthick, Martha (1972). *New Towns In-Town.* Washington, D.C., Urban Institute.

———. (1990). *Agency Under Stress: The Social Security Administration in American Government.* Washington, D.C., Brookings.

Moynihan, Daniel (1970). *Maximum Feasible Misunderstanding.* New York, Free Press.

Peters, B. Guy (1993). *American Public Policy: Promise and Performance,* 3d ed. Chatham, N.J.: Chatham House.

Radin, Beryl (1977). *Implementation, Change, and the Federal Bureaucracy.* New York, Teacher's College Press, Columbia University.

Walker, David B. (1981). *Toward a Functioning Federalism.* Boston, Little, Brown.

Wright, Deil (1988). *Understanding Intergovernmental Relations,* 3d ed. Pacific Grove, Calif., Brooks/Cole.

Transportation Policy and Programs

Traffic Alert and Collision Avoidance System Case

———. (1987). "Collision Avoidance Systems." *Congressional Record,* 133, 28 October, S15255.

———. (1986). "FAA to Require TCAS-2 on Jet Transports." *Aviation Week and Space Technology* 29 September, 34.

Dodd, Lawrence C., and Richard L. Schott (1979). *Congress and the Administrative State.* New York, Wiley.

Jones, Charles O. (1982). *The United States Congress.* Homewood, Ill., Dorsey Press.

Kingdon, John W. (1984). *Agendas, Alternatives, and Public Policies.* Boston, Little, Brown.

Klass, Philip J. (1987). "Carriers Question U.S. Timetable for Mandatory TCAS Operation." *Aviation Week and Space Technology,* 21 December, 42.

———. (1988). "TCAS Comes of Age." *Aviation Week and Space Technology,* 11 January, 9.

Mordoff, Keith F. (1986). "NTSB Study of DC-9 Crash Shows Piper in Area Without Clearance." *Aviation Week and Space Technology,* 8 September, 45–51.

Rhoads, Steven E. (1974). *Policy Analysis in the Federal Aviation Administration.* Lexington, Mass., Lexington Books.

U.S. Congress. Office of Technology Assessment (1989). *Safer Skies with TCAS—A Special Report.* OTA-SET-431. Washington, D.C., Government Printing Office.

U.S. Congress. Senate Committee on Commerce, Science, and Transportation (1989). *Collision Avoidance System for Commercial Aircraft.* S.Rpt. 101–88. Washington, D.C., Government Printing Office.

U.S. Department of Transportation. Federal Aviation Administration (1981). *National Airspace System Plan*. Washington, D.C., Government Printing Office.

U.S. Government Accounting Office (1988). *Air Safety: FAA's Traffic Alert and Collision Avoidance System*. GAO/RCED-88-66BR, February. Washington, D.C., Government Printing Office.

Highway Demonstration Projects Case

———. (1987). "Highway Reauthorization Dies Amid Disputes," *1986 CQ Almanac*. Washington, D.C., CQ Press.

Arnold, R. Douglas (1979). *Congress and the Bureaucracy*. New Haven, Yale University Press.

Buchanan, James M., and Gordon Tullock (1962). *The Calculus of Consent*. Ann Arbor, University of Michigan Press.

Ferejohn, John A. (1974). *Pork Barrel Politics: Rivers and Harbors Legislation, 1947–1968*. Stanford, Stanford University Press.

Greenhouse, Linda (1987). "Senate, for Now, Upholds the Veto of Roads Measure." *New York Times*, 2 April.

———. (1987). "Senate Rejects Reagan Plea and Votes 67–33 to Override His Veto of Highway Funds." *New York Times*, 3 April.

Kau, J.B., and P.H. Rubin (1979). "Self Interest, Ideology and Logrolling in Congressional Voting." *Journal of Law and Economics* 22 (October): 365–84.

Kelley, Ben (1971). *The Pavers and the Paved*. New York, D.W. Brown.

Lave, Charles A. (1985). "Speeding, Coordination, and the 55 MPH Limit." *American Economic Review* 75 (December): 1159–64.

Maass, Arthur (1951). *Muddy Waters*. Cambridge, Harvard University Press.

Mayhew, David R. (1974). *Congress: The Electoral Connection*. New Haven, Yale University Press.

Meyer, John, and Jose A. Gomez-Ibanez (1981). *Autos, Transit, and Cities*. Cambridge, Harvard University Press.

Mills, Mike (1991). "Highway Bill Debate Becomes War Between the States." *CQ Weekly Report*, 8 June, 1487–89.

———. (1991). "Roe Wins Job He's Waited For: Ascent on Public Works." *CQ Weekly Report*, 8 December, 4062.

Rae, John B. (1971). *The Road and the Car in American Life*. Cambridge, MIT Press.

Small, Kenneth A., Clifford Winston, and Carol A. Evans (1989). *Road Work: A New Highway Pricing and Investment Policy*. Washington, D.C., Brookings.

Solomon, Burt (1987). "Staff at Work." *National Journal*, 16 May, 1174–76.

Stratman, Thomas (1991). "The Effects of Logrolling on Congressional Voting." Unpublished manuscript.

Energy and Environment Policy and Programs

High-Level Nuclear Waste Policy Case

Carter, Luther J. (1987). *Nuclear Imperatives and Public Trust: Dealing with Radioactive Waste*. Washington, D.C., Resources for the Future.

———. (1987). "Siting the Nuclear Waste Repository: Last Stand at Yucca Mountain." *Environment* 29 (8): 8–13, 26–32.

Davis, J.A. (1987). "Nevada to Get Nuclear Waste; Everyone Else 'Off the Hook'; Political Deal Cut," *CQ Weekly Report* 45 (19 December): 3136–38.

Green, Harold (1982). "The Peculiar Politics of Nuclear Power." *Bulletin of the Atomic Scientists* 38 (December): 59–62.

Jacob, Gerald (1990). *Site Unseen: The Politics of Siting a Nuclear Waste Repository*. Pittsburgh: University of Pittsburgh Press.

Metlay, Daniel (1978). "History and Interpretation of Radioactive Waste Management in the U.S." In *Essays on Issues Relevant to the Regulation of Radioactive Waste*, edited by W. Bishop et al. Washington, D.C., U.S. Nuclear Regulatory Commission.

Temples, J. (1980). "The Politics of Nuclear Power: A Subgovernment in Transition." *Political Science Quarterly* 95: 239–60.

Thurber, James A. (1991). "Dynamics of Policy Subsystems in American Politics." In *Interest Group Politics*, edited by Allen J. Cigler and Burdett A. Loomis. Washington, D.C., CQ Press.

Thurber, James A., and Timothy C. Evanson (1993). "Subsystem Politics and the Nuclear Weapons Complex: Congressional Oversight of DOE's Environmental Restoration Program." In *Problems and Prospects for Nuclear Waste Disposal Policy*, edited by Eric B. Herzik and Kevin H. Mushkatel. Westport, Conn.: Greenwood Press.

U.S. Congress. Office of Technology Assessment (1982). *Managing Commercial High-Level Radioactive Waste, Summary*, 97th Cong., 2d sess.

U.S. Department of Energy. Office of Civilian Radioactive Waste Management (1988). *Draft 1988 Mission Plan Amendment*. Washington, D.C. (June).

Hazardous Waste Disposal Case

Cook, Mary Etta, and Roger H. Davidson (1985). "Deferral Politics: Congressional Decision Making on Environmental Issues in the 1980s." In *Public Policy and the Natural Environment*, edited by Helen M. Ingram and R. Kenneth Godwin. Greenwich, Conn., JAI Press.

Davis, Charles E., and James P. Lester (1988). *Dimensions of Hazardous Waste Politics and Policy*. New York, Greenwood Press.

Environment and Energy Study Institute and the Environmental Law Institute (1985). "Statutory Deadlines in Environmental Legislation: Necessary but Need Improvement." Washington, D.C. (September).

Florio, James J. (1986). "Congress as Reluctant Regulator: Hazardous Waste Policy in the 1980s." *Yale Journal on Regulation* 3 (Spring): 351–82.

Fortuna, Richard, and David Lennett (1987). *Hazardous Waste Regulation: The New Era.* New York, McGraw-Hill.

Harris, Christopher, William L.Wont, and Morris A. Ward (1987). *Hazardous Waste: Confronting the Challenge.* New York, Quorum Books.

Harris, Richard A., and Sidney Milkis (1989). *The Politics of Regulatory Change: A Tale of Two Agencies.* New York, Oxford University Press.

Landy, Marc, Marc Roberts, and Stephen Thomas (1990). *The Environmental Protection Agency: Asking the Wrong Questions.* New York, Oxford University Press.

McCarthy, James E., and Mark E. Reisch (1987). "Hazardous Waste Fact Book." Washington, D.C., Congressional Research Service.

Melnick, R. Shep (1983). *Regulation and the Courts: The Case of the Clean Air Act.* Washington, D.C., Brookings.

Piasecki, Bruce (1984). *Beyond Dumping: New Strategies for Controlling Toxic Contamination.* Westport, Conn., Quorum Books.

U.S. Environmental Protection Agency. Office of Solid Waste and Emergency Response. *The Nation's Hazardous Waste Management Program at a Crossroads: The RCRA Implementation Study.* Washington, D.C.

U.S. General Accounting Office (1986). *Hazardous Waste: EPA Has Made Limited Progress in Determining Wastes to be Regulated.* Washington, D.C.

———. (1988). *Environmental Protection Agency: Protecting Human Health and the Environment Through Improved Management.* Washington, D.C.

Vig, Norman J., and Michael E. Kraft (1990). *Environmental Policy in the 1990s: Toward a New Agenda.* Washington, D.C., CQ Press.

Wald, Patricia (1990). "The Sizzling Sleeper: The Use of Legislative History in Construing Statutes in the 1988–89 Term of the United States Supreme Court." *American University Law Review* 39 (Winter): 277–310.

Defense Nuclear Weapons Complex Cleanup Case

Barlett, Donald L., and J.B. Steele (1985). *Forevermore: Nuclear Waste in America.* New York, Norton.

Carter, Luther J. (1987). *Nuclear Imperatives and Public Trust: Dealing with Radioactive Waste.* Washington, D.C., Resources for the Future.

Colglazier, E. William (1982). *The Politics of Nuclear Waste.* New York, Pergamon Press.

Jacob, Gerald (1990). *Site Unseen: The Politics of Siting a Nuclear Waste Repository.* Pittsburgh, University of Pittsburgh Press.

Jenkins-Smith, Hank C. (1991). "Alternative Theories of the Policy Process: Reflections on Research Strategy for the Study of Nuclear Waste Policy." *PS: Political Science and Politics* 24 (June): 157–65.

Thurber, James A. (1991). "Dynamics of Policy Subsystems in American Politics." In *Interest Group Politics,* 3d ed., edited by Allan J. Cigler and Burdett A. Loomis. Washington, D.C., CQ Press.

Thurber, James A., and Timothy C. Evanson (1993). "Subsystem Politics and the Nuclear Weapons Complex: Congressional Oversight of DOE's Environmental Restoration Program." In *Problems and Prospects for Nuclear Waste Disposal Policy,* edited by Eric B. Herzik and Kevin H. Mushkatel. Westport, Conn., Greenwood Press.

U.S. Congress. Office of Technology Assessment (1991). *Complex Cleanup: The Environmental Legacy of Nuclear Weapons Production, Summary.* OTA-0-484. Washington, D.C., Government Printing Office.

U.S. Department of Energy. Office of Environmental Restoration and Waste Management (1990). *Environmental Restoration and Waste Management: Five-Year Plan, Fiscal Years 1992-1996.* DOE/S-0078P. Washington, D.C., Government Printing Office.

U.S. General Accounting Office (1981). *Better Oversight Needed for Safety and Health Activities at DOE's Nuclear Facilities.* EMD-81-108. Washington, D.C.

———. (1990). *Efforts to Improve DOE's Management of the Nuclear Weapons Complex.* T-RCED-90-64. Washington, D.C.

Health Policy and Programs

Medicare Prospective Payment System Case

Aaron, Henry J. (1991). *Serious and Unstable Condition: Financing America's Health Care.* Washington, D.C., Brookings.

Davis, Raymond G. (1985). "Congress and the Emergence of Public Health Policy." *HCM Review,* Winter, 61–73.

Fetter, Robert B., David A. Brand, and Dianne Gamache (1991). *DRGs: Their Design and Development.* Ann Arbor, Mich., Health Administration Press.

Guterman, S., P.W. Eggers, G. Riley, T. Greene, and S. Terrell (1988). "The First Three Years of Medicare Prospective Payment: An Overview." *Health Care Financing Review* 9 (Spring): 67–77.

Kline, Janet (1989). "Health Care: CRS Issue Brief." Washington, D.C., Congressional Research Service (March).

Lave, Judith (1990). "The Impact of the Medicare Prospective Payment System and Recommendations for Change." *Yale Journal on Regulation* 7: 499–528.

Prospective Payment Assessment Commission (1985–1990). *Report and Recommendations to the Secretary, U.S. Department of Health and Human Services.* Washington, D.C. (1 March).

———. (1985–1990). *Medicare Prospective Payment and the American Health Care System: Report to the Congress.* Washington, D.C. (1 March).

Robinson, Michele L. (1989). "Power Politics Decides Who Writes Medicare Policy." *Hospitals,* 5 August, 18–20.

Rovner, Julie (1989). "Reconciliation Dominates Policy-Making Process." *Congressional Quarterly,* 29 April, 964.

Russell, Louise B. (1989). *Medicare's New Hospital Payment System: Is It Working?* Washington, D.C., Brookings.

Smith, David G. (1992). *Paying for Medicare: The Politics of Reform.* New York, deGruyter.

U.S. Congress. House Committee on Ways and Means (1991). *Overview of Entitlement Programs: 1991 Green Book.* Washington, D.C., Government Printing Office (7 May).

U.S. Department of Health and Human Services (1982). *Report to Congress: Hospital Prospective Payment for Medicare.* Washington, D.C. (December).

Foreign Affairs and Defense Case References

Defense Policy and Programs

AMRAAM Case

Art, Robert J. (1968). *The TFX Decision: McNamara and the Military.* Boston, Little, Brown.

Carey, Peter (1989). "The Pentagon's Misguided Missile," *U.S. News and World Report,* 1 May, 33.

Fox, J. Ronald, with James L. Field (1988). *The Defense Management Challenge: Weapons Acquisition.* Boston, Harvard Business School Press.

Gregory, William H. (1989). *The Defense Procurement Mess: A Twentieth Century Fund Essay.* Lexington, Mass., Lexington Books.

Hadley, Arthur T. (1986). *The Straw Giant: Triumph and Failure: America's Armed Forces.* New York, Random House.

Holzman, David (1983). "Is AMRAAM Missile Worth the Cost?" *Technology Review,* October, 28.

Kotz, Nick (1988). *Wild Blue Yonder: Money, Politics, and the B-1 Bomber.* Princeton, Princeton University Press.

McNaugher, Thomas L. (1986). "Buying Weapons: Bleak Prospects for Real Reform." *Brookings Review,* Summer, 11.

———. (1989). *New Weapons Old Politics: America's Military Procurement Muddle.* Washington, D.C., Brookings.

Moore, Molly (1990). "Air Force Costs 'Grossly Understated,'" *Washington Post,* 13 February, A9.

Rosenau, William (1989). "The Sword and the Purse: A Guide to the U.S. Congress and the Weapons Acquisition Process." Series 89-08. Cambridge, National Security Program, John F. Kennedy School of Government, Harvard University.

Shapiro, Robert (1987). "One Missile's Lessons." *U.S. News and World Report,* 28 September, 33.

U.S. General Accounting Office (1986). *Missile Development: Status of Advanced Medium Range Air-to-Air Missile (AMRAAM) Certification.* GAO/NSIAD-86-66BR. Washington, D.C.

————. (1988). *Major Acquisitions: Summary of Problems and Systemic Issues: 1960–1987.* GAO/NSIAD/88/135BR. Washington, D.C.

————. (1989). *Weapons Acquisition: Improving DoD's Weapon Systems Acquisition Reporting.* GAO/NSIAD/90/20. Washington, D.C.

————. (1991). *Missile Procurement: AMRAAM's Reliability Is Improving but Production Challenges Remain.* GAO/NSIAD/91/209. Washington, D.C.

Goldwater-Nichols Reorganization of DOD Case

Art, Robert J., Vincent Davis, and Samuel P. Huntington, eds. (1985). *Reorganizing America's Defense: Leadership in War and Peace.* New York, Pergamon-Brassey's.

Caraley, Demetrios (1966). *The Politics of Military Unification: A Study of Conflict and the Policy Process.* New York, Columbia University Press.

Clark, Asa A., Peter W. Chiarelli, Jeffrey S. McKitrick, and James W. Reed, eds. (1984). *The Defense Reform Debate: Issues and Analysis.* Baltimore, Johns Hopkins University Press.

Crackel, Theodore J. (1984). "Defense Assessment." In *Mandate for Leadership II: Continuing the Conservative Revolution,* edited by Stuart M. Butler, Michael Sanera, and W. Bruce Weinrod. Washington, DC, Heritage Foundation.

Hammond, Paul Y. (1961). *Organizing for Defense: The American Military Establishment in the Twentieth Century.* Princeton, Princeton University Press.

Jones, General David C. (1982). "Why the Joint Chiefs of Staff Must Change." *Armed Forces Journal International,* March, 62–72.

Korb, Lawrence (1976). *The Joint Chiefs of Staff: The First Twenty-Five Years.* Bloomington, Indiana University Press.

Lynn, William J., and Barry R. Posen (1985/1986). "The Case for JCS Reform." *International Security* 10 (Winter): 69–97.

Owens, MacKubin Thomas (1985/86). "The Hollow Promise of JCS Reform." *International Security* 10 (Winter): 98–111.

President's Blue Ribbon Commission on Defense Management (1986). *A Quest for Excellence: Final Report.* Washington, D.C., Government Printing Office (June).

U.S. Senate. Committee on Armed Services (1985). *Defense Organization: The Need for Change,* Staff Report. Washington, D.C., Government Printing Office (16 October).

Foreign Affairs Policy and Programs

Foreign Aid and Human Rights Case

Brown, Peter G., and Douglas MacLean, eds. (1979). *Human Rights and U.S. Foreign Policy.* Lexington, Mass., Lexington Books.

Corwin, Edward S. (1957). *The President: Office and Powers,* 4th ed. New York, New York University Press.

Eberstadt, Nicholas (1988). *Foreign Aid and American Purpose.* Washington, D.C., American Enterprise Institute.

Forsythe, David P. (1988). *Human Rights and U.S. Foreign Policy: Congress Reconsidered.* Gainesville, University of Florida Press.

Hill, Dilys M., ed. (1988). *Human Rights and Foreign Policy: Principles and Practice.* New York, St. Martin's Press.

Kegley, Charles W., Jr., and Eugene R. Wittkopf (1987). *American Foreign Policy: Pattern and Process,* 3d ed. New York, St. Martin's Press.

Pastor, Robert A. (1980). *Congress and the Politics of U.S. Foreign Economic Policy.* Berkeley, University of California Press.

Shestack, Jerome J. (1990). "An Unsteady Focus: The Vulnerabilities of the Reagan Administration's Human Rights Policies." Reprinted in House Committee on Foreign Affairs, Subcommittee on Human Rights and International Organizations, *Hearings: Review of the State Department's Country Reports on Human Rights.* 101st Cong., 2d sess.

U.S. Congress. Congressional Research Service (1979). *Human Rights and U.S. Foreign Assistance: Experiences and Issues in Policy Implementation (1977–1978).* Washington, D.C. (November).

U.S. House. Committee on Foreign Affairs (1982). *Executive-Legislative Consultation on Foreign Policy: Strengthening the Legislative Side,* 97th Cong., 2d sess. (April). Committee print.

———. (1988). *Foreign Assistance Reporting Requirements,* 100th Cong., 2d sess. (December). Committee print.

———. (1988). *Required Reports to Congress on Foreign Policy,* 100th Cong., 2d sess. (1 August). Committee print.

———. Task Force on Foreign Assistance (1989). *Report of the Task Force on Foreign Assistance,* 101st Cong., 1st sess. (February). H. Doc. 101-32.

Vincent, R.J., ed. (1986). *Foreign Policy and Human Rights: Issues and Responses.* New York, Cambridge University Press.

Foreign Military Arms Sales Case

Bajusz, William D., and David J. Louscher (1988). *Arms Sales and the U.S. Economy: The Impact of Restricting Military Exports.* Boulder, Colo., Westview Press.

Congressional Research Service (1990). "Trends in Conventional Arms Transfers to the Third World by Major Supplier, 1982–1989." CRS No. 90-298F (19 June).

————. (1990). "Japanese FSX Fighter Controversy." CRS No. 90-309F (20 June).

Farley, Philip J., Stephen S. Kaplan, and William H. Lewis (1978). *Arms Across the Sea.* Washington, D.C., Brookings.

Gast, Philip C. (1987). "The Implementation of the United States Security Assistance Program." *DISAM Journal* 9 (Summer).

Hammond, Paul Y., et al. (1983). *The Reluctant Supplier: U.S. Decisionmaking for Arms Sales.* Cambridge, Mass., Oelgeschlager, Gunn and Hain.

Klare, Michael (1984). *American Arms Supermarket.* Austin, University of Texas Press.

Laurance, Edward J. (1989). "The New Gunrunning." *Orbis,* Spring.

McKalip, H. Diehl (1989). "U.S. Policy Regarding Third Country Sales." *DISAM Journal* 11 (Spring).

————. (1989). "Foreign Military Operations and DOD Relations with Industry." *DISAM Journal* 12 (Fall).

Mortsolf, Larry A., and Louis J. Samelson (1987). "The Congress and U.S. Military Assistance, Part I." *DISAM Journal* 9 (Summer).

————. (1987). "The Congress and U.S. Military Assistance, Part II," *DISAM Journal* 10 (Fall).

Nachmias, Nitza (1988). *Transfer of Arms, Leverage, and Peace in the Middle East.* Westport, Conn., Greenwood Press.

Neuman, Stephanie G. (1989). "The Arms Market: Who's On Top?" *Orbis,* Fall.

Ra'anan, Uri, et al., eds. (1978). *Arms Transfers to the Third World: The Military Buildup in Less Industrial Countries.* Boulder, Colo., Westview Press.

Samelson, Louis J. (1989). "Legislative Constraints on U.S. Arms Transfers." *DISAM Journal* 12 (Fall).

U.S. Arms Control and Disarmament Agency (1990). *World Military Expenditures and Arms Transfers, 1989.* Washington, D.C., Government Printing Office.

Methodology References

Agranoff, Robert, and Beryl A. Radin (1990). "The Comparative Case Study Approach in Public Administration." *Research in Public Administration* 1: 203–31.

Argyris, Chris, Robert Putnam, and Diana McLain Smith (1985). *Action Science: Concepts, Methods, and Skills for Research and Intervention.* San Francisco, Jossey-Bass.

Bailey, Mary Timney (1992). "Do Physicists Use Case Studies? Thoughts on Public Administration Research." *Public Administration Review* 52 (1): 47–54.

Dyer, W. Gibb, Jr., and Alan Wilkins (1991). "Better Stories, Not Better Constructs, to Generate Better Theory: A Rejoinder to Eisenhardt." *Academy of Management Review* 16 (3): 613–19.

Eisenhardt, Kathleen (1989). "Building Theories from Case Study Research." *Academy of Management Review* 14 (4): 532–50.

———. (1991). "Better Stories and Better Constructs: The Case for Rigor and Comparative Logic." *Academy of Management Review* 16 (3): 620–27.

Gersick, Connie (1991). "Revolutionary Change Theories." *Academy of Management Review* 16 (1): 10–36.

Hedlund, Ronald D. (1985). "Organizational Attributes of Legislative Institutions: Structure, Rules, Norms, Resources." In *Handbook of Legislative Research,* edited by Gerhard Loewenberg, Samuel Patterson, and Malcolm Jewell. Cambridge, Harvard University Press.

Linstone, Harold A. (1984). *Multiple Perspectives for Decision Making: Bridging the Gap between Analysis and Action.* New York, North-Holland.

McPhee, Robert D. (1990). "Alternate Approaches to Integrating Longitudinal Case Studies." *Organization Science* 1 (4): 393–406.

Morgan, Gareth (1983). *Beyond Method: Strategies for Social Research.* Beverly Hills, Sage.

Neustadt, Richard E., and Ernest R. May (1986). *Thinking in Time: The Uses of History for Decision Makers.* New York, Free Press.

Oppenheimer, Bruce J. (1985). "Legislative Influence on Policy and Budgets." In *Handbook of Legislative Research,* edited by Gerhard Loewenberg, Samuel Patterson, and Malcolm Jewell. Cambridge, Harvard University Press.

Pettigrew, Andrew M. (1990). "Longitudinal Field Research on Change: Theory and Practice." *Organization Science* 1 (3): 267–92.

Ricci, David M. (1984). *The Tragedy of Political Science: Politics, Scholarship, and Democracy.* New Haven, Yale University Press.

Rockman, Bert A. (1985). "Legislative-Executive Relations and Legislative Oversight." In *Handbook of Legislative Research,* edited by Gerhard Loewenberg, Samuel Patterson, and Malcolm Jewell. Cambridge, Harvard University Press.

U.S. General Accounting Office, Program Evaluation and Methodology Division (1987). *Case Study Evaluations: Transfer Paper 9.* Washington, D.C.

Yin, Robert K. (1989). *Case Study Research: Design and Methods.* Newbury Park, Calif., Sage.

Index